The Reluctant Ally

Michael M. Harrison is associate professor of European studies at The Johns Hopkins University School of Advanced International Studies in Washington, D.C.

The Reluctant Ally
France and Atlantic Security

Michael M. Harrison

The Johns Hopkins University Press
Baltimore and London

The Johns Hopkins University Press, Baltimore, Maryland 21218
The Johns Hopkins Press Ltd., London

Library of Congress Cataloging in Publication Data

Harrison, Michael M
    The reluctant ally.

    Includes bibliographical references and index.
    1. France—Foreign relations—1945-1958. 2. France—
Foreign relations—1958-1969. 3. France—Foreign
relations—1969-   4. France—Relations (military)
with foreign countries. 5. France—Foreign relations—
United States. 6. United States—Foreign relations—
France. 7. North Atlantic Treaty Organization—France.
I. Title.
DC404.H35   327.440182'1   80-8865
ISBN 0-8018-2474-5

For My Mother and Father

Quand je considère cette nation en elle-même, je la trouve plus extraordinaire qu'aucun des événements de son histoire. . . . Un peuple . . . apte à tout, mais n'excellant que dans la guerre; adorateur du hasard, de la force, du succès, de l'éclat et du bruit, plus que de la vraie gloire; plus capable d'héroïsme que de vertu, de génie que de bon sens, propre à concevoir d'immenses desseins plutôt qu'à parachever de grandes entreprises; la plus brillante et la plus dangereuse des nations de l'Europe, et la mieux faite pour y devenir tour à tour un objet d'admiration, de haine, de pitié, de terreur, mais jamais d'indifférence.

Alexis de Tocqueville

Contents

Acknowledgments

This book owes a great debt to a number of people and institutions, only a few of whom can be singled out here. My colleague and friend David Calleo has shown an unflagging confidence in my ability to finish this project successfully, and the achievement is in no small way due to his support and encouragement. My intellectual debt to him has grown beyond easy calculation, so it cannot be adequately acknowledged in mere words of gratitude—which I nevertheless want to express here. Another colleague and friend, Simon Serfaty, has been encouraging and helpful in more ways than I can count. He is particularly responsible for broadening my interests in French and European domestic politics, a development that has enriched this book and my own professional life. The study itself has been much improved because of the wise and thorough criticism of Anton DePorte, to whom I am indebted.

When this study was conceived and first written as a dissertation at Columbia University, it benefited from the judicious counsel of Philip Mosely, the valuable insight of William T. R. Fox, and the advice and assistance of Wilfrid L. Kohl, Robert Paxton, Gordon Adams, and Mark Kesselman. Alfred Grosser shaped my early interest in French politics and foreign policy, and generously helped with this research when I was in Paris. Many other people, including colleagues at The Johns Hopkins School of Advanced International Studies, have helped, encouraged, or inspired me in a variety of ways. They include: Robert W. Tucker, Robert E. Osgood, George Liska, Stanley Hoffmann, Nicholas Rizopoulos (and the Lehrman Institute), James Chace, Serge Hurtig, and Guy de Carmoy. I thank all these people, and others unnamed, for making this a better book. I, of course, carry the entire burden of its defects and any errors.

The Reluctant Ally

Introduction

This is an analysis of France's postwar security and defense policies, concentrating on political-military relations with the United States in the context of the Atlantic Alliance. Only a short time ago, it might have seemed curious to undertake and produce such a study, because many observers were dismissing security issues as less and less relevant for Western industrial societies, and because France, in particular, no longer appeared unduly excited about maintaining an autonomous national defense or a rigorous independence from the Atlantic system. The heroic and, many would say, ultimately futile exertions of the Gaullist era lay in a distant past to be stored safely in museums and archives. They might gather dust there alongside the defense issues that no longer seemed so interesting for Western publics, and were ostensibly being supplanted by economic-welfare or even postmaterialist concerns more in tune with the modern values of societies on the threshold of postindustrial politics.[1] This is clearly not the perspective adopted or represented in this study, which can neither confirm nor deny complicated and ultimately uncertain trends in public values and their implications for elites and policy makers in Western governments. And, certainly, it is unnecessary to assert in detail here the contemporary relevance of defense and security affairs for national policy making in the West, especially at a time when détente is once again waning and defense budgets escalating in response to international and domestic influences.

In the case of France, it is true that defense and security have been less contentious issues in national politics than at any time since perhaps the Versailles Treaty, just as the defense and alliance policies of Valéry Giscard d'Estaing have seemed more compatible with the views and interests of France's allies than those of any previous postwar government in Paris. But the most compelling explanations for this relatively blissful state of affairs cannot be found in a declining concern for security, or in fundamental alterations in French defense policy that amount to a final renunciation of the extravagant claims of Gaullism in recognition of the constraints of Atlantic interdependence. Instead, it is contended here, French security and alliance

1

policies are ceasing to be such divisive issues in domestic politics largely because of the gradual emergence of a national consensus on the value of the Gaullist security model—one based on a certain conception of French independence and symbolized by an independent nuclear force and restrained ties to France's Western allies. And, while it is true that France's relations with these allies have generally improved, this is partly because of the inherent flexibility of the Gaullist model itself and partly because of transformations in the Atlantic system that make it easier to tolerate and accommodate more independence among all allies. For France, such an accommodation is feasible primarily because thirty years of a tempestuous relationship as an ally have left the country in a favorable position to redefine its Alliance role according to shifting domestic and international circumstances. Once viewed by many critics as a unique and deplorable situation resulting from the arbitrary actions of a single-minded leader, France's independent status appears to have become a permanent fixture of the Alliance. Moreover, it has acquired new significance as a model for the more flexible alliance ties required by the complex and fluid international system that emerged during the 1970s.

The principal feature of French domestic politics in this decade was the bipolarization of the political system into competing coalitions of parties grouped on the right and the left of the ideological spectrum. Although conflicts among political allies were often as important and engrossing as their collaboration, and the leftist coalition seems to have collapsed in the course of the 1978 election campaign and its aftermath, it is interesting that debates over security affairs, national defense, and France's formal alliance ties did not figure prominently in the often confused political confrontations of the 1970s. Of course, the neo-Atlanticist leanings of Giscard d'Estaing and his entourage, and the president's willingness to expand some aspects of French military cooperation with NATO allies, periodically earned him the reproaches and hostility of a majority of political forces anxious to maintain the Gaullist legacy of independence. Also, an apparent communist accommodation to the Fifth Republic's nuclear force, and ostensibly to France's special ties with the Atlantic Alliance, was challenged as a subterfuge to secure a controversial neutral position within the West that is unacceptable to most other parties in the country. Nevertheless, despite some legitimate questions about the long-range intentions and motives of French domestic actors regarding national security, it is probably more significant that all major parties and elites have increasingly resorted to Gaullist security policies and perspectives to advance and justify their positions. That such diverse and incompatible political actors as Giscard d'Estaing's centrist coalition, Gaullists, socialists, and communists have felt compelled to promote their foreign policy goals by reference to the Gaullist accomplishment is testimony to the widespread utility of a legacy that is malleable enough to embrace a variety of interests and viewpoints.

In the light of this development, one major task of this study is to reevaluate the Gaullist ideal and its practical implications, to indicate how and why it has promoted a broad national consensus on France's security and defense arrangements. Rather than resort to a narrow and rigid interpretation of Charles de Gaulle's ideas and policies in this domain, the perspective adopted here stresses the essentially ambivalent nature of the independence concept and the quite realistic and pragmatic policies that de Gaulle used in reconciling his abstract ideals with the constraints of the international system and France's own limited resources. This is a different approach from some other analysts, who have chosen to focus on de Gaulle's ambitious rhetoric and his often exaggerated claims for France in a new international order, to demonstrate the absurdity of the ideals and poverty of the accomplishments.[2] Such a task has been easy for unsympathetic observers in the past, although the Gaullist critique of an unstable American-dominated Atlantic system and the vision of a pluralist international order appear more and more compelling as time passes and we experience the long-range transformations that de Gaulle envisaged during the 1960s and earlier. In any case, it seems indisputable that the defense and alliance policies he followed have proven successful enough to merit the commitments of most domestic actors and even to earn the approbation of France's allies as a valued contribution to the overall security of the Western Alliance.

The general reassessment of the security legacy of the Fifth Republic presented here is accompanied by a new perspective on the heritage de Gaulle received from the defense and alliance policies of the Fourth Republic. Whereas de Gaulle and others have generally been contemptuous of the Fourth Republic's policies in this regard, an examination of the motives and expectations that accompanied France's alignment with the West after 1947 will demonstrate the essential continuity in French security goals throughout the postwar period. Thus, the Fourth Republic was a source and inspiration for many of the claims that became so prominent under de Gaulle: the insistence on special privileges in the Atlantic Alliance, the specific demand for a three-power inner directorate to manage Western security affairs on behalf of all allies, the preoccupation with the globalization of American and Alliance support for French interests, the development of a distinctive conception of military threats and defense strategy tailored to French national concerns and incompatible with the orientation of NATO and, finally, the policy of developing nuclear weapons as a vehicle for increasing France's status and her national security.

The Fourth Republic also created or shared many of the contradictions and failures that have since characterized French international policy. One of these was the preoccupation with obtaining a superior and independent military capability in Western Europe, which helped prevent the emergence of a political-military community to complement economic cooperation and enable Europe to assume a more fully independent role in Atlantic and world affairs. Whereas de Gaulle's nationalistic policies are often seen as the source of this dilemma, France's reluctance to encourage or tolerate a crucial military dimension to European unity was actually a decision of the Fourth Republic that de Gaulle was unable or unwilling to reverse. In general, the similarity of goals and security images between republics reinforces the argument that de Gaulle's ideas, actions, and achievements amount to a compelling synthesis of a French security myth built around the ideal of independence and now attracting the sympathy and allegiance of most French elites and the public.

Although the overriding purpose of this study is to explore and explain France's postwar defense and alliance policies, they obviously have a significance that transcends national politics and can clarify certain features of the Western alliance system and European national politics. France has always been the most skeptical of the principal American allies, hence the most willing to stake out independent positions while resisting, with mixed success, the price of excessive dependence. The virtue of this role is that it reveals some prominent characterisitics of an alliance hegemony and particularly its costs in terms of compliance and trade-offs with nonsecurity arenas. In a period when classic security politics can appear to be of diminished significance, it is useful to be reminded of how military alliances still structure power and influence in the West and can be manipulated to secure a broad range of interests. This perspective sheds additional light on the practical value of the Gaullist emphasis on maximum independence in defense affairs, which may be seen as a worthwhile means of protecting a variety of national interests from excessive compromise in the context of modern interdependence.

Finally, the examination undertaken here offers one explanation of why radical and purposeful transformations of the Western international system have been so elusive in the past—whether along the lines of the American-dominated "partnership" sought with persistence by the United States, or the more independent Europe in a multipolar global system sometimes advocated by the French. Both goals have been frustrated by the policies of major allies, particularly these two protagonists, resulting in a stalemate. But the situation is not static, and although the Atlantic Alliance has escaped the grand designs of some allies it seems to evolve slowly into a looser, more obviously pluralistic security system with great leeway and independence for all its members. Thus, they are able to redefine mutual ties and interests according to national and international circumstances that may vary drastically from ally to ally or for a single state from one period to another. It was this kind of flexibility, incipient and begrudged at the time, that finally permitted the redefinition of France's Alliance status without a debilitating crisis and may even have been productive for both Europe and the United States in the long run. Now, as the Atlantic Alliance is taxed by erratic fluctuations in the domestic politics of some members and by escalating conflicts in both the security and economic arenas, it may be useful to offer the French experience (despite its unique aspects) as a prototype of flexible membership. For it suggests the advantages of allowing and encouraging a tolerant adaptation to new conditions confronting allies, thereby avoiding the debilitating confrontations that pose the risk of irreparable damage to a valuable security system.

1 The Fourth Republic: From Alignment to Dealignment in French Alliance Policy

The unhappy and tension-ridden French experience in the Atlantic Alliance began under that equally tormented regime, the Fourth Republic. Successive governments of the Fourth Republic established the goals, conditions, and aspirations that accompanied a hesitant French alignment with the West. They also presided over a growing sense of disappointment and rancour as the Alliance and the United States proved unable or unwilling to meet the exaggerated demands and expectations French elites aimed at their Western partners. Because the pattern of French relations with the Atlantic Alliance was essentially in place before de Gaulle returned to power in the spring of 1958, this period merits a close and careful examination.

In focusing on the Fourth Republic, this chapter will assess the most prominent alliance-oriented goals of French governments after the onset of the Cold War. These aims often seem reasonable when considered separately or in the narrow context of French interests. But the overall pattern is one of unrealistic policies that could not succeed for a number of reasons: France's seemingly irreversible decline in international power and status, and thus her persistent weakness and dependence; the inattention or outright opposition of major allies; and the crystallization of an international bloc structure that subordinated French national goals to the interests of the dominant states and to newly powerful forces such as Third World nationalism.

Rather than adjust to these developments and accept a secondary position within the West, Fourth Republic leaders usually resisted the temptation to accommodate and, instead, tenaciously pursued the role of the most recalcitrant and dissident of the United States' major Western partners. Thus, France was the ally that most resented its position as a dependent in Europe, and the ally that finally proved least capable of modifying its goals and successfully exploiting the United States and the Atlantic Alliance for less grandiose purposes. French discontent and resentment finally crystallized around the bitter and unsuccessful colonial war in North Africa. The Suez crisis of 1956 was the watershed in a process of alienation from the United States and the

Alliance, a development that was reinforced as the situation in Algeria progressively deteriorated. The conclusion suggested by this analysis, then, is that French dealignment from the Atlantic Alliance was not instigated by General de Gaulle under the Fifth Republic. It was the result of a generally unrewarding Alliance experience after 1949, compounded by a particularly profound estrangement from the United States and NATO that began in 1956. Thus, de Gaulle inherited more of an adversary than a firm ally, and was able to capitalize on this situation as reinforcement for his own efforts to enhance French independence and prestige.

A second conclusion emerging from this examination of the Fourth Republic's alliance policies is that, despite the short-sightedness and penchant for subordination ascribed to it by de Gaulle, France's leadership before 1958 pursued international goals strikingly similar to those associated with the Gaullist era of the Fifth Republic. Indeed, the two regimes asked much the same thing of the Western Alliance: guaranteed security against European and global threats to French interests, American recognition of France's rank as a global power, access to the most modern military instrument of security, equality with Britain as a privileged ally of the United States, and French political-military preeminence over West Germany. There were, of course, obvious and significant differences in the international behavior of the Fourth and Fifth Republics. But a high degree of continuity in their security perspectives has been obscured by the distinctive diplomatic style of de Gaulle and a general disparagement of the aspirations and achievements of the Fourth Republic.

It seems, however, that the disparity between the General's international behavior and that of his predecessors was mainly concerned with tactics, means, and the lack of coherence and persistence notable before 1958. By establishing a stronger and more decisive regime, whose external relations were for some time less affected by the vicissitudes of domestic politics, de Gaulle became the first postwar French statesman capable of formulating and pursuing national goals with a consistency unsettling to both domestic and foreign observers. Although perhaps ultimately as unsuccessful as the Fourth Republic in securing many goals, de Gaulle was able to synthesize and organize the incoherent security perspectives of the Fourth Republic into a compelling and flexible model of independence. This accomplishment lay the foundation for a national consensus on French security policy that had eluded most French regimes and may prove to be one of the most lasting and valuable legacies of Gaullism. In addition, de Gaulle transformed the Fourth Republic's aspiration to status and quest for independence into a general and explicit challenge to the structures of both the Western Alliance and the international system. While the lessons and consequences of this aspect of Gaullism are more obscure, they, too, seem especially relevant to the more pluralistic and diffuse international order that has emerged.

The Illusory Alignment: France Joins the West

After World War II, when international politics polarized around two emerging superpowers and eventually forced most free European governments to align with the United States, America's very first ally was among the most reluctant and proved to be the most consistently troublesome for the Western Alliance. Unlike Britain, whose "special relationship" antedated the Cold War and was thought to transcend formal alliances, Fourth Republic leaders had inherited and essentially accepted de Gaulle's prescription for a foreign policy emphasizing French independence as the key to national revival and full restoration to great power status. For de Gaulle, who had fought Vichy, Germany, and the allies with approximately equal energy, French continental supremacy over Germany and a prominent global role were to be secured and protected by an international equilibrium, with France acting as interlocuteur between the Anglo-Saxon and Russian spheres.[1] De Gaulle's collaborators and successors after January 1946 shared much of this perspective and found it to be the necessary international complement to a tripartite government of communists, socialists, and the left catholic *Mouvement républicain populaire* (MRP).

The shift toward alignment with the United States was produced by a combination of international and domestic factors that narrowed the choices of noncommunist leaders. In foreign affairs, MRP foreign minister Georges Bidault found himself forced to rely more on the Anglo-Saxon powers after the Moscow Conference of March-April 1947, when French demands to separate the Saar from Germany were rejected by the Soviets but tolerated by the United States and Britain.[2] The shift in foreign policy was reinforced by the expulsion of the communists from the government on 5 May 1947, when disagreements over wage and price controls ended an always difficult collaboration among the former resistance partners. The internal split was not definitive until the fall of 1947, but French involvement in Marshall Plan negotiations over the summer confirmed the new orientation of the Paris government. French economic dependence on the United States deepened during this period, of course, and adherence to the Marshall Plan program may be considered the most prominent symbol of the new alignment.

Within the governments of this period, members of the MRP were the leading proponents of strengthening the American connection and transforming the economic relationship into a security partnership that could be equally beneficial for France. As early as February 1946, the MRP ministers of foreign affairs and the armed forces had agreed to begin defense discussions with the United States, although the project had to be postponed because of anticipated communist opposition.[3] Once this impediment was removed, and socialist qualms overcome, a security connection became feasible and increasingly desirable for the French and other West Europeans. The first tripartite military conversations were held on Long Island in January 1948. The French representative was General Gaston-Henri-Gustave Billotte, while Generals Matthew Ridgway and Morgan spoke for the United States and Great Britain.[4] These conversations were apparently preliminary and very general in nature, producing no specific results. But the French looked upon this initial example of tripartite security planning, involving global strategic issues, as a prototype of the new relationship they sought with the two Anglo-Saxon powers.

The first formal Western defense arrangements were, however, purely European. France, Britain, and the Benelux countries met in Brussels on 4 March 1948 and on 17 March signed the treaty creating the Western European Union (WEU). The Brussels Treaty was and remains a fifty-year alliance binding all members to meet an "armed attack on Europe" and on any one of them with "all the military and other aid and assistance at their disposal" (Article IV). Germany was mentioned only in the preamble to the treaty; the Soviet Union went unnamed but was clearly the *raison d'être* of the defense arrangement.[5] The overriding purpose of the Brussels Treaty was actually to demonstrate to the United States that the European powers were willing to take the first steps in mutual cooperation for their own defense, thus enabling the American administration to obtain congressional consent to a formal North Atlantic defense treaty. Bidault made the first overt proposal along these lines in a note to the U.S. government on 4 March 1948. The signing of the Brussels Treaty furnished the opportunity for a joint British-French overture to Washington that received the necessary congressional support in the Vandenberg Resolution of 11 June 1948. While the United States was joining in the defense preparations of the Brussels Treaty powers,[6] negotiations on an Atlantic defense treaty opened in Washington on 5 July. A draft document was prepared by November and was subject to further revisions in complicated discussions involving the European governments, the executive branch of the American government, and leaders of the U.S. Senate.[7] The North Atlantic Treaty was ready and signed in Washington on 4 April 1949 and went into effect on 24 August 1949, with the deposit of ratification documents.

Although the Atlantic Alliance was ostensibly a political-military alliance to guarantee mutual security in the event of international aggression, it was internal West European affairs that most preoccupied the diplomats who produced the treaty and the statesmen who signed it. For, despite some nuanced differences in the views of Western governments and among their own different departments, the prevailing attitude in 1948-49 was that there was no imminent, direct Soviet military threat to the security of Western Europe. For countries such as France and Italy, the most immediate danger seemed to come from the political instability accompanying economic deprivation and the agitation of strong internal communist movements aligned with the Soviet Union.[8] There were probably no actual communist plans for fomenting an insurrection in France, but the *Parti communiste français* (PCF) could and did furnish ample evidence of its intention to promote discontent and destabilize the national political economy. These activities sometimes involved foolhardy statements and actions that seemed to substantiate the communist role as a fifth column acting on behalf of the Soviet Union.[9] One result was that noncommunist French elites developed an admirable expertise in utilizing their internal communist menace to expand American commitments to France and Western Europe, and especially to secure economic assistance as a weapon against the appeal of communism to the working classes. This stratagem ultimately had its drawbacks, however, for it also confirmed Anglo-Saxon suspicions about the basic unreliability of a state whose population and government bureaus were laced with communists or disloyal fellow travelers. An underlying reluctance to establish an open and equal partnership with such a country was to plague France's relations with the United States and Britain throughout the Fourth Republic and afterwards.

In 1949, then, the Atlantic Treaty was offered to France and continental Western Europe primarily as an instrument of psychological aid to restore Europe's self-confidence by setting up a security shield for the more important economic reconstruction work of the European Recovery Program (ERP). State Department officials such as George Kennan and Dean Acheson took this view and represented the dominant attitude among civilians in Washington. Thus, Secretary of State Acheson's letter transmitting the North Atlantic Treaty to President Truman stressed that the major purpose of the Alliance was "to contribute to the stability and well-being of the member nations by removing the haunting sense of insecurity and enabling them to plan and work with confidence for the future."[10] There was certainly a Franco-American consensus on this point. But their agreement and mutual understanding of the Alliance commitment was more fragile on the problem of how to meet external threats to French security.

In 1949, the position of the political establishment in Washington was that the Atlantic Treaty represented an important but general signal that Western Europe was considered vital to the security of the United States.[11] It did not, however, guarantee future American military actions on behalf of Europe or a build-up of American forces on the continent. Beyond some plans for material and economic assistance in reconstituting European defense forces, the American security commitment was quite ambivalent. Because of constitutional practices and Senate requirements, the mutual guarantee clause of the treaty (Article V) bound the parties only to consult in the event of an armed attack on one or all of them, and left each ally the sovereign judge of its response to such acts of aggression. As Secretary Acheson stressed to the Senate, "each party retains for itself the right of determination as to whether an armed attack has in fact occurred and what action it deems necessary to take."[12] The American position was dictated in part by the jealously guarded congressional prerogative to declare war, but it also reflected a conviction that military aggression in Europe was unlikely. Thus, outside of the Pentagon, American decision makers did not foresee the necessity or utility of creating a substantial allied military organization or pressing a reluctant Congress to increase the American military presence in Western Europe.

French leaders agreed with their counterparts in Washington and London that the Soviet Union seemed unprepared to initiate an aggressive war against the West.[13] They were, however, more fearful that Soviet intentions might change abruptly later and find the West unable to deter a Soviet attack and incapable of stopping it if it occurred. Invaded three times and occupied twice in the course of eighty years, the French were understandably more pessimistic when contemplating Soviet behavior in an uncertain future.[14] Recent French history also furnished painful lessons about the consequences for France of relying on ambiguous and elusive Anglo-American security guarantees against aggression, so that Versailles and the interwar experience cast a shadow over the value of the Atlantic Treaty.

During the treaty ratification debates in the French National Assembly, the lack of provisions for automatic military assistance in Article V troubled many deputies, who had hoped for a firmer American commitment. Noting the enormous imbalance between Soviet and Western forces in Europe, one deputy expressed the general fear that "without an automatic assistance clause, under present conditions, the Atlantic pact is scarcely a better guarantee of an immediate or late United States intervention than no pact at all."[15] The government, which had pressed unsuccessfully for a firmer commitment, clearly shared the desire for a stronger American engagement and had to admit that the absence of automaticity could be troublesome in the future. The consensus emerging from the National Assembly debates, however, was that Paris expected to circumvent American reservations about making military commitments by creating a set of Alliance institutions that would bind the United States to Europe in the political, economic, and military-strategic spheres.

The French hoped that the future institutions of the Alliance, foreseen in Article IX of the treaty, would constitute the binding military pledge absent from Article V.[16] Whereas Secretary Acheson's comments on Article IX did not favor the growth of a military organization,[17] French rapporteur René Mayer reminded his government that it had an obligation to organize and expand the treaty's military applications, otherwise it would not be worth much more that the Locarno Agreements, Article XVI of the League Covenant, or the Briand-Kellog Pact.[18] The Gaullists in the Assembly attempted to go a step further by defining the kind of defense structure France required for the Alliance and trying to postpone final ratification of the treaty until French demands had been met by the other allies.[19] The government successfully resisted being bound in this matter. But Foreign Minister Robert Schuman openly shared his colleagues' hopes that the Alliance would be the basis for a more concrete American commitment in the form of a military organization closely linking the security interests of all allies.

The issue of institutionalizing the Alliance and reinforcing American military forces would be confronted in 1950 and settled on terms only partially and temporarily satisfactory to France. In addition to a preoccupation with physical security in Europe, however, the French had more complex and problematic goals for the Atlantic Alliance. These goals transcended narrow internal or external threats and focused on the Alliance as a vehicle for reviving France's fallen status in Europe and abroad. Thus, French leaders adapted to the new conditions of the Cold War and perceived the Alliance and its American connection as a cornucopia of opportunity for securing a wide range of French interests. In general, the French were expecting to receive acknowledged first rank within the Alliance and, more specifically, they anticipated an expansion of the Anglo-American duumvirate into a triumvirate bearing primary responsibility for the global management of Western security interests. De Gaulle had already fought for similar status among the victors of World War II, his Fourth Republic successors were carrying on the struggle within the confines of a Western camp, and in 1958 the General would revive the theme again in his "memorandum diplomacy." In 1949, Paris sought privileged access to the Anglo-Saxon club for two reasons. First, because direct influence over American and British strategic planning was seen as a prerequisite for ensuring that French strategic interests were accounted for and adequately protected. Second, because France's leadership hoped that as a part of a Western tripartite oligarchy, it would be in a better position to retain continental supremacy over the Germans and muster American support for French colonial policies.

Despite their growing accommodation to Anglo-Saxon policies after 1947, the French felt they were not being accorded the influence commensurate with their importance and contributions to the West. In particular, they were excluded from the formal and informal Anglo-American military consultations that, in the French view, were decisively laying out the plans and conditions for Europe's defense. Bidault began pressing for inclusion in the Anglo-American military conversations as soon as the communist departure from the government was definite, but Washington and London agreed between themselves to stick to their bilateral format and leave the French out of meaningful participation in their joint planning.[20] French resentment at this treatment was reinforced by the experience in the Brussels Treaty Organization during 1948. There, military planning seemed to turn into a British-dominated enterprise focused on protecting Britain's insular security at the expense of a truly continental strategy. Loose links between the BTO and the United States were another cause for French dissatisfaction, because military liaisons between the two were handled in London and mainly by the British. Paris was naturally suspicious of a system that permitted British officials to act as intermediaries between the United States and continental Europe, and it seized upon the new Atlantic Alliance as a forum for direct and equal access to Washington.[21]

This intention was not a closely held secret in allied circles. Bidault made a very direct bid to join the US-UK Combined Chiefs of Staff in June 1948, but was put off on the pretext that the committee was no longer meeting under this rubric.[22] Later, during the Atlantic Treaty negotiations, the French ambassador in Washington told the secretary of state that, for France, the main purpose of Article VIII (later Article IX) of the treaty would be to set up a tripartite chiefs of staff body, in Washington, and thereby to include France in Anglo-American strategic planning.[23] Although such a body, the Standing Group, was created soon thereafter, its role and powers were to be limited by persistent American (and British) reservations about collaborating with the French. In the United States, the State Department and the Pentagon discussed French demands in February and March of 1949 and, it seems, agreed to give the French formal membership in whatever military control body was established by the Alliance, while taking steps to ensure that this body's functions were limited to narrow and immediate issues of implementing the treaty.[24] As for the French expectation of participating in global security planning, the comments of one State Department official reflected an attitude that was to determine American policy throughout the Fourth and Fifth Republics and be the source of much discontent: "the French," he wrote, "have basically only European and North African responsibilities and inadequate strength to play any role in other theaters and therefore are not entitled to participate in consideration of global strategy."[25]

French expectations of tripartism seemed, in 1949, to encounter a hostile — or at best skeptical — audience with the power to thwart and disappoint the Gallic ally. A similar fate awaited the European side of the French Atlantic design. Expecting to dominate the continental European region of the alliance, the Fourth Republic was to find its interests gradually overwhelmed by a powerful German-American coalition. As the treaty was being negotiated, the French knew that the prospect of a West German revival, backed by the Anglo-Saxons, was already underway and bound to jeopardize the preeminence they associated with security.

Because of pressure from Washington and London, Paris had begun compromising on German issues in 1948 and finally abandoned opposition to the creation of a semisovereign West German state. The Basic Law for West Germany was approved by the military governors on 23 May 1949, and the new government was centralized enough to stir concern in France over the revival of West German nationalism and militarism.[26] Thus, French officials informed the Americans that they considered the Atlantic Treaty to be a security guarantee against Germany as well as the Soviet Union.[27] They also took steps to ensure that the West Germans would be barred from rearming and one day challenging a French hegemony over the Western part of the continent. In July 1949 Foreign Minister Schuman told the National Assembly: "Germany has no army and should not have one. It has no arms and will not have any. . . . It is therefore unthinkable, for France and for all her allies, that Germany could be allowed to adhere to the Atlantic pact as a nation capable of defending itself or of aiding in the defense of other nations."[28] As insurance against these developments, which were already openly discussed, the cabinet arranged for a special amendment to the law authorizing ratification of the treaty. This amendment forbid the government from agreeing to admit new members into the Alliance without parliamentary approval, a stipulation intended to strengthen the leverage of future cabinets should the allies propose expanding the Alliance to include West Germany.[29]

Along with these political benefits of influence and status within the West, the French anticipated two additional "side payments" from the new Alliance and the American connection: increased financial and material aid for rearmament, and some assistance in holding on to France's shaky colonial empire. In addition to substantial sums obtained or allocated under the European Recovery Program, the French had begun receiving American allocations of military spare parts and equipment as early as October 1948, and had filed numerous requests for more aid bilaterally and through the Brussels Treaty agencies.[30] Ratification of the treaty was sped through the National Assembly in 1949 partly in order to facilitate passage of the Mutual Defense Assistance Act then before the U.S. Congress. The French anticipated that this aid program would build up France's armed forces in Europe and provide material support for the ambitious diplomatic goals of the nation's leaders. Furthermore, they hoped this could be achieved at minimum cost to the French economy, which was inflation-prone and bound to experience difficulties in managing an extensive rearmament program along with the burdens of general economic reconstruction and a costly colonial war in Southeast Asia.

The first Indochina War was the immediate source of France's colonial problems in 1949 and a natural preoccupation of the Paris government. The French commitment to an overseas empire transcended that particular conflict, however, and it would be difficult to exaggerate the profound significance noncomminist elites ascribed to colonial possessions and the French Union. Colonies had been identified with national power and grandeur since the early years of the Third Republic, an attitude that was intensified during periods of weakness or instability in the Metropole.[31] Following World War II, France's overseas possessions were perceived as necessary elements of national and international regeneration on nearly every level: conferring political status as a great power, assisting in economic revival, and fulfilling the moral civilizing mission that enveloped a humanitarian mystique around French imperialism.

In the context of the Cold War, French leaders anticipated that the Western allies would applaud and support this mission, which ensured that France's dependents would not fall under the influence of either communism or *"fanatismes nationalistes,"* two ideologies considered indistinguishable in Paris.[32] When the Atlantic Treaty was debated in France, there were regrets expressed in the National Assembly that it was only a narrow regional arrangement barely extended to cover the Algerian departments of France.[33] From the perspective of France's noncommunist forces, it was unfortunate that the treaty did not somehow encompass the entire French Union, and especially Indochina. But the government was already pressing for some form of global cooperation among the three leading Western powers, and would use the earliest opportunity to encourage the United States to extend its support to include France's colonial interests. The dilemma French leaders faced proved to be an unmanageable one for a weakened middle power, namely, how to meet simultaneously both European and colonial commitments, how to manipulate these debilitating endeavors to create the illusion of great power and responsibility, and how to avoid the role of overt dependent and *demandeur* despite heavy and obvious demands placed on the United States and the Alliance. The Fourth Republic, it seems, had ambitions and expectations so extravagant and contradictory that they were bound to create grave disappointments, thereby wounding both national pride and the Alliance tie so highly valued in 1949.

The Organization of Atlantic Defense

In the several years it took to create the defense organization of the Atlantic Alliance, Fourth Republic governments changed composition with enough regularity that it was sometimes difficult for France to formulate and pursue detailed policies with consistency and resolution. Instability took a certain toll in both domestic and foreign policy, particularly because it confirmed the impression abroad of France as an unsteady and floundering ally. It also meant that proposals initiated or favored under one government or minister suddenly had less priority, and they were neglected or even abandoned by the French. This pattern weakened their influence over the development of the Atlantic Alliance organization between 1949 and 1955, when the political and military structure was set up essentially according to American wishes.

It is not certain, however, that more coherent and persistent efforts would have produced radically different results. France's situation as an economic and military dependent in Europe naturally limited her bargaining leverage, which was often used to resist and postpone unpleasant decisions rather than to instigate and be constructive in the defense arena. Furthermore, Fourth Republic governments were at times confronted with relatively clear choices that forced them to establish priorities that did help shape the contours of the Atlantic security system. One priority, finally, was to prefer an Atlantic-centered and American-managed Western defense over a West European continental system linking France more closely to West Germany than to the United States. Another was to sacrifice French military strength in Europe for the sake of overseas commitments in Indochina and later in North Africa, at the expense of the prestige and influence strong European forces might have brought Paris in the NATO commands and in Western policy-making circles. Although the French repeatedly tried to trade off the burdens and sacrifices of their extra-European engagements for status within the Alliance, this was not a very successful ploy. As a result, Paris was never happy with the implications and consequences of its own priorities and choices, because they testified to weakness and an inability to reconcile the contradictions in French foreign-policy goals.

In their attempts to influence the structure of the emerging Alliance security organization, successive cabinets pursued several different policies and themes that conform to the aspirations described above. In a somewhat confusing maze of plans and ideas, the French sometimes put forward complicated projects for close integration of the military forces, defense planning, and financing of Atlantic defense, sometimes favored a diplomatic-strategic version of their trilateral vision either inside or outside the Alliance, sometimes focused on the Standing Group as the vehicle for realizing these aims, or, with the European Defense Community (EDC) project, appeared to favor a close-knit continental body under French tutelege as a basis for European defense. Many of these schemes were pursued simultaneously or sequentially, yet seem incompatible. The French, however, evidently counted on their tripartite connection to the Anglo-Saxons, along with their overseas empire, to enable them to control the political restraints implied by defense integration commitments accepted in NATO or proposed in the EDC. They also sought, with some success, enough of a privileged status to allow France a stubborn pursuit of national interest at the expense of Alliance commitments and the preferences of the dominant American ally.

The French Tripartite Design. Although it was frequently revived in subsequent years, the tripartite scheme for creating a kind of "inner directorate" for the Alliance was an early and principal theme of French diplomacy until the Alliance mechanisms took shape on a different basis after the fall of 1950. The French efforts of 1948-49 were revived by Premier Bidault in a speech at Lyons on 16 April 1950, when he called for the creation of a limited membership "Atlantic High Council for Peace."[34] Subsequent French presentation of this idea combined it with a proposal for common or integrated allied budgeting and planning for rearmament to be administered by an Alliance general staff or secretariat. The plan was first discussed during preparatory sessions for the May 1950 Foreign Ministers Conference in London. In these meetings, Hervé Alphand, then secretary-general of the Quai d'Orsay, stressed the economic planning aspects of this proposed organism.[35] The State Department was skeptical, however, and refused to consider setting up an inner political council comparable to the military Standing Group. Instead, the United States preferred to count on some informal tripartite meetings, as the Western Big Three were already doing, and to expand the consultation role of the full-member North Atlantic Council.[36] Foreign Minister Schuman did bring up the French idea at the conference, but Ernest Bevin and Acheson convinced him, they thought, to abandon both this proposal and the joint budgeting plan, and to accept instead their agreement to hold regular but informal tripartite meetings two or three times a year, supplemented by consulations among each resident foreign minister and the two ambassadors.[37]

The United States and Britain felt they had dealt with this particular French preoccupation, and were annoyed to see it revived in July 1950, when Alphand, then French deputy representative to the North Atlantic Council, again brought up the possibility of establishing in Washington, "where real decisions will be taken," a three-power political "inner council which will parallel the Standing Group on the civilian level."[38] Despite discouraging replies from the secretary of state's office,[39] the Quai d'Orsay persisted in proposing a common defense-budgeting mechanism and the creation, within the Atlantic Council, of "an executive body endowed with the broadest possible powers of decision."[40] In handling these persistent initiatives, the United States finally refused some outright—such as the common budgeting plan—or managed to divert French attention from their tripartite obsession to projects for upgrading the Standing Group, enhancing the work of the full Atlantic Council, and expanding the military forces and command structure of the Alliance. After the fall of 1950, according to available records, the United States was temporarily successful in this endeavor. The tripartite theme would, however, be revived later by the French in reaction to growing Western dependence on American nuclear weapons, and in response to French travails in Algeria when de Gaulle turned to this favorite stratagem of the Fourth Republic and incorporated it into his famous memorandum of September 1958.

Fourth Republic efforts failed partly because the institutionalization of the Atlantic Council mechanism, with regular meetings of permanent representatives, was the preferred American view of how to organize political consultations within a multilateral alliance. This format was given priority because it conformed to the formal egalitarianism of the Alliance, but also because the United States could more easily "lead," or dominate, wider forums where the narrow interests of France or Britain had to accommodate the wishes of Europe's smaller powers.[41] The outcomes, usually, were closer to American preferences and served to maintain Washington's primacy in intra-Alliance decision making. Also, particularly in the formative stages of the Atlantic Alliance, officials in Washington wanted to downplay special American ties with Britain or France and to channel most European security decisions through the infant coalition. Thus, at a time when France was seeking to expand the bilateral Anglo-American "special relationship," Washington was ironically trying to deemphasize this relationship and was consequently unwilling to have it grow to include France as well.[42] Sometimes American officials put off British efforts to reinforce the bilateral connection by noting French and continental sensibilities. Wanting to encourage more of a British commitment to European cooperation, the United States also stressed the importance of discussing European issues in NATO and including the French fully in that forum.[43]

There was, nevertheless, an Anglo-American consensus that the two of them bore special responsibility for protecting Western security interests in most non-European regions, and that France should be barred from directly influencing their decisions concerning areas such as the Middle East and northern Asia. The United States did, therefore, continue to regard Britain as "our principal partner in strategic planning"[44] on a global basis, and relevant issues continued to be examined in exclusively bilateral meetings involving high diplomatic and military officials. Such groups met in Washington in July and October of 1950, for example, to discuss problems in light of the outbreak of the Korean War. This kind of close and ongoing consultation was what Paris wanted to join, but found inaccessible.

Barred from formal and continuous access to Anglo-American collaboration outside the Alliance, or from establishing an inner political directorate, the French could still hope to institutionalize tripartism by building on the foundation of the Standing Group. This three-power committee of national military officers was created in October 1949, and took its place alongside the other main institutions of the Alliance: the North Atlantic Council itself; the Defense Committee, composed of defense ministers or their representations; and the Military Committee, composed of the national chiefs of staff or their representatives. The Standing Group was to function as an executive committee of the Military Committee, and was charged with integrating the defense plans of the five separate Regional Planning Groups.[45] Made up of representatives of the United States, France, and Britain, the Standing Group was the Alliance organism most susceptible to fulfilling French plans for joining Anglo-Saxon strategic planning sessions and securing decisive influence over the allied military defense of France and continental Europe. As their other tripartite formulas broke down, Fench diplomats turned to this institution and sought to upgrade its authority.

After the outbreak of the Korean War, when the Atlantic allies were deciding how to bolster their European defense forces against possible Soviet adventurism, Paris saw an opportunity to ensure that the Standing Group would emerge as the focus of allied military planning. In an important memorandum submitted to the United States in August 1950, the Quai d'Orsay stressed that the Standing Group should become the agency that "like the combined chiefs of staff in the last war, is capable of determining the general strategy from now on and of directing all operations according to a single conception."[46] Rather than limiting the Standing Group's authority to the continental theater, the French wanted to consolidate the separate Regional Planning Groups under the tripartite body. This would have given them a role in determining the defense strategy of the entire treaty area, including the United States, and of zones outside the treaty area alluded to in the August memorandum's stress on "every possible theater of operations."[47] Much of the French package was accepted at the North Atlantic Council meeting in September 1950, which, *inter alia,* provided for a major expansion of the American military presence in Europe, and for a Supreme Commander to direct the integrated Western forces on the continent.

At that time, primarily in response to the French, the Standing Group's functions were upgraded considerably. It was given responsibility for the "higher strategic direction" of the future defense organization, and was to control both the integrated continental force and the Supreme Commander.[48] This formal allocation of responsibility, which went beyond the previous stated intentions of the State and Defense departments, was an apparent victory for the French conception of the Alliance. It might have laid the basis for the kind of inner directorate Paris wanted available to influence the Anglo-Saxons and to solidify France's role as continental Western Europe's spokesman in ruling Western circles. However, the Standing Group did not fulfill these expectations. It was unable to carve out a dominant position within the Alliance defense institutions and was instead debilitated by recurring rivalries, disagreements, and distrust among its members—who functioned primarily as agents of their defense ministries and proved unable to act or plan on the basis of other than narrow national interests.[49] The pattern of noncooperation was set early in the life of the Standing Group. The first British representative, General Morgan, preferred to resort to the usual bilateral contacts with the Americans, while the American member, General Albert C. Wedemeyer, went along because he distrusted officials from countries with a strong communist influence. Their unfortunate French colleague, General Ely, though very capable, could not be effective in alleviating the situation partly because he was held in check by a socialist defense minister, Paul Ramadier, who was suspicious of exclusive committees of military officers.[50] This situation subverted French designs for the Standing Group, while the focus of NATO military planning and influence gradually shifted to the new Supreme Commander and his integrated staff.

France in NATO Military Integration. The post of Supreme Allied Commander Europe (SACEUR) and his headquarters, the Supreme Headquarters Allied Powers Europe (SHAPE), were created in wake of the attack on Korea in June 1950. Although there were already projects to strengthen allied military forces in Europe,[51] this event convinced Western leaders that the Soviet Union had "passed beyond the use of subversion to conquer independent nations and [would] now use armed invasion and war."[52] Allied plans took shape over the summer, and at the September 1950 Atlantic Council meeting the governments agreed to a major build-up of American forces in Europe. This was to be accompanied by an expanded (and American-financed) rearmament effort on the part of the European allies; it was to include, in some unspecified form, a West German military contribution. To coordinate these forces and enable them to put up a defense based on a "forward strategy," the allies also agreed to create an integrated military organization under the centralized strategic direction of the Standing Group and the Supreme Commander. The Allied Command Europe (ACE) was created in December 1950; General Dwight D. Eisenhower was appointed to the post of SACEUR at that time. His headquarters began operating in Paris the following January and was officially installed at Rocquencourt, outside Paris, in April 1951.[53]

The French encouraged and welcomed these developments for several reasons in addition to those already discussed. They fulfilled the aim of securing a firmer American commitment to a strong continental defense as far east of the Rhine as possible—essentially by augmenting the physical presence of American forces committed to the Alliance. Despite the obvious choice of an American to command these forces and other allied troops on the continent, the Standing Group would, it was assumed, provide overall guidance and direction. The post-Korea package also included promises of substantially more aid for the French rearmament program, ensuring that an important French military force would be created to give Paris a major voice in the defense organization. Finally, in the context of the unpleasant American condition of West German rearmament, the French could hope that the planned increase in allied armed forces might obviate the need for West German troops before they actually materialized. And, if French governments were unable to postpone and finally scuttle this calamity, at least they would have a secure and decisive influence through the key French role in NATO institutions.

Numerous developments blocked the fulfillment of these expectations. One was the emergence of an American-dominated SACEUR and SHAPE as the focal point of allied military planning, leaving the French with painfully little influence over their own security in Europe and the allied forces there. The question of SHAPE's role in planning allied strategy and directing allied armed forces is a complicated one and cannot be fully examined here. But some discussion is warranted because Gaullist NATO policy was often aimed at the integration features of this organization and its alleged power to determine the strategy governing French security while subjecting French forces to the orders of supranational commands really controlled by the United States.

The SHAPE staff system was indeed based on the principle of integration rather than the committee system of combined national representatives favored by the British and the Gaullists in France. Eisenhower decided against a nonintegrated structure on the grounds that it was militarily less efficient, would facilitate national rivalries, and would reinforce domination by the three largest allies at the expense of genuine Alliance-wide participation in the mutual defense effort. As a consequence of the emphasis on the international nature of the SHAPE staff, its members and the commanders-in-chief of the principal commands were normally prevented from holding positions of authority in their national armed forces and were discouraged from asserting narrow national interests at the expense of the common effort. The prominent exception to this ban was SACEUR himself, who was also the commander-in-chief of American forces in Europe. This dual role was necessary, among other reasons, to give SACEUR direct authority over the most important military force in Europe and, later, over American-controlled nuclear weapons stationed there.

As SHAPE and SACEUR came to predominate over the planning and implementation of allied defense strategy, a certain mystique was created about the selfless contributions of the staff and its commanders. There was doubtless some value to the staff experience, and the careers of SACEURs such as Lauris Norstad testify to the officeholders' ability to shed their nationalities and become spokesmen for European interests as well as American ones.[54] There were, however, serious imperfections. Along with certain inefficiencies endemic to international bureaucracies,[55] the most glaring defect for the French was the indisputable fact of Anglo-American domination of the staff. SACEUR and the majority of his aids were Anglo-American, with some 30-35 percent of the entire staff Americans, while English was the main language despite the theoretically equal status of French. Americans were perhaps the most serious offenders in relying on each other instead of on the staff hierarchy to get things done quickly, a factor that reinforced the impression that SHAPE, indeed NATO, was very much an American operation.[56]

The superpower hegemony was most evident in the NATO strategic planning process, SHAPE's most important function. One informed French conclusion was that "the superior weight of the American chain of command, acting, of course, in accordance with the Pentagon, has contributed in large measure to depriving Alliance strategy of a truly collective character."[57] This was especially true in regard to nuclear weapons and strategy. Until changes made after 1965, continental allies had minimal access to American plans for the nuclear defense of the Alliance. There was an atomic weapons course for allied offices held at Garmisch after 1952, but it was mainly concerned with the weapons' external characteristics and their effects on battlefield conditions. Although SACEUR had a liaison group at the Omaha defense center and the Strategic Air Command was represented at SHAPE, most French officers felt they received little information about American and British targeting and strategic planning.[58] The circulation of information on these matters at SHAPE was restricted to American or British "eyes only," and even top French commanders of allied forces remained uninformed.

This discrimination was required by the 1946 McMahon Act and regrets were frequently expressed by American officials who had to deal with resentful allies. President Eisenhower wrote in 1966 that the legislation "prevented us from making any workable agreements with our partners in NATO respecting nuclear weapons—indeed, it was difficult and embarassing, because of the restrictions imposed upon us, even to discuss the matter intelligently and thoroughly."[59] This situation was grating enough as long as the Alliance formally depended on plans for a conventional defense of the continent aided by U.S. strategic nuclear power. The shift to a heavy reliance on strategic nuclear deterrence after 1954 was bound to enhance French and continental concern about NATO. For Paris had not obtained a notable influence over planning for theater defense in Europe and had failed to entangle the United States in a defense structure where French authority was substantial. After 1954, both the key weapons and basic strategic decisions for Europe's and France's defense were obviously in the hands of the Americans alone and beyond the purview of the Alliance. The elusive American guarantee still escaped France's grasp.

Gaullists and other critics were quick to note this development during the 1950s and to turn it against French governments as well as against NATO. Another prominent Gaullist charge was that, in addition to turning over strategic control of national security to the Americans, the Fourth Republic had also abandoned control of France's own armed forces by committing them to NATO's integrated commands. While the first charge had substantial merit, the second was based on a simplistic analysis of the NATO system. SACEUR, SHAPE, and the integrated European commands were indeed allocated general formal authority over allied forces on the continent, and this authority was augmented considerably after the demise of the EDC in 1954. Originally, in 1950, each ally agreed to earmark certain forces for NATO, and, furthermore, indicated that these forces would be "organized, equipped, trained, and ready to implement agreed plans" for defense drawn up at SHAPE.[60] Among other incentives, American military-assistance agreements specified that the recipient would develop its armed forces in accordance with NATO defense plans and as a contribution to the integrated defense of the region.[61]

The 1954 Paris Agreements went much further than earlier ones in defining and expanding the powers of SACEUR. They required states in the ACE region to place all their land, sea, and air forces in continental Europe, and particularly those stationed on West German soil, under the direction of SACEUR and the NATO commands.[62] Forces were to be deployed in accordance with NATO's integrated defense plans, and force integration was to be maintained at the army group and tactical air force levels, lower if necessary. It should be noted that the territory of the United Kingdom was excluded from these provisions, so that only British forces stationed in West Germany fell directly under SACEUR.

These agreements and powers were more impressive, however, in council resolutions and NATO rhetoric than in practice. In time of peace, all allied governments retained national control over their armed forces in Europe. The single exception was West Germany after 1955, whose forces were placed directly under NATO in the absence of its own General Staff—but even in this case the Bonn Ministry of Defense exercised most of the normal control functions.[63] SHAPE's contingency planning for crisis and war could count on receiving authority over specified national forces at certain stages of crisis escalation, but no ally was committed to engage in military action under NATO unless it considered that Article V of the treaty was in force. Thus, assignments of forces were often nominal, and national command structures and powers remained intact while they cooperated with the NATO commands as a matter of voluntary national policy.

Such limitations might have been circumvented if the allies had engaged in far-reaching force integration, by mixing national forces down to the lower levels of the force structure. In this case, the national defense system would have lost genuine autonomy because it could not have carried out independent actions without the compliance of other force elements; nor could it have easily resisted engagements involving the entire Alliance defense structure. But force integration in NATO did not penetrate deeply into the national armed forces—it normally extended only to the army group level (200,000 men) for ground forces, and to the tactical air force level for air forces. In practical terms, member forces were only "coordinated," not "integrated," and outside of the SHAPE planning center most military officers and all troops remained under national control and subject to the orders of their national commands.[64]

Despite Gaullist charges, Fourth Republic France is an outstanding example of determination not to accept Alliance restrictions on the use of armed forces, and to retain and manipulate sovereign control over these forces. During the Indochina War, officials in Paris consistently gave this colonial engagement priority over fulfilling military obligations to NATO and helping build up allied force strength on the continent. Although the French intended to devote their armed forces to European defense after the Geneva Accords of 1954, the rapid onset of the Algerian War made the North African theater a more immediate and vital arena for defending French security.[65] In the post-EDC Agreements, the French were careful to insist on qualifying the NATO commitments by excluding forces "intended for the defense of overseas territories and other forces which the North Atlantic Treaty Organization has recognized or will recognize as suitable to remain under national command."[66] Thus, France was later able to withdraw most of her land forces from West Germany and from commitments to NATO, with the virtually automatic consent of SACEUR and the NATO Council. After 1954, then, the bulk of France's army was either abroad or designated for overseas duty and therefore under exclusive national control. General de Gaulle could later capitalize on France's privileged position by keeping his forces outside of NATO jurisdiction even after they were returned to the Métropole.

Because of its marginal active contribution to NATO's military forces, the Fourth Republic's most valuable asset for the Alliance was French territory itself. The principal NATO organs and military commands, many Alliance infrastructure projects, and an extensive American base and supply network were located in France after 1949. In addition to the council and secretariat in Paris, SHAPE was at Rocquencourt (Marly-le-Roi), and the important headquarters of the Allied Forces Central Europe command (AFCENT), with its French commander, was at Fountainebleau. Some 25 percent of NATO infrastructure construction went to France in the course of her membership in NATO, much of it concentrated in the 1950s. Also, some twenty U.S. army facilities were set up in France, including the headquarters at St. Germain-en-Laye near Paris (Camp des Loges). The U.S. Air Force maintained four large air bases at Chateauroux, Evreux, Toul-Rosières, and Laon. These bases included combat units until 1960. The U.S. Navy had a toehold on French soil with its access facilities at Villefranche-sur-Mer.[67] Perhaps the most important American infrastructure facility in France was the 371-mile long Donges-Metz oil pipeline built to service American combat forces in Germany. The pipeline was jointly financed and part of its capacity was made available to the French government.[68] As a positive contribution, this sizable Alliance presence in France deeply implicated the nation in all NATO military activities despite a weak concrete commitment to NATO military strength.

It does not seem, however, that the Fourth Republic unnecessarily or overgenerously dispensed with national sovereignty in granting facilities and privileges for Alliance-related purposes. In 1952, SHAPE and AFCENT were granted extraterritorial rights and status similar to that of diplomatic missions, and were the subject of additional agreements in 1953 concerning technical issues such as communications, finances, immunities, and indemnifications. Although in wartime either party could suspend part or all of the agreement on sixty days' notice, SHAPE was generally assured that it would continue to function "in the case of hostilities involving the application of the North Atlantic Treaty."[69] The status of American (and Canadian) bases and depots in France was regulated by a series of bilateral agreements signed between 1951 and 1958. Among other things, they defined the number of American military personnel that could be introduced onto French territory and the purposes for which the bases could be used.

For example, a 4 October 1952 agreement on American air force facilities required that the USAF supply monthly lists of units and personnel complements at each installation, along with their expected deployments. Each unit's entry into France, and future deployment, was to be cleared in advance with French authorities. The agreement further stipulated that "operations from the bases covered in this Agreement, except in the execution of North Atlantic Treaty Organization missions, will be undertaken only as may be agreed between the two Governments."[70] France specifically retained "territorial" authority over all bases, while the United States had only "operational" control overseen by a French liaison officer present at each facility. Finally, a secret agreement of 8 April 1954, revealed in 1959, stipulated that France would be consulted in advance on any use of American air bases during a crisis, even if the mission planned were under the aegis of NATO.[71] Although controls may have been relaxed and accommodating under the Fourth Republic, it does not seem that Paris actually gave the United States a free hand in France or, as charged by the Gaullists, alienated national sovereignty.

The NATO military organization accepted by the Fourth Republic was not really a leviathan, partly because it was so cumbersome, but also because it operated under numerous constraints imposed by the members. It nevertheless could and did provoke dissatisfaction in France because it tended to consolidate and even emphasize her status as a junior partner with little influence or recognition, despite what the French felt were real contributions and sacrifices. Perhaps this situation would have been tolerable if NATO had been a mechanism for promoting effective allied support for France during her colonial travails, if it had not served as the vehicle for an unwelcome West German rearmament and revival, and if it had adapted more successfully to the national-security dilemma posed by nuclear weapons. But NATO and its dominant member were implicated in frustrating French goals in these matters, and the Alliance became a source of dissatisfaction and

something of a scapegoat for growing French discontent during the
1950s.

France between Atlantica and Europa

While the Atlantic Alliance and the NATO military organization did not
develop in accordance with French expectations, there was a theoretical and
suggestive alternative to the American-dominated Atlantic structure. This
was the necessarily ambivalent ideal of a unified Europe that could pool the
resources of its individual states to form a strong entity relatively independent
of external powers. Many speculated that this Europe, whose prospects ebbed
and flowed throughout the postwar period, might serve as an independent
and stabilizing bloc in an unsteady world, or perhaps as a full and equal
partner of the United States within the West, and as a bridge or mediator
between East and West and even between North and South. French governments have often tended to identify, or confuse, their national interests with
those of such a wider European group because of the assumption, or assertion,
that France is the natural leader of Western Europe. Because France and her
leaders were indeed moving forces behind developments in postwar European
unity, contradictions in French goals and an inability to define clear European
and Atlantic priorities took a heavy toll on West European cooperation,
generally ensuring that it would be subordinate to Atlanticist forces in the
political-strategic arena.

From the standpoint of European unification, one unintended consequence of French policies after 1948 was to encourage and consolidate an
asymmetry between the accomplishments and influence of a West European
economic and political community, on the one hand, and the weakness and
dependence of a European defense effort fully subordinated to an Atlantic
structure, on the other. This awkward and tension-producing relationship was
essentially formed during the 1950s in the course of the debate over the EDC.
Later, it was to confound Gaullist European policy and help undermine the
attack on Atlanticism in the 1960s. It remains an unresolved flaw in the U.S.-
European relationship. Though usually dormant, in a crisis or during periods
of tension it can fester and embitter relations as the United States pits its
defense hegemony against the economic strength and adolescent political
community of the Europeans.

Throughout the Fourth Republic, one uncertainty that at times muddled
French European policy was the rather utopian hope that France—and
perhaps a French-led Europe—could escape the superpower bloc structure
and act as a mediator or, more precisely, an interlocutor between East and
West. This aspiration was implicit in de Gaulle's December 1944 Treaty of
Alliance and Mutual Assistance with the Soviet Union, which symbolized his

determination to forge links with the East in order to resist subordination to the "Anglo-Saxons" in the West. Although the Cold War made it impossible for France to achieve this goal alone, the hope remained in the background that a united French-led Europe could serve as the "necessary factor of compensation and understanding" between the superpowers.[72] Both the Schuman Plan and the EDC were manifestations of the French desire for European unity as a basis for eventual independence from the United States, in that Europe was laying the foundation for a moral and material autonomy that could also provide security against the Soviet Union.[73] Furthermore, by containing West Germany within a framework of European integration, the new Europe could work between the power blocs for eventual détente and European interests in general.

The goals of independence and mediation were often confused in and out of France with more genuinely neutralist sentiments that preoccupied some French intellectuals, and prominent journals and newspapers such as *Le Monde*, and could temporarily join forces with other groups when faced with offensive American behavior or the unpalatable prospect of German rearmament.[74] Sometimes neutralism seemed indistinguishable from the aspiration for independence from the blocs, although the former concept represented a more passive and pacifist conception of France's role than was acceptable to most French elites under the Fourth or Fifth Republics. In any case, in the 1950s most West Europeans and Frenchmen rejected neutrality and did not conceive of European unity as antagonistic to the United States, even though many longed for greater French and European autonomy. This goal was frustrated and deflected, however, partly because the European idea was prematurely tied to a scheme for a supranational political-military community as the device for rearming West Germany. Either development was bound to meet strong opposition within France. Together, they severely damaged the prospects for European cooperation and ultimately reinforced the American hegemony over French and West European security.

Until the Algerian War ushered in the Suez crisis and a newly profound French antagonism toward the United States and the Alliance, the issue of West German rearmament and the European Defense Community was the most prominent source of bitterness and recrimination that lingered long after the matter itself was settled. It was, in effect, a repository of the contradictions in French security policy, exposing them and French weakness in a particularly brutal way. The most significant defeat came at the outset, of course, with the emergence of a German-American alliance committed to rearmament as the solution to Western Europe's conventional military infirmities, on the one hand, and to the problem of the Federal Republic's international status, on the other. Despite the roadblocks and diversions ingeniously created by France, once Washington and Bonn settled on a defense contribution as the locomotive for security and a West German revival, Paris could not scuttle this most disagreeable enterprise. It could only influence the timing and final institutional arrangements. The limitations on the Fourth Republic's freedom of choice in the affair are clear in retrospect, but the long delay in finally accepting them was partly caused by an underlying illusion in France that German rearmament could be avoided altogether.

French government denials of an impending West German military revival were voiced loudly as early as mid-1949, because the idea had already been advanced during the Berlin Blockade and figured in a Pentagon study prepared for the Joint Chiefs of Staff in the fall of 1949.[75] After the onset of the Korean War, negotiations within the Truman administration concluded that American reinforcements in Europe, under a unified Alliance command, should be offered on the condition of a German military contribution in one form or another.[76] Konrad Adenauer had already stated his willingness to rearm in return for concessions granting the Federal Republic equal rights and status in the West.[77] The issue surfaced at the September 1950 meeting of the North Atlantic Council when German rearmament became the explicit condition of an expanded American commitment in Europe. Overriding Foreign Minister Schuman's objections, the council charged its Military Committee with the task of preparing a plan for a direct German military contribution to the Alliance.

Under intense American pressure to abandon its opposition to German rearmament,[78] the government of René Pleven produced a plan of its own and presented it to the National Assembly on 4 October 1950. Pleven and his defense minister, Jules Moch, apparently had three motives for devising this audacious project: to postpone West German rearmament for as long as possible; to ensure that rearmament, if it came, would not give the Federal Republic membership in, or direct access to, the Atlantic Alliance; and, finally, to use the integrationist formula as a control device for keeping Germany subordinate to France. After a complicated set of double negotiations—one in Bonn concentrating on a NATO-sponsored German defense contribution, and one in Paris focusing on the European formula—the Pleven Plan predominated and emerged as the European Defense Community Treaty, signed in Paris on 27 May 1952.[79] The Truman administration was initially very sceptical about the French proposal,[80] but was gradually won over to it as a device for achieving American aims, including the unification of Western Europe. General Eisenhower's sympathies were aroused by Jean Monnet during his term as SACEUR in Paris, and, as president, he and his secretary of state became even more zealous supporters of the EDC than the Democrats had been.

Perhaps the outstanding feature of the proposal and the EDC Treaty in its final form was their extreme complexity, particularly in respect to the controversial force integration and supranational control measures that would have submitted French and other member forces to the authority of a European defense committee and, eventually, to the political community planned in conjunction with the EDC. For its French supporters, a primary advantage of the EDC format was that it could impose restraints sufficient to control a rearmed Germany, yet still leave France in a position to dominate the EDC and sustain both her Anglo-American ties and a global role. This group claimed that only the EDC would prevent German membership in NATO, the reconstitution of an independent German army and general staff, and a direct German-American collaboration that would give West Germany the preponderant military, political, and industrial role on the continent. Alongside the privileges attached to membership in the Alliance and France's global status as head of the French Union, the EDC, French "Europeans" argued, would actually bolster France's claims to act as Western Europe's leader and spokesman in Atlantic councils, while laying the foundation for a united Europe independent of the superpowers.[81]

Opponents of the EDC, on the other hand, and many uncertain supporters, doubted that the supranational formula could successfully promote these aspirations. While Gaullists and the military opposed supranational defense integration on principle, they and many others also feared that the EDC restrictions on West Germany were insufficient, and the corresponding ones on unstable France too great, so that Germany would eventually dominate the community. Paris had had to accept nearly the same encumbrances on its independent military capacity as Bonn, although exceptions were made for armed forces assigned to overseas duty. Arguments and fears were exaggerated in the heat of controversy, but many were troubled and swayed by charges such as the one that the supranational community would become strong enough to take over France's role in the Alliance and even replace the French member of the Standing Group with a West German delegate.[82] While British participation might have quelled some of these fears, neither the Labour Party nor the Conservatives were willing to be drawn into an integrated Europe during this period.[83] As the EDC floundered in the Fourth Republic's political system, the United States and Britain did offer guarantees to retain military forces on the continent and, implicitly, help restrain the Germans. But such offers and some modifications in the EDC framework itself proved to be inadequate remedies for French insecurity and a persistent sense of inferiority and weakness in the face of West German vitality and potential strength.

Critics were also preoccupied with the Defense Community's possible effect on France's overseas interests. Many in France considered the French Union to be a major factor of French preeminence over West Germany in any European arrangement, as well as a basis for equality with the Anglo-Saxons on a global level. In order to maintain the integrity of the French Union, in this view, any European community had to be looser than the ties that bound France to the Union. As an opponent of supranational European unification wrote in 1953: "The truth is that France is not a uniquely European power, but a world power. She cannot merge with nations strictly confined to the framework of the continent. She can only form a partnership with them, coordinate her policy with theirs in certain areas of common interest, and for the rest preserve her personality and her independence."[84] Along with general opposition to the loss of national control over armed forces, and skepticism about the efficacy of integrated multinational units, EDC opponents saw that France would face unbearable choices between concentrating armed forces in Europe to offset West German power, or deploying them abroad to hold together an increasingly shaky French Union.

Despite treaty guarantees added to counter these kinds of arguments, each criticism was compelling enough to weigh heavily on the minds of the uncertain or uncommitted. Finally, in the face of unrelenting and quite undiplomatic American pressures, the EDC died an ignominious death on 30 August 1954, when the National Assembly refused to consider the ratification of the treaty. It was interred by the swollen weight of contradictory expectations, the refusal of irritated allies to make more concessions, the complicated interplay of French party politics, and the exasperation of a prime minister unwilling to jeopardize his government for a dubious cause.

The National Assembly's action meant that the "European" solution to West German political-military recovery had failed. The alternative, developed by Anthony Eden and Pierre Mendès-France, was an Atlantic-oriented package involving revival of the moribund Western European Union and direct German membership in NATO. The appeal of this plan was that it directly associated both the United States and Britain in the control of West Germany. Its principal defect was that the Federal Republic would enter the Alliance virtually as a sovereign state, with an unintegrated (in EDC terms) military potential surpassing that which France could expect to muster for European defense.

To prevent the full resurgence of West German military power, the French government insisted that the Paris Agreements of October 1954 give France an important edge in a number of respects. First, Protocol No. II to the agreements establishing the revised WEU provided for the same maximum levels of armed forces among members as had been in the EDC treaty, that is, rough Franco-German parity with any changes subject to unanimous approval of the members.[85] The restriction was absolute for the Federal Republic, because its troops would only be deployed for NATO's forward defense on its own territory. Troops designated for overseas duty, however, whether actually abroad or in Europe, were exempt from this provision. French governments were therefore free to increase the size of their forces and armaments without restriction or effective control.[86] Second, West German remilitarization was permitted on the condition that Bonn allocate all future military forces to NATO duties under the command of SACEUR and, incidentally, under the French general in charge of the central Europe sector of Allied Command

Europe. Paris, on the other hand, was free to shift its force allocations to overseas categories and maintain them under exclusive national control.

West Germany's dependency status was reinforced in that, of all NATO members, only it was required to accept the presence of foreign troops "of the same nationality and effective strength" as when the agreements took effect, on 5 May 1955.[87] Of course, Bonn actively sought the presence of American, British, and French troops as a physical manifestation of their commitment to West German security, just as France wanted them on the forward line to enhance her own security. Nevertheless, West Germany was bound to accept foreign troops, whereas France served as host to NATO forces as a matter of choice and a policy of extending facilities to the Alliance in order to facilitate the American presence in Europe. French leaders retained the freedom to change their views, expel NATO and the United States from the country, and benefit from the interposition of NATO forces on German soil between France and the East.

As a final insurance of French privilege and status, Paris included severe restrictions on West German access to nuclear and strategic weapons in both the defunct EDC Treaty and the Paris Agreements. Adenauer's commitment for Germany "not to manufacture on its territory any atomic weapons, chemical weapons or biological weapons" was written into the agreements, along with provisions forbidding German manufacture of long-range guided missiles, large warships and submarines, or strategic bomber aircraft.[88] This was a reasonable and broadly supported provision under the delicate circumstances of re-creating a German armed force. But the clear French intention was to compensate for this setback by forever closing the option of nuclear and strategic weapons to the Federal Republic, just as Paris was beginning to develop these arms. If, as it appeared by 1954, nuclear weapons were essential to national security and a major role in the Alliance, then only France would have the material resources and the legal right to manufacture them. This French privilege was a key legacy of the Fourth Republic to de Gaulle, one that he would exploit fully and fight with determination to maintain.

Despite these restrictions on West Germany's military potential, the general outcome of this conflict marked a significant political defeat for French security policy in Europe, because it displayed a debilitating indecisiveness and lack of influence over the United States and Alliance policies. Although the long delay in restoring West German sovereignty and creating the first German military units was an achievement of sorts for the Fourth Republic, it was a Pyrrhic victory that helped create a solid German-American coalition at the core of the Atlantic Alliance. Faced with recurrent disappointments, resistance, and recriminations from the French, the United States naturally came to place more value on the stronger, more stable, and more subservient German ally.[89] For, as many in France had feared, the direct German-American links in NATO progressively reduced French influence in the Alliance as Germany's increased. As one analyst concluded in a study of German-American relations, "Both the circumstances in which Germany's NATO membership was agreed, and the form it took, brought about a much closer American-German alignment than would have occurred if the EDC had actually come into existence."[90] The restraints France had insisted on thus gradually eroded after 1955, until the United States seemed prepared to discard them altogether and offer Bonn access to nuclear weapons in the early 1960s.

Perhaps the least visible but most battered victim of this affair was the ideal of European unity and ultimate independence. The integrationists such as Monnet and Schuman were largely responsible, because they tried prematurely to impose a supranational political-military community on Europe rather than settle on a less ambitious European design. In any case, Gaullists and other critics were probably correct at the time in pointing out that, without legitimacy and public support, an EDC would inevitably be dominated and manipulated by its strongest member or by the United States. After its demise, however, more realistic forms of European political-military collaboration could not be revived, partly because of mutual Franco-German suspicions, but also because the Atlanticist alternative to the EDC reinforced American domination of the European security system via the extension of the NATO network, the expansion of SACEUR's and SHAPE's powers, and the full integration of West German security interests into an Atlantic rather than a European format. The revived WEU proved to be a weak appendage of NATO and, although de Gaulle would later attempt to revive a political-military dimension to European unity, by then both American and most West European interests were locked into the Atlantic Alliance and unable to entertain genuine alternatives.

Curiously enough, until 1954 the United States had supported West European military cooperation as a counterpart to the economic and political community advocated by the integrationists. Perhaps this was on the implicit understanding that such a community would be more pliable and cooperative than its troublesome national governments. After the EDC, however, a European defense system outside NATO became less appealing in Washington because it implied a dangerous and destabilizing diffusion of nuclear weapons. The MLF embroglio finally clarified American priorities in this respect. American officials also began to worry about the consequences of having encouraged European economic cooperation and its extension into a political community. As Western Europe gradually became an economic competitor and a less subservient political ally in many respects, the asymmetry between the Euro-centered economic community and the Atlantic-centered security arrangement became an advantage to be exploited by the United States for a range of benefits. These conflicts erupted in the early 1970s, but the choices made by France and her neighbors in the 1950s appear to

have decisively shaped the subsequent dynamics of U.S.-European relations.

Rearmament and Nuclear Weapons

The general record of disappointment and frustration in achieving French
security goals through the Atlantic Alliance is dispelled only by a success in
obtaining substantial American aid for defense spending during the early
years of the Alliance. This assistance escalated dramatically after the outbreak
of the Korean War and might have helped to create the impressive and influential military machine anticipated in Paris. A strong army in Europe, in turn,
would have boosted France's status in the Alliance and perhaps have reduced
pressures for rearming West Germany as the solution to Europe's conventional
weakness. Although the Fourth Republic did make some progress in rebuilding
its army, this effort was less successful than anticipated because of the inability
of the French economy to bear the strain of inflationary defense expenditures,
and because of a consistent policy of favoring colonial defense requirements
over European forces when choices had to be made. Moreover, it became
increasingly evident after 1954 that nuclear weapons rather than conventional
forces were the essential prerequisites for status and security. These arms
were not, however, available through the Alliance connection.

American support for French and European defense spending was initially
provided by the Mutual Defense Assistance Act of 1949, and later by the
Mutual Security Act of October 1951 and subsequent legislation. A prominent
feature of this legislation, and related bilateral agreements, was the condition
that a recipient's armed forces be equipped for service in NATO and deployed
in accordance with NATO planning.[91] It was also American policy to grant
defense assistance only on the condition that the partner reciprocate by extending numerous privileges and services to the United States, in the context
of their joint Alliance obligations.[92] During the peak years of this aid (1951-
54), the United States furnished sums amounting to about one-quarter of the
entire French defense budget and one-half the equipment expenses of rearmament.[93] Under the Off-Shore Procurement Program alone, France received
$943 million in contracts during this period, out of a total of $2,065 million
granted to all European allies.[94] By the time American military aid to Paris
stopped entirely in 1964, France had accumulated $4,158 million in defense
assistance since 1950, or nearly half of the $10,857 million granted to the
original members of NATO.[95]

This aid was the basis for planning a major expansion and modernization
of the French armed forces. They received a special credit of 80 billion francs
in June 1950, and from 1950 through 1952 the proportion of the budget
devoted to defense rose from 19 percent to 36 percent. Under the bilateral

Franco-American agreements of 1950, the French army was promised equipment and technical aid sufficient for modernizing five of its divisions—three to be stationed in West Germany and two in France. Subsequent programs called for four entirely new divisions to be created with American arms, and a fifth to be equipped with French-made weapons. Planned in accordance with NATO recommendations for compatibility with nuclear war conditions, two of the new and highly mobile *"pentomique"* divisions were set up between 1952 and 1954 and equipped with fifteen-ton AMX tanks and other sophisticated weapons. They were stationed with the French Second Army Corps in West Germany.[96] Old equipment from modernized divisions was to be used to establish four *forces régionales* combat units, so that Paris could meet its overall NATO commitments—which varied from fourteen active divisions in 1951 to twenty active and twenty reserve divisions in the Lisbon goals of 1952. Under NATO plans, then, the French army could look forward to as many as 750,000 active troops, including overseas forces, and approximately 3,600,000 trained reservists.

Through 1954, these extravagant plans were not realized owing to a combination of domestic economic crises, chronic balance of payments deficits, and Indochina War expenses. The combined strains of rearmament and the Indochina War contributed to an inflation rate of 27 percent in the eighteen months after June 1950.[97] In order to cut inflation and stabilize the franc, Premier Pleven had to eliminate some 200 billion francs from the military budget for 1952. Minister of Defense Bidault, an ardent partisan of the French presence in Indochina, saw to it that war expenses went unaffected and instead sacrificed European defense programs. Made with the knowledge that it could not be fulfilled, the Lisbon force commitment was promptly withdrawn. In 1953, France claimed some ten active divisions in Europe, five at 100 percent strength and five at 75-80 percent; but informed sources have reported that there were really only six divisions at 70 percent strength, while the rest existed only on paper.[98] With Indochina taking up between 40 and 45 percent of defense budgets after 1950, and occupying one-quarter of the French officer corps, it was impossible for France to make her anticipated contribution to NATO.[99]

The Geneva settlement of 1954, and French withdrawal from direct involvement in Indochina, gave grounds for hope that rearmament for the European theater could be resumed. A revised program developed in 1955 foresaw that by the end of 1956 France would have a 500,000-man army concentrating the bulk of its forces under NATO for European defense, and that the penatomic division program would be completed.[100] However, these plans were soon interred by the Algerian War, which began with incidents in November 1954. This colonial conflict was far more costly than its predecessor, because army corps in Europe were virtually dismantled and sent to North Africa, leaving a mere skeleton force on the continent. Whereas in June 1954 there were only 117,000 French troops in North Africa, part of them Arab, within fifteen months an additional 400,000 troops were transferred there, mostly from West Germany and France. Only eighteen months after their first maneuvers, the two existing penatomic divisions were transferred from Germany to Algeria, where their sophisticated training and equipment were virtually useless. This was the consequence of a decision made by Max Lejeune, then *Secrétaire d'état à la guerre* in the Mollet government, to sacrifice France's modern European forces for the sake of Algeria, at whatever price.[101] Although the army kept some of its units together in a NATO-type organization, hoping to return them to Europe intact, the General Staff was soon compelled to restructure its forces to meet the requirements of guerilla warfare in Algeria.

By 1960, the French army had 418,000 men in North Africa being trained and supported by most of the 203,000 troops in the Métropole. With another 65,000 serving at other overseas posts, only a small force of 50,000 remained in West Germany as a token presence in NATO. The most important French military contribution untouched by Algeria was one tactical air force, also stationed in Germany. The air force and navy were generally less affected by these developments, except that the entire defense budget was diverted to cover expenses incurred in North Africa.[102] Despite the dubious nature of France's Algerian mission in terms of Atlantic security, Paris continued to count its expenses there as a contribution to the Alliance defense posture, and for a time the United States even furnished France with helicopters and small arms, although it was common knowledge that they would be used in Algeria and not in Europe.[103]

Thus, the French expectation that the Atlantic Alliance would serve as a vehicle for modernizing the armed forces was only partially realized. There had been substantial American aid, but the desired result was not achieved because one demanding and costly overseas engagement followed another. France's priorities reduced her influence in the Alliance in both political and military affairs, and ensured that she would play a secondary role to allies relatively unburdened by an overseas conflict. The situation also testified to the poverty of French claims to great power status, because Paris could not fulfill its European commitments and still maintain a beseiged colonial empire. Another consequence of the French (and general European) failure to rearm was that European security remained essentially dependent on the American nuclear capability to deter and retaliate in the event of attack. Because these weapons remained in American hands and outside the NATO structure, the European allies soon began to realize that they had no direct influence over the key instruments of their own security.

The American shift toward greater reliance on nuclear weapons at the expense of conventional forces was augured by a reevaluation of defense programs undertaken within the Eisenhower administration during 1953 and

1954. As early as July 1954, a SHAPE report was recommending the use of tactical nuclear weapons in Europe, although this decision was put off for two and one-half years. In December 1954, however, the North Atlantic Council did accept the American policy of dependence on U.S.-controlled strategic weapons and authorized SHAPE to assume they would be used in a European war. Thus, the "New Look" doctrine of massive retaliation in response to any attack became the cornerstone of Alliance defense.[104]

Although a coherent French policy regarding nuclear weapons did not emerge until 1958, it is clear that government advisors were quick to realize the implications of these developments. As early as 1952, General de Gaulle had pointed out that the future risk of nuclear retaliation from the Soviets would inevitably weaken the American guarantee to defend Europe.[105] By mid-1954, leading French military figures were giving the same warning to the government of Mendès-France. In August, the French representative to the Standing Group, General Jean Valluy, reported the new American strategic doctrine to General Guillaume, France's Chief of Staff. Acting on this information, Guillaume warned the prime minister that European dependence on American-controlled nuclear weapons effectively deprived France of her hold over the U.S. security guarantee and rendered Western defense "completely dependent on American wishes."[106] Whereas the NATO organization and the presence of American forces in Europe had seemed an adequate fulfillment of French security requirements in Europe, in 1954 Paris began to realize that reliance on nuclear weapons was initiating a fatal erosion of the guarantee sought in 1949.

As interallied conflicts over nuclear weapons and strategy escalated in later years, four possible ways of alleviating Europe's insecurity were to emerge: allied control or influence over the American weapons and strategic planning processes, transforming NATO itself into a nuclear power, the creation of a joint European force linked to NATO, or the construction of national European nuclear forces. One typical French reaction was to consider a three-power, oligopolistic version of the first possibility. In 1954, Mendès-France broached this subject by suggesting to Secretary of State John Foster Dulles that France, Britain, and the United States should jointly shoulder the responsibility for triggering the American nuclear force on behalf of the Alliance.[107] There was evidently no positive response from Washington to this suggestion, and the initiative lapsed until de Gaulle revived it in his 1958 memorandum.

In the meantime, the French set in motion a program that amounted to first steps in creating a national nuclear force. From the point of view of certain military officials chaffing under the Indochina defeat, the acquisition of nuclear weapons seemed essential to their mission, as well as to French status and influence in the Alliance. As General Guillaume told Mendès-France, "Such an arsenal would allow the European nations to invervene in the new warfare with their own weapons, and would give them the possibility of recovering a role of first rank in the direction of the coalition."[108] A memorandum prepared by Jean-Marc Boegner associated the Quai d'Orsay with the military proponents of a French nuclear force such as Guillaume and Charles Ailleret, and with Pierre Guillaumat, head of the *Commissariat à l'énergie atomique*. At an interministerial meeting on 26 December 1954, Mendès-France deferred a final decision, but the effect was to acquiesce in the continuation of a nuclear-energy program that left France the option of producing nuclear weapons.[109] Subsequent premiers of the Fourth Republic allowed the weapons-related research to go forward until, on 11 April 1958, Premier Félix Gaillard made one of the last decisions of the Fourth Republic and ordered a nuclear bomb test for early 1960.

Considering the pattern of French goals and priorities described here, the Fourth Republic's promotion of nuclear arms represented an attempt to seize on a newly available instrument for achieving the status and the security guarantee that had proven so elusive after 1949. By 1954, the Alliance was not developing in accordance with earlier French expectations, and it even appeared that the NATO defense organization was of secondary importance in light of acknowledged dependence on nuclear weapons. Rather than being in a position to enhance control of her own security, a nonnuclear France seemed bound to sink further into dependence as a mere protectorate of the United States. Thus, as the Algerian War escalated and exacerbated French discontents, controversies over nuclear weapons and Alliance strategy also emerged and contributed to an insecurity and antagonism that set the stage for French dealignment.

French Colonialism and the Alliance

Fourth Republic France's obsession with a colonial mission has already served as a background for much of this discussion, particularly as a basis of claims for status and allied support while it drained France's energies and military resources. Although there was another French nationalist tradition opposing colonialism in favor of concentrating resources within the hexagon—and leaders such as Mendès-France did tend to favor it under the Fourth Republic—this view did not predominate until after 1958 and de Gaulle's reorientation of French priorities.[110] Instead, the Fourth Republic's determination to avoid decolonization was a problem that dominated its internal and external politics, finally destroying the regime and ushering in the Gaullist era. It was also the issue that crystallized French discontent with the Atlantic Alliance and initiated the process of dealignment even before de Gaulle came to power and capitalized on the situation he inherited. As already noted, Fourth Republic leaders had hoped that the Atlantic connection would induce the United

States to provide material support for maintaining the French Union. With this in mind, they had also tried to use the Alliance as a foundation for instituting tripartite global cooperation. Indochina and then Algeria were the conflicts that prompted Paris to seek allied backing for France's non-European interests, but in neither case could the French be satisfied with the results of their efforts.

Indochina. The Indochina War was the first occasion on which France sought allied cooperation and a global application of Western resources against communist aggression. Before 1947, Paris's struggle with Ho Chi Minh was based primarily on a nationalistic determination to hold onto the French Union and apply its assimilationist logic to all members. After the onset of the Cold War, however, French leaders saw an advantage in redefining the conflict as an anticommunist one and sought to internationalize it.[111] The argument was that the communist threat was not limited to Europe and, in meeting it, Western unity and mutual support should be extended to wherever Soviet-backed aggression materialized—Korea and Indochina by 1950, later North Africa and the Middle East. Also, because France's involvement in Indochina adversely affected her defense posture in Europe, the two efforts were obviously linked and it was "only fair that those who have the same interests share, in some way or other, the burden the French are obliged to support" in Indochina.[112]

The United States, which had originally opted for a policy of noninterference in postwar Indochina, began taking a more active interest in the dangers of communist expansion there by late 1949 and early 1950.[113] At tripartite meetings held to discuss the situation in Southeast Asia, the French pressed for support by the Anglo-Americans and found the British reluctant while the United States was willing to extend some political and material assistance.[114] The Korean War lent new urgency to the problem and on 27 June 1950, President Truman announced that he would increase American military assistance to the anticommunist forces in Indochina and install a new permanent military mission there. The first American arms shipments arrived in July 1950, and in October an American military mission was set up in Saigon to administer the burgeoning aid program. By early 1953, the United States was paying as much as one-half the costs of the war in indirect aid channeled through Paris and direct assistance administered through Saigon to the forces of the Associated States (Laos, Cambodia, Vietnam).[115] In addition to bilateral support, France received moral and diplomatic backing from the Alliance itself, when the council expressed "its wholehearted admiration for the valiant and long continued struggle by the French forces and the armies of the Associated States against Communist aggression," concluding "that the campaign waged by the French Union forces in Indochina deserves continuing support from the NATO governments."[116]

The French achievement in associating the United States with this conflict turned out to be a mixed blessing, however, because of a basic incompatibility in American and French aims in the region. For Paris was struggling to hold together a close-knit French Union and to maintain a dominant French presence in Indochina. But the United States was uninterested in shoring up a European neocolonial system and, instead, foresaw that the Indochina states would become independent and only loosely tied to France. Thus, Washington used its aid program in Saigon to move the indigenous leaders toward greater independence from both French and communist influence.[117] As the first Indochina War reached a climax in 1954, the United States began to consider the possibility of replacing the unsuccessful French as the main sponsor of anticommunist forces on the peninsula. In early 1954, for example, a National Security Council study registered American determination to oppose a negotiated settlement of the war and to support its continuation with "active U.S. participation and without French support should that be necessary."[118]

Unaware of these projects in Washington, France's final experiences with the Americans in Indochina still furnished telling lessons about the cost of dependence. One came on the eve of the Geneva Conference, when the United States refused to intervene to save the French position at Dien-Bien-Phu, besieged since 11 March 1954. Earlier, when pressed by Washington to spurn negotiations and adopt the risky Navarre Plan, which left Dien-Bien-Phu exposed, the French had requested assurances of direct American intervention if necessary. Late in March, the government of Premier Paul Laniel sent General Paul Ely to Washington in search of a specific guarantee to intervene with B-29 bombers, and the delegation was given the impression that such an active intervention might be possible early in April.[119] When Foreign Minister Bidault formally made the request on 4 April, both to save the garrison and to bolster France's bargaining position in Geneva, Dulles refused due to congressional and British opposition. A second request was made and again rejected at the Paris Atlantic Council meeting on 23-24 April.

While the United States denied France's request for an armed rescue in Indochina, Dulles nevertheless continued to insist that Paris foreswear a cease-fire and negotiated peace at Geneva, and continue to fight on to a military victory. When an exhausted France nevertheless had to accept such a settlement, in the form of a neutralized Indochina with a continuing French presence there, the United States effectively undermined the terms of the Geneva accord and helped eliminate the French presence in Southeast Asia. Thus, for France, one lesson of the Indochina conflict was that a weakened and dependent ally could not be assured that the Alliance and the United States would support and promote French interests abroad, and to invite direct American intervention in an overseas conflict was to risk being undermined and finally supplanted by the superpower ally.

Algeria. The American role in France's Indochina defeat was a prelude to the more serious interallied tensions caused by the Algerian trauma after 1954. Militarily, the Algerian War led to a severe physical, strategic, and political alienation from NATO that reinforced growing doubts about the value of the alliance with the United States. The most obvious concrete effect of the Algerian War has already been discussed: it forced France to transfer European-based army units to North Africa and to redirect her military infrastructure system to servicing this antiguerilla conflict.

France's physical absence from NATO military institutions was accompanied by the emergence of an idiosyncratic strategic doctrine used as part of a broader campaign to convince the Atlantic allies that France was performing an invaluable service to the West and NATO in North Africa. One consequence of a preoccupation with the *guerre révolutionnaire* theory was that the French definition of priority threats to Western security began to diverge substantially from the strategic preoccupations of other members of the Alliance. Although the *guerre révolutionnaire* concept was to be abandoned under de Gaulle, its preeminence in French military circles in the late 1950s contributed to France's growing isolation from the security concerns that were necessarily at the heart of an anti-Soviet alliance. As George Kelly has observed, this doctrine was partly "the French army's answer, its defensive riposte, to the nuclear preoccupations of its Anglo-Saxon allies."[120] But it also contributed to a climate of alienation and dissent in France that nourished the more significant discussions then beginning about the consequences of nuclear weapons on allied solidarity and the value of the American guarantee—discussions that finally led to a distinctive French nuclear strategy incompatible with both American doctrine and NATO itself.

In its outline of general strategy, the *guerre révolutionnaire* theory asserted that national liberation movements in colonial territory were merely one aspect of the international and global communist assault on the West. Communism was one enemy, it claimed, and wherever Western military forces fought it they were serving the interests of the West as a whole. In the light of the Algerian conflict, pan-Arab nationalism was seen as a particularly insidious, cryptocommunist enemy assisting in the effort to undermine the West's strategic position on the Mediterranean.[121] Held back in Europe by NATO, these forces were now attempting to outflank the West from the south and eventually encircle it. Based on the lessons of World War II, French strategy contended that the Paris-Brazzaville axis formed a single strategic theater, or Eurafrica, and France's mission as the West's agent was to hold on to this region. Publicists of the doctrine frequently pointed out that there were important naval bases in North Africa (the Mers-el-Kébir and

Bizerte bases), and American airfields in Morocco that formed part of the European defense network.[122]

In the face of this attempted encirclement of the West, NATO's role was to contain the modern Soviet forces on the European front while, in North Africa, France fought the more active enemy using the techniques of limited war. This was precisely the value of NATO to France and the West, because it provided security in Europe and enabled France to carry out the more pressing and dangerous mission in the Mediterranean basin. As General Ely wrote at the time, "it is because the coalition is fully effective in the face of the European threat that we can direct our principal efforts elsewhere and counter a more immediate threat in North Africa."[123] Thus, in this argument, an *Algérie française* was in the interest of the Alliance, and France was actually performing a crucial NATO task by defending her colonial prerogatives. France was in truth undertaking the most difficult of allied responsibilities. Rather than luxuriating on the placid German front, France was spilling her blood in the more costly and less glamorous venture in Algeria. And, just because she bore this burden, France's leaders insisted that she should be accorded greater influence and stature in the Alliance. "That is what gives France the right to speak sharply to the Americans, as an equal, and no longer, as has too often been the case thus far, as a humiliated and surly debtor."[124]

American opposition to Franco-British actions in Egypt in 1956, which for France were prompted by Abdel Nasser's support of the Algerian rebels, was a painful signal that the French position on the Algerian War was not sympathetically received in Washington. Nor was the NATO military organization enthusiastic about the arguments just described, because its officers were preoccupied by the West's defense posture on the continent and especially the central front. Along with ongoing contacts inside the NATO organization, the French military made several specific attempts to convince its allied colleagues of the value of France's case.[125] These efforts were not very successful, however, and the United States in particular quietly but firmly opposed this strategic doctrine and its policy implications. This situation led many French elites to challenge the value of NATO itself, but at the time the principal aim of military leaders such as General Ely was to associate NATO with France's efforts and extend the security area of the Alliance to cover French territories in Africa.[126]

Contrary to French arguments, however, Washington contended that Algerian nationalism was not a stalking horse for Moscow. On the contrary, it was France's policy of suppression that was dangerous, because it could force the Arabs into the hands of the communists. To the American champion of anticolonialism, the Algerian revolt was essentially part of the Asian-African movement for national liberation that was inevitably and rightfully terminating the outdated imperial systems of European states. This perspective doubtless blinded the United States to the complexities of the situation in

Algeria. Such insensitivity was resented in France, where American policy was often interpreted as a subterfuge for a subtle but insidious brand of dollar imperialism waiting to fill the breach.[127] French elites felt that their position in Southeast Asia had been undermined in this way, and they were determined not to repeat the error in Africa.

The Suez crisis was the event that directly linked French problems in North Africa to her Anglo-American security ties and focused growing doubts about the Alliance's value to crucial French interests. For some time, Paris had blamed the Algerian rebellion partly on Nasser and his brand of Arab nationalism, and the Egyptian seizure of the canal on 26 July 1956 furnished a welcome opportunity to cut off this source of support to the rebels. In collusion with Israel and Britain, France plotted a seizure of the canal that was expected to topple Nasser and ultimately tranquilize the situation in Algeria. While Paris was calling for Alliance consultations to harmonize policies outside of Europe, the governments of Guy Mollet and Anthony Eden kept the United States and the NATO Council in the dark about their plans, in the hope that a *fait accompli* would be accepted in Washington.[128] The scheme misfired from the outset, however, and produced a public confrontation within the Atlantic Alliance. Eisenhower was furious at the October invasion, which distracted world attention from Soviet repression in Hungary and embarrassed him personally during the final stages of a presidential election.[129] The exercise in French and British independence collapsed in the face of oblique Soviet warnings of nuclear reprisals on Paris and London, while the United States insisted on the termination of all military actions and a withdrawal in favor of U.N. forces. Faced with financial collapse from an American-led run on the pound, Prime Minister Eden buckled under at midday on 6 November and Mollet was forced to concur that evening.

This confrontation between the two most powerful West European states in NATO and their American protector produced diammetrically opposite reactions in Britain and France. Whereas Eden's independent policy fell along with him, and Britain learned that it could not undertake military actions without prior American support, Mollet stayed in power and the philosophy behind France's involvement found a new resolve. Tortured by the continuing impasse in Algeria, many in France blamed the Suez fiasco on a Yalta-style Soviet-American conspiracy aimed against European interests. The American reaction to Suez lent new weight to the opinion that a misguided desire to court the uncommitted parts of the world was leading Washington to desert its allies, jeopardize the security of the anticommunist West, and undermine France's most vital interests outside of Europe. As one usually pro-Atlanticist French observer charged, "the United States will not feel any scruple in siding against its loyal allies on behalf of its potential allies, against two essential members of the Atlantic Alliance on behalf of those for whom anti-Westernism is a political, racial, and religious objective."[130]

Thus, France emerged from the Suez conflict with an even stronger conviction that her efforts in North Africa and the Middle East were necessary to her own survival and to Europe. Many in France went further and argued that Suez had also demonstrated the limits the United States placed in its nuclear guarantee to European allies, because Washington had not reacted forcefully enough to Soviet intimations of direct reprisals against the two invading powers.[131] Disregarding the fact that British nuclear weapons had not strengthened London's hand, the Suez crisis furnished additional arguments for those in Paris who were building a strategic theory to promote a nuclear-weapons program. For now they could claim that France, and perhaps the West European states together, had to acquire atomic weapons of their own if they hoped to protect interests that were crucial to them but not, it seemed, to the United States.[132]

In reaction to these signs of American opposition or indifference to French needs, Fourth Republic governments revived earlier themes stressing the need for harmonizing allied policies in regions outside the North Atlantic Treaty area. After the Indochina experience, however, the case was made with some hesitation. Officially, Paris considered the revolt to be primarily an internal affair and had even removed the Algerian departments from SHAPE jurisdiction to ensure that French political and military activities there (including torture) were not openly debated among unsympathetic allies. On the other hand, French governments felt compelled to demand that NATO extend the scope of political consultation to cover communist subversion outside Europe. When Premier Mollet insisted in April 1956 that "the Western powers should reaffirm in every part of the world, a united front, that they should adopt a common policy,"[133] he essentially meant that the United States should openly support French policy in Africa and encourage NATO to do the same. American policy did not come around, however, nor did the Alliance. Instead, Atlantic Council communiqués during this period stressed France's solitary pursuit of her own interests in Algeria, and regretted that the situation there was weakening the common defense in Europe.[134] Although the French case did meet with some sympathy within NATO, particularly on the part of Belgian Secretary-General Paul-Henri Spaak, the gap between French and American perspectives was too wide for reconciliation within the Alliance.[135]

Toward the end of the Fourth Republic, the last functioning government before de Gaulle presided over a series of acrimonious clashes with the Anglo-Saxons that helped undermine the regime itself. During the fall of 1957, the government of Radical Félix Gaillard found itself faced with an apparent revival of the Anglo-American "directorate" working against French interests.[136] In the wake of Suez, the British had worked assiduously to patch up the "special relationship" and had met enough success to arouse suspicion that bilateral meetings between Harold Macmillan and Eisenhower were leaving Paris out of important decisions and even working against France. After one such meeting in October, these fears were confirmed by the Tunisian arms dispute. The Bourguiba regime there was thought to be furnishing aid to the Algerian rebels, and Paris had suspended all arms shipments to Tunis pending guarantees that they would be used only for internal purposes. Bourguiba turned to the United States and Britain, who hesitated but finally agreed to provide arms in order to forestall a Tunisian approach to the East bloc. The shipment was made on 15 November and provoked a bitter reaction in France, where recriminations were magnified by Belgium and Italy's behaving like proper allies and refusing to discuss weapons deals with the Tunisian government.[137]

Reacting to these American and British policies, the Gaillard government's brief tenure was distinguished by a number of initiatives that testified to growing hostility and independence on the part of this dissident ally. The December 1957 North Atlantic Council meeting, at the level of heads of government, was tense because of warnings from Gaillard that the Alliance could not prosper if allies' interests were jeopardized and some members continued to behave as if they were "a bit more equal than others."[138] Bilateral meetings between French and American leaders were also notable failures. Eisenhower and Dulles were unreceptive to Gaillard's insistence on extending NATO consultation and mutual support to cover French interests in Africa, and were angered by his accusations of American "self-seeking ulterior motives" in the region.[139] In this atmosphere of distrust, French resentment spilled over into the nuclear weapons issue as well. Gaillard, who would soon order the first French nuclear tests, set one precedent for de Gaulle and refused to consider accepting American IRBMs or the stockpiling of tactical nuclear weapons in France unless they were turned over to direct French military control instead of to U.S. or NATO authorities.

Another precedent for the Fifth Republic arose during this period, as Gaillard tried to organize French-led factions within the West as a means of bolstering France's influence and prestige. Maurice Faure, an under-secretary of state for Gaillard, opened discussions with the West Germans in November in the hope of forming some sort of continental front against the Anglo-American domination of the Alliance. Perhaps buoyed by the formation of the European Economic Community (EEC), Adenauer was receptive and encouraged Gaillard again at the December Atlantic Council meeting. The possibility of Franco-German collaboration on nuclear weapons-related research and development was even brought up, although it was soon dropped with the collapse of the French regime.[140] Gaillard also launched the idea of a Mediterranean economic and defense community in March 1958, designed essentially as an extension of France's own "Eurafrican" holdings and intended to involve the Alliance in the preservation of French preeminence in this region.[141]

These eleventh-hour efforts to reverse France's declining position in Algeria and the Alliance were stillborn due to the fall of the Gaillard government on 15 April, an event directed in part against the United States. Gaillard had been forced to accept Anglo-American mediation in the dispute with Tunisia over the bombing of Sakiet, a Tunisian village, carried out by French forces on their own authority on 8 February 1958. Both the National Assembly and the army resented this outside intervention in a conflict between France and her former protectorate, over an incident related to the Algerian War. Gaillard was accused (unjustly) of allowing Washington to decide France's policies in North Africa, and was overthrown by a vote of 321 to 255 when he urged that France accept the recommendations of the Anglo-American mediation team.[142] The next government, that of reputed liberal Pierre Pflimlin, proved unacceptable to conservatives and the army, thereby provoking the crisis that brought de Gaulle to power. Thus, indirectly, even the final agony of the Fourth Republic was initiated by an act of defiance against the United States.

Dissent and Dealignment in Two Republics

The record of the Fourth Republic's experience in the Atlantic Alliance is a complex and often inconsistent one. Its most prominent feature is the maze of exorbitant and contradictory aims and expectations that fatally undermined national security and exhausted the regime itself. The incongruities in French policy are apparent: Seeking security in Europe and a decisive role in the Alliance, French leaders instead turned their defense over to an American-dominated defense organization where a weak and overburdened France could not exercise great authority. Expecting to create a powerful and modern European armed force as a key element of security and influence in the Alliance, French military resources were instead diverted abroad, where such an instrument was useless and had to be abandoned. Aspiring to preeminence over West Germany in Europe, French governments progressively sabotaged their own efforts by devoting more attention to overseas possessions than to their power position in Europe and the Alliance. Finally, seeking recognition and deference from the United States, the Fourth Republic instead reacted to its own blunders and incompetence with a sullen and sometimes spiteful resentment that confirmed the impression of France as an unstable, unruly, and ungrateful ally that was not worthy of American confidence and support.

De Gaulle and the Fifth Republic were to remedy two aspects of this dismal situation. The principal contribution was a more stable set of government institutions tailored to facilitate the formulation and pursuit of more consistent policy goals. While the Fourth Republic's security policy dilemmas were not a direct result of the unstable and *immobiliste* political system, its institutions and dominant forces had been unable to impose a clear and cohesive set of priorities. Although de Gaulle's actual accomplishments after 1958 are a matter of controversy, few would deny that he and his regime were able to produce a more forceful and usually more consistent foreign policy. The General's second contribution, of course, was to eliminate the basic incompatibility between France's European and colonial commitments and focus French military resources on a Euro-centered system more suited to the nation's resources and to the dialectics of decolonization.

While curing some of the Fourth Republic's infirmities, and scorning or dismissing its heritage of renunciation and dependence, de Gaulle also was to borrow a surprising number of its aspirations, themes, and ambivalences as unattributed material for his own grand designs. The continuity in goals and policies between regimes is sometimes remarkable. The theme linking French status and security with a tripartite inner council, overseeing Western strategic planning and extending allied cooperation on a global basis, was prominent during the Fourth Republic and dominated the oligopolistic thrust of early Gaullist diplomacy. The threat perceptions and strategic preoccupations of the two French regimes were also similar, for in neither case were they compatible with a strong commitment to NATO. The Fourth Republic had a broad and flexible conception that focused more attention on a global nationalist-communist menace to the French Union than on the Soviet Union itself. And, to the extent that security in NATO Europe was of practical importance, the French were plagued by their suspicions about the American guarantee and, after 1954, began to perceive that NATO and French reliance on American-controlled nuclear weapons was a precarious arrangement that would leave France with little actual control over her own security in Europe.

Although de Gaulle did not discard the traditional global security perspective of France, he did revise the French thesis linking European and global security into a more perceptive and compelling analysis of the risks of military interdependence in the nuclear age. He also focused France's national defense in Europe and exploited issues linking Alliance tensions with nuclear weapons, in order to create a French military establishment outside of NATO. While de Gaulle's disengagement from NATO and frontal attack on Alliance military integration represented an innovation over Fourth Republic policies, it is quite clear that NATO integration had been encouraged and accepted before 1958 only on the assumption that it would measurably enhance French security and function as a restraint on others (West Germany) while it contributed to France's own power and influence. But such assumptions were proving to be incorrect well before 1958. Furthermore, Fourth Republic elites had begun to perceive that nuclear weapons devalued NATO and potentially transformed the American-dominated integrated system into an unwelcome, even dangerous, restraint on France. In any case, the practical effect of integration measures accepted by the Fourth Republic were not impressive and certainly did not prevent the Fourth or Fifth Republics from devoting their military resources to national purposes in conflict with those of most Alliance members.

A final feature shared by the Fourth and Fifth Republics is an uncertain and often unsuccessful European policy that actually reinforced the Atlantic-centered, American-dominated features of the West European security system. The outcome of the EDC debate seems to have set the precedent for France regarding this issue. French governments under both postwar regimes have pursued policies that might allow them to set up a French-led and independent Europe, but they have proven unable to find a tolerable and successful formula for extending European cooperation into the political-military arena. Before 1958, an integrated defense community was offered and then rescinded in favor of the NATO-dominated alternative. De Gaulle could not undo this settlement because other allies acquired a strong interest in it, because the inconveniences of being an American protectorate always seemed preferable to the risks of European cooperation and independence, because de Gaulle himself was unwilling to return to integration formulas already scuttled by his predecessors, and because he was unable to reconcile or conceal the tensions created by the traditional French aim of dominating cooperative efforts in Europe, especially those concerning defense.

The similarities and continuities between these alliance policies of the Fourth and Fifth Republics cannot, of course, lead to a confident assertion that, had it survived, the Fourth Republic would have followed a path similar to the partial dealignment and disengagement managed by de Gaulle. This did not seem to be the intention of most French leaders in 1958. The military, though attached to an *Algérie française,* were also loyal to NATO and the Alliance by virtue of a shared opposition to communism. In their conflicts with the United States over the Alliance, most military and political leaders sought not disengagement, but a French-dominated southern extension of NATO. Even French nuclear ambitions were not generally perceived to be incompatible with NATO, and the final decisions to create a nuclear strike force were motivated largely by the desire to augment French influence in the Alliance and contribute to allied defense capabilities.[143]

On the other hand, it does not seem that the Fourth Republic could have fulfilled these familiar expectations. NATO or American support for a French Algeria was unlikely to be the result of a continuation of Fourth Republic policies in North Africa. Nor is it probable that the Fourth Republic could have been more successful than de Gaulle in obtaining American aid for the French nuclear program, or in reconciling French and American strategic interests within the framework of the Alliance. The gradual accommodation of the Fourth Republic's dominant political forces to much of de Gaulle's security policy framework indicates that their own perspectives have been closer to those of de Gaulle than they tended to realize. In 1958, certainly, one is more struck by the prospect of expanding dissent and disagreement than by the likelihood of reconciliation. As Alfred Grosser noted in 1963, "Algeria dominated everything and explained everything, from Suez to the wave of bitter and xenophobic nationalism which swept across France and carried in its train a deep though veiled crisis which hit deeply into the very heart of the Atlantic Alliance."[144] It seems, then, that NATO's value to France never recovered from the allied failure to support her cause in Africa, from the American reaction to Suez, and from the conviction that the United States had morally and materially turned against France and violated the Alliance tie.

2 Gaullist Perspectives on French Security

For nearly eleven years after General de Gaulle came to power in the spring of 1958, French security and alliance policies were the closely held monopoly of this remarkable man and a few collaborators. De Gaulle's images of international relations, alliance and defense matters, and France's prescribed role in international politics take on additional importance because his ideas and policies seem to have established a standard, or model, that constrains his successors and has proven irresistible even for leftist opponents of the Gaullist regime's domestic policies. The emergence of a broad consensus on security policy has been possible because de Gaulle was able to synthesize the often incoherent goals of the Fourth Republic and organize them into a compelling vision of security and status that has a wide appeal in France. The foundation of this vision is the Gaullist ideal of French independence and grandeur, notions that were linked to a policy of national defense and alliance and were part of a diplomatic strategy aimed at the transformation of France's international milieu.

Independence and Grandeur

Independence and grandeur constitute the dual image permeating all of de Gaulle's references to France. It is nearly impossible to separate these two abstract and almost metaphysical concepts that are purported to be the very essence of France's identity and prerequisites for national self-esteem. Independence, however, seems to be the precondition for grandeur in that it frees France to seek her rightful place in the world.

In the Gaullist lexicon, independence is an ideal signifying the absence of enduring and unyielding external restraints on France's freedom and ability to make policy choices in the national interest. As de Gaulle said in 1966, "independence means that we ourselves decide on what we have to do and with whom, without its being imposed by any other State and by any other

collective body."[1] In this sense, independence is basically a neutral concept
without any prescribed aim or goal. It essentially requires France to remain
free from any form of "subordination" that could penetrate and weaken the
decision-making bodies of the state and acquire a hold over elites and the
population, preventing them from making free decisions based on priority
consideration of French national interests. While international cooperation in
the context of interdependence is not incompatible with this ideal, supranational integration is rejected because it directly and permanently undermines
the autonomy and integrity of national policy decisions.

At times, and particularly in its rhetoric, Gaullist nationalism appeared to
seek maximum feasible independence for external and internal state action in
the service of national goals. But it is probably an error to place too much
stress on an external *action,* or Bergsonian, sense of independence at the
expense of the more Rousseauist notion of conceiving and determining the
general interest or will. De Gaulle fully realized the limitations on France's
foreign behavior in the post-1958 period and, in his regime's constitution and
its foreign policy, gave priority to guaranteeing a coherent and independent
determination of policy—partly as protection against France's limited power
and her constant temptation to mediocrity.[2] In this sense, sustaining the will
and ability to make independent judgments and decisions was actually the
core principle of Gaullism. As Michel Debré noted, it is the essence of a
nation to defend its interest and liberty, a duty that requires above all "an
autonomous will of conception and decision."[3] Another close collaborator of
de Gaulle's, Maurice Couve de Murville, also stresses the prime consideration
of an unfettered will, when he asserts that de Gaulle's policies were based on
the postulate that "France has the right and can have the will to be an independent country, hence to determine its policy and to assert it."[4] This concept
did not exclude that decisions could and often would involve a recognition of
limits and constraints, as well as collaboration for mutual interest. Thus,
according to Couve de Murville, "independence is not the disregard of
realities," although it precludes "their passive acceptance and submission to
the inevitable."[5]

There is another interpretation of the Gaullist preoccupation with independence that equates this notion with a goal of virtual autonomy for France
in her international relations. Edward L. Morse's study of de Gaulle's foreign
policy often adopts this view and, not surprisingly, reaches the conclusion that
de Gaulle essentially failed because complete autonomy is impossible in an
age of interdependence.[6] This is a complex issue that can not and, happily,
need not be resolved here. But it does seem that adopting an extreme and
literal standard for measuring the accomplishments of Gaullist foreign policy
confuses some of the rhetoric with the actual pattern of Gaullist international
behavior. In this context, then, Stanley Hoffmann's assessment of Gaullist
priorities seems the most accurate one: "De Gaulle was never foolish enough

to confuse national independence with self-sufficiency or with a total absence of commitments or ties to other nations. His argument was, rather: never to accept bonds that cannot be removed and that might submit your nation's fate to the decisions of others long after the ties are no longer in your interest."[7]

What de Gaulle sought, then, was enough leverage, or independence, for France to permit her leaders to manage and control the effects of international interdependence, and particularly to reduce the ability of other states or transnational actors to make decisions for France without her free consent and participation. This aim frequently involved building international coalitions, engaging in bilateral or multilateral cooperation, and other collaborative efforts designed to manipulate the conditions of interdependence and enhance the influence of the French state—the only legitimate representative of French interests in the international arena. If such goals were more practical than is sometimes asserted, the results for the Fifth Republic also appear to have been more positive. The defense issue will be discussed below, but the constraints of interdependence on de Gaulle's goals and priorities mainly concern economic and industrial policies. John Zysman's empirical studies indicate that in this arena de Gaulle and his successors have essentially sought "to control and direct the terms of interdependence."[8] They met with mixed success, he finds, but nevertheless have enabled the state to reduce France's vulnerability to many of the dangers and risks of international interdependence. Rather than flaunting the realities of an interdependent world, then, de Gaulle was able to reduce French dependence and put France on more equal terms in a competitive international system.

If there is disagreement about the meaning and results of de Gaulle's policies, there is a consensus that Gaullist tactics were a darker side of independence that often contributed to the failures of French foreign policy. The tactics, or style, of Gaullist diplomacy was the arena where de Gaulle's own historical personality and experiences found expression in a mode of statecraft that was often self-defeating because it stressed conflict and confrontation rather than reconciliation and cooperation. The crucial lesson for de Gaulle came from his experiences during World War II, especially in his relations with Roosevelt and the United States, when he learned that power and struggle were the plasma of interstate relations. His assessment was "that in foreign affairs, logic and sentiment do not weigh heavily in comparison with the realities of power; that what matters is what one takes and what one can hold on to; that to regain her place, France must count only on herself."[9] But how can France, chronically weak, make herself independent and powerful in a struggle that inevitably matches her against states stronger than herself? The theme permeating the third volume of de Gaulle's war memoirs is that only through tactics of refusal, obstruction, intransigency, and manipulation of *faits accomplis* can France hope to guarantee her own interests.

To de Gaulle, this diplomatic style was as necessary after 1958 as during the war, because France still found herself in a relatively weak position. For Gaullists, weakness and the justice of her cause gave France a special right to intransigence. Truly great powers can afford largesse and compromise with others because it costs them little in the long run. But a weak middle power can give away nothing because each compromise brings greater dependence in its wake. And, with dependence, France would cease to be her "true" self and follow her "unnatural" but persistent inclination toward decline, disorder, self-effacement, and renunciation of responsibility. The Gaullist diplomatic style, therefore, was not only a bulwark of independence and a shield preserving France's personality against a hostile world, it was also a protection against the inclinations of the French to undermine their national identity: "This will allows [France] to preserve her personality, to be respected and understood, finally to preserve her image in her own eyes and in those of the world, and to continue truly to exist."[10]

In practice, intransigence meant the refusal to act as "*demandeur,*" one who seeks favors from the rest of the world, and to insist on being treated as an equal partner in any international enterprise—or as more than equal, to compensate for a lack of concrete power. Recognized status in terms of prestige is the presumed reward of intractability, because other nations will then have to ask favors of France. Thus, in order to become a leader in the world, to acquire independence and rightful status, de Gaulle's France was often to behave according to the General's prescription for successful leadership. French statecraft was to be like that of the "man of action," who "scarcely imagines himself without a strong dose of egotism, pride, firmness, and cunning."[11] To achieve the greatness required for self-esteem, France would have to confront events and by force of will transcend them. She would have to strive for an awareness of superiority that leads to respect, if not love. Above all, France was to cultivate ambition—not for mundane personal gain, but for "the hope of playing a great rôle in great events."[12] In this formula, ultimate success matters less than the very act of striving, of leaving a mark on the world, because, for nations as for great men, "their fame is subsequently measured less by the utility of their endeavor than by its dimensions."[13] These guidelines for leadership were ones that de Gaulle adopted for himself in his public role as charismatic leader of the French people, and they were the hallmark of his diplomacy in the world beyond France. A particular style of behavior was thus elevated to a principle of statecraft and, in Hoffmann's words, "personal intransigence became France's intractability."[14]

The aims and tactics associated with independence were used above all to recapture France's grandeur, a fundamental aspect of the permanent national interest encompassing "not only the political, economic, and defense interests, or others, but also the image of France in the world and the principles of which she is the natural representative."[15] Grandeur is secured when France receives the homage of the world and her status is recognized and confirmed in the behavior of others. Rather than emulate the concrete power of a great state or superpower, which was beyond France's resources, de Gaulle often seemed to follow the Hobbesian prescription, "reputation of power is power; because it drawth with it the adherence of those that need protection."[16] Like Louis XIV, de Gaulle sought grandeur, or glory, for France and equated it with power in that "it is, so to speak, power recognized by others, power whose fame spreads across the world."[17] International recognition of France's importance was, then, the indispensible compensation for a decline in power in real terms. If this recognition could not be obtained from France's allies, the United States and Western Europe, then it could be sought in France's "universal mission" as she occupied "the chair of director of the world's conscience."[18]

De Gaulle sought grandeur not only because he believed that such "vast enterprises" unite the French and give them a sense of common purpose, but also because he found that an active and assertive France was welcomed and applauded abroad. In his image of France, her pursuit of the national interest was not narrow and self-serving, but was in the interest of all humanity because it evoked those particular French values that have inspired the world. As de Gaulle said in reference to his policy of decolonization and independence for Algeria: "International life may be transformed by this, in the direction of our spirit, which is that of liberty, of equality and of fraternity. By adopting this vast and generous plan, the French people are going to contribute, once more in their history, to the enlightenment of the world."[19] Thus, France's revival and her recovery of independence are supported by the world because her freedom is a sign that other countries can aspire to and obtained their own independence in the more flexible, more pluralist international system fostered by France.

Moreover, a strong and prestigious France is needed and welcomed because her universal mission induces her to use her power for the benefit of others, "power and grandeur which, according to the genius of France, are directed towards the welfare and fraternity of man."[20] France did not, according to de Gaulle, threaten or seek to oppress anyone—unlike the superpowers who aspired to place the world "under the yoke of a double hegemony that would be agreed upon between the two rivals."[21] France is loved precisely because de Gaulle and other Frenchmen had, in his words, "no ambition of extending [them]selves beyond the soil where [they] are sovereign,"[22] because they are satisfied with their frontiers (unlike West Germans), and because they have no desire to dominate the world ideologically, politically, or economically (unlike the Americans and Soviets). When France serves her national interests, then, she is also serving the cause of humanity; France is not imperialist but aims at her natural mission of peace and restoring equilibrium to a world suffering under the hegemony of the superpowers.

However extraordinary such rhetoric and reasoning may appear, the conceptions expressed by de Gaulle and his close associates do not distinguish them radically from other French elites in terms of beliefs and value systems. The notions of France's special mission in the world, her right to a prominent international role, her desire for independence and superior status, were shared by most French elites even if they could not agree on the best means of securing and maintaining these goals. Also, noncooperation and obstructionism as a behavior pattern and a means of retaining privileged interests have long been noted as regular practices among French political groups. Individualism, or an integrity of the self confronting a hostile environment, has been one prominent characteristic of the French value system and has been used as a key to explaining social and political behavior in France.[23] In this sense, de Gaulle carried on a distinctly French pattern in his foreign policy behavior and, by force of personality and conviction, was the most French of Frenchmen. Nor were the tactics unique to the Fifth Republic. As Raymond Aron reminds us, both the Fourth and Fifth Republics "had in common the rare use of discussion and the frequent use of obstruction. The Fourth Republic's obstruction was often founded on the blackmail of the weak. The Fifth Republic's obstruction was based on claims to greatness."[24] Where alliance politics were concerned, one particular result of Gaullist diplomacy was that the normal bargaining rules for disputes and negotiations among allies were constantly violated.[25] Expectatations of flexibility and compromise would not be fulfilled by Gaullist France when basic issues of prestige and independence were thought to be at stake, a fact never fully understood by France's NATO partners throughout the 1958-66 period.

Finally, although a Gaullist policy based on independence and grandeur naturally focused on external relations, it is important to note that it had a significant internal function as well. For de Gaulle believed that status and recognition were essential to avoid an internal decadence that would "subjugate [France's] soul, destroy her stature, and sooner or later overwhelm her in a system foreign in every respect."[26] Rather than simply subordinating internal politics to a virtuoso foreign policy, then, de Gaulle assumed that an active and influential France was essential to the moral and psychological well-being of the French themselves. It was partly this insight that made Gaullism a powerful force in French politics, because it offered the French a sense of dignity based on France's international status and prestige. What de Gaulle brought France was the novelty of resolute leadership and the pride of an ambitious program for making France a respected world power. He also, of course, used this program and its alluring rhetoric to disguise or cushion the psychological impact of France's decline and the transformation from a genuine great power to a middle-range state of moderate significance in the world.

An Independent National Defense

The Gaullist position on national defense was derived from the ideal of French independence and the preference for limited forms of international cooperation consistent with the overriding need to uphold the integrity of the national state. To de Gaulle, the principal guarantee of independence was a firm will on the part of citizens, governors, and armed forces to preserve the integrity of the state in the final resort to arms.[27] This determination is a prerequisite for independence because the threat of war and other menaces to national security are constant factors in interstate relations, while decision-making autonomy across a wide range of issues may be impaired unless national leaders feel capable of defending the state effectively without excessive dependence on others. Moreover, a secure and efficient national defense is particularly necessary for a country such as France, whose chronic political weakness makes her susceptible to a dependence on others that can only be offset by constant attention to armed strength. As de Gaulle wrote in *The Army of the Future:* "The sword is not only the last argument in her quarrels, it is also the only thing that makes up for her weakness. Everything that is ill-adapted in her territory, infirm in her character has, in the last resort, nothing to offset it but the warlike arms, the skill of the troops, the sufferings of her soldiers."[28]

National defense is more than simply protecting a nation from foreign pressures and aggression. It is, in Gaullism, the essential condition for maintaining the authority and legitimacy of the state and government in the eyes of the population: "The defense of the country is the first duty of the State. It is even its raison d'être."[29] If French rulers are not in control of their own means of defense, they lose their authority and are eventually unable to maintain themselves in power. In his Ecole Militaire speech of 3 November 1959, de Gaulle maintained that all French regimes from the Merovingians through the Fifth Republic had justified themselves primarily by their preoccupation with national defense. If a regime shirked this duty, he claimed, "it would no longer be possible to maintain a State. The government has as its raison d'être, in all periods, the defense of the independence and integrity of the territory."[30]

De Gaulle's classic formulation of an objective priority to an independent defense has been the object of much criticism and of charges that he was "blatantly anachronistic" for adhering to an idiosyncratic and outmoded view of the importance of a strong national defense.[31] In particular, de Gaulle is said to have based his policies on a distinction between "high" and "low" politics, giving a misplaced priority to security and defense policy and ignoring the more significant economic-welfare politics that are increasingly susceptible to international forces associated with interdependence. Even if defense independence were a feasible goal, the argument runs, it was largely irrelevant because the most important issues and constraints on policy choices are now found in the "low" politics basket.

On the other hand, it is clear that de Gaulle did not neglect the economic, industrial, technological, and monetary aspects of French influence and independence—though his efforts met with varying degrees of success and failure. Nor does his concern for national defense seem to have been misplaced. As the analysis below will indicate, de Gaulle was certainly justified in worrying about the great risk of depending on another state for defense guarantees, particularly in the nuclear age, when the potential costs of such dependence have escalated and assumed an unprecedented urgency. He also saw that nuclear weapons were an available and relatively inexpensive means of maximizing defense independence and acquiring more leverage within the international security system. Precisely because France's influence in non-security arenas seemed potentially weaker than her influence over European regional defense, de Gaulle doubtless saw a modern national defense system as a factor of compensation. Thus, a strong defense system would increase French status and prestige, traditional elements of power. They would also be a source of influence in the newly complex international system in which states are not only mutually dependent, but find that dominant influence in the context of one arena can be manipulated to compensate for weakness elsewhere. Rather than an excessive and obsessive concern with security politics at the expense of "low" politics, then, it seems that de Gaulle perceived a direct relationship between the two arenas and felt that a strong defense system could help minimize the potential costs of dependence across a spectrum of issues.

If attention to national defense must be a constant vigil of the French state, and its main claim to legitimacy, it is clear that the state cannot turn over this responsibility to external authorities and must keep firm control over the instruments of defense, the armed forces. For de Gaulle, there was one logical formula for organizing the defense of France, and it was an exceedingly simple one that served as a guide for his policy toward NATO and the Alliance, namely, "the principle that dominates everything is that an army fights for its country, under the authority of its government and under the orders of its leaders."[32] De Gaulle was bound to reject the defense integration associated with NATO because he felt it would weaken the will of the government and people, deprive the state of its decision-making independence, and finally subordinate France to the interests and policies of the strongest power in the alliance.

More specifically, the General claimed that an integrated command system such as NATO's deprived the military of its sense of supreme responsibility to France, thereby damaging its reliability and usefulness to anyone. Also, the population was bound to become reluctant to support a defense effort that had no clear relationship to the national interest and the legitimate government. "How indeed in the long run could a Government, a Parliament, a people give their money and their services with all their heart in time of peace, and make their sacrifices in time of war, for a system in which they are not responsible for their own defense?"[33] Military integration had an even more malicious and debilitating effect on the armed forces, which must bear the main burden of protecting the state. According to de Gaulle, an integrated command system can deprive the military of its fundamental reason for fighting, which is and must be to serve the nation. As he said at the Ecole Militaire in 1959, if foreign elements are directing French troops, those with the responsibility to command lose their authority and dignity before both the nation and their soldiers: "As for the military command, which must have the unrivaled responsibility of commanding on the field of battle, where it answers for the fate of the country, if it ceased to hold this honor and this responsibility, if it were no more than one element in a foreign hierarchy, this would mean the rapid end of its authority, its dignity, its prestige before the nation and, therefore, before the armed forces."[34] Thus, in an integrated military system dominated by other states, the armed forces lose their supreme responsibility to France, are deprived of the national mission so essential to their sense of duty and integrity, and the nation soon finds that it has lost its own guardians. Independence is impossible under these conditions, and the state, in de Gaulle's definition, ceases to exist as such.

Gaullist Alliance Policy

As in his doctrine of an independent national defense, de Gaulle's view of alliances and his critique of the Western alliance system were well developed and publicized before he returned to power in 1958. The kind of alliance most compatible with the Gaullist image of France was, not surprisingly, a classical one in which the value of the alliance is measured by its contribution to national goals and not by its beneficial effects on an ill-defined superior community interest. Alliances are, or should be, flexible and temporary instruments of statecraft, designed to support the aims of the separate member states.[35] In particular, de Gaulle believed that each alliance member should retain maximum freedom to undertake independent actions when its interests diverge from the common interest or the wishes of the most powerful members.

This aspect of de Gaulle's alliance policy, which set him firmly against military integration, seems to have been shaped by his wartime experiences. Under the difficult circumstances as leader of a subordinate member of a winning coalition, de Gaulle often found that the external goals of an alliance (vis-à-vis the enemy) were a secondary consideration to intraalliance issues of relative prestige and divergent interests among the allies. The General's main concern during the war, especially toward the end when victory was assured, was to use the coalition as a vehicle for acquiring security, status, political influence, and independence for France in the postwar period. Because of France's weak position, he adopted an intransigent attitude to defend French interests against the designs or thoughtlessness of the United States and Britain. Devoid of the idealism that seemed to guide, or cloak, the aims of the "Anglo-Saxons," de Gaulle assessed allied military actions primarily in terms of their potential effect on France's postwar position in Europe and overseas. British and American arguments based on military efficacy generally failed to sway de Gaulle's conviction that military-strategic concerns were secondary to the pursuit of higher national interests and status. For him, the alliance existed to serve France. This interest assumed the defeat of Germany by coordinated allied forces, but only on the condition that their actions would "produce, on the national territory, specific results of direct interest to France."[36]

After the liberation of most of France, when French territory was serving as a base of allied operations and French troops were participating in increasing numbers, de Gaulle felt that these contributions entitled France to an equal role in coalition decision making. Instead, he found that "Washington and London claimed exclusive rights to strategic leadership," a position that "was indeed unjustifiable."[37] The General's reaction reveals the limits he placed on alliance collaboration. "To compensate for this abuse," he wrote, "I would, on occasion, have to force their hand and even employ our troops outside the Allied framework."[38] In other words, if France is denied her rightful status, she resorts to the first weapon of the weak, intransigence, and if that fails, she in effect temporarily withdraws from the coalition in defense of her own interests. De Gaulle's recounting of his clash with Eisenhower over the proposed allied retreat from Strasbourg reveals how very stubborn and convincing he could be on behalf of France.[39]

This incident is also an example of de Gaulle's belief that, even in wartime, French cooperation depends on an alliance's value to national interests even at the expense of its general purpose of a militarily efficient victory. When the two are in conflict, he asserts, formal commitments to allies cease to be binding: "The excuse a policy of resignation might find in the fact that the Allied command was responsible for military operations had, in this case, no validity. For if the French government could entrust its forces to the command of a foreign leader, it was on the formal condition that the use made of those forces be in accord with the nation's interest. If not, the French government was obliged to resume command of its forces."[40] Such experiences reinforced de Gaulle's convictions about the danger of material dependence on others for defense, and about the risks involved when foreign commanders are in charge of French armed forces. Although circumstances had forced him to accept this situation during the war—just as weakness and the Soviet threat led the Fourth Republic to accept NATO integration and dependence on the United States—de Gaulle considered that these conditions were only temporary and to be discarded in periods of revival.

In the postwar era, de Gaulle shared many of the security goals of the Fourth Republic's leaders, but was unsparing in his criticism of the regime's weakness and many failures. The General welcomed the prospect of an alliance with the United States in 1948, but qualified his approval by noting that the practical value of the new coalition would depend on France knowing the exact conditions under which her allies would provide aid against aggression.[41] Like many in France, de Gaulle was disturbed by the lack of an automatic assistance clause in Article V of the Atlantic Treaty and feared that the Anglo-Saxons might once again come to France's aid too late. Sensitive to the immense destructive capacity of nuclear weapons, he frequently expressed the fear that the Alliance might concentrate its forces in the peripheral zones, leaving the heartland of Western Europe open to a destructive sequence of conquest and liberation. This was inadmissable. "We will consider criminal a policy and strategy which, on the pretext that destructive atomic bombs exist elsewhere, would deliberately abandon the soil of the Métropole first to the invasion of some, then to the bombardments of others."[42] In 1949 and 1950, de Gaulle joined those who called for the presence of substantial American forces on the front line as a deterrent to such an invasion and a guarantee of an immediate and forceful American defense. But he saw this as a temporary solution, for in the long run French security could be assured only if her own national defense capabilities were revived, and if she secured the major role in Alliance decision making that would enable her to protect the national interest. Like his political opponents, then, de Gaulle expected the Alliance to restore France's strength, prestige, and her capacity for making an independent and valued contribution to the coalition.

When these shared expectations were not fulfilled, de Gaulle was the first and most articulate critic of the inadequacies of the Fourth Republic and the Alliance. Instead of restoring France to her rightful status, he noted, the Alliance was keeping her in a position of dependence and subordination to the policies of Washington and London. In return for meager arms deliveries, the irresponsible governments of the Fourth Republic were ceding bases in France and her possessions to the United States, agreeing to an integrated NATO organization that put French troops under the command of American officers, and consenting to the further destruction of France's national defense with the EDC scheme—all without obtaining the requisite defense guarantees and a determinant role in formulating Western strategy. As a result, according to de Gaulle, the French found themselves with no part to play except "that of subordinates, even concerning the Rhine, Paris, the Loire, North Africa. Thus we risk, according to the circumstances, being invaded by the adversaries and dominated by the allies."[43]

The NATO integrated military organization was, of course, in contradiction with France's most vital interests. American control of SHAPE and an American SACEUR in charge of continental defense meant that the most basic decisions about French security were taken without her participation as an equal. France had become "a kind of protectorate" subject to foreign control or, at best, unwarranted and intolerable interference in her defense, foreign policy, and economy. There was not even a guarantee that "the protector would protect us," because the United States was under no strict obligation to defend French territory or maintain troops in Europe. Finally, in this state of dependence, France was unable to defend her own policies in Europe and abroad, but instead had to bow to American wishes and policy, which, on many points, "in no way conforms to our own interests."[44]

General de Gaulle did not limit himself to attacks on the Atlantic defense system and France's debased position within it. In a series of statements usually tied to the EDC debate, he also proposed reforms in the Alliance to make it conform to his views. Although these proposals are vague on some points, the broad outline of a "Gaullist" Atlantic Alliance does emerge from them. It furnishes the background for the General's single formal proposal for Alliance reform, the 1958 memorandum, and is a necessary complement because the memorandum's meaning is unclear unless it is interpreted in light of the earlier position.

In place of the integrated NATO military organization with a Supreme Commander and international staff, de Gaulle preferred a combined interallied general staff with authority to handle common strategic planning under the direction of the separate allied governments. The governments were to control the combined staff through some "higher organism," which might be a committee of heads of state.[45] Each member would naturally maintain its complete autonomy in the alliance while voluntarily cooperating with others. There was to be a common overall strategy agreed upon by the governments, filled out and applied by the combined staff, and ensuring that the vital interests of each member were protected. Because de Gaulle excluded a supreme commander with his own staff from this plan, he felt it would leave "our own leaders the authority over all forces ensuring the direct defense of our own territories."[46] Thus, the defense of France would no longer be in the hands of foreigners, the armed forces would be responsible only to French ministers and generals, and only French officials would exercise authority over French territory and its military bases.[47]

This Gaullist alternative to NATO appears to be a classical alliance of states that have carefully reserved their sovereign autonomy. Such a description is only partly accurate, however, because de Gaulle linked the alliance proposals to his design for a European confederation. Thus, the new Atlantic system was to be distinguished by a group of European states coordinating its defense with the North American branch of the alliance. Instead of the supranational EDC and expanded powers for SACEUR, which constituted a supreme renunciation of French independence for de Gaulle,[48] he wanted a confederation to establish "a truly European alliance" in which West German rearmament would be handled to suit the interests of Europeans, and not as the platform for a special German-American relationship.[49] The European pillar was to be directed by a council of heads of government meeting periodically. Like the alliance as a whole, the European confederation was to have its own combined general staff charged with coordinating the plans and material resources of the members. Each state would be bound to aid another in the event of aggression, although a declaration of hostilities would depend on the (unanimous) consent of the council. The council, to include Britain, would also regulate Europe's relations with the United States within the broader Atlantic Alliance framework.[50] De Gaulle did not specify the exact nature of the links between the European and American poles, but it is clear that they were to be equal in status and that American influence over Europe and individual European states would be held to a minimum.

Although this European security community was ostensibly a confederation of sovereign and equal states, de Gaulle remained true to French tradition and policy by insisting on a privileged, superior position for France, and restraints on Germany. French preeminence was to be guaranteed by entrusting general responsibility for the defense of continental Western Europe to Paris and a French general. De Gaulle first brought this up in November 1948, when he proposed the global application of a Western alliance and carefully assigned the European and North African theaters to French command, because "from the moment that it is a question of the defense of our territory, which is first of all essentially the defense of Europe, only the French can be responsible for it."[51] In later attacks on the EDC and the role of SACEUR, de Gaulle clung to the view that a French commander naturally should have sole authority over all land, air, and sea forces for a region extending from the Baltic to Africa.[52]

Germany's precise role in these arrangements was left undefined before 1958, but it appears that the Federal Republic and its rearmament were to be controlled by European members of the confederation and by a Franco-German entente.[53] A proposal made by the Gaullist party during the EDC controversy seemed to handle the German problem and reconcile the European combined general staff with a French commander for Europe. In this plan, the European confederation was to delegate authority to the French commander-in-chief, who would work in conjunction with an international staff of advisors. West German rearmament was limited to a "shock force," which would always have fewer divisions in Europe than those of France.[54] Finally, de Gaulle was an early advocate of the French nuclear weapons pro-

gram as a key to equality with other great powers—a goal he realized was beyond the resources of most other continental states and unimaginable for
West Germany.[55]

These early proposals were clearly the ancestors of the 1958 memorandum
and de Gaulle's subsequent attempts to construct a European political-military
confederation dominated by France. Under the Fifth Republic, de Gaulle
pursued his earlier designs in yet another sense: He attempted to extend the
Alliance into a global operation to protect France's extra-European interests.
In November 1948 de Gaulle had insisted that any future war would be global
in scope, and the West should be prepared to fight in the three theaters of
operation. France was to be responsible for Europe and North Africa, Britain
for the Middle East and East Africa, while the United States' role would be
mainly in the Far East.[56] Later, at the height of the Indochina conflict,
de Gaulle expressed the sentiments of many of the French when he said that
the Atlantic Alliance should be expanded to "the global level" to guarantee
the interests of its members wherever they are challenged.[57] Again, as France
faced retreat from Tunisia and Morocco and rebellion in her Algerian departments, he stressed the overwhelming need for NATO to guarantee France's
position in North Africa. French independence and status as a world power
depended on her African possessions, he said, whose strategic value could not
be distinguished from that of the Métropole itself. Because French interests
were global in nature and confronted a generalized communist threat, and
because the value of the Alliance lay in its ability to protect these interests,
de Gaulle insisted that the restricted regional character of NATO should be
abandoned in favor of a mutual guarantee applicable around the world.[58]

These arguments were familiar ones under the Fourth Republic. Starting
in 1958, however, de Gaulle's insistence on the global interdependence of
allied security focused primarily on the strategic importance of nuclear
weapons. These views, which were based on more than just narrow French
interests, fed a growing controversy within the Alliance. They also enhanced
the credibility and appeal of de Gaulle's claim that the NATO defense system
and its inherent American hegemony had been a serious error for both
France and Europe. In seeking to revise this security arrangement after 1958,
de Gaulle also developed a strategy for transforming the Western bloc and
the international system to make them more compatible with his images of
national security and international equilibrium.

Transforming the Atlantic System

Under de Gaulle's stewardship from 1958 until 1969, French security policy
followed a number of tactical variations and strategic turns according to

domestic and international circumstances. Despite important shifts in emphasis, de Gaulle was generally consistent in his opposition to political or military integration, in his determination to secure an independent defense system for France outside of NATO, and in his efforts to restructure European, Atlantic, and eventually global politics to enhance French independence while contributing to a more flexible and stable international system. Although Gaullist Alliance diplomacy was exceedingly supple and could exploit policies and themes whenever useful, it does fall into four convenient periods for analysis: from 1958 through 1961, from 1961 to early 1965, from 1965 to mid-1968, and the final months of de Gaulle's presidency.[59] The first stage was dominated by the memorandum proposal for a tripartite directorate set above the Alliance, the second by attempts to organize an independent European security system around a Franco-German understanding, the third by a temporary withdrawal into semiisolation while proselytizing for a new global system, and the last by a partial accommodation to the Atlantic system. The alliance and defense aspects of these periods will be analyzed in some detail in subsequent chapters. The purpose of this section's discussion is to describe briefly the most salient general characteristics of Gaullist security policy and provide a setting for the often confusing convolutions of French diplomacy.[60]

In the first phase, from 1958 through 1961, de Gaulle essentially continued with earlier themes from French Alliance policy, consolidating and clarifying the Fourth Republic's goals in his memorandum of September 1958. This period was characterized by an emphasis on transforming the Atlantic Alliance into a three-power oligarchy deemed more compatible with France's independence and her security interests in Europe and abroad. Although the General pressed for British and American acceptance of his proposals during this period, he probably doubted the success of his stratagem from the outset and simultaneously prepared to use other means to secure his aims, especially European policy and the nascent French nuclear force.

For de Gaulle, doubtless the most significant achievement of this period was the internal stabilization and revitalization of France, which was the prerequisite for ending her dependence on outside powers. De Gaulle's first priority, then, was to replace the unstable and indecisive Fourth Republic regime that had followed a course of national self-abnegation and abasement. He did this with the support of a new constitution and political system, including a dominant Gaullist party, that guaranteed presidential control over the making and implementing of security policy decisions.[61] Once the Algerian problem began moving, however tortuously, toward a settlement, de Gaulle had more and more freedom from internal restraints or unrest and could focus attention on French European policy and the construction of a modern armed force equipped with nuclear weapons. The more active and influential France of the Fifth Republic was possible, then, because the regime was able to abandon a debilitating colonialist policy, restore domestic economic and political stability, and, in de Gaulle's words, discover an unaccustomed ability "to demand and to act" in pursuit of France's own interests.[62]

The memorandum phase of Gaullist Atlantic diplomacy was not an aberration in French Alliance policy, as is often assumed, nor was it a mere tactical ploy to establish a pretext for later moves against NATO. But the proposals were unacceptable to both the United States and France's European partners, who preferred that political-military affairs be handled within the NATO framework. As an alternative to this brand of Atlanticism, which de Gaulle saw as a pretext for American hegemony, the General began to stress his second option of a "European" Europe independent of the United States. The Fouchet negotiations of 1961-62 were the principal forum for the attempt to extend European cooperation to include political and even military issues, and to shift from the integration format to an intergovernmental one based on periodic meetings of heads of state or government. When this effort proved abortive, de Gaulle turned to a "small Europe" of Franco-German cooperation in late 1962, hoping that it would be the embryo of the wider community he sought. When this, too, had gone amiss by 1965, Gaullist France continued to hope that Western Europe would soon follow her lead and eventually adopt a united policy of building an independent pole of power in world politics.

De Gaulle's conception of European unity was clearly the fulcrum of French Atlantic and global politics for much of his tenure in office and thus merits a close examination. His serious interest in European cooperation dates back to World War II. This is, at least, the view expressed in the final volume of his war memoirs, which was completed after the General's return to power in 1958, and therefore constituted a declaration of future intention as well as an interpretation of past behavior.[63] In this work, the prominent role of European cooperation in the Gaullist design for the postwar world was sketched in broad and unambiguous strokes:

> I intended [in 1944] to assure France security in Western Europe by preventing the rise of a new Reich that might again threaten its safety; to cooperate with East and West and, if need be, contract the necessary alliances on one side or the other without ever accepting any kind of dependency; to transform the French Union into a free association in order to avoid the as yet unspecified dangers of upheaval; to persuade the states along the Rhine, the Alps, and the Pyrenees to form a political, economic, and strategic block; to establish this organization as one of the three world powers and, should it become necessary, as the arbiter between the Soviet and Anglo-American camps.[64]

This seems to be an accurate description of de Gaulle's European goals before the full brunt of the Cold War was felt. Through 1946 and even 1947, de Gaulle clung to the hope that a united Europe could act as "the necessary element of compensation and understanding" between the two superpowers, whose competition posed a risk for French independence equalled only by the menace of a joint condominium over Europe.[65]

In subsequent years, de Gaulle developed three themes that dominated his views and, after 1958, his policies on European cooperation. They were: first, that France is the natural leader of a unified Western Europe; second, that the form of cooperation should be a confederation of independent states and not a single integrated unit; and third, that this French-led Europe ought to become an independent force in international politics. The proposition that France should occupy the key position in Europe did not distinguish de Gaulle from his Fourth Republic opponents, but the Monnet-Schuman vision of an integrated federalist Europe was anathema to him.[66] This was partly a question of basic philosophy, for de Gaulle's more traditional perspectives embraced a profound conviction that the only legitimate and viable actors in world politics were sovereign states, a concept indistinguishable from his image of independence and grandeur as essential attributes of France herself.

De Gaulle's opposition to federalist integration was also prompted by his conviction that an integrated, stateless Europe could never become an independent force in world affairs and would, of necessity, be a satellite of the United States. Precisely the opposite assumption underlay the integrationist measures promoted by Fourth Republic leaders, who had acted on the conviction that only a supranational Europe could muster the resources and harmonize policies to secure independence from the United States and acceptance as both an equal partner in the West and a major global actor. De Gaulle, however, believed that supranationalism would debilitate Europe and perpetuate the subordination of France. His critique on this subject was similar to the charges leveled against NATO and military integration. Integration in both NATO and European institutions, he said, had been accepted by the states of Europe because they were weak at the time and unable to defend their independence against American policies. Just as NATO integration was a system designed to perpetuate American control over the security of Alliance members, European integration facilitated American economic and political domination of Europe.

Thus, de Gaulle contended that an integrated Europe without strong nation-states would inevitably lack the political will necessary to escape American hegemony and play a great role on the world stage. Moves against integration in any sphere of activity involving France were linked by the persistent tendency to equate the existing forms of European and Atlantic cooperation with subordination to the United States. This theme was especially prominent after the failure of the Fouchet negotiations in 1962, while Washington was publicizing its support for European integration as the prerequisite for an Atlantic partnership. De Gaulle saw this as a subterfuge in which Washington was promoting the kind of Europe that it could most easily dominate.

After his return to power in 1958, de Gaulle did initially accept the integrationist European Economic Community, although it had been vehemently attacked by Gaullist politicians.[67] As Roger Massip has explained, de Gaulle's toleration for the EEC probably stemmed from a realization that French leadership in this enterprise granted her a measure of international prestige and influence surpassing even the economic advantages of the Community.[68] Toleration was, however, accompanied by a determination to modify the Community to make it more compatible with the Gaullist image of European unity. In the opening shot of a 1960 campaign to redesign the European union, the General made it clear that he had not altered his view that the nation-states were the only solid foundation for building Europe:

> Now, what are the realities of Europe? What are the pillars on which it can be built? The States are, in truth, certainly very different from one another, each of which has its own spirit, its own history, its own language, its own misfortunes, glories and ambitions; but these States are the only entities that have the right to order and the authority to act. To imagine that something can be built that would be effective for action and that would be approved by the people outside and above the States—this is a dream.[69]

Dismissing the EEC Commission as a mere technocratic institution "which cannot have any authority and, consequently, any political effectiveness,"[70] de Gaulle proposed that European political cooperation should rest on intergovernmental organs coordinating the political, economic, cultural, and defense policies of the separate states. The focal point of the scheme was "organized, regular consultation between responsible Governments," by which he meant periodic meetings of the six heads of state or government and their ministers. The Fouchet negotiations of 1961-62 were the setting for de Gaulle's attempt to shift from the integration format to an intergovernmental and, eventually, confederal one. Although not the most prominent issue at the time, an important feature of these discussions for de Gaulle was his hope that the new European institutions would foster defense cooperation outside the American-dominated NATO framework. The expectation that an independent, non-Atlanticist defense system could replace NATO was also a feature of the Franco-German entente stressed by de Gaulle between 1962 and 1965. Both of these European efforts proved unsatisfactory, however, and de Gaulle had to abandon them temporarily. Thus, he stirred up a major crisis in EEC affairs in mid-1965, and manipulated it to block supranational voting measures due to take effect in early 1966.

De Gaulle could and did prevent the further development of European cooperation along integrationist or supranational lines, and the subsequent course of European cooperation indicates that the Gaullist formula of cooperating, interdependent, but still separate states is closer to the complex reality of Europe than the early supranational formulas. However, de Gaulle's own efforts to create a more cohesive bloc and to extend European cooperation to cover defense issues failed for a number of reasons. One, certainly, was de Gaulle's own distinctive personality, style, and sense of diplomatic tactics that provoked crises and inevitable resentments in Europe. These characteristics also tended to confirm and feed suspicions that the Gaullist European order was being promoted less for its value to the community than to make France the pivotal European state, managing Europe's relations with the United States, the Soviet Union, and the Third World. The tripartite proposal of 1958 cast a long shadow over de Gaulle's European diplomacy, reminding France's partners of the undaunted French drive for preeminence.

In that de Gaulle's critique of the bipolar order and superpower hegemony necessitated the construction of cooperating groups of states as alternative centers of power, his diplomacy often seemed especially ill-suited to the requirements and task he so clearly and forcefully outlined.[71] De Gaulle was thus conspicuously unable to make any progress in extending European unity to include defense cooperation and the harmonization of security policies. In this effort, however, he was hampered as much by the realities of Europe's military weakness and the structure of the international system as by his own failings. While the arguments about the growing unreliability of the American guarantee and the danger of the new flexible response strategy fell on receptive ears in European capitals, the proposals for European defense autonomy and reliance on French nuclear weapons for protection always strained credulity and faced decisive resistance. French European policy was also undermined by one of its own prominent contradictions, between the aspiration for political-military unity and French strategic concepts that emphasized national autonomy and the divisibility of security even among continental European states. De Gaulle's arguments that European independence would require a defense counterpart to economic and political cooperation were unassailable in their logic, and may yet appear to have been prophetic. But, at the time, they were premature because there was no feasible way of managing and protecting the dangerous transition from an Atlantic-centered to a Euro-centered security system. The Gaullist European design faced skepticism and finally had to be set aside because France's potential partners were unwilling to risk unravelling the Atlantic connection while embarking on an uncertain European adventure.

Unable to transform the Atlantic system from within, and always aware that France enjoyed its protection, however diminished, de Gaulle's security policy after 1965 was marked by a retreat on one level—to a nationally oriented, semiisolated, and autonomous defense system with minimal links to NATO and Western Europe—and, on another, by increasing global activism on behalf of the pluralist, multipolar system that de Gaulle felt was bound to succeed the bipolar order. De Gaulle had, of course, been an early critic of the emerging superpowers' domination of global politics and their tendency to condominium, which was so conveniently symbolized by the Yalta agreements. By the early 1960s, he found the hegemony of the superpowers increasingly intolerable, because it oppressed the states within each bloc, and dangerous, because it threatened general destruction as local conflicts anywhere on the globe tended to engage superpower interests and might then escalate to regional or global levels. As an alternative to this system, de Gaulle used his talents and French influence on behalf of a global order based, in Edward A. Kolodziej's analysis, on a "multipolar strategic and diplomatic system, characterized by diverse and competing centers of state political authority, strategic powers, and diplomatic initiative."[72] This new structure was, de Gaulle thought, inevitable because of intrinsic changes in world politics, desirable as a source of freedom and flexibility for third states, and beneficial for everyone because it would mitigate the global competition of the superpowers and the latent threat of nuclear conflict between them.

De Gaulle's arguments and his challenge to the old international order seemed plausible and often even compelling because, during the 1960s, the bipolar system was indeed changing, slowly and asymmetrically, into a more flexible structure with many of the characteristics emphasized by de Gaulle. In the course of the decade, the strategic stalemate between the United States and the Soviet Union provided a setting with more freedom of maneuver for less powerful states, and encouraged them to challenge openly the global hegemony of the superpowers. The Sino-Soviet conflict, the emergence of a more independent and assertive Third World, the vague possibility of more autonomy for Eastern Europe—all lent credence to Gaullist logic.[73] In the context of Atlantic politics, Western Europe's growing economic power and potential for political cohesion challenged the American role and seemed to open new possibilities for revising the East-West settlement in Europe. Thus, the Gaullist design for a new international equilibrium also held out some promise of a more generally satisfactory European order.

This aspect of the scheme was understandably never very clear, but it seemed to advocate a Europe "decoupled" from direct dependence on the superpowers and from their confrontation, and to assert that this more independent Europe could erect a new security structure designed to contain Germany and reunite East and West within a framework of cooperating nation-states. As David Calleo interpreted de Gaulle's long-range plans, an independent Western Europe was to restrain West Germany within a loose structure, while the Soviet Union gradually gave more freedom to the satellite states.[74] The Franco-German entente would be complemented by a Franco-Soviet "understanding" about Germany, which might permit closer relations between two separate German states and exercise military control over them and their denuclearized status. In a "concentric ring" approach to European security, then, the two superpowers are still active as guarantee states because the United States and Western Europe would remain linked in a loose alliance arrangement to compensate for the geographical preponderance of Soviet power.

Perhaps the most striking and authentic feature of this Gaullist grand design was the considerable feat of uniting an attractive and often logical view of the emerging international order with a pivotal role for France. The coincidence of French national interest with a transformed global system and a revised East-West settlement in Europe brought French diplomacy unprecedented attention in the 1960s and gave it a universal appeal unmatched in the postwar era. De Gaulle himself was convinced that France's self-appointed role as challenger of the "Yalta system" was the great enterprise through which she could recapture the grandeur so necessary to national self-esteem. Recovering her own independence and universally admired, France seemed the natural champion of the international peace and equilibrium that were to accompany a détente between the blocs and their eventual disappearance. As de Gaulle wrote in his review of the Fifth Republic's achievements: "In short, if there was a voice that might be listened to and a policy that might be effective with a view to setting up a new order to replace the Cold War, that voice and that policy were preeminently those of France. But only on the condition that they were really her own and that the hand she held out in friendship was free."[75] France's independence was thus to contribute to the new international order, and in return multipolarity would keep that independence intact and accord France grandeur as the instigator of the new system.

De Gaulle himself and French diplomacy undoubtedly did assist in the erosion of the bipolar world during the 1960s, also promoting the process of détente in Europe that has transformed some aspects of East-West relations. France could not, however, alter the essential features of two blocs in Europe, one held under tight control and the other more independent in many respects, but still subordinated to the United States for military security purposes. The extent of the Gaullist challenge to this settlement was not apparent until after 1962, when the setbacks in European politics led him into a more vehement campaign. Previously, the construction of an independent Europe had been proposed as a partnership with the United States. After the failures of the memorandum and Fouchet initiatives, however, the theme of partnership gave way to growing hostility as de Gaulle saw that attempts were being made to reinforce American control of Western Europe and to solidify a tight bipolar system based partly on a Soviet-American condominium.

The first trend was confirmed by Washington's rejections of the 1958 memorandum demands, by the Nassau Agreement of December 1962, which reaffirmed "Anglo-Saxon" domination of the Alliance, and by the MLF scheme of 1963-64, which would have sabotaged European unity and an independent defense. Evidence of the second trend could be found in the Cuban missile crisis of October 1962 and the Test-Ban Treaty signed in July 1963. The coincidence of these events seemed to indicate that the superpowers had stepped back from their confrontation over Cuba, determined to end the risk of nuclear war between them. In that the Nassau Agreement, the MLF, and the 1963 treaty were all aimed, in part, against the independent French nuclear force, and by extension against Europe's independence, it seemed that stricter American control over the policies of its allies was part of the bargain. Perceiving a growing threat in the revival of an obsolete Yalta formula, de Gaulle's press conference of January 1963 became the occasion to vent his firm rejection of the "Atlantic Community" concept as a stalking horse for reinforced American hegemony and a superpower condominium.

It is also possible that after 1963, instead of a revived bipolarity, de Gaulle saw the Soviet Union as actually in retreat before an aggressive American policy that complicated widening cleavages within the Soviet bloc.[76] In this interpretation, the outcome of the Cuban crisis had been a victory for the United States and had induced the Soviet Union to sign the Test-Ban Treaty as an armistice agreement permitting Moscow to concentrate on problems within its sphere of influence, leaving the United States free to extend its domination outside a defensive Soviet bloc. American imperialism in Vietnam was thus an example of the attempt to solidify a preponderant world role for the United States, a policy that posed the risk of miscalculation and a nuclear escalation engulfing Europe and the world. Although de Gaulle was never very clear on this issue, his speech in April 1965 did claim that French independence stood in opposition to an American impulse for universal domination. "The fact that we have reassumed our faculty of judgment and action in regard to all problems sometimes seems to displease a State which may believe, by virtue of its power, it is invested with supreme and universal responsibility."[77]

One aspect of de Gaulle's détente policy, then, may have been to restore an international equilibrium by offering Moscow the mediation of France in establishing links with an independent Western Europe and embracing a positive role in a Europe "from the Atlantic to the Urals." This phase of French diplomacy, after 1965, coincided with a Soviet interest in encouraging dissidents in the West, and both states could envisage some benefits from dual (but uncoordinated) pressures on the evolution of the German problem. The high point of this collaboration was de Gaulle's tour of the Soviet Union in June 1966, triumphantly heralded by a withdrawal from NATO that established French credentials to carry on an independent dialogue with the Soviet Union on the future of Europe. The progress of détente was, however, severely limited by the Soviet resolve not to risk its own empire in Europe for the sake of new ties to the West. Events in Czechoslovakia in 1968 only reaffirmed this and brutally demonstrated that France's celebration of détente had been somewhat excessive and premature. In any case, French resources and capabilities were insufficient to carry off the ambitious role of interlocutor between the Soviets and the West. Détente depended much more on the United States and West Germany, the two powers who could offer concrete and valuable concessions to the Soviet Union. Thus, while neither the risks nor the accomplishments of French détente policy proved to be very significant, and Paris certainly did not contemplate a "reversal of alliances," de Gaulle was probably instrumental in paving the way for the more productive American and West German efforts toward the East.

The 1965-68 period was in some ways the most audacious in postwar French foreign policy, because the emphasis on an isolated defense system was combined with a remarkably perceptive critique of American policy, and its consequences for Europe and the international system as a whole. But this period was not the zenith of Gaullist foreign policy because isolation or autonomy within Western Europe was not de Gaulle's aim. On the contrary, this situation was only a temporary expedient due to the risks ascribed to NATO and the unavailability of a constructive European alternative acceptable to France. Finally, in 1968, the accommodation to an Atlantic status quo based on France's role as a partial ally did constitute an acknowledgment of failure because Europe remained Atlanticist, détente was elusive, uncertain, and unlikely to transform international politics in the foreseeable future, and the domestic stability and resources required for a virtuoso foreign policy had collapsed in a debilitating domestic crisis that fatally wounded the Gaullist adventure. The opportunities offered by the looser international system that emerged during the 1960s had been tested and exploited to the maximum by de Gaulle, but they proved to be inadequate materials for the more creative and constructive aspirations associated with independence and grandeur.

3 Challenging Atlantic Hegemony

Dilemmas of Atlantic Security

Between 1956 and 1966, French security policy took shape in the context of a growing and finally widespread malaise over changes in the political and strategic contexts of Atlantic defense. The sense of insecurity in both Western Europe and the United States was the result of an unfavorable shift in the strategic balance between the United States and the Soviet Union. It marked a first step in the erosion of American preponderance and led the United States to adopt the controversial flexible response strategy and, furthermore, to emphasize its role as director of a more centralized Western Alliance. West Europeans, on the other hand, had every reason to question American intentions, and they sought to bolster their security in various and often contradictory ways: by enhancing the role of a more independent and European-controlled NATO, by developing national nuclear forces as supplements or perhaps alternatives to the American guarantee, by encouraging European defense cooperation for the same purposes, or, finally, by encouraging NATO-wide sharing of nuclear information and augmenting European influence over the American strategic planning process.

During this period, security politics within the Alliance were complicated by Western Europe's development into an economic community with political and perhaps even military potential that could be wielded in partnership with the United States or in the service of a more independent Europe foreseen by de Gaulle and others. During the Kennedy-Johnson administration, the emergence of a grand American design for U.S.-European relations was based on Europe's subordination in terms of defense. It constituted the first serious American effort to limit the independence of the emerging European entity, an effort later revived with even greater vehemence by Henry Kissinger. Détente was another factor complicating the politics of this earlier period. Soviet-American cooperation sometimes posed the risk of collusion and condominium at the expense of European states, but it also seemed to lessen the risks of the bipolar struggle and reduce the direct military threat to Western Europe, which was, after all, the *raison d'être* of the Atlantic Alliance. The actual implications of unfavorable shifts in the strategic balance were thus unclear and subject to contradictory trends and assessments. Détente was, moreover, only partial and open to setbacks, so that the full globalization of the Soviet-American confrontation often seemed more of a reality than at the height of the Cold War, and the risk of condominium was sometimes outweighed by the threat of American adventurism in Southeast Asia, which could have escalated into a global war and engulfed Washington's allies.

A simple and coherent discussion of Alliance politics in this period is obviously elusive, partly because the strategic and political issues are themselves so complex and subject to divergent interpretations, and partly because the main actors—individuals as well as large governments—often pursued multiple and seemingly contradictory strategies. De Gaulle, for example, at one time sought a reorganized Atlantic Alliance under tripartite direction, simultaneously developed the theme of West European political-military cooperation outside the NATO arena, yet invested in nuclear weapons and strategic doctrines that seemed to emphasize a national defense isolated from both NATO and Western Europe. The United States, on the other hand, sometimes appeared to be willing to assist in the development of national nuclear forces in Europe, sometimes to oppose them in favor of a NATO nuclear capability subject to American controls, and sometimes to promote European nuclear defense cooperation as the embryo of a more equal Atlantic partnership. But Washington finally abandoned any potentially drastic changes in the Atlantic status quo in favor of continued emphasis on NATO as the safest vehicle for managing Western security problems while still preserving American leadership. This Atlanticist outcome, which was the most tolerable one for all allies except France, predominated over the Gaullist options and left the General with a semiautonomous defense as the only recourse after 1965.

Strategic Issues. With roots firmly planted in a European preoccupation over excessive dependence on distant American nuclear weapons and an American-managed Alliance, the Atlantic strategic conflict was nourished by the Suez crisis and blossomed with the launching of Sputnik in 1957. Soviet intercontinental ballistic missiles heralded the end of American territorial invulnerability and forced Washington to revise an all-or-nothing deterrence strategy for defending Western Europe. The massive-retaliation doctrine had always faced criticism and reservations within the American government and military establishment,[1] and by 1957 influential critics such as Kissinger were arguing for a strategy emphasizing limited war, graduated response, and critical thresholds between conventional and nuclear weapons.[2] Albert Wohlstetter exerted perhaps the most significant influence on the evolution of

American strategic doctrine during this period. He argued that bipolar nuclear deterrence was inherently unstable and depended on the United States maintaining large, centrally controlled strategic nuclear forces with an assured second-strike capability and enough flexibility for sophisticated manipulation of threats throughout the escalation cycle. Wohlstetter also emphasized the importance of a major conventional response capability to give decision makers more leeway before resorting to nuclear weapons.[3]

Some of these preoccupations were reflected in policies followed by the Eisenhower administration during 1957 and afterward, but it was not until 1961 that they were assembled into a comprehensive strategic doctrine with relatively clear policy guidelines. This was accomplished in a review group headed by former Secretary of State Acheson, which reached its conclusions in March 1961. The Acheson recommendations stressed: (1) increasing NATO reliance on conventional forces to raise the nuclear threshold; (2) enhancing American operational control over all NATO forces, conventional or nuclear; (3) acquiring more freedom for the global application of American-based strategic nuclear forces; (4) avoiding a European veto or control over the management and triggering of American nuclear forces, except perhaps those deployed in Europe; and (5) increasing American control over the nuclear weapons deployed by European powers, while discouraging the development of truly independent nuclear forces. These recommendations, known as the Green Book, were approved as administration policy in a National Security Council directive issued in April 1961; they subsequently shaped American policy on most Alliance security issues.[4] In the context of this discussion of Alliance politics, three aspects of the elaborate and perhaps overly subtle strategy of "flexible response" stand out as significant: first, the stress on conventional forces as a preferred option for allied regions, so as to decrease the likelihood of triggering a nuclear war that might escalate to involve American territory; second, the emphasis on centralized management and control of Western military power, because all forces were to be part of a complicated manipulation of threat, both global and regional; and, third, the explicit opposition to independent nuclear forces among allies and neutrals.

As a guideline for enhancing American security, the flexible response strategy was essentially a "damage-limiting" one designed to avoid all-out nuclear war and to increase the number and kinds of options available as military responses to different forms of aggression. For the United States, the doctrine posited an increase in strategic nuclear capabilities to make these forces invulnerable enough to survive a first strike and then retaliate. Under the "counterforce" theory, it was often suggested that nuclear weapons would be used against military targets rather than civilian population centers, in the hope that the enemy would behave in the same manner.[5] For both the United States and the Alliance, flexibility required that localized, nonnuclear aggression in Europe should be met by adequate conventional forces, in order to avoid an unnecessary escalation to nuclear weapons. As a result, the United States increased its own conventional capabilities for global action and urged that its allies make this their main contribution to defense in Europe. American officials stressed that the Alliance should not be forced to choose between "suicide or surrender" and that a threat of nuclear retaliation was not a credible deterrent except in response to "a challenge to our most vital interests."[6] Thus, "the use of nuclear weapons must be reserved only for the most desperate circumstances."[7]

European allies, of course, had some difficulty understanding how the Americans might define "vital interests" beyond the clear-cut case of a nuclear attack on the United States itself. They had already been traumatized in 1957, by an American devaluation of strategic nuclear deterrence in favor of a "pause" concept emphasizing conventional forces reinforced with tactical nuclear fire power based in the European theater. By 1961, the Kennedy administration had followed this logic to its conclusion and downgraded even the European-based tactical nuclear weapons, only recently brought in to reassure allies that a conventional Soviet assault would indeed confront some sort of nuclear response. Although actual American strategy was somewhat ambivalent, partly because flexibility meant eschewing commitments to specific forms of military response, it was clear that the crucial distinction had now been drawn between the conventional and tactical nuclear levels, not between the latter and a resort to strategic nuclear arms.

Another aspect of this strategy, one stressed by Defense Secretary Robert McNamara, was an emphasis on the need for a centralized and carefully controlled response to any aggression against American or allied forces. McNamara pointed to this in his important Ann Arbor speech in 1962 when he said that the new strategy "magnifies the importance of unity of planning, concentration of executive authority, and central direction."[8] He and other Defense Department officials made it clear that this centralized control was to lie in the hands of the United States and its president. Deputy Assistant Secretary of Defense Alain C. Enthoven said, in February 1963, that American defense policy was based on the "controlled use of force," adding that one of the objections was to provide "freedom for the President to select and apply the amount and kind of force appropriate to the threat at hand."[9] Although the response was to be carefully regulated, its exact nature was not predetermined for every eventuality, because one point of the policy was to deter the enemy by keeping him unaware of the exact risks involved in any aggression, or at least of the point at which he would trigger a nuclear escalation.

Flexible response was thus essentially based on a manipulation of uncertainty as the foundation of deterrence, but the price of inducing apprehension and caution in an opponent was increased insecurity and concern of allies who had depended on relatively clear-cut commitments and understandings about fulfilling guarantees. The new policy sought maximum discretion for

American decision makers to determine how, when, and where to respond to various kinds of Soviet pressures or attacks, but it also seemed to minimize the discretion, influence, and choices of dependent allies who had always perceived their security in terms of leverage over the United States and the use of American military power. A certain depreciation in the American nuclear guarantee, combined with the insistence on augmenting American direction of allied forces, naturally enhanced European concern about the intentions, and eventual responses in a crisis, on the part of the United States and an American-controlled NATO.

The French were particularly quick to grasp the implications of changes in American strategy, and had even sensed the new policy coming for some time.[10] Some French strategic analysts had long argued that, to Washington, Europe was only a bridgehead for American security and necessarily of secondary importance.[11] They saw the Kennedy-McNamara doctrines essentially as confirmation of trends evident as early as 1959, when Secretary of State Christian Herter made his famous comment that he could not "conceive of any President involving us in an all-out nuclear war" unless the facts clearly showed the United States to be "in danger of all-out devastation."[12] By the early 1960s, others in Europe could share France's malaise because the United States was indeed making a crucial distinction between the kinds of military responses suitable for the European and North American theaters; it appeared to many that the only event envisaged as a trigger for strategic nuclear weapons was an actual attack on American territory. The concurrent devaluation of tactical nuclear weapons was equally disconcerting, especially for West Germany, which, since 1957, had counted on the immediate use of TNWs as part of NATO's forward defense system. Like most continental allies, West Germany was traditionally more concerned with absolute deterrence than with defense, and it looked upon American conventional forces and TNWs in Europe more as trip wires for American strategic weapons than as essential parts of a graduated defense system. Thus, for Europeans, one result of the exaggerated American emphasis on flexible response and graduated deterrence tactics for the European theater was to undermine the perceived value of NATO and the American guarantee, especially because allies did not have direct access to, or influence over, detailed American contingency planning.

European Nuclear Forces.   Ambiguous on many points, the Kennedy administration defense policy seemed clear in its vigorous opposition to independent nuclear forces within the Alliance. McNamara stated that these forces were incompatible with the precepts of the flexible response doctrine because they were vulnerable, could only be used as a first strike and anticity force, and encouraged nuclear proliferation. With a characteristic self-assurance, arrogance, and exaggeration easily matching that of de Gaulle, he branded allied nuclear forces as "dangerous, expensive, prone to obsolescence, and lacking in credibility as a deterrent."[13] Just as the Alliance's defense was indivisible in the face of a common enemy, the secretary of defense artfully claimed, so should its nuclear armament be unified under centralized direction and a single chain of command to control targeting and firings. In other parts of a campaign against allied nuclear forces, administration officials also insisted that such forces were politically undesirable because they accentuated rivalries among allies, decreased confidence in the United States, and would finally undermine Western security and the stability of NATO itself.[14] Based on these assumptions, American policy not only advocated tighter NATO defense integration as part of an enhanced American capability for global crisis management but also sought to bring allied nuclear capabilities under Washington's direction, whether bilaterally through integrated schemes such as the MLF, or indirectly via the NATO mechanism.

One ostensible consequence of the Kennedy policy, then, was to resolve a nagging uncertainty in Washington about how to treat the French and, to a lesser extent, the British nuclear weapons programs. After the war, the United States had foresworn aiding the nuclear development programs of either country, in order to prevent proliferation, to maintain a monopoly on weapons development in the West, and, especially in the case of France, to prevent the leaking of technical secrets to communist agents. This policy was redrafted in favor of Britain as early as 1954; it changed substantially in March 1957, when Eisenhower and Macmillan reached an agreement in Bermuda that led to modifications in the McMahon Act to permit sharing of military nuclear technology under a "substantial progress" clause. Although there was a private understanding that exchanges of nuclear technology and weapons systems would not be shared with third parties,[15] the agreements on direct assistance (signed 2 July 1958) gave Paris grounds to hope that meeting the "substantial progress" requirement for assistance would entitle France to the same benefits. The McMahon Act amendment encouraged this belief, because it mentioned "other friendly countries" as potential recipients. French hopes were not to be realized, however, because the unstated condition of aid to Britain was that its nuclear weapons would never be truly independent of the United States and would conform to American strategy and targeting doctrines. The French program, particularly under de Gaulle, was based on quite different assumptions and could not qualify for assistance.

The issue first arose during the December 1957 Atlantic Council meeting, which was marked by Franco-American tension over the Algerian War. Premier Gaillard and Defense Minister Jacques Chaban-Delmas attempted to strike a deal similar to the one the United States had offered Britain, by indicating that France would house American IRBMs (outside of NATO controls) if she were also granted aid for her nuclear program.[16] No agreement was reached, however, and the proposal was revived by de Gaulle when he met with Secretary of State Dulles in July 1958. De Gaulle was even firmer than his predecessors in requiring French control over any American nuclear weapons to be stationed on French soil, so there was complete disagreement on this problem. The two statesmen also discussed possible American assistance to the French nuclear weapons program, and de Gaulle's reconstruction of this meeting indicates that Dulles made some sort of offer to sell atomic weapons to France.[17] Other sources indicate, however, that Dulles's reply was basically discouraging, and tempered only by a promise to look into the possibility of selling a nuclear submarine reactor along with enriched uranium fuel.[18]

Certain members of the Eisenhower administration did actually favor extending some nuclear aid to France, largely in the hope that it would induce de Gaulle to be more cooperative within NATO. This was a minority view, supported only in the Pentagon and the Paris Embassy, and could not prevail over the opposition of the Joint Committee on Atomic Energy (JCAE) and Admiral Hyman Rickover.[19] De Gaulle's own policies did not advance his case in Washington. The March 1959 withdrawal of the French Mediterranean fleet from NATO coincided with the emergence of the debate in the United States, and this move was cited as clinching the arguments against providing any nuclear submarine data to France.[20] The only assistance offered Paris was a supply of 440 kilograms of enriched uranium fuel for a compact submarine reactor to be developed by the French. The agreement was signed on 7 May 1959, but the American decision represented a significant blow for France compared to the more extensive aid granted Britain.

Under Eisenhower, this policy of denying significant assistance to France was perhaps not irreversible. It did, however, establish the precedent of an American preference for aiding allies it could control and depend on, or of "sharing" nuclear capabilities through NATO mechanisms also dominated by the United States. De Gaulle understood this and quickly clarified the issues in public, confirming that the French nuclear force would be an independent instrument and not subject to direct or indirect American controls. The General's Ecole Militaire speech of September 1959 insisted that, however obtained, a nuclear force had to belong entirely to France and be at her unfettered disposal.[21] The following December, the consequences were spelled out by Minister of Armed Forces Guillaumat when he told the French Senate that the ensemble of military forces, centered on the nuclear force, "must be powerful enough to be feared at the international level, well equipped enough to be a sought after contribution in a coalition, and coherent enough to keep the autonomy that would on occasion permit it to act outside the framework of an alliance."[22]

Such fundamental differences in French and American perspectives and interests also influenced the assistance policy of the Kennedy administration, whose strategic doctrines were in any case opposed to a French force, and even revived some old qualms about helping the British.[23] The French problems arose again in March 1962, in connection with the visit of a French military procurement team headed by General Gaston Lavaud. The team was not seeking complete weapons systems, only components to fill out the French nuclear program;[24] it found the American government divided once again. There were still those who felt that a positive response might make de Gaulle more cooperative and, incidentally, make the French force dependent on American technology.[25] Others advanced the administration's nonproliferation dogma, as well as the more valid and realistic opinion that de Gaulle's cooperation in NATO could not be bought.[26] In the midst of the debate, General Lavaud's requests were turned down when he could not promise that a sale would enhance French cooperation with NATO. By mid-April, Kennedy apparently sided with the status quo group and decided not to help the French.[27] Nevertheless, in the later summer of 1962, due to pressures from Boeing Aircraft and a balance of payments problem, Washington approved the sale to France of a squadron of KC-135 jet tankers, which extended both the range and the credibility of France's Mirage-IV nuclear delivery system. This sale, negotiated at the time McNamara was attacking the *force de frappe* as expensive and prone to obsolescence, indicated considerable confusion within the government. The impression was confirmed by revelations the following October that Deputy Secretary of Defense Roswell Gilpatric had brought up a potential sale of atomic submarines during a September visit to Paris. In the midst of this disorder, the Nassau Agreement arose to further complicate matters.

The Macmillan-Kennedy meeting in the Bahamas (19-22 December 1962) was a confused affair, held in the wake of an American decision to cancel the Skybolt missile program, which Britain had depended on to lengthen the life of its obsolete V-bomber delivery force. In the spirit of on-the-spot improvisation, without adequate preparations or consultations with allies,[28] the Anglo-American "special relationship" was revived in favor of the British. After considering various alternatives, Britain was offered Polaris missiles (to be mounted by British warheads) instead of Skybolt, as well as assistance in building its own fleet of nuclear submarines. This force was to be assigned to a prospective multinational NATO nuclear force and would be used on behalf of the Alliance in all circumstances, unless Britain decided "that supreme national interests [were] at stake."[29] This was what Macmillan had been interested in—maintaining a theoretically independent force—but paragraphs seven and eight of the communiqué added a confusing reference to a multilateral (integrated and nonnational) NATO Polaris force that was being pushed by the American State Department. Almost as an afterthought, and reportedly over British objections,[30] the United States immediately offered the Polaris missiles to France under the same conditions that Britain had accepted, including a national interest clause. The president and his advisors hoped that this might reconcile de Gaulle to nuclear cooperation with NATO. The president followed the public announcement of the offer with a private memorandum to de Gaulle. This was scarcely a formula designed to please the status-conscious General, who had not been consulted or informed beforehand and once again found himself placed on the sidelines of an Anglo-American venture.[31]

De Gaulle was justly wary of this unexpected development, but showed some interest in whether warheads might be included in the missile offer to France. The French nuclear program did not plan to develop missile warheads before 1970, and without them the Polaris missiles themselves would have been useless. De Gaulle had Ambassador Alphand sound President Kennedy out at Palm Beach on 29 December but Kennedy's replies were judged to be purposely evasive.[32] At a meeting with American Ambassador Charles Bohlen on 3 January 1963, the General himself raised the question of warheads and France's desire to acquire nuclear submarines, but Bohlen could not give a definite reply, and de Gaulle apparently concluded that such items would not be part of the American package.[33] The integrated and multilateral force aspects of the Nassau Agreement were stressed to the French during George Ball's visit to Paris on 9 and 10 January, and this doubtless reinforced their distaste for the project.

De Gaulle finally rejected the Nassau offer at his press conference on 14 January 1963. He also vetoed British entry into the EEC, a decision purportedly linked to the Nassau Agreement, and launched a strong attack on the American vision of an Atlantic Community as a subterfuge for hegemony. The Nassau offer was unacceptable, according to the General, because French nuclear technology was not advanced enough to make use of Polaris missiles and because France's policy of military independence prevented her from entering into a multilateral arrangement. Even with a "supreme emergency" clause, he added, the withdrawal of such a force would be impossible in the midst of a crisis or nuclear war, or such an action would paralyze the entire system just when it was most needed.[34] Although Kennedy subsequently initiated a last attempt to barter American nuclear assistance to France in return for cooperation with NATO and de Gaulle's signature on the Test-Ban Treaty, by 1963 Franco-American estrangement over European policy precluded any rapprochement on Alliance and nuclear weapons issues. De Gaulle rejected this overture in July and confirmed his determination to continue building and testing his independent defense force.

In 1964, under President Johnson, the United States reacted to French obstinancy with a particularly strict interpretation of its obligation, under Article I, paragraph 2 of the Test-Ban Treaty, not to assist other states in atmospheric testing. In late 1964, the United States ceased deliveries of enriched uranium fuel for the French atomic submarine program, providing only 171 kilograms of the 440 kilograms promised in the 1959 agreement.[35] Other nuisance measures included an embargo on advanced computers, which might have been used in a nuclear weapons program, and the prevention of overflights by French planes involved in Pacific atmospheric bomb tests.[36]

In retrospect, it is difficult to arrive at a definitive judgment on American policy toward France's nuclear weapons during this period, because the conflict of basic interests was so pervasive that each party can appear justified in its behavior. The United States, on the one hand, was not obliged, even as an ally, to assist in the development of independent national nuclear forces designed to act outside of NATO and perhaps contrary to American interests. The French nuclear force was guided by an unshakable independence that precluded aid on the British model, which was predicated on Britain's loyalty to the Alliance, an active participation in NATO, a willingness to make British soil available for American and NATO defense purposes, and a commitment to use nuclear weapons in conjunction with American strategic plans. It seems that no American largesse could have altered de Gaulle's Alliance policy, induced him to join a multilateral or multinational arrangement linked to the Alliance, or prevented him from finally taking France out of the NATO integrated military structure. Coordination with the French force could have been achieved only outside the NATO framework, along the lines of the tripartite organization proposed by de Gaulle and turned down by the United States.[37]

On the other hand, a more enlightened American policy during this period might have recognized that a virtual American monopoly on independent nuclear capabilities within the West was perhaps not in the United States' long-range interest; thus, it would have been wiser to focus stringent nonproliferation measures against future nuclear states and allies rather than actual ones such as France.[38] As the United States finally recognized by 1974, the French nuclear force was not a destabilizing element in East-West relations, but had indeed contributed to security in Europe and had not itself encouraged other states in Europe or elsewhere to develop nuclear weapons. Perhaps modest, sensible, and imaginative appraisals of French policy were unlikely in the heady and tense Atlantic diplomacy of the 1960s. But at least the United States might have avoided the inconsistent and, as one critic noted in reference to the Nassau fiasco, "unusually maladroit" diplomacy that exacerbated conflicts and certainly confirmed de Gaulle's worst fears about American intentions.[39] Although American refusal to aid the French program probably did not change the course of French Alliance policy, Washington's efforts to tighten controls over NATO and create European or NATO nuclear alternatives to the French example definitely exacerbated Alliance conflicts and encouraged de Gaulle to cut military ties in 1966.

Nuclear Sharing and Atlantic Partnership.   American approaches to resolving
the Alliance's crisis of confidence, and to the risk posed by the proliferation of
independent nuclear forces in Europe, went through several mututations before relatively modest information-sharing measures were adopted after 1965.
During the Eisenhower years, the policy was to move theater nuclear weapons
into Western Europe to increase available firepower and to raise the possibility
of creating some sort of NATO nuclear capability under joint allied control.
In reaction to the alleged "missile gap" between the United States and the
Soviet Union in 1957, the United States decided to station Thor and Jupiter
IRBMs in Europe, where they would be capable of reaching Soviet territory.
Secretary of State Dulles brought this proposal, along with an earlier one to
furnish NATO forces with American-controlled tactical nuclear weapons, to
the North Atlantic Council meeting in December 1957.

Both offers posed insurmountable difficulties for Franco-American relations. The Thor and Jupiter missiles were vulnerable because of the length of
their launch-preparation time and were useful only for a first strike. According
to the American offer, the missiles themselves were to be under the control of
SACEUR for targeting purposes, although the host country would have actual
custody. Nuclear warheads were to remain in American hands and would be
activated by a joint U.S.-host country decision. These restrictions, and fears
that the missiles were inviting targets for a Soviet preemptive strike, made the
offer unappealing to Gaillard's government and to most allies.[40] The
prospect of housing tactical nuclear weapons met with French scepticism for
similar reasons. The host country was to purchase the arms, but was to have
little control over them because the United States and SACEUR retained
both custody and the authority to release warheads from American depots to
NATO troops.[41] Moreover, NATO, not the host country, was to determine the
logistics of stockpiling the warheads and deploying them and their launching
platforms. This, in turn, would have affected Soviet targeting against the host
country and the deployment of national troops within that country. Thus,
indirectly, American and NATO intervention in national defense structures
would have been reinforced.[42] Setting the precedent for de Gaulle, Premier
Gaillard refused these offers unless France was given more direct control over
the weapons as well as aid for her own nuclear program. This was also the
sentiment of the National Assembly, which passed a unanimous resolution in
December 1957 requiring parliamentary approval before stationing "any
military equipment not controlled by the French government."[43] In his meeting
with Dulles the following July, de Gaulle merely confirmed and expanded on
Fourth Republic policy in this respect, insisting on direct control of such
weapons by French authorities rather than by NATO or the United States
and, furthermore, setting a new condition of French participation in Anglo-
American global strategic planning.[44]

The Eisenhower administration continued with the policy of assigning nuclear weapons for Alliance duties and in December 1960 offered to allocate five American nuclear submarines to NATO by 1963. This policy was later confirmed by Kennedy, and, because American control was not in question, it was uncontroversial. The elaborate, somewhat fantastic, and eventually very divisive schemes for multilateral or multinational nuclear force systems also arose during this period, in part to discourage allies such as France from building independent national forces. Until the Multilateral Force (MLF) emerged in 1962, the most prominent idea was the one advocated by General Norstad, then SACEUR, of making NATO itself a nuclear power. He based his suggestions on SHAPE studies made after 1957. They included projects for mixed-manned battalions equipped with TNWs and a NATO land-sea strategic force built around Polaris missiles.[45] These ideas figured in Secretary of Defense Thomas Gates's suggestion in April 1960 that the United States might be willing to sell allies a modified version of the Polaris missile, to be mounted on barges and railroad flatcars and furnished with jointly controlled warheads activated and launched by SACEUR under American presidential authority.[46]

Although de Gaulle was not at all interested in these plans,[47] Norstad's ideas were embraced quite enthusiastically by Chancellor Adenauer, in the hope that they might serve to integrate French nuclear ambitions into a wider European-NATO framework. Adenauer made several attempts to convince the French that some sort of NATO nuclear force would be in their joint interest, going so far as to claim that Washington would consider creating such a force and allowing it to operate without an American veto.[48] Despite French skepticism, West German enthusiasm encouraged the United States to propose that NATO study the possibility of setting up a multilateral IRBM force; this was discussed at the December 1960 North Atlantic Council meeting. The French (and the British) were still dubious, their worries doubtless confirmed by reports that one purpose of the American proposal was to subvert the French independent nuclear force.[49] No firm decisions were made or expected in respect to this early version of the MLF, because the newly elected Kennedy administration needed to take office and study the projects before committing itself.

The idea of making NATO a nuclear power was kept alive in Atlantic politics by Norstad and a somewhat confused American policy, but it was the untimely revival of the multilateral-force concept in 1962 that created destructive tensions within the Alliance and doubtless affected de Gaulle's resolve and the timing of his NATO withdrawal. The MLF project was worked out early that year by State Department figures who were ardent proponents of European integration and Atlantic partnership. At the time, they saw defense collaboration as one way of cementing the European enterprise and binding the United States and Western Europe despite escalating conflicts over trade and economic issues.[50] The idea was approved for interallied discussions by Kennedy and incorporated into the Nassau Agreement in an ambiguous and indiscriminant fashion; it soon received a strong impetus as a State Department anti-de Gaulle campaign, after the General had declared war on their cherished ideals of an Atlantic Community and an integrated Europe in January 1963.[51] The MLF was thus conceived as an example of Atlantic partnership in nuclear defense affairs. Some figures in Washington broadly hinted that it might evolve into a more independent European force, thereby expressing the hope for eventual equality between American and integrated European pillars of the Alliance.[52] The State Department came to view the idea as a vehicle for reviving European unity in spite of the French, as a diversion for a presumed German appetite for nuclear weapons, and as a European alternative that might absorb the theoretically independent British force. The proposal itself went through various forms until it finally emerged in March 1963 as a proposed mixed-manned fleet of twenty-five surface ships, each armed with eight Polaris missiles. These ships were to be assigned to NATO under SACEUR's authority, but a decision to fire the missiles would have required the unanimous consent of all participating states.[53]

The complicated story of the MLF's blossoming and sudden demise is unimportant in this context. What is significant is that the French and other Europeans soon perceived it to be part of an irrational and excessive American campaign against France. Because the United States and West Germany turned out to be the only states seriously interested in the scheme, Paris soon decided that Washington was reacting to the Franco-German Treaty by offering Germany the dangerous lure of access to nuclear weapons—a prospect never contemplated by the French in their courtship of the Federal Republic. Couve de Murville explained French concerns directly to President Kennedy on 23 May 1963, pointing out the grave risks of the MLF giving West Germany the desire and the means to become a nuclear power. Kennedy replied that France had set the example for Germany, but de Gaulle's foreign minister demurred and maintained that at least his government had no intention of satisfying such a craving.[54] As the MLF controversy approached a climax at the end of 1964, French spokesmen attacked it from every angle. On 5 November 1964, Premier Georges Pompidou told a group of journalists that the project was incompatible with the Franco-German Treaty, contrary to the French conception of Europe, "and finally more or less directed against France."[55] It was also suggested in the French press that the setting up of the MLF would lead to a grave crisis in the Atlantic Alliance that might end with a French withdrawal from NATO. The Gaullist *La Nation* reported that an MLF would so minimize NATO's conventional forces that France would have no reason to keep her army in NATO and, furthermore, would symbolize such a complete lack of agreement on NATO defense posture that the presence of allied bases in France would be jeopardized.[56]

European leaders sensed a grave crisis pending if the mixed-manned force were to go beyond the discussion stage; and growing West German reservations about risking such a conflict with Paris finally helped convince President Johnson to table the idea in December 1964. Johnson apparently went out of his way to stress that French sensitivities were a factor in this decision.[57] The MLF project was not completely interred, however, until the Johnson-Erhard meeting a year later. It remained alive enough in Atlantic politics to reinforce de Gaulle's resolve to halt the progress of European integration in 1965 and to begin planning the NATO withdrawal early in the same year. European, and particularly West German, interest in the MLF had convinced the General that Atlanticist formulas for defense cooperation were more compelling than his own design, a situation that left him with no practical option other than partial disengagement.

During the same crucial year of 1965, the United States and other allies began developing a more constructive and ultimately successful information-sharing approach to calm Europe's nuclear anxieties. One problem with earlier American policies had been an inability to perceive that much European insecurity was due to the U.S. penchant for developing defense policies and strategies in isolation rather than as a result of a process of consultation with allies.[58] The flexible response doctrine emerged in this way and was representative of "the reluctance of the Americans to accept the others' genuine participation in the making of NATO strategy and the reluctance of the Europeans to accept a strategy in whose formulation they have played no significant part."[59] In this case, there had been no prior consultation or meaningful effort to build support for an extremely complex set of ideas that virtually revolutionized Western defense. Although American officials were aware that allied confidence required multilateral participation in the American strategic-planning process,[60] in practice they focused on ill-considered devices such as the MLF, which were militarily superfluous and politically ineffective because they did not confront the key issue of reassuring allies about how the American strategic force would be used on behalf of Europe. The MLF, with its multiple-veto system, was thus an expensive and divisive American concession that confused symbolic control of hardware with significant allied participation in the making of American strategy decisions. After the MLF had been placed on the sidelines, NATO did move in this direction, and decided to confront the problem of reforming nuclear consultation mechanisms.

On 31 May 1965, Defense Secretary McNamara proposed the formation of a special NATO committee to improve consultation on issues related to nuclear weapons. Ten members decided to join the "McNamara Committee," which first met on 27 November 1965, and later set up three working groups concerned with communications, data exchange, and nuclear planning itself. The working groups began their operations in February 1966, and, after France's withdrawal from NATO defense activities, they received official

NATO status in December 1966. The most important new forums were the restricted-membership Nuclear Planning Group (NPG) and the plenary Nuclear Defense Affairs Committee (NDAC). They proved to be moderately successful devices for educating Europeans about the complexities of nuclear weapons and the strategic options governing their use, especially for TNWs based in Europe. These groups were not designed to secure rigid guarantees about how American power would be used in a crisis involving Europe, but the process of multilateral planning and consultations seems to have conditioned and shaped American responses in a direction more favorable to European interests.[61]

France had no interest in a project designed to restore confidence in American leadership in NATO, and opposed it until the 1966 withdrawal prevented any further obstruction. The McNamara proposal of May 1965 was billed as an Atlantic alternative to French policy, and the favorable response of most allies confirmed the failure of France's own European defense initiatives during this period. This development probably influenced the timing of French preparations for the NATO withdrawal. The Elysée staff was then requesting preliminary studies from government ministries concerning the nature and effects of a withdrawal, and favorable prospects for the new American idea were taken as a final indication that France would have to strike off on her own course, since other allies were incapable of shedding American hegemony in the near future. None of the American approaches to issues of mutual confidence-building proved satisfactory to de Gaulle, who had promoted different options for reorganizing the Alliance during these years. This was because American ideas had been based either on an artificial egalitarianism with the Alliance that preserved the domination of the United States or on integrated defense formulas bound to repel de Gaulle. Instead, the General proposed his own ideas for oligarchical leadership and European defense cooperation, but he found that the appeal of Atlanticism left France isolated and largely impotent.

Memorandum Diplomacy and Tripartite Stalemate

Background to the 1958 Memorandum. In the face of the American policies described above, de Gaulle's Atlantic diplomacy was characterized by two complementary strategies, which were conceived as alternatives to the Atlanticist formulas that finally prevailed. In sporadic pursuit of the aims outlined in the September 1958 memorandum to Eisenhower and Macmillan, de Gaulle sought to realize the French oligarchical vision of tripartite Western cooperation, while on the continental European level he tried to lay the foundation for political-military cooperation under French leadership. The latter could have bolstered France's tripartite and global roles in line with the memorandum initiatives, or it could have fostered a Europe more independent of Atlantic ties.

After the May crisis, and his investiture as the Fourth Republic's last premier on 1 June 1958, General de Gaulle's natural preoccupation with the situation in Algeria did not prevent him from devoting attention to the collateral problem of France's Atlantic ties. De Gaulle raised the major issues with Anglo-American leaders in meetings held early in the summer. At the end of June, he saw Macmillan and Foreign Minister Selwyn Lloyd in Paris and issued his familiar complaint about NATO and the integrated military-command system. He also reiterated the French case for global policy consultation between the three most important Western powers, specifically suggesting that the tripartite Standing Group in Washington ought to be given more authority.[62] The more important meeting was with Dulles on 5 July when, as Couve de Murville later described the situation, the immobilism of American hegemony faced its most determined opponent in the West.[63] De Gaulle again made a case for tripartite "cooperation on the level of global policy,"[64] insisting that there was "nothing more important for the French people than to be made to believe again that France [was] a great power."[65] Forewarned by the British of de Gaulle's pretensions, Dulles replied that France's great power status could best be revived by domestic reforms. He also alluded to the problems and resentments any tripartite group would cause within NATO and among nonaligned countries.[66] The meeting was also marked by the disagreements on nuclear weapons issues already described, thereby establishing the wide gap between French and American perspectives at the outset of de Gaulle's tenure.

The summer of 1958 was also notable for two international crises that apparently furnished the main impetus for the September memorandum, by linking together issues of global policy consultation and strategic interdependence. One was the Anglo-American military intervention in Lebanon and Jordan in July. De Gaulle interpreted this as a typical bilateral action undertaken without consulting France, which had historic ties to Lebanon and was partly responsible for the status quo in the Levant under the Tripartite Declaration of 1950. Although the French had been informed of Anglo-American intentions to take some action in the region, they apparently expected further consultations to allow France to become a partner in the intervention itself.[67] Instead, with only a few hours advance notice, the best Paris could muster was to send the cruiser *Brest* to take care of French residents in Beirut.[68] In addition to the blow to French prestige, Moscow's reaction to the intervention doubtless impressed upon de Gaulle that uncoordinated Anglo-American actions outside Europe could pose a direct risk to France. Along with Eisenhower, Macmillan, and Nehru, the General was subjected to a typically passionate communiqué from Khrushchev, contending that Western intervention in the Middle East had put the world "on the brink of military catastrophe," when "the slightest imprudent move could have irreparable consequences."[69]

A similar problem arose a few weeks later, on 22 August, with the initiation of a Communist Chinese bombardment of the coastal islands of Quemoy and Matsu. This seemed the possible prelude to a full-scale invasion of Formosa that certainly would have engaged American military forces. Secretary of State Dulles mentioned the possibility of American military action on 4 September, and a bellicose Kremlin declared on 8 September that any attack on the People's Republic of China would be considered an attack on the Soviet Union itself—a circumstance that would necessarily have involved NATO and triggered a military confrontation in Europe. The dangers of escalating military action seemed even greater when, later in September, it was learned that the United States had placed atomic weapons on Quemoy and had augmented existing stockpiles on Formosa. Thus, the summer passed with two major crises outside Europe that involved the United States, and a risk, however minimal, of a military escalation affecting France. In neither case, de Gaulle felt, had France been effectively consulted in advance about American actions. This deplorable situation served as an appropriate occasion to consolidate French grievances and proposals in a memorandum to his principal Atlantic allies.

The memorandum, dated 17 September 1958, consisted of two apparently identical documents delivered on 25 September to President Eisenhower and Prime Minister Macmillan, each accompanied by a personal note from de Gaulle.[70] The first draft was evidently prepared by Jean-Marc Boegner, a *Conseiller diplomatique* attached to the presidential office; de Gaulle put it into final form.[71] Neither the diplomatic services of the Quai d'Orsay nor the Council of Ministers were directly informed of the contents of the memorandum, although de Gaulle did mention its existence to his ministers shortly after it had been delivered.[72] The memorandum opened with a reference to the crises in the Middle East and the Formosa Straits, contending that they demonstrated that the "existing organization of the Western alliance no longer [met] the conditions necessary for security, as far as the whole of the free world [was] concerned." De Gaulle went on to suggest that France, Britain, and the United States should form a tripartite organization, "at the global political and strategic level," charged with two specific tasks:[73] the coordination of global security policies and the formulation and application of plans for the use of nuclear weapons. Along with these two issues, a reorganization of NATO was implied, but the connection between the tripartite organization and the Alliance itself was not specified in the memorandum. These proposals became the subject of recurrent diplomatic exchanges between the three governments directly concerned, also spilling over into French domestic politics and interallied conflicts in NATO. The French memorandum initiatives lapsed completely by 1962, when de Gaulle apparently concluded that there was no point in pursuing this chimera any longer.

Global Policy Coordination. The possibility of coordinating the general foreign policies of the three powers in regions outside of the Atlantic Treaty area, long a concern of the French government, became the focus of most tripartite diplomatic exchanges and meetings after September 1958. On a limited scale, this proved to be the only positive American response to the Gaullist initiative. It was, however, insufficient for de Gaulle, who consistently and unsuccessfully sought to expand the discussions to include global security and strategic issues, particularly in respect to nuclear weapons, and to create a more permanent and visible tripartite forum as the locus of discussion and eventual policy coordination. Although Britain might have gone along, it seems that the United States was quite unwilling to move seriously in de Gaulle's direction, so he finally renounced these efforts. It is likely that the General actively pursued this tripartite goal as long as he did mainly because it was useful for domestic purposes and, for a time, lent French diplomacy some weight and additional prestige, which was helpful in Europe and in the settlement of the Algerian War.

The memorandum itself focused on this issue as a failing of NATO, which was limited to the Atlantic treaty area, "as if what happens, for example, in the Middle East or in Africa did not immediately and directly affect Europe, and as if the indivisible responsibilities of France did not extend to Africa, the Indian Ocean and the Pacific, for the same reason as those of Great Britain and the United States." To remedy this situation, de Gaulle suggested that a new tripartite organization be set up that would, along with managing nuclear weapons, "take common decisions on political questions touching on global security." The memorandum also foresaw the creation of different regional theaters of operation subordinated to the tripartite organization, specifically mentioning the Arctic, Atlantic, Pacific, and Indian oceans.

President Eisenhower's response, dated 20 October 1958, focused on the problems associated with global policy harmonization and virtually ignored the memorandum's references to joint nuclear and military-strategic planning.[74] The president agreed with de Gaulle on the global nature of the menace to the West, asserting "that our policies should be adapted to deal with the worldwide nature of the threat." But he stressed that the need was already largely fulfilled by NATO, SEATO (of which Franch was a member), and America's other alliances. Although Eisenhower was willing to consider tripartite discussions, he took a dimmer view of setting up a formal organization or of linking it to expanded geographical responsibilities for NATO. Establishing the policy that was to predominate amidst twists and turns in American relations with France, Eisenhower wrote:

> We cannot afford to adopt any system which would give to our other allies, or other free world countries, the impression that basic decisions affecting their own vital interests are being made without their participation. As regards NATO itself, I must in all frankness say that I see very serious problems, both within and

outside NATO, in any effort to amend the North Atlantic Treaty so as to extend its coverage beyond the areas presently covered.

He did, however, conclude with the observation that "a community association" had to evolve according to circumstances, and he was prepared "to explore this aspect of the matter in appropriate ways."

De Gaulle considered the reply evasive,[75] but Eisenhower was nevertheless willing to go ahead with three-power consultations, as long as they did not acquire an organic character and were limited to political, not military, issues. Instead of working through the Standing Group, as de Gaulle had suggested, Eisenhower instructed Dulles to set up a tripartite ambassadorial committee in Washington. During November, arrangements were made for this committee to initiate meetings attended by the French and British ambassadors and Under-Secretary of State Robert Murphy.[76] The first sessions were held in December, but did not go well because Ambassador Alphand made it clear that France was less interested in political discussions than in associating France with American military-strategic planning on a global level. According to Robert Kleiman's account, Alphand proposed that the three sides transfer discussion of global, strategic war planning to a combined chiefs of staff, and was turned down.[77] Secretary Dulles then saw de Gaulle in Paris on 15 December, during a NATO ministerial session, and, reportedly as a diversion from military issues, suggested that the tripartite group take up African policy.[78] De Gaulle agreed, and in an attempt to upgrade the meetings sent M. Daridan, director-general of political affairs at the Quai, to spend February in Washington for talks on the Far East, while long-time Gaullist Louis Joxe made the trip in April for discussions on Africa. The exchanges, particularly those in April, continued to be marked by strongly divergent views about the ultimate purpose of the meetings. The United States had agreed to them only on the understanding that there would be no pressure for agreement on joint actions, or for preparation of binding strategic plans. Instead, Alphand continued to press for joint contingency planning and was again rebuffed.[79] During this impasse, Eisenhower evidently decided that concessions were in order and offered to extend the scope of the talks to cover some military-strategic questions. It is unclear from available evidence, however, whether this suggestion was meant to cover global strategy or only military problems in Africa.[80]

In any event, de Gaulle had not been satisfied with the progress of the negotiations. While the talks were still going on, on 11 March 1959, he announced that the French Mediterranean fleet was being withdrawn from assignment to NATO and put under a separate and new French command covering the Mediterranean and North Africa. In a private letter to Eisenhower, dated 25 May 1959, de Gaulle explained his action as a response to threats to French security not covered by the Western Alliance.[81] He also linked the new command to the memorandum's proposal for dividing the world into strategic theaters, indicating that this French security zone, and another one for sub-Saharan Africa, might be subject to cooperative arrangements with Washington and London, or with NATO, just as France was prepared to cooperate in the Indian and Pacific Ocean areas. With these suggestions, which were combined with an insistence on coordinating nuclear weapons strategy and triggering, de Gaulle clarified his intentions regarding global political-military cooperation. Faithful to his pre-1958 ideas, the General wanted to divide the sensitive regions of the world into strategic theaters, where each of the three powers was to have autonomous authority and responsibility while it coordinated actions with its partners. France could thus determine Western policy in the western Mediterranean and in French Africa, with full backing from London and Washington, and further enhance her own prestige by association with Anglo-American actions elsewhere.

De Gaulle concluded this important letter by inviting Eisenhower to visit France, and discussions on these subjects abated until their meeting in Paris in September 1959. At that time, de Gaulle pressed his case for a tripartite organization and for joint strategic planning and administration of nuclear weapons; he also indulged in extensive criticism of NATO's integrated military system, expressing his conviction that such integration damaged patriotism and the sense of national responsibility for defense. From Eisenhower's report of this conversation to Macmillan, it is doubtful that there was much mutual understanding.[82] Shortly thereafter, however, Eisenhower appears to have decided to try and break out of this impasse. At a Western summit meeting in the Rambouillet chateau, on 20 December 1959, he abruptly agreed to institutionalize the tripartite talks on a higher level, as long as they were "clandestine" and completely disassociated from NATO. The three leaders decided that machinery for regular discussions should be set up in London, with high-level representatives from each power.[83] The American decision appears to have been made on the spur of the moment, without benefit of staff advice, and Macmillan quickly agreed so that there would be no chance to reconsider. The prime minister's enthusiasm was prompted by an expectation that France would help Britain obtain EEC trade concessions in exchange for assistance in winning over the Americans to de Gaulle's scheme.[84]

De Gaulle, however, did not fulfill his agreement to follow through with concrete suggestions for setting up the group in London, perhaps because he was waiting for the first explosion of a French atomic device (on 13 February 1960) to bolster his bargaining position. All governments were also distracted by preparations for the Big Four summit on Berlin, held in Paris in May 1960. This disastrous summit may have revived a momentum to push ahead with tripartite consultations, which Macmillan proposed on 25 May with identical letters to his two colleagues. He suggested that they carry out the Rambouillet agreement and set up scheduled meetings of their foreign ministers, as well as the three heads of government. In Macmillan's plan, each foreign minister was to designate a special officer responsible for coordinating, preparing, and following through on the meetings, although this was not to be regarded as "constituting a formal secretariat."[85] Eisenhower's response was positive, and he agreed to appoint Livingston Merchant, then under-secretary of state for political affairs, as the American official charged with these responsibilities, but he was careful to insist that no official apparatus should be created that might lead the NATO allies or African neutrals to believe that an "inner directorate" had been formed. In order to allay suspicion, Eisenhower wanted to keep other NATO members generally informed of the talks.[86]

De Gaulle predictably found these restrictions unappealing, and his distaste was reinforced by Macmillan's indication that the three-power discussions would again have to focus on political, not military, issues. In a public speech, the General replied that strategic coordination was the real issue, warning about the mortality of an alliance "*presently* necessary to the security of France and of other free peoples on our ancient continent," who should be organized into an independent European structure in defense and other affairs.[87] In letters to Eisenhower and Macmillan, dated 10 June, de Gaulle passed over offers of global political consultation and returned to the theme of military-strategic talks. To Macmillan, he said that the consultations ought to be extended to defense issues in meetings between ministers of defense or chiefs of staff. Instead of coordination by Foreign Ministry officials, he suggested that the Standing Group in Washington should perform this function.[88] To Eisenhower, de Gaulle noted that the real issue was "global strategic cooperation" and reminded his wartime colleague that France wanted nothing less than "an equal voice in the joint decisions on the use of nuclear weapons."[89] For this purpose, he proposed a high-level planning group similar to the one described in the note to Macmillan.

Eisenhower's reply of 2 August struck a conciliatory tone, but did not give de Gaulle what he wanted. Eisenhower reminded the General that the United States had been willing to include military-strategic issues in the April 1959 meetings on Africa, but the French side had never followed through and taken up the offer.[90] Eisenhower was once again disposed to renew the effort, apparently on a global basis and not just restricted to Africa, but on the condition that Washington be represented by "an appropriate general officer who ha[d] no connection with the standing group itself." France could use her own representative to the Standing Group if she so desired. But, for European military problems, Eisenhower was careful to insist that NATO was the proper forum for discussion, and tripartite talks could not be allowed to infringe on its perogative.[91]

The renewed Anglo-American willingness to engage in three-power military-strategic negotiations represented a major concession and was the closest Washington ever came to accepting de Gaulle's own view of these talks. It was, however, unacceptable to the French president, who, by mid-

1960, was interested only in concessions on nuclear strategy and administration of nuclear weapons and saw that consistent American unwillingness even to discuss these matters meant that tripartite conversations would deal with peripheral issues. Instead of trying to work within the framework of Eisenhower's proposal then, de Gaulle virtually precluded further negotiation, by replying that the tripartite organization had to be set up in conjunction with a general reorganization of the entire Alliance itself, and only a summit conference could reconcile the positions of the three powers. He wanted the conference held in Bermuda in September 1960.[92] Macmillan was willing, but Eisenhower, who was then in the midst of a presidential election, saw no useful purpose in taking up a reorganization of NATO until Paris had put forward more specific proposals. This was the Eisenhower administration's last attempt to cope with de Gaulle, and diplomatic maneuvers evidently ceased, pending Kennedy's oath of office.

The conclusion of Eisenhower's term of office signaled the end of an always dim hope that France and the United States could reconcile their differences over the Atlantic Alliance, global consultations, and nuclear weapons issues. Eisenhower had set limits to what Washington was prepared to concede on tripartite political and strategic planning, but de Gaulle's view of diplomacy prevented him from accepting such concessions, and manipulating them in the hope of achieving his grander aims. Until their memorandum diplomacy virtually ceased in January 1962, Kennedy and de Gaulle did continue negotiations, but the views of the two leaders were too far apart for any viable solutions to emerge. Kennedy's Grand Design and de Gaulle's European Europe were irreconcilable visions of a future order. Nor, on the issues of nuclear weapons and defense, could the French goal—an independent force and joint administration of the Western strategic armory—be adjusted to harmonize with the emerging American policy of centralizing Washington's control over all nuclear weapons in the West.

Such basic differences in perspective were exacerbated by Franco-American conflicts over the Congo and, more importantly, over the Berlin crisis in 1961, which found France and West Germany aligned in fear of irresponsible American concessions to Soviet pressures. Thus, an atmosphere of distrust surrounded the Kennedy-deGaulle meeting in Paris, from 31 May to 2 June 1961, although Kennedy did indicate that he was willing to carry out Eisenhower's policy of tripartite planning on a limited range of military issues. The president had Paul Nitze prepare a proposal for a military contingency-planning group to discuss Laos, the Congo, and Berlin. The inclusion of Berlin was an innovation, because all previous American plans for tripartite discussion on this level had excluded European issues. De Gaulle reportedly made a favorable response and promised to take steps to implement the proposal.[93] There was, however, no further action taken by either party, probably because of conflicts over Berlin after the construction of the wall. De Gaulle reverted to his grander vision of tripartite collaboration in a letter, sent to Kennedy in August 1961, that dealt with Berlin. Kennedy did not reply directly until 31 December 1961, and apparently did not even deal with the issues raised by the French leader. Discussion of de Gaulle's memorandum proposal virtually ceased with a final letter from the General, dated 9 January 1962, which simply restated the necessity of instituting a permanent three-power organization, with a combined military staff to prepare "common decisions and common actions."[94] Kennedy did not respond to this by then tiresome French theme, and the Franco-American stalemate was complete.

By 1962, no actual misunderstanding clouded relations between these allies, because de Gaulle understood American resistance too well, and Washington, if confused about its priorities in Atlantic security policy, had nevertheless defined limits for concession in dealing with extravagant French demands. Earlier, however, de Gaulle's interest in global and strategic cooperation had often been assessed primarily in terms of the French involvement in Algeria; so there was a persistent assumption, in and out of France, that Gaullist policy was really pursuing the recent and narrower Fourth Republic aim of obtaining allied support in North Africa, rather than the longer-standing French interest in a tripartite oligarchy to manage the Alliance, and general Western policies around the globe.

The "Algerian interpretation" of the memorandum was widespread within France, and de Gaulle let it flourish because it strengthened his hand as he moved away from a rigid *Algérie française* position. Premier Michel Debré, a fervent supporter of a French Algeria, was de Gaulle's spokesman for this interpretation, and in numerous speeches and meetings with allied diplomats he insisted that "unconditional" allied support for French policy in North Africa was part of the memorandum package of prerequisites for further cooperation with the Alliance.[95] Debré's stand received support from within the government and from non-Gaullist political leaders. As Chief of Staff, General Ely had long associated himself with French Eurafrican geostrategic views, so he and other military figures viewed de Gaulle's efforts with favor, as an attempt to secure Anglo-American backing in North Africa.[96] Ely, and much of the French military establishment, favored extending NATO military cooperation to cover Algeria and the French Community, and for a time misinterpreted de Gaulle's demands as identical with their own perspectives. Thus they approved of special three-power consultations on global problems, but did not share de Gaulle's absolute priority of a formal directorate covering political as well as strategic-nuclear issues. Political elites also misunderstood the full scope and significance of de Gaulle's initiatives, arguing that he sought French participation in global defense planning essentially to obtain a coordinated Western response to Soviet-inspired subversion in Algeria and the French Community.[97] Such assumptions, widespread until de Gaulle gradually emerged with a more flexible position on Algeria after the fall of 1959, led many to underestimate the extent of France's revisionist claims against the United States and the Alliance.

It is unclear how important the Algerian issue was within the overall framework of the General's early memorandum diplomacy, partly because the Gaullist "art of the deliberately ambiguous statement" makes it difficult to trace the evolution of his Algerian policy.[98] He did, however, come to believe that Algeria was really a peripheral issue for France, which had been a great power before conquering the region and could become one again without it.[99] By late 1959, de Gaulle apparently began to see the advantages of moving closer to a liberal stand on North Africa and, in his September meeting with Eisenhower, the French leader offered a preview of his speech of 16 September, which opened the way to negotiations and even to a right of self-determination for the Algerians. This confirmed what allied officials had already been told by the Quai d'Orsay and Couve de Murville himself, namely, that the Algerian matter was not the heart of French Atlantic and memorandum diplomacy, despite Debré's assertions to the contrary.[100] De Gaulle's slow evolution toward a reasonable solution in North Africa probably elicited an unusual American toleration for his other, less reasonable demands, in order to avoid undermining an enlightened French decolonialization policy.

Although de Gaulle abandoned the extremist French position on Algeria, he nevertheless shared the prevailing image of France as a power with special interests in Africa and the Mediterranean basin, and this was one basis of his request for tripartite consultations on problems in these areas. The French Community was born on 26 September 1958, at the same time the memorandum initiative was launched. De Gaulle's correspondence with the Anglo-Americans confirms that he expected the proposed tripartite organization to help perpetuate a shaky French preeminence in the region because, as he told Dulles in December 1958, any Western policy in Africa would naturally be determined by France. While slowly abandoning the overt colonialism of the Fourth Republic, then, de Gaulle nevertheless continued to seek status through France's overseas "mission" and overt backing by the Anglo-Saxons.

Nuclear Weapons and Strategy. The most striking innovation of de Gaulle's memorandum diplomacy was to link more traditional French security concerns with the new strategic issues festering within the Atlantic Alliance since the Suez crisis and Sputnik. De Gaulle went beyond the narrow colonial or continental perspectives of the Fourth Republic and perceived clearly that coordination of Western policies would be both unproductive and an insufficient guarantee unless it were extended to include the manipulation of nuclear deterrence on a global scale. Long before the Kennedy administration arrived at a similar view—with antithetical policy conclusions—de Gaulle had realized that European security and the American nuclear guarantee would increasingly depend on a truly global confrontation of superpowers that would reduce Europe's status in the bipolar struggle, making it a subordinate theater rather than a primary stake. Thus, the risk that the guarantee would be withheld or ineffectively implemented was enhanced, and supplemented, by the new threat that irresponsible American actions outside Europe would escalate and involve the NATO area. De Gaulle concluded that self-interest required the Europeans to control any nuclear weapons placed on their soil by the Americans and to acquire a significant voice in how U.S. military force elsewhere was used.

The September memorandum raised this point in connection with the proposed tripartite administration of strategic planning on a global scale, indicating that the three-power organization should "establish and, should the occasion arise, apply [administer] the plans for strategic action, notably concerning the use of nuclear arms." As justification for this proposal, de Gaulle cited the new weapons technology, which invalidated the limited scope of an organization such as NATO:

> On the other hand, the range of ships and planes and that of weapons make such a restricted system militarily obsolete. It is true that it had at first been granted that nuclear weapons, obviously essential, would remain for a long time a monopoly of the United States, which could seem to justify that, at the global level, defense-related decisions were in practice left to the government in Washington. But, on this point too, one must recognize that such a situation is no longer really valid.

The memorandum was still vague on details, however, and the scope of French demands on this issue was only gradually clarified in public and in private. By October 1958, Couve de Murville was said to be confirming to allies that de Gaulle wanted a tripartite planning organization that would give France and Britain an actual veto over U.S. nuclear forces, except when used for self-defense.[101] The issue was also discussed by de Gaulle and Dulles the following September, but contradictory rumors continued to circulate.

De Gaulle's letter to Eisenhower in May 1959 could have left no doubt in Washington about French requirements. Expressing resentment that the United States refused to share nuclear secrets with France, the General said he could accept this, with regrets, but he could not accept Washington's exclusive control of the West's nuclear arsenal. He pointed out that

> we are tied together to such a point that the opening of this type of hostility [atomic war] either by you or against you would automatically expose France to total and immediate destruction. She obviously cannot entrust her life or her death to any other state whatsoever, even the most friendly. For this reason, France feels it is essential that she participate, if the case were to arise, in any decision which might be taken by her allies to use atomic missiles or to launch them against certain places at certain times.

Meeting with Eisenhower the following October, de Gaulle again pointed out that the issue of direct French participation in American and British strategic planning and administration was the heart of his memorandum proposals.[102] He may also have been more specific and, alluding to the Suez, Lebanon, and Formosa crises, suggested that the three powers draw up a mutually binding list of casus belli.[103]

Faced with continued American intransigence, and an obvious unwillingness to confront this aspect of his memorandum proposals, by 1960 de Gaulle may have hoped that France's formal accession to the nuclear club could force the Anglo-Saxons to take him and France more seriously. This had been an important rationale for the French nuclear program all along, and by late 1958 French officials were explicitly tying the prospect of a nuclear force to the memorandum's tripartite design. In an unpublished address to the *Institut des hautes études de défense nationale* in November 1958, a high official of the Quai d'Orsay, François de Rose, justified France's nuclear armament as "likely to be immediately exploitable for France on the political level," even before it was militarily efficient, in that "it [would] perhaps facilitate our accession to this role of *codirecteur de l'alliance* which is necessary for the protection of our interests."[104] On 13 February 1960, the first French atomic device was exploded at the Reggane testing center in the Sahara, an event that French leaders used to justify their demands vis-à-vis the Anglo-Saxons. Thus, Premier Debré told the National Assembly in October 1960 that France's independent efforts to develop an atomic force were bound to bring her more influence within the Alliance.[105]

That same month, in a speech at Grenoble, de Gaulle made his most explicit public explanation of the kind of control that his government sought over American nuclear weapons. "France considers that if, unfortunately, atomic bombs were launched in the world, none would be launched from the free world without her having accepted it, and that no atomic bomb be launched from her soil unless she herself makes the decision."[106] Later, on 11 April 1961, de Gaulle added that France and Europe also expected to have a positive role in determining if, how, and when American weapons were to be employed in Europe's defense. "For the European states of the continent, which are by far the most exposed, must know exactly with which weapons and under which conditions their overseas allies would join them in battle."[107] In other words, de Gaulle first wanted a veto over the use of American strategic arms except for national self-defense, to prevent the United States from initiating a nuclear war outside Europe that might spread and eventually involve NATO and France. He also wanted France, acting on behalf of continental Europe, to be in a position to ensure that American nuclear weapons would be used when necessary to defend French and European interests. This control was to be reinforced by an independent French nuclear force, coordinated with the Anglo-American weapons through the tripartite organization, and by French authority over any American nuclear weapons that might be stationed in France. If the tripartite organization had been created along Gaullist lines, it presumably would have established joint crisis-management procedures and contingency plans, to satisfy de Gaulle's requirements and to allow France to act on behalf of Europe. Coordination of global policies on nonstrategic issues would have helped to harmonize general policies and prevent conflicts among the Western oligarchy and subordinant members of the Atlantic system.

Given the scope and audacity of these proposals, it is not surprising that de Gaulle was unable to bring his memorandum scheme to fruition. His unwillingness to accept small concessions from the Americans, his insistence on a functioning and visible tripartite committee to manage the free world's security interests, and his determination to dismantle NATO military integration in due course could scarcely be reconciled with the interests of the United States and key allies. De Gaulle's preoccupation with the credibility of the American nuclear guarantee to Europe was widely shared among NATO members, but his oligarchical solution was unacceptable to continental allies. The United States was unwilling even to consider granting any other state shared control over American strategic planning or the strategic nuclear forces themselves. The record of Franco-American discussions on this question indicates a complete inability to grapple with the issue. De Gaulle raised it with Kennedy for a last time in June 1961, but their conversation produced no concrete results and only confirmed that the memorandum goals were inaccessible.[108]

NATO and the Alliance. The relationship between the proposed tripartite organization and the European region covered by NATO and the Atlantic Alliance has always been a matter of controversy, partly because of deliberate French efforts to obscure the connection. The French position was that the proposals of 1958-61 were only for global political-military cooperation on a tripartite level; this cooperation involved non-European regions excluded from NATO, and nuclear weapons strategy and administration, also outside the scope of NATO because the United States and Britain had maintained exclusive possession and control. In this context, then, France had not raised issues directly affecting NATO or the Alliance. As Couve de Murville said of the memorandum in April 1966, "that was something which went beyond the Atlantic Alliance, because it involved only the three powers with world-wide and nuclear responsibilities."[109] On the other hand, de Gaulle and his subordinants made no secret of French objections to the NATO military organization during this period, and the memorandum demands were broadly tied to an eventual reorganization of NATO itself. De Gaulle said on 11 April 1961, for example, "What I question, therefore, is not the Atlantic Alliance, but the present organization of the Atlantic Alliance."[110] Such statements were only half true, however, because French diplomacy actually sought to do both, that is, dismantle NATO (the military organization) and revise the Atlantic Treaty itself.

A review of French proposals during this period supports such a conclusion. As far as the original Atlantic Treaty is concerned, de Gaulle sought an extension of the North Atlantic Treaty for the three leading powers of the Alliance—in some instances, to cover much of the non-Communist world. Linking the initiative to the treaty, the memorandum specifically notes that France envisaged invoking the revision procedures of Article XII, to secure both this geographical extension and the establishment of the tripartite organization. Furthermore, de Gaulle's insistence on an absolute and irrevocable American commitment to defend Europe with nuclear weapons, and an appropriate institution to administer the commitment, would have completely altered the mutual defense guarantee in Article V, which left it up to each member to determine its own reaction to an attack on an ally. Finally, the French design certainly implied significant changes in the Alliance's political and military structure. De Gaulle appears to have foreseen a new defense organization with regional military theaters, starting with a French-managed Mediterranean and African zone, where each of the three allies was to have supreme authority. Cooperation in these theaters was to be administered by the tripartite organization. Although de Gaulle focused his efforts on areas outside of Europe, there can be no doubt that NATO Europe was eventually to be included as well. The initial memorandum, for example, includes "the Atlantic" as a potential theater, subject to the new institutions. It is also revealing that de Gaulle wanted NATO's Standing Group to be the military-strategic nucleus of the system. This was the only exclusive three-power group in the Alliance structure, and a logical starting point for placing Europe, as well as the external regions, under the tripartite system. The General was quite persistent in his efforts to enhance this organ's functions in the context of tripartite diplomacy. General André Beaufre was assigned to the Standing Group in 1960, with express orders to revive its status in NATO: his successor, Admiral M. Douguet, continued in these vain efforts to revive it at the expense of other NATO bodies concerned with defense questions.[111]

Thus, the tripartite organization, with its revitalized Standing Group, combined general staffs, and institutionalized meetings of defense ministers and heads of state or government, was to supplant SACEUR, SHAPE, and the Military Committee and eventually to supercede even the Atlantic Council as the locus of Alliance decision making. To de Gaulle, the loss would not have been a great one, because he considered these integrated or multilateral organs to be mere instruments of Anglo-Saxon hegemony over the Alliance. As he candidly explained in his memoirs, he was simply insisting that France be coopted into the Alliance's ruling elite. "I therefore proposed that the alliance should henceforth be placed under a triple rather than a dual direction."[112] De Gaulle doubtless also contemplated that continental Europe would return to a system of nonintegrated national armies, generally supervised by a nuclear-armed France representing the tripartite organization.[113] A nonnuclear West German force could have been controlled by the European and tripartite organizations, while serving as an advance guard on the continent, with France as the main defense and the United States a reserve and final recourse. Britain was to find her European role in the northern sector and perhaps the Low Countries. Such a design was compatible with de Gaulle's images of France, her national defense, and her rightful role in Europe and the world. It gives the period of memorandum diplomacy a logical and consistent place in the development of his overall international strategy for France's revival.[114]

The audacity of such a design has led many observers to conclude that the memorandum and related moves were actually an elaborate scheme designed to provoke dissension and an American refusal, thereby justifying France's withdrawal from NATO at a choice moment in the future. De Gaulle's sometimes disingenuous Fifth Republic memoirs do present the memorandum as one stage of a policy of disengaging France from NATO, though not from the Alliance, while bringing about a détente with Russia and building an independent nuclear force. He writes that he expected evasive replies to the memorandum and that afterward "there was nothing to prevent [the French government] from taking action."[115] It is of course true that de Gaulle expected a great power such as the United States to guard its independence and even its hegemony, so he could have had few illusions that France would be granted what Wilfred L. Kohl noted was "so extravagant a demand as a veto power over the use of American nuclear weapons anywhere in the world."[116] After all, France had no nuclear bomb of her own until the primitive device exploded in February 1960 and did not acquire even a rudimentary delivery force before 1964.

Nevertheless, de Gaulle's realistic skepticism about the likelihood of success does not justify the prevailing judgment that the memorandum initiative was essentially "a clever tactical instrument to help justify France's eventual withdrawal from NATO,"[117] or that it was presented only "with the idea of provoking a refusal which would then justify France in her gradual resumption of freedom of action."[118] Instead, in the context of postwar French diplomacy, the memorandum demands appear to express representative goals of French security, an updated Gaullist version of early Fourth Republic expectations for the Alliance. De Gaulle did indeed want a formal, public tripartite organization to guarantee France's security, legitimize her claims to great power rank, and ensure her preeminence in Western Europe and Africa. This was the easy route to grandeur, and, not surprisingly, the way was barred. After 1961, the Elysée pursued similar ends by way of its European policy and developments in Franco-Soviet relations. But the General's memorandum diplomacy was neither an aberration nor a clever tactical ploy; it must be accorded a legitimate role in the evolution of postwar French security policy and the Gaullist design.

An Independent European Defense

France and the European Alternative. De Gaulle's design for a European confederation of nation-states, eventually constituting a new pole of economic, diplomatic, and military power in a reorganized global system, was another prominent feature of French diplomacy in this period. The idea was malleable enough to suit the tripartite formula emphasized from 1958 through 1961, then to advance the cause of European independence from Atlantic hegemony and, finally, to accommodate the brief and equally unsuccessful Franco-German entente formed at the beginning of 1963. The very ambivalence and flexibility of the European idea has allowed it to survive repeated assaults and setbacks. It was, however, severely strained by de Gaulle's attempt to clarify the political-military dimension of Europe and to direct it against NATO and the "Atlantic partnership" design of the Europeanists in the Kennedy administration.

As previously noted, de Gaulle opposed this idea and the counterpart of an integrated federalist Europe, favoring instead a confederal system, sometimes called a *"Europe des patries."*[119] He condemned supranational integration on the grounds that nation-states were the only viable sources of political legitimacy and because he viewed integration as a vehicle for American domination of Europe. European and French independence was the predominant Gaullist goal, and a central feature of French European policy was the proposition that Europe could become independent only if it established a defense system separate from that of the United States. De Gaulle's classic view was that political autonomy was largely a function of an independent defense; thus, the Europeans had to create "in the political domain—which is first that of defense—an organization, certainly allied to the New World, but which would be truly theirs, with its objectives, its resources and its obligations."[120] European cooperation, therefore, implied the eventual replacement of the NATO system with a separate defense organization for Western Europe, loosely linked with the United States through the Atlantic Treaty and perhaps the tripartite organization. In this aspect of his European policy, de Gaulle attempted to revise the settlement of 1954-55, which had turned European defense resources over to an American-dominated NATO. Fifth Republic policy, then, was to return to part of the EDC ideal, which involved a more autonomous European military structure, but without the supranational and integrationist features and with a more overt French preeminence based on exclusive possession of nuclear weapons on the continent.

The political justification for a separate European defense system was that, without it, Europe could never escape subordination to the United States and never emerge as an independent world power capable of asserting its own interests and of restoring balance to an unstable and oppressive bipolar system. In purely military terms, de Gaulle insisted that continued dependence on the United States and NATO posed grave risks for West European security, for two reasons mentioned earlier. One was the familiar French and continental fear of the American penchant for tardy interventions in European conflicts, now reinforced by a North American vulnerability to strategic nuclear attack in retaliation for assistance to Europe. During the period of memorandum diplomacy, de Gaulle sought the clear and institutionalized nuclear guarantee unavailable through the Atlantic Treaty and NATO. When this proved unavailable, and the Kennedy administration's defense doctrines seemed to confirm the decoupling of American and European security interests, de Gaulle concluded that France and Europe could never count on Washington to commit itself to nuclear destruction for the sake of allies. As he argued in the spring of 1962, during the Fouchet negotiations: "America and Soviet Russia are capable of striking each other directly and, doubtless, of destroying each other. It is not certain that they will take this risk. No one can tell today when, how, or why one or the other of these great atomic powers would employ its nuclear arsenal."[121] Maneuvers such as the stationing of American-controlled tactical nuclear weapons in Europe were insufficient indications of Washington's intentions, because under the McNamara strategy there was no way of knowing when, and under what conditions, they would be released for battlefield use.[122] Moreover, given the density of Europe's populations, the use of tactical weapons after the failure of deterrence would involve unacceptable levels of destruction.

The Cuban missile crisis of October 1962 was cited by de Gaulle as additional proof that Europe's privileged position in American strategy had given way to primary concern for the security of the United States itself, because during that affair strategic forces were said to have focused on defending the American homeland rather than Europe, which itself faced the risk of an attack.[123] This crisis enabled de Gaulle to wield another argument against European dependence on the United States and NATO; namely, the danger that Washington would involve Europe in a war started elsewhere on the globe, without any allied influence over the course of events. This thesis was a prominent feature of the private memorandum diplomacy among the three leading Western allies. After 1962 it emerged more often in public, and by 1965 Paris was issuing frequent warnings about the possibility of a nuclear escalation in connection with the Vietnam war. De Gaulle apparently believed then that American power was quite out of hand, with the United States intervening all over the world and most tragically in Vietnam, while the Yalta duopoly was failing because it could no longer restrain the superpowers and ensure minimum security to their dependents. The remedy of a Europe independent in its defense was necessary not simply as a means of restoring international equilibrium but also as relief and restraint for a United States dangerously strained by the burdens of hegemony.[124]

In raising such questions about the American commitment to Western Europe's security, de Gaulle was often acting as the most articulate spokesman for European uncertainties about changes in U.S. defense posture and strategy. But de Gaulle went beyond merely clarifying issues, because he advocated replacing NATO with an independent European defense system based on French nuclear weaponry. This aspect of the Gaullist design was perhaps least convincing, for France could not provide Europe with an effective alternative to dependence on the United States, however uncertain the benefits of the status quo. Nor were French and general West European security interests as compatible as de Gaulle maintained during this campaign, because French military policy and defense strategy posed conflicts of interest on this scale similar to those that existed between the United States and Europe on the Atlantic level.

The Fouchet Plan and the Veto of Britain. The Fouchet negotiations were an outgrowth of de Gaulle's intention to divert European cooperation from the integrationist forum of the EEC into a confederal system of cooperating states, one that would include defense affairs. A first attempt to introduce defense and foreign policy affairs into a non-NATO European setting, made in 1959, was unsuccessful because France's partners could not agree to deal with these problems outside the Alliance network.[125] Undaunted, de Gaulle renewed his effort late in the summer of 1960. He held a series of meetings with heads of government from the EEC states, notably with Adenauer, on 29-30 July 1960, and sounded them out on a future European union and the possibility of upgrading their cooperation on security affairs.[126] The General publicly unveiled his plans at the September 1960 press conference and, after some delays, a committee headed by Christian Fouchet was formed, in March 1961, to initiate studies on European union. A formal French proposal for a "Union of the States" was submitted on 19 October 1961, and negotiations continued through the spring of 1962.

The details of these proceedings are beyond the scope of this discussion.[127] The participants arrived at an impasse on 17 April 1962, and the prospects for a political confederation died despite some later attempts to revive them. A major reason for the failure was the presentation of an entirely new French draft treaty for the union in January 1962, one that altered the generally acceptable document already under examination. The new plan threatened the integrity of the EEC Commission by placing economic affairs within the competence of the union's intergovernmental organs; it also virtually precluded the possibility of evolution toward a more centralized, possibly supranational, organization.[128] The eventual political orientation of the union was another important source of disagreement, especially between a Dutch-Belgian coalition and the French. Foreign Ministers Luns and Spaak finally broke off the negotiations because Couve de Murville would not accept British entry into both the EEC and the union, as a concession for the postponement of an integrated and supranational Europe.[129] General suspicion of French motives was enhanced because, whereas the original Fouchet Plan had stated (Article 2) that the union's common defense policy would serve to strengthen the Atlantic Alliance, de Gaulle's January text ominously contained no reference to cooperation with NATO.

Although the NATO issue was only a secondary cause of overt disagreement among the negotiators, de Gaulle's evident intention of using the union as a vehicle for separating a West European security system from the United States and NATO was then, and afterward, the crux of the problem. As de Gaulle said later, in reference to the Fouchet discussions, "this attempt was unsuccessful because at that time our partners, as a whole, did not consider that Europe could exist by itself and deal with questions of policy and defense outside of NATO."[130] Thus, the Fouchet experiment demonstrated the difficulty of leading Europe out from under the American hegemony. It also confirmed de Gaulle's belief that the supranational Europe implied by EEC institutions would be a device to ensure continued subservience to the United States. Later, in 1965, he was to take drastic steps to ensure that this did not happen.

British entry into the proposed union and the EEC was a major obstacle to an agreement during the Fouchet negotiations. London's applications to either forum were opposed because de Gaulle wanted to spare his project for an independent Europe from an obvious Trojan horse with privileged ties to the United States. Despite some concessions from Macmillan, discussions over the memorandum proposals had doubtless affirmed that British governments put the vestiges of the "special relationship" before their more fragile European vocation. For de Gaulle, this assessment of future British policy apparently took precedence over the likelihood that British membership in European institutions would provide a sure ally against supranational integration.[131]

The Gaullist veto of British membership in the EEC, issued on 14 January 1963, stemmed from a general conviction in Paris that Britain was diplomatically and economically unsuited to the kind of Europe foreseen by de Gaulle. Negotiations following the British application in October 1961 had indicated to the French government that London's economic policies and preferences were incompatible with EEC institutions and procedures. There were also ill-timed indications that British security policy remained unacceptable. This aspect of the problem apparently arose as a result of a meeting between de Gaulle and Macmillan at Rambouillet on 15 and 16 December 1962. The French later maintained that, in the course of these talks, the British prime minister had suggested close cooperation between the French and British nuclear force programs within a European framework, and then perfidiously backed down at Nassau by renewing dependence on Washington.[132] According to other accounts, Macmillan had vaguely raised the issue of European defense cooperation during an earlier meeting (in June 1962 at the Château des Champs), but the subject did not come up again at Rambouillet except when de Gaulle alluded to a possible joint missile-development program.[133] Most likely, as Couve de Murville indicated later, the Nassau Agreements were essentially a final confirmation of French doubts about the British application, because the Polaris missile deal reaffirmed that the "special relationship" was still more valuable to London than independence and membership in France's version of Europe.[134] Strengthened by domestic electoral successes, de Gaulle was able to issue a unilateral veto of British membership and denounce the enlargement of the Community as a scheme to sustain American hegemony in Europe. "It is foreseeable that the cohesion of all its members, who would be very numerous and very diverse, would not hold for long and that in the end there would appear a colossal Atlantic Community under American dependence and leadership which would completely swallow up the European Community." This was "not at all what France wanted to do and what France is doing, which is a strictly European construction."[135] After de Gaulle's earlier setbacks, then, the veto was a holding action on one front, to keep an unsatisfactory status quo in Europe, while he turned to West Germany in the hope that an independent Europe could be relaunched and soon joined by others.

The Franco-German Entente and European Security.   De Gaulle thought that he had found in West Germany, and especially in Chancellor Adenauer, a more malleable partner for building an independent Europe. The reconciliation of the two states was in any case a prerequisite for European unity, and Adenauer had seemed to de Gaulle to be a kindred spirit ever since their first meeting, at Colombey, on 14 September 1958. The chancellor was equally impressed by the French president's loyalty to European unity, an impression evidently sustained later by Adenauer's inability to grasp the full scope of de Gaulle's revisionist policies on NATO, the Atlantic Community, and European security. This coalition of elder statesmen was periodically reinforced by West German fears that the United States and Britain were insufficiently rigorous in defending the West German position on Berlin and reunification. During the extended Berlin crisis of 1961-62, Kennedy's willingness to explore compromise solutions, in cooperation with Britain and the Soviet Union, damaged relations between Bonn and Washington, while the French fed West German suspicions that another Yalta agreement, at West Germany's expense, was in the offing. De Gaulle earned Adenauer's gratitude by refusing to participate in these initiatives and by insisting that the West adopt a hard line toward the Soviet Union.[136] It was partly because of such German-American tensions that the chancellor suggested to de Gaulle, in September 1962, that the reconciliation of their two states be crowned by a formal agreement. This was most convenient for de Gaulle, who perceived a means of bringing West Germany under France's wing and debilitating NATO with German complicity.

Signed in Paris on 22 January 1963, the Franco-German Treaty was in effect a scaled-down version of the defunct Fouchet Plan.[137] It provided for regular meetings between heads of state or government, their ministers, and other officials—all coordinated by a joint interministerial commission. Because the agreement was part of the French policy of weaning the Federal Republic away from NATO, there were significant provisions for extending cooperation on defense matters. West German troops were already training at French facilities, under an agreement of 25 October 1960, and the French and German general staffs had been meeting regularly, since June 1961, to discuss strategy and logistics. The 1963 treaty foresaw regular meetings of defense ministers, while the two chiefs of staff and their subordinates were to hold meetings every three months. Exchanges of military personnel and cooperation in arms production were also scheduled. Finally, the two governments promised to consult each other before taking decisions of any importance in regard to NATO, the EEC, or East-West relations, and further agreed to attempt to harmonize their military strategy and tactics for European defense. In conversations with Adenauer at the time of the signing of the treaty, de Gaulle made it apparent that he envisaged this bilateral military cooperation as a step toward reducing Europe's dependence on the United States and NATO.[138]

This French aspiration was marred from the outset by domestic West German reaction to the treaty. Incensed by de Gaulle's veto of British membership in the EEC and by renewed French attacks on NATO, the West German Bundestag accepted Socialist leader Herbert Wehner's suggestion that a preamble be attached to the treaty, to confirm the document's compatability with the West German commitment to European-American cooperation within the framework of NATO. Adopted on 16 May 1963, the preamble noted the Federal Republic's desire for "close association between Europe and the United States of America" and its resolute support for "common defense within the framework of [the] North Atlantic Alliance and the integration of armed forces of member states of that Pact."[139] De Gaulle naturally rejected the West German parliament's blemish on his entente; nevertheless, the preamble reflected prevailing German policy and interests and was a warning of the limits of Franco-German cooperation. In the realm of military security, West Germany was firmly linked to the United States and NATO. If forced to choose between the Atlantic Alliance and the Gaullist vision of European security, Bonn was bound to opt for the former.

For this reason, after January 1963, Franco-German military cooperation did not expand dramatically. It was limited to modest extensions or amplifications of previous agreements on personnel exchanges, German access to French training facilities, and minor joint arms-production ventures. Although the prescribed bilateral meetings on defense policy took place, German defense officials assiduously avoided in depth discussion of strategy and tactics and instead relegated such issues to the NATO forums, or meetings with their American counterparts.[140] Rather than grow closer to France, then, West Germany's defense establishment actually reinforced its ties with the United States. It was assisted in this endeavor by an American government determined to repair the bond between Bonn and Washington at the expense of Paris. The battle for the allegiance of the Federal Republic was opened by Kennedy's highly successful visit to there in June 1963, when the president reassured Adenauer that the United States would face any risk in keeping its promise to defend Europe with nuclear weapons.[141] Shortly thereafter, in August, the United States and Germany agreed to a joint tank-production project, which had originally been conceived as a Franco-German affair. The crowning success of the American offensive was the agreement on German arms purchases from the United States, signed on 14 November 1964 by defense ministers McNamara and Kai-Uwe von Hassel. As one analyst noted, this agreement "in effect made the German armed forces dependent on the United States for their military equipment."[142] By that time, the West German Atlanticist orientation had completely triumphed in the government set up by Chancellor Ludwig Erhard after he replaced Adenauer in October 1963. Under Erhard and his foreign minister, Gerhard Schroeder, the laudable goal of eventual European independence, even in partnership with the United States, became a low priority in West Germany, and relations with France inevitably suffered.

This development was particularly apparent in conflicts between Bonn and Paris over the MLF and the French alternative of an independent European nuclear defense arrangement. The difficult, and finally impossible, task confronting the French was to convince the West German government that a French nuclear guarantee for Europe, or an eventual European nuclear force emerging from the French one, was a more reliable instrument of European security than NATO, the MLF, and American protection.[143] One argument was that, by virtue of the geographical proximity of European states, a French nuclear force was automatically valid for the defense of West Germany and Western Europe as a whole. De Gaulle himself frequently stressed the natural unity of French and West German military systems as one aspect of the two states' rapprochement, as when he told West German military officers that "the organic cooperation of our armies with the aim of

a single defense is therefore essential to the union of our two countries."[144]
Prominent Gaullist supporters of the *force de frappe* such as Alexandre
Sanguinetti insisted that West Germany fell within France's most intimate
defense perimeter; thus, "any attack on West Germany is a physical attack on
France."[145] The lure was most explicitly proferred by Premier Pompidou
during defense-budget debates on 2 December 1964. After criticizing the
flexible response strategy, a devalued American nuclear guarantee, and the
MLF, Pompidou told the National Assembly that the French force was
intended as insurance that any form of aggression against Europe would meet
a nuclear response on the aggressor's homeland, thereby triggering the American strategic forces. He concluded that the French guarantee covered all of
Europe. "But it must be observed that, by the very fact that France is in
Europe, her strength works fully and automatically on behalf of Europe,
whose defense is physically and geographically inseparable from her own,
which is not the case for powers, even allied, outside of the European continent."[146]

A collateral French thesis was that the *force de frappe* constituted an
investment for the time when a politically unified Europe could assume a
collective responsibility in defense matters. Minister of Armed Forces Pierre
Messmer alluded to this possibility in 1963, in an important article outlining
the government's military policy: "In order for Europe to exist," he wrote, "it
will have to assume the burden and the responsibility of its defense and, for
that, possess nuclear weapons. When we reach that point, we shall see that
France's possession of national nuclear weapons will be a keystone in the
building of Europe and, by reason of this, the subject of the most impassioned
debate."[147] Premier Pompidou, in the speech previously cited, also referred
ambiguously to "an integrated European defense" as first requiring European
political and defense unity, which was "an ideal that we not only foresee but
also desire." In the meantime, he added, France would continue to build an
atomic force, "which by the very fact that it is French is already European."
Perhaps the most direct overture of this kind was made in September 1963 by
a member of Pompidou's cabinet, Michel Habib-Deloncle, when he speculated
before the Council of Europe that European political unity could lead tò a
common defense based on Franco-British nuclear collaboration as the nucleus
of European security.[148]

While moving further into the American orbit, the Erhard government
did not ignore these maneuvers and attempted to clarify its understanding of
French intentions regarding a European defense system. In doing so, Erhard
was in part responding to pressures from the so-called Gaullist wing of the
CDU-CSU, led by Adenauer and Franz-Josef Strauss, which tended to support
an independent European defense based on an integrated nuclear force.[149]
After a December 1963 visit to President Johnson in Texas, Erhard and his

ministers met with French leaders in Paris the following February and confirmed their intention to participate in the MLF. According to one report, de Gaulle countered this with a firm promise to use the French nuclear force "in the first moment of a conflict for the defense of Germany."[150] Erhard later contended that he also broached the subject of a joint Franco-German nuclear force, but de Gaulle demurred.[151] At still another de Gaulle-Erhard encounter, in Bonn in July 1964, the chancellor again raised the question of a concrete West German participation in the management of the French force, and de Gaulle again refused to give an affirmative reply.[152] After this encounter, the Bonn government apparently concluded that France had no tangible offer to make and a European nuclear force was an unlikely prospect for the foreseeable future.[153] As for depending on a unilateral French nuclear guarantee, the military value of the small and untested French force was deemed negligible by comparison with what the United States offered through the Alliance. Nor was there any reason to believe that Europe would be more secure depending on French promises rather than those of the United States. As Fritz Erler noted, "the other European nations will undoubtedly have more influence on the American force than on the French. By de Gaulle's definition, any foreign influence on the French atomic force is excluded."[154]

The West German assessment was essentially correct then, because Paris had no serious intention of denationalizing the *Force nucléaire stratégique* and somehow sharing it with Europe. Thus, French efforts to seduce the Germans with ambivalent hints of joint nuclear security arrangements were undermined by the more credible Gaullist thesis that defense in general, and nuclear weapons in particular, were susceptible only to national control. De Gaulle applied this precept to European as well as Atlantic defense cooperation, as when he stated in October 1960: "To the European peoples, France proposes to cooperate and coordinate their political activity to serve common goals. But France intends not to lose [her] identity. She intends, in particular, that her defense have a national personality."[155]

Despite some indications to the contrary, the views of de Gaulle's government did not really change later on and, as Couve de Murville stated in June 1963, the possibility of European cooperation in nuclear weapons amounted to little more than hypotheses and hopes.[156] This was especially true in respect to West Germany, because the French force was partly designed to ensure France's preeminence over West Germany, and any significant bilateral or multilateral sharing would have diluted the advantages of a politically symbolic deterrent useful, in any case, only for national purposes. Finally, as the next chapter will demonstrate, French military strategy at this time was an obvious, even flagrant, violation of the supposed unity and coherence of French and West German security interests. For, instead of a single Franco-German defense zone, French strategic doctrine emphasized a "two battles" strategy, in which the national nuclear force was to be engaged only when Soviet forces had invaded West Germany, were approaching the Rhine barrier, and posed a clear threat to French territory.

It does not seem that the results of Franco-German diplomacy materially changed Bonn's policies in the 1963-65 period, because the West German government was evidently not prepared to alter its commitment to the NATO security framework. Although Bonn, like Paris, had been disturbed by changes in American strategy and new Soviet-American dialogues, the reaction by Erhard and his colleagues was to intensify cooperation with the United States, in an effort to bolster Atlantic ties. Thus, the MLF and other aspects of Atlantic cooperation were pursued by the Germans primarily as political instruments that could reinforce the American commitment to West European security.[157] Perhaps the most salient West German fear during this period was that French intransigence, and Gaullist attacks on the United States and NATO, might actually precipitate an American withdrawal from Europe, a contingency that the Germans wanted to prevent at all cost. From West Germany's vantage point, then, a Gaullist Europe was of questionable value for the immediate future, and excessive speculation was possibly dangerous.

At the root of this conflict between Bonn and Paris were quite divergent security perspectives that effectively prevented a fruition of the Gaullist design.[158] For, since 1955, the NATO system had provided a foundation for West Germany's reemergence to international respectability and, whereas France had come to resent the Alliance as a symbol of declining status in the world, for Germany it was a key factor of revival. The very existence of West German armed forces legally depended on NATO and, unlike those of France, they were thoroughly integrated (materially and psychologically) into the Atlantic defense system. More tangibly, NATO had become the only acceptable framework for ensuring West Germany's military security vis-à-vis the East. As a divided nation bordering on the Soviet empire, the Federal Republic was less sanguine than France about both the Soviet threat and the realities of Western Europe's military dependence on the United States. It wanted the most reliable and tangible political and military security guarantee available, and the options held out by France were unacceptable.

West German perspectives and policy were thus determined by the asymmetrical European solution of the 1950s, which allocated economic and many political issues to a European community, but channeled defense and security to an Atlantic arena managed by the United States. Because the German problem and West German policy were actually the principal unresolved issues of European security, the failure to realign the Bonn regime meant that the Gaullist challenge to the Atlantic order was neutralized. De Gaulle realized this by mid-1964, and his bitter disappointment was expressed during a press conference on 23 July 1964, held after an unsatisfactory meeting with Erhard earlier that month. De Gaulle listed areas of conflict with Germany, notably over relations with Eastern Europe and China, as well as different views on the Indochina War and EEC agricultural policy.[159] Instead of following France's lead in European policy, de Gaulle complained, "Bonn has not believed, up to now, that this policy should be European and independent."[160] Preparing the way for the EEC crisis of 1965, de Gaulle declared that the failure to under-write a new status for Europe jeopardized the future of the EEC. Hoping that West German leaders might change their perspective, France clearly would not, and instead intended to pursue "by her own means, that which a European and independent policy can and should be."[161] But an independent Europe was not imminent: de Gaulle began preparations to strike out on his own.

Prelude to Disengagement: French European Policy, 1965-1966. In reaction to the collapse of his plans for the Franco-German entente, de Gaulle initiated action on three difference fronts: he attempted to disable the Common Market and free France from integration in an American-dominated European organi-zation; he began final preparations for a unilateral withdrawal from NATO; and, finally, he sought a bilateral dialogue with the Soviet Union, as recognition of France's independence and superior status in Western Europe. The EEC crisis of 1965 was ostensibly over the Community's financing and institutional control of its agricultural policy, but the more profound causes can be traced to the collapse of the Gaullist European design.[162] Unable to convince West Germany and other members to follow his ideas, the General rejected an audacious commission scheme for extending the Community's supranational powers and, instead, tried to dilute the Rome Treaty and ensure that an inde-pendent France would not be subject to the will of a pro-American majority.[163] After the breakdown of negotiations on 30 June 1965, and the beginning of a French boycott of Community institutions, the French government concluded that, in the absence of a European consensus supporting Gaullist policy goals, the Rome Treaty provisions for majority voting in the Council of Ministers could not take effect as scheduled in January 1966.[164] Confirming this interpre-tation of French actions, Couve de Murville told the National Assembly, on 16 June 1965, that there could be no further progress on European unity until the other states agreed to adopt the French policy of independence.[165] Gaullist deputy Christian de la Malène was even more specific when he told a *Union pour la nouvelle république* (UNR) rally at Strasbourg on 25 November that "as long as France's partners, notably Germany, refuse a defense that is autono-mous and independent from the United States, Europe will not be feasible."[166]

Rather than simply apply some brakes to European integration, however, de Gaulle also seemed to contemplate major alterations in the EEC frame-work. His ministers noted that the more blatant supranational clauses of the Rome Treaty needed revision, and they indicated that the French government could foresee and tolerate a total breakdown of the EEC itself.[167] These extreme possibilities did not materialize, however, partly because of the strong adverse reaction in France, and de Gaulle's disappointing performance in the presidential election of December 1965.[168] During the last stages of the election, there was an abrupt change in the French position and, in January, certain compromises among the Six, including an informal agreement not to institute majority voting, permitted the Community to function again. But the crisis was resolved at the expense of progress in European unity, which was slow to recover from the French attack. In the context of this discussion, the 1965 European crisis was a prelude to the impending announcement of France's withdrawal from NATO, for both actions were facets of the overriding goal of ridding France of subordination to the United States.

While he was engaged in offensives against European integration and NATO, de Gaulle embarked on a major effort to build up French ties with the Soviet Union. Relations between the two states were improved during and after 1964, as exchanges of government officials developed, and the process of *"détente-entente-coopération"* was crowned by de Gaulle's visit to the Soviet Union in June 1966. As suggested earlier, de Gaulle's Eastern policy was part of a natural evolution in his global strategy to augment France's stature and influence in the world. It was not a reversal of alliances, but an example of cooperation à la carte with East and West, making France the fulcrum of evolving East-West contacts and a future resolution of European security problems. By freeing France from NATO and American military domination, de Gaulle was indicating to the Soviet Union that France, and potentially a French-led Europe, was not a satellite, and had to be dealt with in its own right. De Gaulle had already received indications that Moscow would welcome a French partnership in remaking Europe, and the perception of a direct Soviet threat to Western Europe had declined measurably by the mid-1960s. Both parties found their policies coinciding on issues such as U.N. activities in the Congo, the MLF, and Vietnam; and both could see that their cooperation might be mutually beneficial in ensuring that West Germany be controlled and managed for their purposes.

By late 1964, then, de Gaulle was indicating that a settlement of the German question could be considered and, given the tensions between France and West Germany at the time, he appeared to be using his Eastern policy as leverage against Bonn. This interpretation, which was sometimes exaggerated,[169] was partially confirmed during de Gaulle's press conference on 4 February 1965, held after an unsatisfactory Erhard visit to Paris on 19 and 20 January. In response to questions about Franco-Soviet relations and postwar European security, the General replied that the German problem had to be settled and guaranteed primarily by Germany's European neighbors, who were most affected by the division of the continent. Envisaged as part of a general and complex process of East-West détente, such a settlement, he said, would require Germany to accept supervision of its frontiers and armaments, in an accord with its Eastern and Western neighbors.[170] It was unnecessary to add that the major guarantor powers should be France and the Soviet Union, the only continental states with nuclear weapons.

In raising this issue, de Gaulle was doubtless attempting to offset the ascendant German-American connection, by warning Bonn that its future status depended more on the policies of other European states than on the United States. And he was indicating sensible conditions that the Federal Republic would have to accept if better relations with the East were to develop. But de Gaulle was also pointing out that any acceptable solution to the German problem ought to leave France in a superior position vis-à-vis her old enemy and new but often unfaithful partner. One need not conclude from this that de Gaulle was himself basically anti-German, or convinced that West Germany threatened France directly.[171] Like his predecessors, the General was attempting to counter Germany's inherent economic strength with an unassailable French political-military advantage in determining the future of European security. This was not so much a Gaullist goal as a persistently French one. Nor was it unreasonable.

Although trying to establish a position as the Soviet Union's privileged Western interlocutor on European security issues, French détente policy was not dangerous or destabilizing, because Paris essentially continued to support the West German position on most outstanding issues, or to point the way toward acceptable solutions on problems such as boundaries with Poland. But de Gaulle's expectation of fostering an East-West settlement in Europe against NATO and the Atlantic system seems to have been based on the incorrect assumption, or hope, that West Germany could be induced to accept a new relationship with the East while simultaneously loosening security ties to the United States and NATO and accepting in their place a French guarantee and Franco-Soviet understanding. In reality, however, West German accommodation to détente, and the concessions to the East incorporated in Ostpolitik, depended on a sense of security that required a strong NATO system and American support for Germany's Eastern diplomacy.

The structure apparently envisaged by France for managing the détente process would have been too uncertain and too weak to provide sufficient assurances for the necessary and drastic changes in West German policy. Gaullist actions and pronouncements certainly opened new perspectives and helped the West Germans begin their accommodation to the postwar territorial and political settlements in central Europe, a development that may or may not lead to the loosening of the East bloc foreseen by de Gaulle. But French leadership of an independent Europe, disengaging itself from the United States, was an unrealistic model for controlling these developments in the face of Soviet power. Gaullist détente policy was also somewhat premature by its own standards, because de Gaulle recognized that significant progress would depend on a liberalization of the Soviet Union's totalitarian domestic system, as well as on changes in the paranoid and defensive attitudes governing Soviet relations with other states.[172] But internal reforms were terminated with the fall of Khrushchev in 1964, and the 1968 intervention in Czechoslovakia was conclusive evidence that France's freedom in the West could not be duplicated in the East. A communist Soviet Union never shared de Gaulle's view that it should behave like a state devoid of ideological responsibility for managing the affairs of fellow socialist regimes. This inclination coincided with Russia's historical ambition to dominate its neighbors for security reasons. These two factors together made ambitious Gaullist designs for a European settlement seem utopian except in the distant future.[173] France, in any case, found herself on the sidelines of the détente process after 1968, when de Gaulle's bid for center stage in Europe was fatally undercut, and West Germany began exploring the leading role it was to assume at the expense of French ambition.

4 French Military Independence and Dealignment, 1958-1968

Whereas Gaullist diplomacy after 1958 offered France's allies limited forms of military collaboration, tripartite or European or both, the main lines of de Gaulle's armed forces policy and defense strategy placed such an emphasis on independence that they often seemed to preclude meaningful international cooperation in this domain. The formation of a national defense structure outside of NATO and incompatible with most Alliance policy and institutions, and the development of a defense strategy emphasizing national autonomy in the nuclear age, were obvious problems that burdened French policy in Atlantic and European forums. De Gaulle's military policy and strategy were, however, useful in mustering domestic support for a sensible but innovative French defense structure focusing almost entirely on the Métropole for the first time since the colonial expansion of the nineteenth century. Nor was this transformation undertaken at a great risk to French security. For, while he emphasized an independent national defense at odds with NATO, de Gaulle profited from European geography, and NATO's protection, to build his independent defense under the cover of Alliance security.

This privileged position and apparently ungrateful stand were a constant irritant to the United States and other allies during the brief period (1965-68) of extreme French alienation from the Atlantic system. In the long run, however, France's defense capabilities and semiautonomy have been recognized as a positive contribution to European and Atlantic security, while the status of an independent and partial ally has proven flexible enough to accommodate a gradual shift back toward cooperation that began under de Gaulle in 1968. The most recent trends in French military policy will be discussed in chapter five. The first section below contains a brief description of Gaullist armed forces policy and defense strategy during the period of emphasis on maximum independence.[1] The second section describes how this military policy was reinforced by France's partial withdrawal from NATO and expulsion of allied military forces and institutions from French territory.

An Independent and National Defense

Restoring National Defense and Civilian Political Authority. Under the Fourth Republic, France's armed forces concentrated their material resources and strategic doctrines in a priority defense of their overseas mission and colonialism. One of de Gaulle's most significant and enduring legacies to France was to terminate this costly and unrewarding endeavor, and redefine the military's mission in terms of a national defense of the Métropole, based primarily on nuclear weapons. This was the major theme of de Gaulle's speech before the Ecole Militaire on 3 November 1959, which announced important changes in French military policy.[2] Later, the official "Ordre aux Armées," issued on 1 January 1962, called on the army to wind up its activities in Algeria and prepare for a permanent return to Europe and to those "great warrior actions that could be imposed on the nation and on its allies."[3] A continental mission might have meant a return to NATO and European defense cooperation, as many officers hoped, but this was ultimately excluded by the Gaullist view that cooperation, while possible and desirable, was subject to the condition that "France must keep for herself her will, her personality, and her army."[4] A return to the integrated commands of NATO was thus out of the question.

In addition to the concept of a Métropole-centered defense, nuclear weapons were the keystone of this policy, because it was only by drastically modernizing the armed forces that they could serve de Gaulle's international policy, and meet the responsibility of defending France without direct reliance on NATO. De Gaulle emphasized this in the 1959 Ecole Militaire speech, and during the withdrawals from Algeria he again offered the *Force nucléaire stratégique* (FNS) as the instrument fulfilling the armed forces' national mission. In May 1962, de Gaulle stressed that a modernized army would rely primarily on "a French atomic deterrence force" that was developing "ceaselessly" as the vehicle of the national mission he offered:

> The gradual return of our military forces from Algeria is enabling us to acquire a modernized army; an army which is not, I daresay, destined to play a separate or isolated role, but one which must and can play a role that would be France's own. Finally, it is absolutely necessary, morally and politically, for us to make our army a more integral part of the nation. Therefore, it is necessary for us to restation it, for the most part, on our soil; for us to give it once again a direct responsibility in the external security of the country; in short, for our defense to become once again a national defense. It is indispensable, I repeat, both morally and politically.[5]

Edgar S. Furniss concluded from this that de Gaulle developed his nuclear force primarily to provide the armed forces with their requisite mission and an acceptable status within the nation.[6] Others have felt, however, that this motive was supplementary to the broader purposes of a nuclear force, in terms of independence and a world role for France.[7] These explanations are actually complementary because independence and grandeur were deemed possible only if France had an independent means of defense, which depended on her armed forces taking up a mission that was France's own. A national nuclear force responded to all these needs, because it brought France prestige, justified her divorce from NATO, and provided the armed forces with the requisite national mission.

One ironic consequence of de Gaulle's abandonment of the French military's Algerian and Eurafrican role was that it enabled him to reduce the influence of French officers most loyal to NATO, because they were also the most fervent colonialists, who were finally subdued and discredited. Prominent officers, such as Generals Jean Valluy, Jean-Simon Chassin, and Maurice Challe, favored more NATO military integration, along with an extension of the Alliance security zone, to protect French hegemony in Algeria and Africa. De Gaulle manipulated this attitude to generate military and popular support for his memorandum proposals, and the Mediterranean fleet withdrawals from NATO, in 1959. After the Barricades Revolt of January 1960, however, these officers realized that de Gaulle was prepared to sacrifice a French Algeria, and the army's colonial mission, for the sake of a nuclear defense of the Métropole outside the NATO framework.

Generals Valluy and Challe emerged as the principal military spokesmen opposing both aspects of Gaullist policy. Valluy often spoke out after his retirement as NATO's Commander-in-Chief on the Central Front (CINCEUR) on 15 May 1960.[8] General Challe, Valluy's replacement in this post, was transferred there from Algeria largely because of his personal commitment to the cause of a French Algeria. Even while serving as CINCEUR, Challe gave interviews opposing Gaullist NATO policy and condemning his government's emphasis on an unintegrated and national defense structure.[9] From early 1960 through the attempted army coup in April 1961, some figures in this group harbored the unrealistic hope that they could replace de Gaulle, and the United States would be so gratified by a revival of French loyalty to NATO that, in return, France would finally be given support and assistance in North Africa. This attitude played a role in that abortive revolt, especially for Challe and Salan.[10]

The bulk of France's officer corps was, however, reconciling itself to de Gaulle's policies by 1961, and refused to underwrite the adventurism of some figures.[11] Thus, the French army accepted the renunciation of its Eurafrican mission, the establishment of rigorous civilian political authority over its activities, and its separation from the NATO commands. The cherished strategic doctrines of French colonialism were definitively abandoned by de Gaulle during a speech to eighty generals and admirals, and two thousand other officers, gathered at Strasbourg on 23 November 1961. He maintained that the military would still have a limited overseas role through the *Forces d'intervention*, though he denounced adherents of the *guerre révolutionnaire* doctrine, and sections of the army who had "formed a conception limited to their immediate wishes and to the terrain in which they were operating."[12] Fifth Republic strategy soon emphasized a rigid distinction between Métropole defense and the maintenance of French interests in Africa, and, under de Gaulle, capabilities for external interventions were sacrificed to the nuclear force and the Europeanization of all sectors of the armed forces. Some forces for intervention abroad were kept intact, however, and have been strengthened under Giscard d'Estaing, as a French military role in Africa experiences a limited revival.[13]

The April 1961 coup attempt, and the army's reluctance to follow de Gaulle's Algerian policy before then, may have had some effect in bolstering his government's resolve to end France's participation in NATO military integration. Couve de Murville doubtless reflected de Gaulle's views when he held NATO indirectly responsible for the army's adventurism in Algeria, because NATO relieved the army of its defense responsibilities at home, and encouraged it "to lose the sense of its essential mission, which is found on the national soil" and not abroad.[14] De Gaulle himself saw the coup attempt of April 1961 as proof that the Algerian experience had sapped the army's loyalty to France, and only a national defense mission could be effective in recalling the army to her service. As he told NATO Secretary-General Dirk Stikker, obedience could be assured only if the military sensed that it was fighting for France herself: "Since the insurrection in Algiers, I cannot rely on my generals and officers. That has to be changed, but loyalty can only be restored if the army and the officers know what they are fighting for, that is France; they cannot fight, or be loyal to some philosophical concept like NATO, and they cannot be loyal to some unknown American general or admiral."[15] Thus, de Gaulle required the armed forces to return to obedience to the state and genuine service to France, by embracing a national identity and mission incompatible with either a self-imposed role abroad, or service to an integrated and American-dominated Alliance.

Along with the Fifth Republic's Algerian and NATO policies, the fulfillment of this Gaullist design required the restoration of effective and responsible civilian political authority over the armed forces. Such authority had eroded badly under previous regimes, to the point where army cadres had become a virtually independent force capable of vetoing political decisions and finally overthrowing the Fourth Republic. Before 1958, partly because of ministerial instability, neither the prime minister nor the minister of armed forces had exercised close and consistent authority over the military; a bureaucratic organ, the *Secrétariat général permanent,* was responsible only for general administration.[16] To rectify this situation, de Gaulle set out to restore state, or civilian, control over the armed forces, and to centralize that authority in the office of the president and officials directly responsible to him.

From 1959 to 1962, during the Algerian War, the prime minister was given apparent responsibility for directing national defense under the basic ordinance of 7 January 1959, but the actual determination of defense policy (as opposed to administration) was in the hands of the Council of Ministers presided over by the president.[17] Specific decisions affecting the goals of defense policy, and their implications for the armed forces, were relegated to the *Comité de défense restreint,* consisting of the president, the prime minister, and other officials. Reinforcing the president's central position in this structure, he also presided over the *Conseil supérieur de défense,* which studied defense problems and established the groundwork for formal decisions. De Gaulle's unassailable personal control over defense policy was institutionalized by a decree of 18 July 1962, under which the presidential organs just mentioned supplanted the prime minister in general responsibility for defense policy, direction of national defense, and conduct of war.[18] Whatever the formal committee structure and necessary delegation of responsibilities, until 1969 there was never any doubt that the president made the important decisions in this *domaine réservé.*

The centralization of decision-making power in the hands of de Gaulle and his subordinates was reinforced by a reduction in the military's direct influence over higher policy making in defense and military affairs. The Fourth Republic's *Etat-major général des armées,* equivalent to the Joint Chiefs of Staff in the United States, was replaced in 1959 by an *Etat-major interarmée* reduced to handling simple liaison work between the three services, while the service chiefs of staff themselves were placed relatively low in the administrative and policy-making hierarchy. The general lines of defense and military policy, set by de Gaulle, were defined and applied by the *Etat-major général de la défense nationale* (E.M.G.D.N.), set up by Premier Debré, in February 1959, as part of the Hôtel Matignon apparatus. E.M.G.D.N. was headed by the military Chief of Staff, then General Ely, but was a mixed civilian-military body, to emphasize that defense policy was no longer an exclusive domain of the officer corps. Whereas relations between France's armed forces and the NATO commands had previously been handled by the *Etat-major général des armées,* the mixed E.M.G.D.N. took over this function after 1959. The policy consequences of de Gaulle's NATO decisions were normally worked out by this group, in the course of regular meetings with officials of the Quai d'Orsay's *Service des pactes,* which handled NATO political affairs for France. The president's and premier's offices received copies of all E.M.G.D.N. documents, in order to verify that their policy directives were being followed. In the reorganization of July 1962, E.M.G.D.N. became the *Secrétariat général de la défense nationale,* and carried out its work under the direction of air force General Michel Fourquet.[19]

France's highest military officer, the *Chef d'état-major des armées,* was under the immediate supervision of the *Ministre des armées* and, in the reorganization of July 1962, was charged with elaborating "the directives, plans, and decisions for the use of forces and resources of the armed forces in the national and interallied frameworks."[20] His actual authority over the three heads of services was somewhat unclear for a while, because he was not authorized to issue orders on his own behalf, and could only transmit those emanating from the president. This was the situation under General Ely and his successor, General Ailleret, who held the post from 11 April 1962 until his death on 10 March 1968. The ambiguity was cleared up on 26 April 1968, after General Fourquet had assumed the post. A decree of that date put the service heads under his orders, and he was given extensive delegated authority from the *Ministre des armées* to define the missions, organization, armament and budget allocations of each service.[21] Although it was not published in the *Journal officiel,* it was generally assumed that the *Chef d'état-major* was also the predesignated wartime commander of France's ensemble of nonatomic forces in the Métropole-Mediterranean theater of operations. Until the partial withdrawal from NATO in 1966, this included all such forces except the two land divisions in West Germany and the First Tactical Air Force (*1er Commandement aérien tactique*), both of which were technically assigned to NATO.[22] In January 1964, France's atomic delivery force, designated as the *Forces aériennes stratégiques,* was placed under the direct orders of the president, in his capacity as President of the Defense Council and constitutional Head of the Armed Forces. They could thus be engaged following a command to this effect issued by the president to the air force officer in charge.[23]

A Modern National Armed Force.   As French military activities in Algeria were progressively eliminated, the national defense structure in France underwent a far-reaching reorganization, dictated by the decision to concentrate on protecting the Métropole primarily with nuclear weapons. The results of this effort had been foreseen during the Fourth Republic by figures such as General Ely, who had proposed a post-Algerian military structure based on a French nuclear deterrent, along with a capacity for mobile intervention forces for domestic or overseas actions.[24] The structure that emerged under de Gaulle between 1959 and 1968 was characterized by: first, the absolute priority given to strategic nuclear forces; second, a consequential reduction in the size and strength of conventional forces; and, third, the integration of the three services along functional lines determined by the nuclear defense system. This three-fold division included the *Force nucléaire stratégique et la défense aérienne,* the *Forces d'intervention,* and the *Défense opérationnelle du territoire.*

Because the early history of the French atomic weapons program has been mentioned earlier, and is analyzed in some detail in other sources, the following discussion is primarily concerned with the planned development of the *Force nucléaire stratégique* during de Gaulle's tenure.[25] The first French atomic bomb was exploded on 13 February 1960, with a force of 60-70 kilotons. There were three more tests at the Reggane center in the southwest Sahara through April 1961. These tests prompted numerous protests from African and Arab states surrounding the site. The 50-60 kiloton prototype atomic device for the Mirage IV delivery system was first tested on 1 May 1962, at an underground site at Inn-Edder, Hoggar. Algerian independence prevented further use of either of these facilities, and all subsequent tests, including thermonuclear ones after 1968, were carried out at the Pacific atoll of Muroroa.[26]

The first generation nuclear delivery system created by de Gaulle consisted of fifty Mirage IV bombers. The plane had a range of 1,550 miles without refueling, which was extended to 2,975 miles by the 1964 purchase (from the United States) of twelve KC-135 tanker aircraft, each capable of servicing four bombers. A Mirage IV carried one A-bomb equipped with an electronic arming device activated by signals from the Chief of State.[27] Originally conceived for a normal flight altitude of 18,000 meters, the Mirage IV planes were subsequently lightened and adapted for low-level penetration flying. This part of the French deterrent first became operational in the fall of 1963, when plutonium bombs were delivered to six of the bombers.[28] Divided into two bomb wings and scattered over nine airfields, the projected force was in operation by 1966, with thirty-six aircraft on alert. Although questions were raised in the 1960s about the planes' vulnerability to a first strike, and their ability to penetrate the Soviet air defense system, the likelihood that a few would survive to deliver their bombs could not be discounted.[29] The disadvantage of only five-to-seven minutes warning time for a strategic missile attack on France from the Soviet Union could have been countered definitively only by constant airborn alert, which was feasible during the crisis that probably would have preceded such an attack. Otherwise, the security of the planes rested with an air defense system geared to detect an air force attack from the east. The detection system consisted of eight French radar centers, France's access to NATO's NADGE warning system, and automatic data processing and analysis through a STRIDA II computer.[30] The command and control center for the nuclear force and air defense was established at Taverny, although backup resources were said to exist at other locations. Through 1966, the Air Defense Command (*Centre d'opération de la défense aérienne,* CODA), charged with protecting the nuclear force, maintained six interceptor squadrons of super-Mystères B2s, two fighter squadrons of Mystère III and IV fighters, and two fighter squadrons of Vautour-N planes.[31]

The second generation of the French deterrent planned by de Gaulle, but not in the original 1960-64 program law, consisted of two squadrons of SSBS (*Sol-sol ballistique stratégique,* or IRBM), each counting nine missiles with a range of almost 1,900 miles, and warheads equivalent to 150 kilotons. The two 89,000-acre missile sites were set (amidst fields of lavender!) in a rocky, gullied section of the Plateau d'Albion in Haute-Provence. Under the program finally completed in 1972-73, the solid-fuel missiles, which were placed in hardened silos 24 meters deep, were subject to launch orders from subterranean command posts at Rustrel and Reilhanette.[32] Three missile groups were planned in the 1965-70 program law, but budgetary cuts after 1968 prevented the last squadron from being established.

Missile-launching nuclear submarines have made up the third, and eventually most important, generation of the French nuclear force. Credits for developing the submarines were included in the 1960-64 program law, but progress was slow because of the need to design (unaided by the United States) an efficient reactor engine, and to await the production of enriched U-235 fuel from the Pierrelatte plant, which began operations only in 1967. The program originally envisaged three submarines, each carrying sixteen 1,500-mile range MSBS (*Mer-sol ballistique stratégique*), with the first sub entering service by 1969. But delays and budget restraints after 1968 meant that the first sub, *le Redoutable,* was not operational until 1971, and the second, *le Terrible,* until 1973. *La Foudroyant* and *l'Indomptable* subsequently joined the expanded fleet, and the fifth scheduled nuclear missile submarine, *le Tonnant,* was launched in September 1977, and entered service in May 1980.[33]

The *Forces d'intervention* were designed as the land-air-sea conventional wing of the Fifth Republic's armed forces system. Because of the budgetary priority accorded the nuclear delivery system after 1960, conventional forces, especially in the army, underwent drastic cuts in personnel and a slow modernization effort.[34] Between January 1962 and January 1967, the army was reduced from 1,023,000 personnel to 581,000, a loss of 43 percent. By 1971, all active members of the French armed forces totaled 557,832, reduced from 1,046,883 in 1960.[35] This loss of personnel, concentrated in army enlisted men, but also affecting the other services, was a natural consequence of the end of hostilities in Algeria, and de Gaulle's decision to base France's defense on strategic nuclear weapons and limit the conventional forces essentially to a support function. This role was defined succinctly by General Ailleret. "The classic forces of infantry, aviation, armor, artillery of a nuclear army [have] no more than the role of covering, exploiting, and concluding atomic actions."[36] France's intervention forces were thus granted only the limited missions of assuring the security of the nuclear reprisal forces, of attacking in conjunction with a nuclear strike, and of mopping up the enemy following such a strike.

For the army's share in this system, the 1960-64 program law foresaw five divisions of the "1959-type," or combined infantry and armored brigades capable of carrying on a self-sustaining battle in a nuclear environment.[37] In 1963, Armed Forces Minister Pierre Messmer indicated that these divisions would not be constituted at their full strength, but would approach the size of the 1959-type. At that time, only the two divisions in West Germany (six brigades) had been partially modernized, and three light divisions (two brigades each) set up in France, mostly with old equipment.[38] All five divisions were scheduled for completion in 1965, but a failure to produce enough armored vehicles and light tanks prevented this and, in 1966, only four of the new divisions existed. Severe budget restrictions for conventional forces in the 1965-70 program law led the government to decide, in July 1967, to create a fifth division by reducing the other four to 80 percent of their strength. Thus, a division counted only 14,000 men equipped with AMX-30 medium and AMX-13 light tanks. Deliveries of AMX-30 tanks were far behind schedule, however, so that by 1970 the army had only 496 of the 995 tanks foreseen in the 1965-70 program.[39] In addition, the army had a sixth division equipped for overseas action, and about 15,000 troops stationed in Africa.

The air force's share of the *Forces d'intervention* consisted of two tactical air forces (CATAC). The first CATAC was based in northeastern France and, until 1966, was integrated into the NATO air defense system. By 1963, it was equipped with a reconnaissance squadron, seven fighter squadrons (F-84, RF-84, F-100, and Mirage III planes), and two brigades for launching Nike missiles. The second CATAC was slowly formed out of matériel brought back from Algeria, then progressively modernized. Finally, naval forces were withdrawn from the Mediterranean under de Gaulle and reconstituted as a primarily Atlantic fleet of 250,000 tons and 270 naval aircraft. Its role was to guard France's coastal areas and, eventually, to protect the nuclear missile-launching submarines due to be stationed at Brest. Because of the priority accorded to nuclear submarine construction, the strength of conventional naval forces suffered along with that of the army. This situation was the object of much discontent and led to the resignation of the naval Chief of Staff, Admiral Patou, in 1970.

Whereas the air force and navy had relatively clear and defined roles in the nuclear-centered defense system, with their Mirage IV planes, missiles, and nuclear submarines to operate and defend, the same was not true of the army. The integration of the services mandated by the new structure presumably gave all three branches a closely coordinated mission in the nuclear defense of the Métropole, but the army confronted the special dilemma of ending its traditional reliance on manpower without the compensation of a clearly defined position in either the defense structure or strategy. The reliance on strategic nuclear deterrence and quick retaliation left little scope for the combat activities of the five land divisions, which were, in any case, too few to defend single-handedly France's eastern border. Close cooperation with NATO might have circumvented or mitigated this problem, but it was not an available option. Another way to give the army a more satisfying and potent share in the new defense system would have been to provide it with tactical nuclear weapons, even though French strategy had no real mission for them—because the government then officially eschewed anything approaching the American doctrine of flexible response, or an extended ladder of escalation. Although tactical nuclear weapons were not included in the 1960-64 program law, army pressure led Messmer to promise in 1963 that they would be developed.[40] General Ailleret later indicated that this was to compensate the army for extensive reductions in its manpower.[41] After a dispute between the army and the air force, both services were granted tactical nuclear weapons, although the original target date of 1970 was postponed until 1973-74.[42] These weapons have posed a strategic dilemma for successive French governments, a problem that will be discussed in chapter five.

The third part of France's military defense structure, the *Défense opéra-tionelle du territoire* (D.O.T.), was of minor significance in the nuclear-centered Gaullist defense system. According to Messmer, the mission of the D.O.T. was one of "annihilating emeny elements that would succeed in gaining a foothold on national soil or which would attempt to penetrate it under any form and by any means whatsoever."[43] If France were invaded or occupied, the D.O.T. was to wage guerrilla warfare, as the Resistance had done in World War II; also, General Ailleret indicated it could counteract (presumably leftist) subversion in times of crisis.[44] The most pressing motive for the projected 500,000-man D.O.T. force was to keep the army in business and sustain compulsory military service, as a device for implanting patriotic values in French youth. Most draftees were to have gone into the D.O.T. after 1971, leaving the professional *"armée de métier"* for volunteers. But delays in organization and matériel subverted this goal, and by 1972 the D.O.T. had only 56,000 troops dispersed among two alpine brigades, twenty-five infantry battalions, three armed cavalry regiments, and one artillery regiment. Nor was the army able to solve the problem of how to put its conscripts into profitable and interesting work in an increasingly technical and professional military service—a dilemma that led to an extended crisis in the ranks during the 1970s.[45]

After 1960, then, the components of the *Force nucléaire stratégique* progressively became the focus of France's national defense, and both conventional and tactical nuclear capabilities were developed in accordance with the emphasis placed on strategic nuclear deterrence. Although progress in all three defense sectors was subject to delays for a variety of reasons—research problems, competing budget priorities, and the financial and fiscal crisis after May 1968—the distinct trend was to sacrifice interventionary and territorial defense in favor of the strategic nuclear force. Despite questions that might be raised about the nuclear force's military-strategic value, France's defense structure virtually dictated reliance on it, for both deterrence and defense purposes. Such a force structure was the consequence of a political decision to separate the defense of France from that of her NATO allies. This becomes apparent in the light of developments in French strategic thought about how and when the national forces are to be used, and what their relationship to the allied defense system ought to be.

National Nuclear Deterrence. The defense system described above was established for a number of political and strategic motives guided by the Gaullist insistence that a modern and independent military force was the prerequisite for France's revival. As an official defense policy statement asked rhetorically, "What other solution would permit France to survive as an independent political entity on the international scene?"[46] There was also, however, a somewhat unstructured body of French strategic views and doctrines that reinforced political motivations, and justified the creation of a national nuclear force independent of close alliance ties and restraints.

General Pierre Gallois's concept of "proportional deterrence" was perhaps closest to the official position that emerged during the 1960s, because it stressed absolute national deterrence—to the exclusion of mutual defense—in an alliance. Gallois argued that the atom was a "power equalizer" (*égalisateur de puissance*) that made even a small nuclear force an absolute deterrent because it could inflict unacceptable damage on a superpower.[47] The relative size of a nuclear force is unimportant, according to this theory. The only requirement is that the "destructive potential" of the reprisal be sufficient to make the risk of an attack incommensurate with the value the larger aggressor might place on the reward. If France could thus credibly threaten to destroy a number of Soviet cities in retaliation for Soviet aggression against the national territory, the deterrent is valid, even though all of France might be leveled in subsequent warfare.[48]

The logical corollary of this doctrine is that nuclear weapons are triggered only when an aggressor reaches the national territory, or clearly indicates his intention to attack it; thus, these weapons are a certain deterrent only for the defense of the state actually possessing and controlling them. According to Gallois, then, the deterrent threat is not valid unless the national state fully controls the means of reprisal. And, because the consequences are so destructive, the deterrent is credible only as a threatened response to an attack on that state's "vital interests," or the national territory.[49] It was this proposition, which Gallois applied to superpowers and medium powers alike, that invalidated an interdependent alliance defense and dictated that France should build her own nuclear force in the absence of a sure American guarantee. Carried to its extreme, the argument was that no state can depend on another for defense because each one's vital interests are distinctive in the nuclear age.

Although the French government never advocated the widespread proliferation of national nuclear forces implied by Gallois's theory, the notion of proportional deterrence was at the heart of official government strategy. General de Gaulle himself was not greatly concerned with providing elaborate strategic justifications for his defense programs, but he did, for example, adopt a minimal or proportional deterrence doctrine during a press conference on 23 July 1964. He said that France could not equal the nuclear strength of the United States or the Soviet Union, "but once reaching a certain nuclear capability, and with regard to one's own direct defense, the proportion of respective means has no absolute value. Indeed, since a man and people can die only once, the deterrent exists provided that one has the means to wound the possible aggressor mortally, that one is very determined to do it and that the aggressor is convinced of it."[50] The French government also underwrote the relative national isolation stressed in Gallois's views, as in a defense policy statement that asserted, "at the basis of deterrence by a medium-sized power, therefore, is found the clearly-expressed political will to defend, in the strongest sense of the term, the interests that it considers vital."[51] Gaullist diplomacy sometimes intimated that France's "vital interests" encompassed the territory to her east, in a way that the security of all of Europe could never be vital to the United States. But, as explained below, French strategy drew the critical line at the national border and made important distinctions between how and when to defend national and non-national territory.

The rather abstract and rigid views of General Gallois were subject to much criticism in and out of France. The critique was based partly on widespread doubts about the will and determination of a government with limited means to accept massive destruction as the consequence of responding with nuclear weapons to a less than massive attack.[52] Perhaps a more valid, subtle, and interesting French theory, which also supported the creation of a small nuclear force, was the one developed by General André Beaufre in various articles and his book *Deterrence and Strategy*.[53] Beaufre advanced the notion of "multilateral deterrence," arguing that a small independent nuclear force increased the uncertainty of a potential aggressor by confronting him with multiple centers of decision making, thereby enhancing the overall deterrent effect of the West's nuclear weapons. In a conflict between the superpowers, or between one of them and a third allied nuclear power, the latter, according to Beaufre, "has strategic consequences out of all proportion to [its] nuclear strength," because an aggressor cannot take the risk that a small ally will not trigger the nuclear force of its great power ally.[54] Thus, the existence of small nuclear forces in Europe counteracts the natural tendency of the superpowers to avoid a nuclear confrontation between themselves, and restores security to zones of marginal interest to a superpower protector such as Western Europe.

This argument was specifically predicated on the assumption that the superpower and its small nuclear-armed ally remain linked through an alliance, and it posed an "absolute prerequisite" that the national nuclear forces be voluntarily coordinated. Rather than requiring absolute autonomy, Beaufre said, a situation of multilateral deterrence called for increased cooperation among allies, because without it the deterrent value of the third force was severely weakened.[55] This was in apparent contradiction with official French doctrine, as was Beaufre's contention that deterrence at the strategic nuclear level was enhanced by linking it with both conventional and tactical nuclear weapons. Nevertheless, from a practical point of view, French strategy did coincide with Beaufre's theories more than those of Gallois, because French security policy always rested on the (sometimes invisible) assumption that an Atlantic Alliance and a (weakened) American nuclear guarantee would continue to cover Western Europe and France. Thus, while a French nuclear force might always expand and eventually become a more genuinely independent deterrent, its actual value was to serve as a semiautonomous trigger for the massive American strategic armory.

Although they emphasized the politically useful and theoretical independence of the French nuclear force, General de Gaulle and other government figures never lost sight of its more realistic function as a potential trigger for the American deterrent. Premier Pompidou told the National Assembly, late in 1964, that the Atlantic Alliance was doubtless a guarantee of final victory in a war, but the United States' own vulnerability prevented it from fully deterring an attack on Europe. Thus, although the French nuclear force could not altogether replace the American guarantee, it did reinforce an eroding American protection.[56] A report by the National Defense Committee of the National Assembly, written by Alexandre Sanguinetti, contained even blunter statements to this effect, stressing that France wanted "to be able to deny the great powers the delights of conventional war on the soil of Western Europe, considered the private preserve of the rivalries of champions thereby safeguarding their own territory."[57] Even during the acme of French alienation from the United States, over the Vietnam intervention and its risk to global peace, de Gaulle argued that his nuclear weapons protected France, not in isolation, but because they ensured that a war in Europe would rapidly escalate to the global strategic level and involve the homelands of the superpowers. If the superpowers intended to use Europe as a surrogate battlefield, he said in 1967, "France would not automatically be the humble auxiliary of one of them and would spare herself the chance of becoming nothing more than a battlefield for their expeditionary forces and a target for their exchanges of bombs."[58] Gaullist security policy, then, took the maintenance of some alliance ties for granted as the basis for linking semiindependent national means with the benefits of an Atlantic security zone. Unlike Beaufre, however, de Gaulle decided that the coordination of nuclear forces proposed in his 1958 memorandum was not feasible, or even desirable, during a period of antagonism with the United States, when maximum autonomy was a preferable basis for security. This did not preclude closer cooperation, or informal coordination, when interests were more in tandem, as was the case again after 1968; but France's independent status to decide when and how to collaborate was considered her most valuable and enduring contribution to European and general Western security.

Until 1969, French strategic views stressed an absolute form of deterrence reminiscent of the discredited massive retaliation doctrine of an earlier era.

This was partly in reaction to the unpopular American flexible response guidelines for warfare in Europe, partly because the notion of proportional deterrence required the menace of immediate reprisal against an aggressor's cities, but principally because the small and nuclear-centered military capability of a France outside of NATO virtually required a theoretical reliance on absolute deterrence rather than on more sophisticated alternatives. As General Ailleret told the NATO Defense College in June 1965, the flexible response strategy was inappropriate for the densely populated and narrow West European theater, given the imbalance of forces there and the massive destruction a conventional or tactical nuclear defense would entail.[59] Nor was the threat of escalation through several levels of response a valid defense strategy, he contended, and instead advocated reliance on immediate and massive nuclear retaliation that would also spare Europe from a prolonged war. Most Europeans, especially the West Germans, shared French reservations about U.S. doctrines and favored relatively rapid recourse to at least tactical nuclear weapons, but there was little support outside France for the nearly instantaneous strategic warfare included in French planning.

For France, however, the threat of a counter-city retaliation, for an aggressor's violation of the national territory, was the only feasible basis for national deterrence in the 1960s. Armed Forces Minister Messmer dismissed American counterforce ideas as a luxury unavailable to France, because "with [France's] means, the only objectives that have a deterrent value are the population objectives; to aim for missile sites would be an absurdity."[60] Immediate and full reprisal was therefore necessary and, once deterrence had failed, the French strategic force was designed "to strike within the shortest possible time with the most powerful nuclear explosives the designated enemy objectives."[61] Ailleret was willing to admit, in 1967, that a full range of armaments and escalation strategies was useful from the point of view of the superpowers, because "no one can know for sure how a conflict might arise today in which either or both of the giant powers could participate." But, he added, a small power like France, with limited resources, could only depend on a strategic nuclear force.[62]

French defense strategy was, therefore, left with a narrow range of alternatives, because nonintegration in NATO precluded active and continuous cooperation with other forces, and because France's own limited military resources were focused on creating an independent strategic nuclear force suitable only for instantaneous attack on population targets. Such an inadequate range of responses to aggression against France and nearby territory was a sort of nuclear Maginot line that potentially left the government with uncomfortable choices between surrender or annihilation. This was never the real case, however, because NATO's position between France and the only feasible aggressor guaranteed that an attack would meet other forms of response, and engage American forces before French national security was directly at stake. Paris was quite aware that geography and the American presence in West Germany protected the country. In a memorandum circulated at the Quai d'Orsay at the time of the NATO withdrawal, France's reliance on American protection in the event of a nonstrategic Soviet attack was quite explicit: "If the hypothesis (practically impossible) of a Soviet conventional aggression is nevertheless evoked, it would evidently not first aim at France. Germany is situated in front of France, and there the presence of American troops could not fail to throw the United States into the conflict."[63] Considering the realistic assessments that underlie Gaullist rhetoric, France's austere and tenuous deterrence strategy, and apparent isolation in Europe, were primarily political weapons dictated by poverty of resources and transitory international circumstances. Indeed, French policy was soon modified as a wider range of French military resources became available and as conflicts with Atlantic allies subsided in scope and intensity under de Gaulle and his successors.

Until 1969, however, adherence to the rigid doctrine of automatic strategic nuclear retaliation led government spokesmen to downgrade the role of national conventional forces and to draw awkward distinctions between national and external security zones. Through General Ailleret's tenure as chief of staff, French conventional forces were limited to protecting the strategic nuclear force and meeting advancing enemy units, determining their intention to attack French territory, and thereby triggering a nuclear retaliation against the homeland of the aggressor.[64] The initial engagement of conventional armed forces was to determine if an attack was an *"aggression caracterisée,"* the first stage of an extensive penetration into Europe and onto French soil, or an *"aggression apparentée,"* a mere frontier incident. A government defense policy statement described the role of air defense in similar terms: "Their maneuvers must by priority aim at establishing a threshold whose violation cannot be the result of an error of a mere foray, but of a clearcut aggression."[65] In other words, under these guidelines, *any* attack, conventional or nuclear, clearly heading toward France would automatically trigger the national nuclear deterrent. By unmistakable implication, *only* an action actually threatening France herself could engage France's armed forces, and eventually the nuclear force. This was quite different from the distinction the United States and NATO drew between major and minor aggressions; major aggressions were actions aimed at the occupation of a strategic point in Western Europe. For France, an attack on West Germany was "major" only if it was definitely headed for the Rhine, with no sign of stopping before it reached French soil. This strategy was distressing for the Federal Republic, because it presupposed the prior destruction of much of its territory before France could be counted on to enter the fray. To be sure, NATO's doctrine of forward defense designated France as a supply depot and source of reserve forces, but her battle-ready air and land units had been expected to meet an aggression across the German frontier, along with the rest of the allies. By the mid-1960s, however, the unity of Western Europe as a strategic theater, particularly on the central front, was disrupted as the critical line of defense for France was drawn at her own eastern border and the Rhineland approaches.

This aspect of French defense strategy could not be stated forthrightly by Paris, especially before 1966, but it was hinted at in references to "two battles" for Europe, the first of which was the "battle for Germany." General de Gaulle seemed to endorse the concept during a February 1963 speech before the Ecole Militaire. He mentioned as a prospect "the battle of Germany, the first battle of the war," and added that if it should go badly, with or without atomic weapons, France would then be invaded. Referring to the second battle, of France herself, he cited it and it alone as the reason why France had to have her own atomic weapons, or "the capability of confronting the invader, should the occasion arise, with a national resistance on our own territory."[66] There were also more concrete indications that France was adopting this concept before the withdrawal from NATO in 1966. During 1963, for example, French army maneuvers in the Jura region were based on plans that envisaged bombarding West Germany while French forces remained out of direct fire on the western side of the Rhine. This war game scenario was the object of protests from West Germany.[67] Later, in June 1965, another dispute erupted over France's failure to station her troops in accordance with NATO's forward defense strategy. At a meeting on 4 June, between defense ministers Messmer and von Hassel in Bonn, the latter complained that France had not moved a portion of her forces to the Straubing section of Bavaria nearer the Czech frontier, as had been planned. He rejected the French excuse that adequate installations were not available, because American facilities there had only recently been vacated. It is clear that the troops were not moved because such a position had no logical role in a defense policy already predicated on a withdrawal from NATO and noninvolvement in a West European forward defense.

There were suggestions that, after 1965, this aspect of Gaullist strategy and defense policy raised the possibility of political-military neutrality as a feasible status for a France outside of NATO.[68] Although de Gaulle himself dismissed and denigrated the role of armed but passive neutrality on the Swiss, Austrian, or Swedish models, he did evidently want to provide France with the capacity to exercise an option of nonbelligerency in the event of a military conflict in Europe in which the nation's vital interests were not engaged. This was not neutralism, because an independent and nuclear-armed France had the means of entering a conflict in strength or, according to government decisions based on the particular circumstances, the nation could avoid the automatic engagement implicit in full NATO membership and, through nuclear deterrence, attempt to remain aloof or apart from military exchanges.

The option of nonbelligerency, in the event of an American-inspired war reaching into Europe, was indeed cited by numerous French leaders as a prominent motive for withdrawing from NATO. As explained earlier, de Gaulle had perceived such a danger as early as the 1958 incidents in the Middle East and Asia, but the Vietnam War presented the timely and compelling example of a remote local conflict that could escalate into a global nuclear war. During the presidential election campaign in December 1965, de Gaulle linked French opposition to this war with both the national nuclear force and the imminent withdrawal from NATO. Referring to the need to end all armed conflicts that could escalate into nuclear exchanges, he said that France was acquiring her own means of deterrence and protection, and therefore could refuse to be "integrated in a war that she had not wanted, on the pretext of European or Atlantic integration."[69] The specific fear, expressed later to justify the actions against NATO, was that the United States might be led into armed hostilities with China, which could provoke a Soviet intervention in Asia and quickly spread to involve all American allies and territory hosting American troops. Premier Pompidou cited this hypothesis in 1966 as a reason for the expulsion of NATO and American forces from France.[70] Vietnam and unchecked American global activism were evidently important factors behind the General's NATO decisions, for he stressed in February 1966 that, whereas a world war was unlikely to start in Europe, American conflicts in Korea, Cuba, or Vietnam "risk, by virtue of that famous escalation, being extended so that the result could be a general conflagration. In that case Europe—whose strategy is, within NATO, that of America, would be automatically involved in the struggle, even when it would not have so desired."[71]

In the context of such considerations, the 1966 partial withdrawal from NATO, backed by national nuclear weapons, was undertaken partly to enhance the possibility that France might remain aloof from hostilities in Europe if her own territory were not immediately attacked or her own interests at stake. As outlined by one close observer, the French position was that in a crisis France was initially protected by the Alliance, but, being outside the military organization, she was not in immediate danger and might, therefore, play the role of mediator. If armed conflict broke out, Paris could consider declaring neutrality, backed by the threat of strategic nuclear retaliation, or of joining NATO forces with or without engaging the *force de frappe,* depending on how close the fighting came to French soil. An all-out spasm nuclear war would obviously involve France immediately, and she would have to join in with all her resources.[72] This was a loose and flexible form of alliance engagement, in which the state's political and military orientation may be decided according to particular circumstances and conflicts. De Gaulle expressed the new policy in a modification of French commitments under Article V of the North Atlantic Treaty. His formula first appeared in a handwritten note to President Johnson, dated 7 March 1966, in which he noted that despite the withdrawal France would remain a member of the Alliance and would "fight at the side of her allies in the event that one of them would be the object of *unprovoked aggression.*"[73] This new position was not in conflict with the vague obligations of the Atlantic Treaty but, under the circumstances, the expression did lend an additional dimension to the NATO withdrawal by emphasizing that an independent France had acquired the right to assess carefully future casus belli and then decide on her own reactions.

The globalization of Gaullist diplomacy, and the arguments just outlined, are evidence that the withdrawal from NATO was in part precipitated by the feeling that, in the age of intercontinental nuclear weapons, the physical security of France and Europe could be affected by events anywhere in the world. Thus, security in the narrow NATO forum, as de Gaulle had asserted in his memorandum policy, could not be reconciled with the dangers of global nuclear escalation. Nor, when there was such a variety of possible threats, could France's military strategy and defense focus exclusively on confronting an attack from the East. Such a limited perspective was particularly inappropriate in an era of Franco-Soviet détente and, in 1966, one French accusation against NATO was that the Alliance envisaged only this kind of threat. In the course of explaining the reasons behind the withdrawal, an information bulletin of the Armed Forces Ministry noted that "France is a medium-sized power that has maintained her own interests throughout the world. The military policy of France, which is only one aspect of her general policy, wants to avoid NATO crystallizing forever the hypothesis of a Soviet aggression in Europe as the only possible military problem."[74] Because French military strategy was, the ministry noted, increasingly concerned with "some other hypotheses that could become more real," full membership in NATO had become a burden. Following the 1966 withdrawal, then, additional efforts were made to divert French military thinking away from NATO's limited horizons.

The consequence of this effort—the short-lived notion of a French defense structure directed against attacks from anywhere on earth—was, of course, scarcely an innovation in France. Extra-European threats not covered by NATO had preoccupied the Fourth Republic, were a focus of de Gaulle's memorandum diplomacy, and had long been a subject of discussion within the French general staffs. A global defense policy had been de Gaulle's announced aim since at least 1959, when he noted that because France could be destroyed from any point on the globe, its "force must be made to act anywhere on earth."[75] But the concept achieved a sensational notoriety principally because of General Ailleret's article of December 1967, entitled "Défense 'dirigée' ou défense 'tous azimuts.'"[76] Ailleret noted that whereas the possibility of Soviet aggression in Europe had declined greatly, nuclear proliferation and instability in Asia, Africa, the Middle East, and South America made it increasingly likely that a war could originate in parts of the globe other than Europe. Thus, France faced the risk of attack by an adversary "who wanted to use [her] territory or [her] resources in the struggle," or could be "attacked and destroyed from a distance by one of the belligerents who wanted to prevent his enemy from using [France's] soil and resources." He offered the conclusion that France had to possess a nuclear force of ICBMs capable of deterring "anyone acting in any part of the world, who wanted to make use of [France] or destroy [her] in order to assist the achievement of their war aims." This force, the French Chief of Staff wrote, should be capable of striking anywhere, i.e., in "all directions."

This article and the policy options then under consideration had important implications for the future development of France's military forces and her political alignments, but none of them was realized; the entire project was stillborn despite initial publicity. An "all-direction" defense system for the armed forces was indeed confirmed as official policy by de Gaulle on 28 January 1968,[77] and Pierre Messmer later stated that the government was considering the development of an ICBM force as a third-generation nuclear deterrent, subject to financial considerations.[78] A number of possibilities were then being contemplated, including land-based missiles with a 5,000-6,000 mile range, sea-based missiles, or a combination of the two. There were, however, no plans for taking immediate production decisions, and the government was only considering the possible allocation of research credits in the budget program law for 1970-75.[79] One reason for caution was the emergence of strong opposition to the project within the government. De Gaulle and Ailleret favored it, and the latter had even decided to sacrifice tactical nuclear weapons for an ICBM force if that proved necessary for budgetary reasons. But Messmer, Couve de Murville, and Debré (then Minister of Economy and Finance) were all skeptical of France's financial ability to support such an ambitious and expensive program. During this period, Debré told de Gaulle that the missiles were a financial "impossibility" for France and, furthermore, were militarily unnecessary for the conceivable future.[80] De Gaulle's support would doubtless have carried the project forward in this initial stage, but the economic and financial crisis after May 1968 had a debilitating impact on the budget and government resources, and thereby completely eliminated the ICBM option. Instead, the government decided to study the more feasible idea of increasing the range of the IRBM force already under development.

The political-strategic rationale for the Ailleret doctrine was to convince France's armed forces that they could no longer orient their defense efforts toward one overriding menace from the east—once Germany, more recently the Soviet Union.[81] Associates of General Ailleret indicated that China and the Arab states were the menaces that most preoccupied him. But Ailleret's references to deterring attacks by any state wanting to use France as a surrogate battlefield were reminiscent of Gaullist charges against Washington, and led to speculation that the United States was a possible, or even likely, object of a global French deterrent force. Because in 1969 the French could legally denounce the Atlantic Treaty and sever all remaining ties to the Alliance, the *tous azimuts* doctrine was interpreted as a possible step toward armed, active, and full neutrality.[82] There is no convincing evidence, however, that such a drastic move was seriously contemplated. In any case, the ICBM force was quickly interred and, more important, the invasion of Czechoslovakia in August 1968 refocused French attention and strategy on the Eastern threat and restored a lagging interest in the Alliance. Although the Ailleret doctrine had almost no practical significance, it did subsequently become a symbol of the most extreme neutralist strand in French diplomacy and strategy. It has been adopted by the communist left and interpreted as a diplomatic posture of maximum alienation from the United States, West Germany, and the Alliance, and as a military strategy eschewing predesignated targeting against the Soviet Union and the East bloc.[83] The Gaullist regime evidently did not contemplate such a drastic isolation and withdrawal from the West, but it did furnish the slogan and a theory of independence subject to this exaggerated interpretation.

The French Withdrawal from NATO

Military Noncooperation, 1958-1965.   According to political, military, and strategic trends in French policy under de Gaulle, "independence" entailed the exclusion of foreign influence over France's foreign policy and required that she recover control over the armed forces to reinforce and serve the political decisions of the state. Furthermore, it implied that a resolve to engage in hostilities along with the allies should depend on a free decision reached by responsible civilian authorities at the time. There could thus be no binding prior commitments and no blind submission to the force of events, because of either military integration or the presence of foreign military installations in France. The full consequences of this policy were spelled out clearly in 1966, but well before then the consequences had guided developments in strategy, force structure, and successive restrictions placed on France's participation in NATO. The years before 1966, then, were marked by a steady effort to reduce French involvement in NATO defense activities. The policy of noncooperation included a refusal to permit the deployment of American-controlled tactical nuclear weapons, restrictions on French integration in NATO's air defense network, the withdrawal of the French navy and naval personnel from NATO, and other measures that foreshadowed the major actions of 1966.

The tactical nuclear weapons issue was brought up earlier in this study, in connection with Fourth Republic policy and the 1958 memorandum. The problem arose as a result of the North Atlantic Council decision of December 1957 to supply allies with the arms, stockpiled under American guard and released only by American presidential authority. The principal motives were to compensate for the West's inferior military strength in Europe and their lack of intercontinental missiles, and to enable NATO to resist a Soviet move without immediate recourse to strategic weapons. French policy, set by the Gaillard government, was not to accept the arms except under conditions of actual French control and perhaps American aid to the French atomic weapons program. De Gaulle confirmed these demands and expanded them in his memorandum. The impasse over the tripartite proposals led to a final government decision, in early June of 1959, not to allow the arms on French soil.

One result of this decision was the first major transfer of NATO military forces from France, when General Norstad decided he had to move some 250 American Supersabre fighter-bombers from bases in France (Toul, Etain, and Chaumont) to an ally where they would have access to TNWs. After consultations with Whitehall, it was agreed that most of the planes would be stationed in England, with a double-key control system for their atomic weapons. SHAPE also considered a plan under which the planes would have returned to France periodically under a rotation system, without nuclear warheads, but it was apparently vetoed in Washington as impractical.[84] It was later revealed that in 1959, and again in 1960, during tense moments over the Berlin situation, SHAPE requested permission to supply remaining American planes in France with TNWs, but was turned down by the Paris government.[85] De Gaulle's decision on this issue was consistent with his subsequent policy of denying French territory to foreign military agents or arms if they might endanger France or restrict her independence. The outcome also reflected the pragmatism that was to characterize French military relations with NATO. For, while de Gaulle kept American atomic arms off of French soil, he was quite willing to let French forces stationed in Germany accept them. According to military sources, this was a concession to the air force's wish to obtain training in handling atomic warheads and delivery systems. In the summer of 1960, then, France's First CATAC units in West Germany formed a Nike missile batallion under American supervision. Of the two types of missiles furnished, the "Ajax" and the "Hercules," the latter could carry an atomic warhead.[86]

Problems arising from the need to integrate West Europe's air defense facilities were more complicated than those that surrounded TNWs, although similar compromises between French and NATO interests were also reached here. SHAPE had long recognized that the small size of European countries, the high speed of jet planes, and NATO's proximity to Soviet air bases in East Germany made integration of national capabilities a practical necessity. Plans for the integration of detection, information processing, air alert, and retaliation procedures under SACEUR's authority had been developed by 1957, but implementation was held up first by the Fourth Republic and then by de Gaulle's own opposition to including France in these plans. The need for speedy decision making in the event of a crisis and attack made tighter defense integration seem necessary to figures at NATO, but to de Gaulle it was an additional infringement on national political control over the actions of France's armed forces. The French military, including Marshall Juin, did attempt to sway the General's thinking, and in the summer of 1958 General Norstad made an elaborate presentation that he thought had won de Gaulle over to including all of France in the proposed system.[87] As part of this campaign, French air force generals, first Chassin and then Pélissié, were appointed "air defense coordinators" for the Central Europe command at Fontainebleau, although a British air marshall was still their superior.[88]

De Gaulle resisted these efforts but, at an Atlantic Council meeting in December 1958, his government did consent to place its First CATAC of approximately 250 planes, already under NATO authority, within the framework of an extended air defense command. The apparent concession was hedged with important qualifications, however, for Paris had reserved the right not to follow SACEUR's orders in a crisis if they failed to coincide with French decisions. This was confirmed on 6 December 1959 by the First CATAC's commander, General Brohon, who stated that, for France, NATO integration stopped at the power to order deployments and issue a command to open fire.[89] France's special status remained essentially the same even after a 1960 Atlantic Council decision to create a fully integrated air defense system under the command and control of SACEUR. According to the France-NATO agreement signed in September 1960, only a small sector of northeastern France was included in the geographical scope of the new command, and French planes there and in West Germany were "integrated" only up to the order to open fire, an act that would require the express consent of the French government.[90]

Although this move contradicted de Gaulle's general guideline of not undertaking new engagements in NATO or the Alliance unless his political demands were met, France evidently joined the air defense arrangement mainly because she needed access to the new allied early-warning system. Installed between 1960 and 1963, the first generation NADGE (NATO Air Defense Ground Environment) was a chain of high performance radars that functioned as a coordinated air detection system. Data from this network and its American 412-L computers were automatically fed into the French Strida-II computers at the national air defense center at Drachenbronn in the Vosges. The French system received only reports from NADGE, however, and was designed to cut out at the point where SHAPE's four regional air defense headquarters began issuing commands and controlling allied air responses.[91] The dependence on NATO for warnings of an enemy air attack enabled France to overcome political reservations about the link, and this form of cooperation was to be maintained even after 1966.

The withdrawals of the navy and naval personnel from assignment to

NATO were important precedents; first, because they were the initial steps in removing forces from NATO integration and, second, because the postwithdrawal relations between the French navy and NATO commands were similar in nature to those set up after 1966 for all of France's armed forces. The withdrawal of the Mediterranean fleet in March 1959 was preceded by much speculation that France was about to request an extension of NATO activities in the region, though under French control. The Gaillard government had been considering a reorganization of Mediterranean defense when efforts were cut short by its demise on 16 April 1958. General de Gaulle's first initiative in this respect was to create the French post of Commander-in-Chief for the Mediterranean in December 1958. Its first occupant, Admiral Auboyneau, was charged with responsibility for the Mediterranean fleet and for maritime security along the strategic triangle of Toulon—Mers-el-Kébir—Bizerte, considered by France strategists to be part of the "grand axis" of Paris-Brazzaville-Dakar.[92] Because the admiral was also part of NATO's AFSOUTH command and, in this capacity, partly responsible for interallied forces in the western Mediterranean,[93] his appointment to the new French post fed speculation that de Gaulle wanted him placed in charge of a new, upgraded NATO zone in the western Mediterranean.[94] Much of the French military had for years been agitating for NATO to establish a second full Mediterranean command and allocate it to France;[95] thus, French officers revived the idea at SHAPE in February 1959 and carried on several weeks of discussions about it there. The government itself, however, did not make such a request of NATO and apparently never intended to, because de Gaulle was not interested in the creation of a new integrated NATO command, even one headed by a French officer. Thus, after what de Gaulle saw as the failure of the February tripartite discussions in Washington, he decided to remove the Mediterranean fleet from NATO jurisdiction altogether—or, more precisely, the third of it that had actually been "earmarked" for NATO duties in time of crisis.[96]

Official French explanations for the move concentrated on France's North African priorities, noting that the action had almost no practical effect and only meant that in wartime all the French fleet in the area would remain under national command, although it could still cooperate with allied naval forces.[97] General de Gaulle echoed these justifications, adding that France was only emulating the United States and Britain, both of whom kept most of their fleets outside of NATO.[98] Later, he added that France could scarcely have allowed her fleet, destined to maintain links with Africa, to remain under the authority of an organization exclusively concerned with defense in Europe.[99] Because the fleet withdrawal was mostly a symbolic maneuver with little actual effect on allied activities in the region, the reaction in NATO circles and Alliance capitals was subdued.[100] During the summer of 1959, the French fleet participated in NATO naval exercises as usual, although its maneuvers were combined with a grand tour of North African cities, which was arranged to demonstrate French grandeur in the Mediterranean to both NATO and the Algerians.[101] The following February, NATO and the French navy arrived at an agreement for coordinating their activities in the region; this established the guidelines for French participation in future allied naval maneuvers.

Although Couve de Murville told the National Assembly that the Mediterranean fleet action was the only change the government could foresee in its ties to NATO,[102] four years later, in 1963, the Atlantic fleet was also removed from the authority of the Alliance. As with the previous action, there was no advance warning or consultation. The government simply eliminated its Atlantic ships from a 15 June reply to the routine Annual Review questionnaire, designed to indicate which forces would be at NATO's disposition during the coming year.[103] The report was received just before President Kennedy was to leave for a European tour, and was doubtless intended to remind him of France's determination to pursue equality in the Alliance. The decision to recover national authority in the Atlantic was also prompted by long-range plans to move a major part of the Mediterranean fleet and station it on the Atlantic Coast at Ponant.[104] These ships had not been under NATO since 1959, but Paris seemed to be clearing the books in anticipation of a greater French presence in the Atlantic, which was eventually to include nuclear submarines. Again, the effect on NATO was a minor one. Within the Atlantic Command (SACLANT), which was responsible directly to the Standing Group and not to SHAPE, France had handled only the small Gulf of Gascony sector; her Atlantic fleet in 1963 consisted of only five submarines and a light escort squadron, both based at Lorient.[105] Further minimizing the impact of the withdrawal, after 1963 these submarines remained closely linked to SACLANT headquarters at Norfolk, Virginia, and continued to participate in NATO Atlantic exercises.[106] After the withdrawal took effect on 1 January 1964, the submarines took their usual place in NATO's "teamwork" maneuvers, under cooperation guidelines signed by SACLANT and the French Commander-in-Chief for the Atlantic on 14 February 1964.

Once the entire French navy had been relieved of all formal NATO authority over its activities, the assignment of French naval personnel to NATO staffs no longer served any purpose. Paris left the post of Naval Deputy to SACEUR unfilled after the death of Admiral Barjot late in 1963, and began to boycott the regular meetings of the Channel Committee in early 1964. It was therefore no surprise when Admiral Douguet, French representative to the Standing Group, notified his colleagues, on 7 April 1964, that all French naval personnel were to be withdrawn from the integrated staffs because the navy was no longer under NATO authority.[107] The change did not affect Admiral Douguet, but it did withdraw NATO titles from French officers in the Atlantic, Mediterranean (SHAPE), and Channel commands. A French government communiqué on 28 April noted that close liaison arrangements would be set up between the navy and NATO, although Pierre Messmer added that "henceforth no French naval command will have any kind of subordination to or participation in an organ of the NATO command."[108] For the naval officers concerned, however, the altered status amounted largely to a change in title—from "allied officer" to "national representative"—or liaison between the French naval staff and the NATO commands. They and their successors remained at their posts and continued to perform much the same tasks as before.[109]

Although this was the last overt French military withdrawal from NATO before the main event in 1966, there were some final examples of military noncooperation during 1965 that augured a more significant disengagement. The most important was France's refusal to participate in the NATO fall military exercise for allied general staffs, named "Fallex '66." Fallex had been planned since 1964, over repeated French objections because it was based partly on a flexible response strategy for defending Europe. French representatives to the Atlantic Council had vetoed this as official Alliance strategy ever since the United States first proposed it in November 1963, and NATO remained theoretically committed to the massive retaliation doctrine. Designed to test allied communications networks and alert systems, Fallex violated the doctrine by planning a nonnuclear defense against Soviet aggression. The technical details of France's absence from the exercise were worked out by General Lyman Lemnitzer (SACEUR) and General Ailleret, in an agreement that kept all but a few French officers at SHAPE out of the process. A second signal of impending action was a change in the command structure of France's First CATAC, which was stationed in France and West Germany and integrated into NATO. A decree published on 4 August in the *Journal officiel* abolished the two command positions that had distinguished the First CATAC from the Second CATAC (national and unintegrated), putting them both under a single officer directly responsible to the Minister of Armed Forces. Although there was no immediate practical effect, the decree did lay the foundation for bringing the entire air force back under exclusive national command. Finally, officials in NATO's Defense Planning and Policy Division were made aware of a change in attitude at the end of 1965, when they received the French Armed Forces Ministry's response to questionnaires connected with the Annual Review planning process. Whereas the French had previously been at least as cooperative as other allies, this time only aggregate force levels were supplied and questions essential to NATO's long-range force planning were left unanswered.

Because of these signals and de Gaulle's numerous warnings, allied civilian and military officials were not caught entirely offguard in 1966, even though the disengagement came sooner and was more extensive than they anticipated. There were, however, very few specific precautions that could have been taken in the absence of a formal notification of France's intentions. Despite the steady decline in France's military and political cooperation with NATO, she remained a full member of the Alliance, and the others could not openly plan in advance for an eventual separation. There was, for example, no formal discussion at NATO about defense plans that excluded French participation, although it was the subject of much private speculation. By 1965, Washington had drawn up contingency plans for defending Europe without a French contribution, but they were not communicated to NATO and were discussed privately with only a few allies.[110]

The United States also began taking preliminary steps to reduce its own dependence on French territory as a supply base, and to plan a more extensive evacuation. As early as Kennedy's European tour in the summer of 1963, the president asked General Lemnitzer about moving the oil pipeline out of France, but the idea was rejected as too costly.[111] Instead, an American logistics base at Verdun was closed later that year and moved to Bremerhaven, which was being transformed into a major American depot.[112] During 1965, the Defense Department apparently drew up detailed studies for a complete withdrawal of both American forces and allied military headquarters from France. Pending the necessity of implementing these plans, the Pentagon considered restoring some of its bases to French control and inquired of Belgium, the Netherlands, Britain, and Italy if they would become new hosts for the bases.[113] Three small airfields were turned back over to France in November, and the U.S. Army and Air Force headquarters buildings in Paris were shut down then, even though new sites had not yet been selected. Finally, in January 1966, McNamara announced a large-scale closing of 160 American military bases, including 23 abroad. This move affected several installations in France whose removal the following spring was not directly connected to the French ultimatum in March. Valid economic reasons were cited for this and other reductions in the American military presence in France, but it was scarcely coincidental that firmer allies in Europe were the recipients of transferred personnel and matériel which were not returned to the United States.

Disengagement and Crisis in the Alliance.   Before 1966, France's incremental withdrawal from NATO military activities, and de Gaulle's ritualistic denunciations of the Alliance's military integration, were thought by many to be part of a carefully managed scenario leading up to a grand formal proposal for revamping the whole Alliance structure.[114] This proposal was expected sometime before 1969, when the Atlantic Treaty could be denounced by any of its signatories. Most observers agreed with *Le Monde* that de Gaulle would not try "to withdraw in a spectacular fashion from the North Atlantic Treaty Organization. Such a development, with the disquieting consequences that it entails, would certainly be very badly accepted by the country."[115] The prevailing assumption that de Gaulle would have to present a formal and detailed *plaidoyer* and negotiate a revision in NATO was, however, an illusion. It is clear that the General made his one and only attempt to transform the Alliance by interallied diplomacy, rather than *fait accompli,* in the 1958 memorandum and its sequels. Nor did he intend to present a project directly to NATO, preferring to deal with the Alliance's dominant powers and France's natural interlocuters, the Anglo-Saxons, or to negotiate a European alternative with the continental allies outside of NATO forums.

The tripartite memorandum negotiations constitute, therefore, the only French attempt to transform the Alliance and eventually dismantle the system of military integration. No direct proposals along these lines were made then or afterward, however, because of obvious American unwillingness to consider them and because the hostile reactions of France's European partners to the memorandum proposals confirmed the impossibility of altering NATO from within.[116] The French were subsequently pressed several times to place their specific complaints about NATO and any proposals before the Atlantic Council, as Paul-Henri Spaak did in an exchange with Couve de Murville in May 1964. The unflappable French diplomat replied, however, that he had no criticism of Alliance political institutions and saw no sense in pursuing the problem of the military organization because there was no ground for compromise or agreement. Spaak received no support from the other foreign ministers present, evidently because they preferred the uneasy status quo to precipitating a formal break.[117] Later, Couve de Murville told the National Assembly that France had made her conception of the Alliance known to everyone, but the breach between her views and those of other allies was too wide to permit negotiations and compromise.[118] The memorandum proposals had been de Gaulle's design for a new Atlantic Alliance. When it became apparent that neither the Anglo-Saxons nor France's European neighbors were willing to consider it, there was no point in carrying out the memorandum's threat to invoke Article XII of the Atlantic Treaty and initiate a long and fruitless negotiation.

Apart from the partial and limited measures taken before 1966, de Gaulle's unilateral preparations for a more drastic rupture with NATO were not begun until the spring of 1965. Some of the reasons for the timing of these preparations have already been suggested: the failure of tripartite discussions by 1961; the collapse of French projects for a European union and eventual defense cooperation in 1962; the rapid demise during 1964 of the Franco-German entente because of the MLF and other issues; the onset of the crisis over the European Community and supranational integration in the spring of 1965; and the good prospects for expanding French ties to the East and even the Third World. The United States and the rest of Europe had demonstrated their determination to maintain NATO in its existing form and confirmed it by the welcome given to the American plan for nuclear consultation in May

1965. The potential success of what was to become the Nuclear Planning Group was apparent by the end of the year and marked France's isolation within the Alliance. The unsatisfactory denouement of France's Atlantic and European efforts argued for new tactics on a global scale, and the prospects for them were bound to be enhanced if accompanied by an impressive seizure of independence from the Atlantic and NATO hegemony. Another factor was French opposition to American military actions in Southeast Asia, which became more important after the bombing of North Vietnam had started in February 1965 and which seemed to enhance the risk of global escalation.[119] Other aggressive and ill-considered uses of American military power, especially the intervention in Santo Domingo in May 1965, only reinforced de Gaulle's fears.[120]

From the point of view of France's own military capabilities, de Gaulle could not have considered a substantial withdrawal from NATO before the end of the Algerian War in 1962 and until the new national defense structure had been set up. The first stage of a national defense was in place by early 1966, when the Mirage IV part of the nuclear deterrent became fully operational. The year 1966 was also convenient in terms of French domestic politics. It followed the presidential elections of 1965, which confirmed de Gaulle's mandate to carry out his policies, yet preceded the National Assembly elections of March 1967 by enough time to ensure that a NATO withdrawal would not still be a burning issue in France. Finally, de Gaulle's advancing age (he turned seventy-six on 22 November 1965) made it desirable to disengage France from NATO as soon as possible, to make this aspect of independence an irreversible accomplishment for his successors.[121]

Within the French executive offices and ministries, the process of determining how to manage a disengagement from NATO was begun in late May or early June of 1965. The entire operation was carried out in great secrecy. Only General de Gaulle, Couve de Murville, Pierre Messmer, and some of the small staff at the Elysée knew about its full scope and purpose. The relevant government services were asked for both general and detailed technical studies about the methods and consequences of a "possible" withdrawal from NATO or from the Alliance itself, the latter to include a denunciation of the Atlantic Treaty. According to one source, the documents that were produced posed a series of options, which extended from remaining in a NATO military organization with greater French authority over all allied forces in West Germany, to a complete separation of France from NATO itself, but not from the treaty.[122] According to the *conseiller diplomatique* at the Elysée who assembled the reports, the technical studies by the *Service des pactes* emphasized the difficulty of severing relations with NATO due to the various treaties, agreements, and military arrangements linking France to the Alliance system. The General himself was quite uninterested in such matters, and left it up to his own advisers to decide on the details of the partial disengagement, which was subject to his guidelines and final approval. The secrecy was so complete that, even after de Gaulle's first announcement in February 1966, the rest of the government remained uninformed about his actual plans. According to Harlan Cleveland, the Quai d'Orsay offices then began to prepare plans for a gradual French withdrawal and drew up notes to allies "suggesting" that NATO installations might consider relocating to other countries.[123] The crisper and more extensive Elysée project was not released until the notes to allies, dated 10 and 11 March, were given to the Quai for distribution to the recipients. The cabinet was given a general briefing on 9 March, and it was only at that point that the rest of the government was brought into the proceedings.[124]

Preoccupied by the EEC crisis between June and January and by an unexpectedly difficult presidential election campaign in the fall of 1965, de Gaulle and his associates made only a few discreet references to the NATO project before it was actually announced as a unilateral decision. In late August, de Gaulle told George Ball that within a year the status of foreign military bases in France would have to be changed; they would be closed or put under the command of French military officers.[125] Remarks made during a presidential press conference on 9 September 1965 indicated that Paris was contemplating a change in France's status in NATO, but de Gaulle gave no indication of imminent action and only mentioned 1969 as the outside date when he would terminate "the subordination known as 'integration' which is provided for by NATO and which hands [France's] fate over to foreign authority."[126] In December, NATO Secretary-General Manlio Brosio left a meeting with de Gaulle convinced that no decision had yet been made, and that one was not contemplated before the spring of 1968.[127] Further confusing France's allies, Couve de Murville had told Dean Rusk in October that France's position would be clarified the following spring, most likely in March.[128]

The results of the policy review initiated the previous spring were finally revealed in three stages: de Gaulle's press conference of 21 February 1966, the notes and memoranda distributed to allies between 7 and 11 March, and the detailed instructions to the other fourteen NATO members distributed by the Quai d'Orsay on 29 March. At his press conference, de Gaulle was not specific about the decisions that had been taken, but concentrated on justifying them in advance with his familiar analysis of the "new conditions" in international politics and in France's will to independence that naturally led her government to question the application of the Atlantic Treaty. Thus, he said, he had decided to modify the conditions governing France's participation in the Alliance beginning immediately through 4 April 1969, although the actions taken would not affect France's adherence to the basic treaty. As a hint of the practical consequences to follow, de Gaulle indicated that "it means re-established a normal situation of sovereignty, in which that which is France as regards soil, sky, and [armed] forces, and any foreign element that would be in France, will in the future be under French command alone."[129] This was characterized not as a rupture, "but a necessary adaptation," which would be taken in stages and be accompanied by new French-allied arrangements to facilitate cooperation in the event of conflict in Europe.

More specific consequences of this announcement were provided in messages written personally by de Gaulle, first to President Johnson on 7 March, followed by similar notes sent on 9 March to the heads of state or government in Britain, West Germany, and Italy. On 10 and 11 March, Hervé Alphand, secretary-general of the Quai d'Orsay, distributed more detailed memoranda to the ambassadors of the fourteen allies. This set the precedent for France's insistence on handling major problems raised by the withdrawal with allies bilaterally or multilaterally, and avoiding dealings with the Atlantic organizations as such (the council or secretariat). These notes outlined the consequences of the French government's decisions regarding its ties to NATO: (1) the termination of the assignment of all French land and air forces to Allied Command Europe and France's withdrawal from the integrated commands handling these forces, ACE and AFCENT; (2) the transfer of the two commands' headquarters from French territory; and (3) to the United States and Canada, notice that under present conditions France would no longer accept "any foreign units, installations or bases in France being responsible in any respect whatever to authorities other than French authorities," and an invitation to study "the practical consequences" of the new French position.[130] This plainly meant expulsion, because the note mentioned the possibility of making the bases available to the United States and Canada in the event of a conflict in which both they and France participated.

The memoranda also indicated a willingness to set up liaison arrangements between NATO and the French commands and to determine the conditions under which French forces, particularly those in West Germany, would participate in joint wartime actions. Paris indicated that it would be willing to keep forces in Germany under the terms of the convention of 23 October 1954. Questions concerning France's relationship to the Military Committee and the Standing Group were also raised. Although a willingness to discuss the application of these decisions was expressed, the notes clearly constituted an ultimatum, and the allies were expected to comply and not try to negotiate. Negotiations, the memoranda stated, "would be doomed to failure, since France's partners appear to be or assert they are all advocates of maintaining the *status quo,* or else of strengthening everything which, from the French viewpoint, appears henceforth unacceptable."[131]

The responses and replies of the fourteen confirmed France's assessment of their intractability, and requests for more precise instructions were met with another memorandum distributed on 29 March. Once again, the fourteen texts were identical except for insertions applying specifically to the United

States, Canada, and West Germany. De Gaulle's demands were specified as follows: (1) on 1 July 1966, the assignment of French ground and air forces to ACE would be terminated and all French personnel withdrawn from SHAPE, AFCENT, and AFSOUTH; (2) French staff and students would be withdrawn from the NATO Defense College in Paris at the end of the term (23 July 1966); (3) 1 April 1967 was suggested as a feasible date for the removal from French territory of SHAPE, AFCENT, and the Defense College; (4) to the United States and Canada, the date of 1 April 1967 was also suggested as "appropriate" for completing the transfer of military forces and supply depots to other countries, although a longer period could be arranged for some of the more complicated American moving operations, and France offered to make a special provision enabling the United States to continue using the oil pipeline; and (5) to the Federal Republic, an offer was made to continue the stationing of French ground and air forces in West Germany, but only by virtue of the convention of 23 October 1954.[132]

The reactions of France's NATO allies to de Gaulle's decisions were at first somewhat tentative, then reflected a natural anger and exasperation in some quarters, but finally were subject to a general determination to cope with de Gaulle by not aggravating the situation unnecessarily. After the first notes were received, the permanent representatives at NATO met in an unofficial group of fourteen, without France, chaired by the Belgian André de Staercke. After ten days of debate, they put together a common declaration, which was published on 18 March.[133] It was a surprisingly weak affirmation of NATO's utility to their mutual security, perhaps because some members were then still uncertain about how far France was prepared to go and wanted to avoid making matters worse. The Netherlands urged the fourteen to take a very critical position, but countries such as Denmark, Canada, and Portugal preferred a cautious approach at the time.[134]

Responses from some of the individual governments were naturally more forthright. American policy was established right away by President Johnson, who wrote, in response to de Gaulle's personal communication of 7 March, that the French decisions raised "grave questions regarding the whole relationship between the responsibilities and benefits of the Alliance."[135] In a second reply, Johnson presented the American view that only the Alliance's organization ensured that the members would honor their commitments to aid each other in the event of an attack. The organization, he noted, also deterred such an attack by demonstrating both "military coherence" and "political unity of purpose." The United States did not consider that military integration impaired its sovereignty, nor that of France, because it contributed to their security. For this and other reasons, the president concluded that the military organization of the Alliance was indispensable. "For our part, we continue to believe that if the Treaty is to have force and reality, members of the Alliance should prepare the command structure, the strategic and tactical plans, the forces in being, and their designation to NATO in advance of any crisis and for use in time of crisis."[136]

When the full scope of the French decisions became apparent at the end of the month, the American government proved to be divided over how to meet this gravest French challenge to a cherished bulwark of American security and hegemony. Secretary McNamara and Pentagon officials seemed relatively unconcerned with the political implications of the move; nor did they believe that the prospective loss of French territory to NATO was of decisive military importance. Always cost-conscious, the McNamara Defense Department soon perceived de Gaulle's action as an opportunity to streamline both the American military presence in Europe and the NATO defense structure.[137] At the State Department, however, many dogmatic Atlanticists and partisans of European integration tended to react quite emotionally to the French move, doubtless because of years of frustration and defeats in their dealings with Gaullist France. Particularly forceful American reactions were urged by George Ball, then under-secretary of state and a violent critic of de Gaulle; Robert Schaetzel, deputy assistant secretary for European Affairs; and Henry Owen, acting director of the Policy Planning Council. Secretary of State Rusk, more involved in Vietnam than European issues, confined his statements to specific refutations of French charges against NATO and generally appeared to take a moderate position.

Within the State Department, policy suggestions from the hard-line group included a formal denunciation of any American treaty commitment to defend France, an adherence to obstructionist tactics in future negotiations over the French decisions, and a revival of some kind of European integration initiative in the hope that de Gaulle would be unable to manage simultaneous crises in the NATO and EEC forums.[138] Ball was reported to have told a meeting of the fourteen in Paris on 29 March that the United States was planning to challenge the eviction of its bases on legal grounds and to ignore the deadlines, that France should be made to pay for the costs of the eviction or be denied access to NADGE, and that NATO should revise procedures for sharing military intelligence with Paris.[139] Some of these proposals did figure in later negotiations, but the virulent and petulant tone was missing by then. Ball's public speeches on the NATO crisis reflected a similar approach and were surprisingly direct and undiplomatic in their recriminations.[140] These efforts proved to be a poor imitation of tactics that de Gaulle had mastered and used so well, and were finally abandoned when the Pentagon's good sense and pragmatism prevailed over de Gaulle's enemies in the State Department. Early in May, President Johnson took the side of the moderates and directed his administration to avoid excessive and bitter language in references to France. A calmer and more constructive atmosphere prevailed after this intervention.

While Washington was spending April deciding on its posture during the crisis, the European allies gradually formulated their own positions. British policy was characterized by a practical concern for keeping NATO together, and the Labour government's foreign secretary, Michael Stewart, formulated the first proposals for transferring the entire Alliance machinery out of France and streamlining it in the process. In a speech before the Western European Union (WEU) Assembly on 15 March, Stewart set the tone for London by stressing the seriousness of the French action without indulging in a diatribe. He made it clear, however, that a calm and dignified approach to the problem was accompanied by a firm British commitment to continue with NATO and its integrated military system. In general, London was profiting from the situation by taking the lead among European allies, a role that France had long denied to Britain.[141] Among other allies, the Netherlands had a characteristically bitter reaction against France. Foreign Minister Joseph Luns took the opportunity to attack de Gaulle's European policy, advocate an Atlantic political union, and vent a fear that France's new isolation would inevitably elevate West Germany to a dominant position in Western Europe.[142] Canadian Prime Minister Lester Pearson tended to be more critical of the United States than France in the affair, and blamed Washington for not having outflanked de Gaulle by increasing Europe's share in the control of the Alliance.[143] Finally, in Bonn, the principal issue was how to approach future negotiations to regulate the status of the French forces on West German soil. Although Foreign Minister Schroeder was to prove intractable in the matter, the initial March reaction of both government and opposition was to try to preserve both Franco-German ties and the NATO link to the United States.[144]

Despite some diversity of diplomatic approaches among France's Atlantic allies, the common element in the allied reaction was a unanimous resolve not to let the French action destroy or irreparably damage NATO and the military organization. Crises of this type have an advantage of clarifying interests while they force a settlement of usually irreconcilable positions and prevent even more debilitating conflict in the future. As the American ambassador to NATO in 1966 has pointed out, the French withdrawal did apparently force the other allies to pause and reconsider their vested interests in maintaining NATO.[145] Their conclusion was that the Alliance and its military integration were the only feasible means of organizing Western Europe's defenses and of keeping the United States in the picture. Doubtless the most important reason for European support of military integration and the NATO structure was that the United States considered their survival the condition of an American military presence in Europe and the collateral nuclear guarantee. This had been the policy since 1950, and it remained as valid, of not more so, in 1966. President Johnson reaffirmed it in his 23 March note to de Gaulle; other American officials were soon reminding the allies that without integration there could be no American guarantee to Europe.[146] NATO and military integration could, however, survive the French withdrawal and, during the rest of 1966, agreements were reached and arrangements made that met de Gaulle's requirements and removed the most tangible sources of friction between France and NATO itself. Despite the apparent gravity of the French decisions, the details were worked out with a minimum of difficulty. As a result, France was granted special status as a partial ally, which subsequently kept her in the Alliance and even proved flexible enough to permit a gradual and satisfactory reconciliation between the claims of French independence and the requirements of Atlantic security.

Sovereignty Restored: The Allied Evacuation from France. De Gaulle's invitation to the allies to leave French soil led to the departure of all American and Canadian forces, NATO's military commands and, though not at France's request, the NATO council and secretariat. American bases posed the most difficult physical problem. In 1966, there were thirty American military bases and depots on French soil. The U.S. Air Force held title to nine of them, four of which were important for air support, reconnaissance, and logistics activities, and the other five were only small supply depots.[147] The U.S. Army had twenty installations, including the General Staff Headquarters at St.-Germain-en-Laye (Camp des Loges), three communications centers, a helicopter supply depot, and fifteen other depots for matériel and fuel. The navy had an access facility at Villefranche-sur-Mer on the Mediterranean. There was, in addition, the 550-mile oil pipeline from Donges on the Atlantic to Huttenheim in West Germany. It served some 1,200 fighter planes and the land vehicles of the U.S. Seventh Army in West Germany. A total of 26,000 military personnel and 1,300 American civilians worked on these installations; they had also brought 37,000 dependents into France.[148]

In its reply to the French ultimatum, Washington's basic (and legally correct) contention was that most of the base and communications agreements could not be denounced unilaterally. "In view of the attitude of the French Government," the United States was willing, however, to make a concession and leave France within two years instead of meeting the French deadline of 1 April 1967.[149] Paris's position on the legal issue was elegantly simple. The bases were in France, it contended, by virtue of France's membership in the NATO military organization. Because this was to be terminated as of 1 July, and NATO was leaving on 1 April 1967, all prior agreements were inoperative. After some bilateral exchanges and discussions among the fourteen about where the American facilities could go, technical negotiations on the evacuation began on 21 June between Robert McBride for the United States and Jacques de Beaumarchais for France. The French position was adopted, and by September Robert McNamara was able to announce that the United States would meet the French deadline.[150]

The American departure began in August 1966, when six air reconnaissance units started to move out. Three went to Britain and, in a cost-cutting move, one unit was dissolved and two were reclassified as "dual-based" and moved to the United States, with a second home at Stuttgart, West Germany, where the U.S. Army headquarters was also relocated. With dual-basing and reductions in forces, McNamara was later able to claim that the withdrawal from France had resulted in a net reduction of 18,000 American military and civilian personnel stationed abroad, as well as 21,000 dependents.[151] The last American facilities in France were officially closed on 14 March 1967 and turned over to General Louis Dio, inspector-general of the French Land Forces. The two small Canadian air bases near Metz were also evacuated and their forces redeployed in Germany. There was some talk in 1966 of reaching an agreement whereby American forces could return to their former bases in France during a conflict, a possibility raised in the French memoranda. It was evidently a subject of discussion between Ambassador Charles Bohlen and Couve de Murville at a 18 July meeting and on subsequent occasions. No agreement could be reached, however, because the United States was interested only in guaranteed access during a crisis short of actual war, and Paris would not grant reentry rights under these conditions. Bohlen informed Couve de Murville of this on 22 November and the subject was closed.[152] The United States did, however, retain access to the crucial oil pipeline, under an agreement signed on 24 March 1967. The United States was given unrestricted use of the facility, although a protocol stated that "the question of the utilization of the pipeline system in time of war is reserved by the French Government."[153]

The move out of France cost the United States an estimated $912.7 million in facilities left behind, plus construction costs at new sites amounting to approximately $225 million. The figures do not include the unrevealed costs of closing down the facilities and moving personnel and matériel. The base agreements with France provided for negotiations on the residual value of the installations, which were taken over by the French armed forces. Talks were held, but by early 1968 France had agreed to pay only $13 million for portable surplus matériel left behind.[154] In September 1968, and again in January 1969, Washington submitted claims reportedly amounting to $350 million for the value of evacuated facilities and moving expenses, but the issue remained unsettled until December 1974, when the United States accepted $100 million as final payment for all outstanding claims.[155]

For the French, another financial problem, and the only concrete domestic repercussion of the NATO actions, concerned the localized economic impact of the allied retreat. In April 1966, there were 18,703 French personnel employed at allied installations, and some 4,000 to 5,000 additional jobs depended directly on contract labor for the allies.[156] In 1965, the foreign military installations had furnished a total of 270 million (new) francs in salaries to local national and allied personnel, who were therefore an important source of revenue for local commerce. To minimize the economic and political repercussions of the expulsion, a bureau was set up in the prime minister's office to develop retraining and industrialization programs for the less prosperous areas losing bases.[157] It was a long-standing government policy to channel industry out of Paris into underdeveloped regions, and the bureau's activities were coordinated with those of other agencies, to encourage firms to move into the affected areas by offering investment and tax incentives. This effort was a modest success, and towns such as Chateauroux were to benefit from major installations built by French and foreign industry.[158] Thus, there were no important political protests about this aspect of the NATO decisions, and by 1968 the most pressing economic strains caused by the allied departure had been handled successfully.

The transfer of American forces out of France clearly raised no serious problems. The expenses involved, even without much compensation from France, were partly recovered by cuts in forces stationed abroad and by reductions in the number of American military installations in Europe. The principal value of French territory to the United States, that of a staging area for supplying and reinforcing American troops in West Germany, had markedly declined by the mid-1960s. A second value accorded to French territory, that of strategic depth for the central front, had also lost much of its importance. As Secretary McNamara told the Jackson Committee in 1966, "neither the United States nor its allies have [sic] ever contemplated a war in which falling back upon French soil through the battlefield of Germany was an acceptable strategy for the alliance."[159] In terms of logistics support for the forward area, much of the matériel for forces there had been funneled through Benelux and West German ports for several years. The large supply depots with stocks for many months of warfare, which had once existed in France, were unnecessary because NATO did not foresee or plan for such a long war of attrition. The problem of securing adequate oil and fuel was offset by continued access to the pipeline across France. It is not an assured supply in the event of a crisis, because France could cut it off at any time, but there are alternate arrangements for providing American forces with local fuel from Belgium, Holland, and West Germany.

The one indisputably serious problem raised by the loss of regular military access to French territory concerned NATO's overflight rights. The air space above France was practically indispensable as a link between the northern and southern halves of the Alliance. Swiss and Austrian air lanes were naturally closed to foreign military traffic, and all NATO aircraft moving between AFCENT and AFSOUTH had to cross France. The alternate route—through the Channel, across the Bay of Biscay, and through the Straits of Gibralter (or perhaps across Spain)—was generally impractical and too long a distance for some aircraft to fly without refueling. French air space was also used for flights between the United States and Europe, between Britain and the

Mediterranean, for American forces moving between West Germany and Spain, and as training space for German and allied air units that could not stray too close to the Eastern frontier.[160] All in all, some 100,000 allied flights traversed France each year under a series of agreements dating from 1951. The most recent, signed on 30 April 1963, had continued the previous practice of renewing allied overflight rights quasi-automatically on a yearly basis. Each flight required only a routine traffic clearance from French authorities.

On 3 May 1966, however, Paris informed the allies that as of 1 June overflight rights would be subject to monthly rather than annual renewal. A monthly renewal schedule was considered unacceptable by the fourteen because it presented NATO with the constant threat of losing its vital air links. It soon became apparent, however, that this restriction was essentially a French tactic to secure concessions from NATO in other areas of interest to France. Specifically, the government and Chief of Staff Ailleret wanted to ensure that they would have continued access to the NADGE air alert system, which was essential to French national security. Both NADGE and the overflight problems were discussed by Ailleret and General Lemnitzer during a meeting on 23 Novermber, held to determine the future status of military cooperation between France and NATO. As a result of their meeting, France retained access to the air alert system and pressure from other European states, especially West Germany, soon produced a modification of the overflight regime. On 3 August 1967, Paris informed Washington that, as of the following January, American military flights would again be permitted on an annual basis. After a second Ailleret-Lemnitzer conference, on 17 September 1967, the annual regime was extended to all NATO forces. How these accords would operate in a major crisis is an open question, however, because France could withdraw the authorization at any time. Like all aspects of French military cooperation with NATO after 1966, overflight rights are subject to political decisions that cannot be predicted with confidence.

The move of the NATO commands themselves proved to be quite uneventful once the fourteen, in their unofficial meetings at the Palais de Chaillot headquarters, decided to accept the situation and not further aggravate France. There was some discussion about possible new sites for SHAPE, and the British interest in serving as host was finally disappointed, because most allies felt that SHAPE should remain on the continent for symbolic reasons and because of the practical matter of retaining close communications with the forward area.[161] Belgium finally agreed to accept SHAPE at an Atlantic Council meeting on 7 June 1966, though not without some misgivings about the eventual cost of preparing new installations.[162] On 22 July, Brussels offered SHAPE some land at a former army training area at Chièvres-Casteau, fifty kilometers southwest of the capital. The offer was accepted by the Atlantic Council in September, despite some misgivings among SHAPE personnel used to the amenities of the Paris region. The headquarters closed its facilities at Rocquencourt on 20 March 1967, two days before the deadline, and on

1 April the still-unfinished buildings at Chièvres-Casteau were opened with the raising of fourteen flags. In a gracious and ironic gesture, de Gaulle held a banquet for General Lemnitzer at the Elysée on 16 March and decorated NATO's SACEUR with the Grand Cross of the Legion of Honor.

The three European commands under SHAPE were moved out of France during the same period. At the June 1966 session of the Atlantic Council, the affair was used as an opportunity to simplify the Central Europe command structure and combine the three Fontainebleau headquarters (AFCENT, LANDCENT, AIRCENT) into a single unit. This action had been under consideration for some time, and the withdrawal of French personnel facilitated cutting staffs while keeping an equitable distribution of senior posts.[163] A suitable site for the new combined AFCENT was not found until October 1966, when the allies settled on the Limburg province of the Netherlands, close to the Belgian and West German borders. Part of AFCENT's Central Army Group (CENTAG) and Northern Army Group (NORTAG) was placed in the buildings of an abandoned state mine at Brunssum, and the rest went to army barracks twenty-five kilometers away at Maastricht. The remodeled installations were officially inaugurated on 1 June 1967. As the last NATO military organ, the Defense College also evacuated its home at the Ecole Militaire in Paris and moved to Rome in October 1967. The Eternal City was scarcely a center of Alliance activity, and the Defense College's move there was testimony to NATO's dispersal upon its departure from Paris.

Although it was a foregone conclusion that all of NATO's military organs would leave France, the fate of the North Atlantic Council and the staff-secretariat was not immediately apparent. The French government made no mention of the council in its memoranda because, as Couve de Murville told the National Assembly, the withdrawal did not involve the council, which was "political in nature" and whose "creation had been foreseen by the Treaty of Washington itself."[164] Some of the fourteen, however, felt that NATO's political head could not remain isolated in Paris while the military body left for other parts of Europe. In this view, it was dangerous and unwise to leave the council so distant from the military commands, because constant and secure communications were required in times of tension or crisis. The possibility, however remote, of French neutrality in a conflict involving the rest of NATO made Paris seem unsuitable as a headquarters. The United States and Britain were strong partisans of transferring the council, and the latter suggested that London might be an ideal location.[165] The French left the decision on this issue up to their colleagues, some of whom still felt that if the council were left in Paris it would one day be easier for France to return to NATO.

After some months of debate, the United States took a firm and decisive position on the issue. Testifying at the Jackson Committee hearings on 16 June, Secretary Rusk said that the council had to be close enough to SHAPE for day-to-day contact and "to remove any doubt in peacetime as to which is the controlling body of the Alliance." He felt "certain" that the others would soon see his point.[166] On 3 October, Rusk told Couve de Murville that doubts about France's position during a war made it imperative that the council be moved,[167] and on 26 October the United States overcame West German reluctance and secured agreement that the council and secretariat should leave France. London was impractical for the proximity agruments already noted, and an earlier Belgian offer to take the Alliance's political organs was revived and accepted. On 10 October 1967, the council and staff were officially installed in temporary buildings at Evère, a suburb of Brussels. A permanent installation was originally foreseen, but because of the antici- pated expense and other considerations the prefabricated buildings at Evère were merely reinforced; the council has remained there, on an isolated fringe of Europe's expensive and dreary capital city.

NATO and France's Independent Armed Forces. In 1966, the only French land forces assigned to NATO were two divisions of the Second Army Corps, consisting of six mechanized and armored brigades, two batteries of Hawk surface-to-air missiles, and four batteries of Honest John surface-to-air missiles. The 65,000 troops in these units were stationed in southwest Germany (near the French border) and constituted a reserve force in NATO planning. More important for NATO defenses was the First CATAC, with its 450 modern Phantom and Mirage planes, 120 Nike missiles, and 23,000 troops. Approxi- mately one-half of this force was stationed in West Germany and the rest was in France. The eight squadrons of Mirage II-E and F-100D fighter-bombers, some equipped with Nike-Hercules missiles and American-controlled nuclear warheads, were a substantial part of SACEUR's nuclear striking power; the prospective loss of the French air units faced NATO with a breach in its air defense. Thus, a crucial military question raised by France's disengagement was what future role her armed forces might play within the NATO defense system.

The French memorandum of 29 March stated that the assignment of French forces to NATO was to be terminated on 1 July 1966, but left their future status unclear, although it envisaged arrangements whereby French forces "could participate in time of war in joint military actions [with NATO], as regards both command and the operations as such."[168] One issue confronting the allies, then, concerned the kind of arrangements that could be made for peacetime and wartime cooperation between France's armed forces and those of NATO. A second issue, closely linked to the first, was whether the French forces then in West Germany would remain there and under what conditions. From the outset, France and the fourteen disagreed over the linkage of these two problems. Paris contended that they were entirely separate; thus, France's military presence in West Germany should be regulated by a bilateral agreement between the two states themselves, whereas the nature of future military cooperation between France and NATO forces should be settled independently by the respective military commanders. The fourteen, on the other hand, contended that France's right to station troops in West Germany depended on their role within NATO; thus, the two problems had to be resolved together. As with most other issues posed by the disengagement, the French position ultimately prevailed, and the allies adapted to it rather than push France further out of the Alliance than necessary.

The initial position of the fourteen was worked out in Bonn between mid-April and early May, by a tripartite working group made up of West German State Secretary for Foreign Affairs Karl Carstens and the American and British ambassadors, George McGhee and Sir Frank Roberts. Their efforts produced a note submitted by West Germany to France on 3 May. The position stated there was that the French troops were stationed on German soil by virtue of the network of treaties and resolutions providing for West German accession to sovereignty and NATO membership—namely, the final act of the London Conference of 3 October 1954, the NATO Council resolutions of 22 October 1954, and the Paris Agreements of 23 October 1954. France was reminded that the 22 October resolution bound all member states to place forces intended for European defense under SACEUR, and that it was on this assumption that France, West Germany, the United States, and Britain had concluded the 23 October agreement on the presence of foreign forces in the Federal Republic.[169] The crux of the argument was that France's withdrawal nullified this convention as far as the French forces were concerned, "for it makes an essential difference whether the foreign forces stationed on Federal territory are placed under a joint command in which the Federal Republic of Germany participates in an appropriate degree, or whether these forces are solely under the national command of their state of origin."[170] The German note suggested that new bilateral agreements could be drawn up, provided a satisfactory arrangement was concluded about the future role of the French forces in NATO defense.

The French completely rejected this position. On an earlier visit to Bonn on 18 April Couve de Murville had already informed his West German counterpart, Schroeder, that his government considered the 23 October agreement to be still valid in its own right, and that the troops would remain in Germany after 1 July unless Bonn invited them to leave.[171] Upon receipt of the German note, de Gaulle's spokesman dismissed the possibility of continuing with any kind of NATO authority over its armed forces and said that France had no particular desire to keep troops in West Germany and, if necessary, they could be evacuated within a year after 1 July.[172] As Messmer had already told German Defense Minister von Hassel earlier in May, the strength of France's position was that she was not a *"demandeur"* in this affair, and the entire responsibility for the outcome rested on Bonn, which only had to agree to de Gaulle's terms.[173]

Thus, West German officials found themselves in a difficult position, torn by competing international priorities and even different viewpoints within the government. The Federal Republic was politically and legally committed to NATO military integration, because it kept American forces on the forward line and because the 1954 agreements had granted it a fully equal status in the Alliance only as long as all other allied forces in Europe and on West German territory fell under NATO, along with the Bundeswehr.[174] On this point, sovereignty and status were as much at stake for Germany as for France. On the other hand, most in Bonn still wanted to maintain amicable relations with France despite the NATO crisis and, it turned out, to keep French troops in West Germany at all costs as a symbol of continued four-power responsibility for the future of Germany—and as a visible French commitment to West German security at a time when French intentions were very much in doubt. Within the government, Foreign Minister Schroeder was perhaps the least inclined to compromise with the French, and insisted on some form of guarantee that the French troops would be automatically engaged in the event of a war or crisis.[175] Chancellor Erhard was, however, less committed to securing such a precise role in NATO and went out of his way to allay the impression given by Schroeder that West Germany was indifferent to whether the troops stayed. During a speech before the Bundestag on 26 May, he said that Bonn "unequivocally" desired the presence of French land and air forces and transitional arrangements could be made if suitable agreements were not reached before 1 July.

This cleared the air and permitted the two governments to initiate serious discussions on 1 June. However, because no agreement was reached in these early talks and the French began projects to move some forces back to France, Erhard was forced to offer Paris an interim agreement to allow French troops to remain in West Germany after 1 July.[176] A German note dated 30 June stated that the units could remain beyond the deadline, assuming that they would continue to fulfill their basic NATO defense duties pending a definitive agreement.[177] Paris had no serious objections to this formula, particularly because it had already decided to let the unintegrated French forces carry out their NATO missions for a short time while SHAPE made other arrangements.[178] Thus, on 1 July, the French forces were formally removed from NATO's authority, and France's General Jean Crépin passed on the command of the central front to General Johann von Kielmansegg, his German successor. On the same day, American nuclear warheads assigned to French forces were withdrawn because access to them was determined by NATO commitments.[179]

The first round of bilateral Franco-German talks, between Jacques de Beaumarchais and Herman-Meyer Lindenberg, had ended on 6 June without resolution, and the next session, begun on 13 June, was equally unsuccessful. The negotiations continued sporadically through the year, but remaining points of contention were settled only after the Erhard government fell in November and was replaced by the new Kiesinger-Brandt "grand coalition" on 1 December. The two sides decided on 13 December that the troop issue would be settled by a simple exchange of letters between the two foreign ministers, Couve de Murville and Willy Brandt. In these notes, they avoided the legal issue by agreeing that the 23 October Convention on the Presence of Foreign Forces in the Federal Republic did not "rule out" the continued presence of French forces. The French position was, in effect, upheld because the notes implied that the convention was still in force. In a second letter of the same date, Couve de Murville announced certain modifications in the regulations for the troops in Germany. They stipulated that: (1) both French and West German flags would henceforth fly over the bases; (2) the bases would remain at their present locations, and any proposed changes would be subject to future bilateral agreement; (3) France would report to West Germany annually on the strength, structure, and matériel of the forces; (4) German liaison officers for the French forces would be informed fourteen days in advance of any troop movements at or above the regimental level, and West Germany would have seven days to raise objections except that the time limits would be shortened under conditions of urgency; and (5) the procedure just mentioned would also be followed for French frontier crossings. With the exception of these modifications, the NATO Status of Forces Agreement was to remain in effect for the forces in question.[180]

This exchange of letters marked a complete victory for France in the affair. The presence of her troops in Germany was maintained independent of any NATO role they might fulfill, and no political or military conditions were attached. The forces would stay simply because Bonn wanted them there and because it suited Paris for the time being. They were to remain close to the French border and could be withdrawn at any time, particularly if a conflict developed in which France decided to remain on the sidelines. As Couve de Murville interpreted the agreement for the Council of Ministers in Paris, France was, therefore, without unpleasant obligations: "Under this agreement, if the Germans wish the French troops to leave the Federal Republic, it is their right and we will leave. This does not mean, inversely, that if France one day were to decide to withdraw her troops, she could not do so. She would have the possibility, should it so happen that the French Government felt this to be necessary."[181] France's independence and freedom from obiligations was further confirmed by the lack of any substantive French military commitment to NATO, which was the result of exchanges in that forum.

At the North Atlantic Council, the permanent representatives of the fourteen had since early June tried to induce the French to negotiate on military cooperation agreements. In particular, the fourteen sought to pin the French down on the level of forces they intended to leave in West Germany, what missions they would assume for NATO, whether they would be available to NATO in a crisis or in wartime, and if France was willing to accept the principle of NATO command over the forces at a predefined stage of alert or warfare.[182] The French representative, Ambassador François de Leusse, was instructed by the Quai d'Orsay that the entire matter had to be left up to military representatives of France and NATO. The council finally capitulated, and a meeting between Lemnitzer and Ailleret was arranged for 23 November. In addition to military cooperation and the specific issue of France's role if NATO were to call a general alert, the two men were to discuss allied overflight rights, French access to the NADGE air defense warning system, and unresolved technical details of liaison between commands. In respect to France's military commitments to NATO, the results of the Ailleret-Lemnitzer talks remain secret in principle, but it is clear that they were not especially satisfactory for NATO. Ailleret's instructions made this a foregone conclusion, for he was empowered to reach agreement only on missions that *might* be assigned to French troops *if* France made the political decision to participate in common military actions. The missions could be based on contingency plans worked out in advance and according to various hypotheses about enemy actions and allied responses. But in no event could there be provisions for automatic French engagement in a crisis or war, because such commitments would necessarily depend on decisions made in the light of particular circumstances and French interests.[183]

After Ailleret explained these guidelines at the 23 November meeting, French and NATO military officials met to formulate sets of contingency plans providing for French participation in common military responses to different aggressive acts. Ailleret and Lemnitzer also agreed that French forces would be able to participate in NATO training exercises, maneuvers, and war games, and that their roles would be allocated according to the agreed contingency plans. According to an authoritative French military source, after 1966 the French and NATO commands worked out several sets of military contingency plans that assume French participation in concert with the armed forces of NATO.[184] For the French side, each set and all subsequent modifications have had to be approved at the political level, by the offices of the president and minister of defense. Each separate joint maneuver is also subject to political approval. In a crisis in which the plans might be activated, French participation is naturally contingent on political consent. Despite some initial indications to the contrary by Ailleret,[185] the French made no firm commitments to subject their forces to SACEUR's orders even if they agree to joint actions. Thus, the contingency plans represent the only guarantee that the forces in question would act in a manner compatible with SACEUR's directions. In the event of French neutrality or military noninvolvement during a crisis, the agreements evidently stipulate that French ground forces in West Germany could not engage in any action whatsoever except to withdraw back into France. At best, the procedures could be cumbersome during a crisis and would only add to SACEUR's problems in managing his forces along the narrow German front. Nor is it certain that the French would abstain from any unilateral military actions on West German territory, because some contact there with an advancing enemy is specifically foreseen by French national war plans. One could easily conjure up scenarios of various troops acting at cross purposes and introducing general confusion into the defense of the central region. Nor, of course, do any of these understandings cover France's strategic nuclear force (or her TNWs), the use of which might be expected to be incompatible with NATO's own defense plans.

For SACEUR, the effect of this uncertainty has been that plans for Europe's defense must be drawn up in two forms, one including and one excluding French participation. Under de Gaulle and Pompidou, at least, it was impossible to predict how Paris might decide to act during a crisis, and SHAPE authorities had to accord operational priority to military plans that excluded France. As General Lemnitzer said, in an interview in late 1966, he could no longer count on the French forces and considered them a potential danger because they might interfere with allied military actions during a crisis.[186] He was also unhappy that the loss of French fire power, along with NATO's general conventional inferiority, was requiring SHAPE to assume an earlier recourse to TNWs than had once been foreseen.[187] This development may have disturbed the United States, but most European allies were obviously not traumatized by the deterrent value of a low nuclear threshold.[188] In any event, NATO's inability to depend on France was not a sudden innovation in 1966. It had been apparent for some years that de Gaulle's military policies made France an uncertain factor, and under Article V of the treaty no member was obliged to fight alongside its allies. Although France's status was ambivalent and her position in NATO flexible enough to change in the future, in 1966 the balance had to swing to a presumption of French nonparticipation if NATO's military forces and plans were to retain their effectiveness and cohesion.

Alliance Adaptation.   In addition to its military consequences, France's disengagement led to a number of important changes in Alliance institutions, in their ties to the French, and in the general nature of France's membership status. Specifically, the withdrawal was the occasion for the creation of a new status for French military personnel assigned to NATO commands, for the abolition of the Standing Group and modifications in the Military Committee, for changes in the council's procedures for handling political and military questions, and for the introduction of a special membership status to accommodate France's selective participation in Alliance activities and agencies.

As Paris had announced in the memorandum of 29 March, the assignment of French military personnel to SHAPE and its subordinate commands was ended on 1 July 1966.[189] These officers were replaced by liaison missions posted to SHAPE and the allied commands in the central and southern sectors. At SHAPE, the role was performed by an expanded office of the French National Military Representative (NMR), with the new designation of French Military Mission. The National Military Representatives had served at SHAPE since 1951 as channels of communication between allied military organs and national defense authorities. They protected members' national interests at NATO and ensured that national defense officials were kept informed of allied military planning and other activities. Major-General Robert Lancrenon had been the French NMR to SHAPE since February 1966, and on 29 July he was officially named head of the French Military Mission.[190] On the same date, Brigadier General Michel Deveaux was appointed to head the newly created mission posted to AFCENT, then still at Fountainebleau. With French forces remaining in West Germany, it was also necessary to maintain links with other allied military units in the area, and these offices were set up at the same time.[191]

These various missions generally serve as communication channels between French and NATO commands, and, when the need arises, they work out the terms and details of French participation in NATO maneuvers and training exercises. It is evident that the Military Mission to SHAPE also represents its general staff in negotiations on some aspects of contingency planning, although the liaison with the Military Committee (see below) bears the main responsibility in this area. Under de Gaulle and Pompidou, the French liaison officers were given little free rein, and all but the most elementary decisions had to be approved by the Ministry of Defense. This situation did not prevent frank and wide-ranging exchanges between French liaison officers and their allied colleagues, but political control was tightly exercised.[192]

A French liaison mission also represents its government to the Military Committee, an organ that underwent some modifications as a result of the withdrawal and the council's decision, on 16 June 1966, to abolish the Standing Group. Paris had announced that it would withdraw its representative to the Standing Group, General Jean Housay, on 1 July, which presented the fourteen with the dilemma of what to do with this rather ineffective executive body for the Military Committee. Under pressure from the smaller powers, the council decided to replace the Standing Group with a more egalitarian and integrated International Military Staff (IMS), which was drawn from all member states except France and Iceland. The director, of three-star rank, is nominated by the members and appointed by the Military Committee. The IMS is charged with ensuring that the Military Committee's orders are implemented as directed, and with initiating military policy studies for NATO.[193]

Because the IMS and the Military Committee took over the functions of the Standing Group and were directly involved in laying guidelines and plans for the integrated defense of Europe—according to a strategy (flexible response) incompatible with that of France—Ambassador François de Leusse announced on 14 September that his country's representative to the Military Committee would be withdrawn on 1 October and replaced with a simple liaison mission. Following this action, the Military Committee began to meet under two different formats. Most of the time, thirteen national military representatives are present, along with a civilian representative from Iceland and the head of the French Military Mission to the Military Committee. France is not a statutory member of the committee, but when her representative is present he takes part in the deliberations along with the other officers. He may not, however, participate in the taking of decisions, and he is permitted only to advise the others of his government's views. Committee sessions that include France are called "Part One," and those that do not are called "Part Two," the agenda having been set at the previous full session. Here, the French officer indicates which parts of the agenda he is interested in and they will be discussed first. The Military Committee is also the focal point at NATO for allied exchanges of intelligence on military developments in the Eastern bloc; France found it desirable to retain access to this information because her own resources were inadequate compared to the American information supplied to NATO. In 1966, under American prodding, the fourteen set the condition that French access was to depend on Paris's willingness to swap secrets,[194] a criterion that was subsequently fulfilled. The head of the French mission was then granted access to the MC161 file containing NATO's intelligence reports. On the other hand, the United States insisted in 1966 that all documents and NATO discussions dealing with information Washington furnishes about its nuclear weapons and strategy may not be made available to France. Because information-sharing on this subject increased measurably after 1966, the American condition has been the most important barrier to France's access to allied defense policy planning activities.

Although France naturally remained on the North Atlantic Council and continued to participate in its subsidiary bodies concerned with nondefense issues, the council itself underwent a transformation as a result of the French withdrawal from Alliance military activities. Because France was no longer to take part in most of NATO's defense affairs, the problem arose of finding a satisfactory forum where the other members could discuss and take decisions on defense issues in the name of the Alliance, but without France. For, as Rusk noted during the June council meetings, France's disengagement naturally meant that she could no longer obstruct defense decisions and activities on the part of the other allies.[195] A formula for institutionalizing this situation was found in the ad hoc arrangement that had been functioning since March. Under the chairmanship of Ambassador André de Staercke, the fourteen permanent representatives had met without France to coordinate their positions. The French delegate had tacitly consented to this unprecedented procedure. The format was accepted as permanent at a ministerial session on 15 December, when Couve de Murville agreed to split the council into two parts: the fifteen-member council proper, which was to concern itself with issues of a primarily "political" nature, and a fourteen-member Defense Planning Committee (DPC) with a mandate for defense problems.[196]

Following procedures similar to those used in the Military Committee, the dual council has been equally flexible in managing a somewhat awkward situation. In general, agenda items of interest to France are taken up in the council, whereas matters that focus on NATO strategy or the integrated defense system are relegated to the DPC. With the exception of any American nuclear data, barred from France in this forum as well, the procedure for dividing the agenda has usually been informal. As chairman of both bodies, the secretary-general normally checks with the French deputy permanent representative to see which topics the delegation wishes to discuss in the full council. Or, if a question arises in the DPC that the fourteen feel calls for French participation, the French delegation can be asked to join in the deliberations. The secretariat and all national delegations are housed in the same building, and such matters have usually been settled with ease and informality. Furthermore, through continuous personal contacts, the French have been able to make their views known on DPC issues and can influence decisions taken in that forum. The French delegation is also granted access to most DPC minutes and documents and, therefore, remains well-informed about defense discussions among the fourteen. As one very concrete benefit for the fourteen, France's self-imposed isolation from defense issues allowed the others to circumvent the French veto on changes in alliance strategy and nuclear information-sharing through the Nuclear Planning Group (NPG) and Nuclear Defense Affairs Committee (NDAC). As late as December 1966, Couve de Murville tried to block the evolution of the "McNamara Committee" into these permanent NATO organs, but the decisions were relegated to the DPC. The fourteen were thus able to set them up as vehicles for improving allied participation in NATO nuclear planning and drafting guidelines for the use of tactical nuclear weapons under the flexible response strategy.

France's continued participation in other NATO specialized agencies and programs after 1966, even those with military functions, was determined by French interest and the other allies' decision to maintain as much cooperation with France as possible. For the French, the only criterion was self-interest, as long as participation did not entail any military commitments or substantive loss of national control over defense. Thus, although the French did cease to participate in activities such as the Defense Support and Infrastructure Program, they retained membership in other defense agencies deemed useful for France's own defense programs. NADGE and the existing air alert system, "Ace High," fell in this category, as did the NATO Pipeline Agencies and the air defense telecommunications systems. In addition to these specific infrastructure projects, France remained in a number of joint research, production, and maintenance programs that operated under NATO auspices.[197] In 1966, they included (1) the NATO Maritime Patrol Aircraft program ("Atlantic"), (2) the HAWK weapon system program, (3) the NATO Maintenance and Supply Organization (NAMSO), (4) the AS30 Missile program, (5) the new Conference of National Armaments Directors (CNAD) and some of its weapons projects, (6) the SHAPE Technical Center at the Hague, and (7) the Advisory Group for Aerospace Research and Development (AGARD, which even stayed at its Neuilly-sur-Seine location). Along with NADGE and the air defense telecommunications systems, the last three organizations in this list fell under the aegis of the Military Committee and, with the exception of NADGE and AGARD, received all or part of their funding from NATO's military budget. France, however, ceased to contribute to the military budget on 1 January 1967, because it also covered the expenses of the IMS, SHAPE, SACLANT, and other military commands. After that date, France paid her share of expenses on a program-by-program basis. The precise figures are not available, but it has been estimated that, after the withdrawal, France's share of the military budget was reduced from 17.1 percent to 8.5 percent.[198]

As a result of the 1966 withdrawal, then, France's status in the Alliance became that of an ally accorded an original, even privileged, role. Secretary-General Brosio admitted this in November when he said: "Because she participates in certain organisms of the Alliance and abstains from participating in others, France has established herself as an ally enjoying a special status."[199] Although some aspects of France's postwithdrawal participation in NATO were the result of indirect negotiating tradeoffs, for the most part Paris determined what was to be kept or discarded. Ambassador de Staercke aptly characterized this policy as one of "NATO à la carte." The special arrangement was obviously one-sided to a large extent, but did not present serious inconveniences for either side. A privileged status had not been the first inclination of some member states, notably the United States, which considered "punishing" de Gaulle by reducing France's Alliance role to a minimum bordering on exclusion. This was not done for a number of sensible reasons, including the hope that "after de Gaulle" a France only partially dealigned might find it easier to return to more extensive collaboration with NATO activities. In addition, despite the French government's policies, the Atlantic Alliance, if not "NATO," had important sympathizers in France, and it was preferable not to create an irreparable breach and lose touch with them. Such judgments abetted the creation of a more flexible kind of Alliance after 1966, one that could accommodate shifts in the NATO policies of France as well as of other allies who decided to follow some Gaullist precedents for their own reasons. The Atlantic Alliance has thus been able to withstand the strains of an increasingly pluralistic international arena and more volatile domestic politics within some members, which might otherwise have irreparably damaged the Atlantic security system.

5 The Partial Ally: France and the Alliance, 1968-1980

The brief period between 1966 and mid-1968 amounted to an extreme and ephemeral manifestation of the Gaullist policy of independence and grandeur. France's relative isolation within the West was offset by a spectacular, but essentially symbolic, global policy with intimations of a semineutral Paris rallying Third World victims of superpower oppression and shaping the terms of a future East-West settlement in Europe. But fulfilling these aspirations would certainly have required more concrete resources and influence than France could hope to muster alone under the most favorable conditions. Even the rhetorical appeal of de Gaulle's critique of the international order depended (to a certain extent) on a stable domestic political economy, which was severely undermined by the collapse of civil order in May 1968. This crisis eventually led to de Gaulle's departure the following April. In the meantime, it debilitated the French economic position through lost production and the onerous wage increases that unions obtained in lieu of the romantic student vision of radical social transformation. The debilitating effects that domestic turmoil had on France's international independence and flexibility were compounded by the Soviet invasion of Czechoslovakia in August 1968. The invasion was a setback to détente and an affirmation that the necessary transformation of the East bloc into a more pluralistic system similar to the West's was a very uncertain and distant affair.

These internal and external events, combined with changes of policy and administration in the United States, resulted in conditions favorable to a reduction in tensions between France and the American Alliance during the final months of de Gaulle's tenure as president. This reconciliation to the Atlantic Alliance under de Gaulle amounted to an acknowledgment of the coalition's continuing utility to French and general European security, as long as France could maintain the privileged role of partial ally that was the fruit of the 1966 withdrawal. Although de Gaulle may have flirted briefly with the possibility of a more drastic break with the Alliance, his final and altogether realistic accommodation on these terms established the precedent followed by his successors. Both Pompidou and Giscard d'Estaing have, of course, had to maintain France's independent nuclear defense and autonomy from the NATO military organization as unchallenged principles of French security policy. As under de Gaulle, France's relations with the United States and the Alliance have naturally fluctuated according to domestic and international conditions and issues. Despite a general trend of cooperation, Pompidou and his foreign minister, Michel Jobert, felt constrained to resist American efforts in 1973-74 to revive a lagging American hegemony over Europe by reformulating the Kennedy design for "partnership" on the basis of explicit trade-offs between economic and security concessions among the Atlantic states. Although France successfully opposed the more obvious institutional and policy concessions sought by the Nixon administration as a price of Europe's security dependence, the 1973 Middle East War and the ensuing energy crisis gave the United States the upper hand anyway and soon undermined French resistance to American policies.

The economic crisis after 1973 had a strong effect in France, as in other Western countries, focusing attention and energy on domestic economic problems as well as on the management of various international constraints that constitute dependence or interdependence, depending on one's point of view. The French penchant for an obstinant and obstreperous independence in the European and Atlantic arenas has obviously been tempered by these new economic circumstances, among other reasons. The unfamiliar pattern of more accommodating French behavior is also due to Valéry Giscard d'Estaing's election as president in April 1974, which marked the onset of the most amenable French administration in postwar history. Since that time, most Gaullist tactics have disappeared from the French international repertory, and cooperation and conciliation have become hallmarks of French policy in both European and Atlantic affairs. Giscard's neo-Atlanticist tendencies are, however, held in check by certain sacrosanct Gaullist standards and principles, especially concerning defense and NATO. He also has to contend with the constraints of a revived and flourishing domestic political system that now accords less freedom to French governments and even to the chief of state. Although Giscard has instituted changes in French defense strategy and force structure that make them more compatible with NATO, and perhaps with participation in broader West European defense efforts, his policies are circumscribed by the recent emergence of a domestic consensus supporting the Gaullist principles of an independent and essentially national defense focused on nuclear weapons. This national consensus on defense and security, along with stable political institutions, appears to be one of the most lasting and valuable Gaullist legacies to France.

Parameters of Independence

Accommodation with the Alliance. The withdrawal of 1966 had left in abeyance the matter of whether France would remain in a state of partial dealignment, or if de Gaulle would follow his course to its most extreme conclusion and leave the Alliance altogether in the near future. At the time, De Gaulle provoked speculation on this issue because he referred to 4 April 1969 as the "last date" for France's Alliance obligations, which was the case only if France chose to denounce the Atlantic Treaty.[1] Otherwise, there is no expiration date for membership. In his letter of 7 March 1966 to President Johnson, de Gaulle stated that France would remain a party to the treaty after 1969, "barring events that in the next three years would happen to change the fundamentals of the relations between East and West."[2] Later, in October, de Gaulle was asked directly if he intended to quit the Alliance, but his evasive response left the issue unresolved.[3] It was partly to forestall a complete break that the fourteen allies let France retain the NATO ties most useful to her, a situation that was also expected to make it easier for a post-Gaullist regime to slip back into full membership or at least more extensive co-operation.

Nevertheless, after 1966, there were numerous reports from highly placed sources that membership in the Alliance was a liability for France that would soon be discarded altogether.[4] The Ailleret strategic doctrine of *tous azimuts*, announced at the end of 1967, was another indication that the partial withdrawal had been only an intermediate stage on the road to full neutrality. Just when the complete break might occur was in doubt, because it was unclear whether, under Article XIII of the treaty, a denunciation could take place in August 1968 or in August 1969, and then become effective one year later.[5] Whatever the precise date, 1968 was generally considered in France to be the crucial year for this decision. There is no reliable information about how de Gaulle was leaning on this issue before mid-1968, although one can speculate about the factors that might have swung a decision one way or another. In general, it is difficult to imagine what he might have expected to gain by leaving the Alliance. France's special status put no formal restrictions on her decision-making freedom and at least kept her in touch with other states that shared her security interests. Leaving the Alliance would have reinforced France's isolation from European security affairs and belied the claim that Paris was preparing the way for European independence. And, however devalued American nuclear protection was, there was nothing to be gained by formally renouncing it. The withdrawal of 1966 had not jeopardized the security afforded by NATO and no advantage could be had by doing so in 1968.

A full dealignment might also have had more serious domestic repercussions than the actions of 1966. The Gaullist majority in the National Assembly had been reduced from 350 seats to 242 for the UNR in the elections of March 1967. Giscard d'Estaing's pro-Atlantic Independent Republicans were taking a more independent *"oui, mais"* stand vis-à-vis the Gaullists and had more leverage due to the close parliamentary balance. There were also signs that the public was much more apprehensive about the possibility of leaving the Alliance itself than it had been about severing ties with the NATO military organization. A poll conducted by the *Institut français de l'opinion publique* (IFOP) in September-October 1967 showed that 54 percent of the public preferred to remain in the Alliance, while only 12 percent advocated a full withdrawal. Among the various political families, it was not surprising that the center (75 percent versus 7 percent) and the Federation of the Left (66 percent versus 4 percent) favored the Alliance, but the figures for the Gaullists (61 percent versus 11 percent) showed relatively strong opposition to a final break with the Western security system. Even the Communist Party electorate (44 percent versus 30 percent) wanted to maintain the American connection.[6] Although a strong government campaign could perhaps have turned public opinion around, it might also have crystallized the undecided against the government and mobilized a majority who felt that France could not manage a completely isolated defense.[7]

Such considerations were, however, overshadowed by other developments during 1968, which ensured that leaving the Alliance could not be entertained as a serious option. First, as already noted, the domestic disturbances of May and June nearly toppled the regime and severely weakened de Gaulle's personal image and France's international position. The domestic economy and France's trade and monetary advantages were undermined, and there was a natural tendency for the leadership to turn inward and focus on domestic reforms rather than undertake audacious new foreign policy initiatives. Also, the communists were widely but unjustly blamed for these events, making it even more unlikely that France would sever ties with important bastions of anticommunism such as the United States and the Atlantic Alliance.[8] Thus, 1968 marked an important defeat of the radical and revolutionary left in France, but it also lay the basis for a gradual revival of socialist forces and the creation of successful electoral alliances among left-wing parties that conditioned French politics until the legislative elections of 1978. The emergence of a strong leftist challenge to Gaullism and its conservative allies, and to the capitalist order in France, naturally tended to promote government cooperation with European and Atlantic capitalist states. This tendency was notable under Pompidou and has been a subtle leitmotif of Giscard d'Estaing's as well.

Domestic developments in 1968 coincided with notable improvements in Franco-American relations that made full neutralism less desirable or necessary. President Johnson withdrew from electoral politics in the United States on 31 March and simultaneously announced a halt to the bombing of North Vietnam, an act that de Gaulle praised as one "of reason and of political courage."[9] Soon thereafter, on 10 May, it was announced that Paris was to be the site of negotiations between the warring parties in Vietnam, a situation that obliged France to respect "a strict reserve and the utmost calm throughout the talks."[10] A remarkable change in de Gaulle's attitude toward the United States was evident on 15 May when, in the midst of the civil disturbances, de Gaulle told the new American ambassador (Sargent Shriver) that France and the United States "were bound together in all the great tragedies" and "must remain so." Disagreements are mere episodes "and at the bottom, we are, you and we, in the same camp of freedom."[11] Relations continued to improve through the Johnson administration and were marked by generous American support of de Gaulle's decision not to devalue the franc in November. Finally, the new Republican administration in the United States gave every indication that it intended to sustain the Franco-American détente. President Nixon, with his own pretensions to a de Gaulle-like role, was an avowed admirer of the General's and journeyed to Paris in February 1969 to offer hommage and a relatively modest, even Gaullist, view of the American role in Europe and the Alliance.[12]

A denunciation of the Atlantic Treaty seemed quite unlikely by midsummer in 1968, then, and it was certainly precluded by the Soviet occupation of Czechoslovakia in August. De Gaulle condemned this event as "absurd compared to the perspectives of European détente," noting that the consequence "demonstrates to our eyes the maintenance of the Eastern bloc and, through that, of the Western bloc in a most injurious manner for Europe."[13] After this affair, France confirmed her continued adherence to the Western Alliance. At a special ministerial session of the North Atlantic Council in November, Foreign Minister Debré cautioned the allies that détente would proceed in spite of the Czech situation, but he joined in a communiqué that condemned the Soviet action and stated that it "aroused grave uncertainty about the situation and about the calculations and intentions of the USSR," an uncertainty that demanded "great vigilance on the part of the Alliance." In the light of Soviet behavior, the council and France declared: "The North Atlantic Alliance will continue to stand as the indispensible guarantor of security and the essential foundation for the pursuit of European reconciliation. By its constitution the Alliance is of indefinite duration. Recent events have demonstrated that its continued existence is more than ever necessary." After this statement, Debré inserted a clause noting that, barring a radical change in East-West relations, "the French government considers that the Alliance must continue as long as it appears to be necessary."[14] This amounted to a French affirmation of the Alliance's durability.[15]

Subsequently, French government officials reaffirmed that France would not leave the Alliance, but would remain apart from NATO integration. Debré's presence in Washington on the twentieth anniversary of the signing of the North Atlantic Treaty was, as he said at the time, proof that the treaty had not lost its *"raison d'être, "*[16] De Gaulle's resignation on 28 April 1969 ended all speculation on this issue, as his successor was clearly unwilling to engage in spectacular and unilateral foreign policy actions. After 1968, then, the Alliance did not appear to be an onerous burden on French independence, but was an additional factor of security that could not be discounted or readily replaced.

The improvement in French relations with the United States and the Atlantic Alliance continued during President Pompidou's administration, until the abrupt revival of tensions as a result of the American "Year of Europe" campaign and the Middle East War of 1973. Before then, Pompidou's own inclinations were apparently to protect the essential Gaullist creation of an independent nuclear defense, but to cooperate with NATO and individual allies when useful and feasible. Pompidou was also more preoccupied with domestic economic and social issues and, although he kept close presidential control over foreign policy, concentrated his efforts on a revival of European political and economic cooperation. Pompidou could not, in any case, have easily tampered with the terms of France's NATO ties because of the close attention the opposition and wary Gaullists paid to any sign of a *"glissement vers l'OTAN."*

Until his resignation from the post of Minister of National Defense in 1973, arch Gaullist Michel Debré's guardianship of France's defense structure was additional insurance that de Gaulle's somewhat suspect dauphin would respect the heritage in this domain. Despite some modifications in French strategic doctrine and quiet repairs in military relations between the French and NATO commands, Debré's security views were virtually the same as those of his mentor.[17] Both condemned military integration as a form of protectorate and domination by a greater power that left smaller states potentially helpless. Only an independent nuclear defense could provide genuine security to France, according to Debré, because without it the enemy would question her will to defend herself and, therefore, would not be deterred from an attack. In the end, France could only count on herself for deterrence and protection because of the conditions governing the use of force in the nuclear age. This situation did not invalidate alliances, especially the Atlantic Alliance, but Pompidou's defense minister insisted that interallied cooperation was consistent with national security only if France retained her autonomy of decision making and exclusive control over her armed forces. In practical terms, this meant that the French armed forces command could not be divested of their national character and strict control by French political authorities. It also meant that interallied cooperation on matters such as joint targeting, discussed at the time, was ruled out as impractical and dangerous because it would have reduced the credibility of the small but independent French nuclear force.

Subject to these guidelines and limitations, many aspects of French military and political cooperation with NATO were improved and normalized under Debré and Pompidou. In January 1971, General Fourquet made the first visit of a French Chief of the General Staff to SHAPE since 1966, and his conversations with General Andrew J. Goodpaster, the SACEUR, were a sign of the détente between France and the allied commands.[18] General Fourquet's successor, Air Force General François Maurin, who occupied the post between June 1971 and July 1975, was openly disposed to remove unwarranted obstacles to joint military efforts between an independent France and the NATO forces.[19] Discreet joint planning for cooperative actions in the event of French participation in allied defense actions was facilitated and extended to cover more contingencies during this period. The NATO and French general staff headquarters instituted regular exchanges of information on new or updated plans for possible concerted military action, and both sides became well-informed about each other's various contingency plans.[20] Subject to political restrictions, France revived her participation in some NATO land maneuvers on the central front. Even when such maneuvers focused on a conventional defense in violation of French doctrines, Paris began sending observers to keep up to date on allied battle plans. Naval cooperation in the Mediterranean became especially pronounced, because of the growing Soviet presence there and because it did not have the same ramifications for nuclear strategy implied by close connections between French and allied land and air forces.

Growing French interest in Soviet penetration of the Mediterranean led to modifications in the format of Atlantic Council discussions as well. While this issue was normally handled in the Defense Planning Committee as a problem of Soviet military behavior, French interest in the matter gradually induced the council to discuss it in the "political" council proper, where French views could be aired. Alliance discussions about the MBFR talks in Vienna underwent a similar transformation. These technical negotiations of arms control measures were officially classed as "political" at NATO to permit a French contribution there, despite Pompidou's decision to boycott the talks themselves. None of these subtle and unpublicized shifts in French policy amounted to more than a normalization of better relations among allies, but they did indicate that Gaullist independence was not synonymous with isolation. They also testified to the wisdom of the allied accommodation to France in 1966.

Resisting Hegemony: The Year of Europe. While Pompidou normalized relations with NATO and the United States, and removed unnecessary points of friction in Alliance matters, the focus of his foreign policy was a revival of French efforts to foster West European political and economic cooperation and unity. The expansion of the European Community to include Britain was a departure from Gaullist precedents, although de Gaulle had fluctuated on this issue through the Soames affair, and by 1970 the French could perceive an advantage in British membership as a way of compensating for West

Germany's growing economic and political weight within the European Community. Pompidou also seemed to recognize that a revival of the Gaullist European option was bound to be a slow and arduous affair that could progress only in small and relatively discreet steps. Thus, rather than follow de Gaulle's generally unrewarding precedent of defining Europe according to cooperation in the "high politics" arena, Pompidou's France stressed economic, industrial, and monetary cooperation and proposed relatively modest formulas for institutionalizing unity, such as the (unsuccessful) European Political Secretariat idea of 1972 and the creation of regular European summit meetings. The regional rather than global thrust of post-Gaullist French diplomacy, and the internment of the often arrogant and grating Gaullist tactics toward allies and partners, seemed, therefore, to inaugurate a calmer and more reasonable era in Atlantic politics.

This was the case until 1973, when American policy shifted and rekindled moribund fears of unwarranted American inteference in European affairs. In the midst of the awkward Atlantic controversy over the "Year of Europe" campaign, the October War in the Middle East and its aftermath set off the most serious and acrimonious Franco-American confrontation since the nadirs of the mid-1960s. One reason that the French mounted a particularly strong resistance to the Kissinger design was because, as it unfolded and was transformed by the Middle East conflict, events tended to confirm the most classic Gaullist themes about the dangers of dependence and American hegemony. Thus, the Kissinger-Nixon strategy of linkage and trade-offs between security and economic affairs bluntly asserted that henceforth the price of American defense protection would be economic and commercial concessions amounting to an official American veto over EEC decisions. De Gaulle had foreseen that Europe's defense dependence could be costly across a spectrum of issues, but American policy after the spring of 1973 provided the first overt and coherent attempt to capitalize on such trade-offs by institutionalizing a new European-American relationship.

The inconvenience and potential danger of this asymmetrical connection was verified by two additional developments during this period: first, the June Nixon-Brezhnev agreement on avoiding nuclear war, which savored of condominium; and, second, the American military engagement during the Middle East War and the autonomous alert of global American forces on behalf of Israel during that crisis. The danger that Europe might be dragged into an external conflict was obvious, and, at the very least, American actions implicated European states on behalf of Israel despite their neutrality and tendency to support the Arab political position. In such circumstances, it was natural for the French to mount a Gaullist-style resistance to the renewed American threat. The principal and revealing difference between the Pompidou-Jobert effort and those of de Gaulle was that, by 1973, France could no longer afford or manage an isolated defense of her own and Europe's rights and prerogatives. Instead, she had to try and galvanize European unity and independence in the face of this multiple American challenge, which sought to capitalize on a security hegemony for economic concessions of special interest to Pompidou's France. Although Paris met with some minor successes, European unity was still too weak to avoid more than the most obvious concessions to American demands. Also, the Middle East conflict and the energy crisis created conditions favorable (temporarily) to a revived American ascendancy over a Western international political economy dominated by oil politics and political-military influence in the Middle East. The independent French position was thus, once again, effectively isolated and disarmed until Giscard d'Estaing began to preside over a French accommodation to the new Atlantic order.

These conflicts were launched by a speech Kissinger made in New York to the Associated Press in April 1973.[21] The initiative came from a small group of policy makers in the National Security Council who were apparently attempting to revitalize and restructure American relations with key allies in the wake of the Southeast Asian debacle.[22] One ambiguity in need of clarification concerned the European implications of the Nixon Doctrine, which had emphasized a looser American relationship with allies who were expected to assume greater responsibility for their own defense and security affairs.[23] This notion, which was really only an Asian policy, along with the Kissinger theme of a five-power global power structure, seemed to raise the possibility of enhanced European independence and a new relationship of equality between the two Atlantic poles. The Year of Europe exercise, however, was designed to insure that the rhetorical American vision did not materialize into a serious West European (or Japanese) challenge to the United States in vital issue areas. For Kissinger and his colleagues assigned a clear priority to the Soviet-American bilateral relationship, and in 1973 they were undertaking to ensure that stability at this level would not be undermined by unruly allies capable of upsetting delicate superpower restraints and understandings ostensibly required for détente and global equilibrium.

One of the greatest potential challenges to this imperial "structure of peace" was certainly the menace of a united and expanding European entity capable of protecting and enhancing the shared economic and political interests of its member states. In his April address, Kissinger posed three correctives to what he later termed the potential disintegration of the West. These interconnected palliatives were: first, a working distinction between states with global and purely regional responsibilities; second, the linkage between American military protection and European political-economic concessions; and, third, a proposed acceptance of mutual restraints on autonomous actions. Kissinger's prescriptive image of Europe's actual and proper role was one of a European Community with "regional interests" that too often came into conflict with the "global interests and responsibilities" of the United States. The two perspectives had to be reconciled, Kissinger said, and he suggested that the American condition for continued support of European unity was for the Community to serve as "a means to the strengthening of the West." "We shall," Kissinger noted, "continue to support European unity as a component of a larger Atlantic partnership." According to this "unifying framework," then, Europe was apparently expected to subordinate its identity to the vaster and American-dominated Atlantic system. This was essentially a reformulation of a long-standing American goal that, ever since the Kennedy formulas, had implied the preeminence of American over European interests and the denial of a genuine pluralist order in the West.

As a means of achieving the grand design that had escaped his predecessors, Kissinger turned to the veiled threat implicit in the linkage of political, military, and economic issues in Atlantic relations. This notorious concept was to weigh heavily upon European-American conflicts following the Middle East War, but it was a dominant American theme well before then. Apparently borrowing the idea from a report by former Secretary of Commerce Peter Peterson, Kissinger asserted in April that these issues were "linked by reality, not by our choice nor for the tactical purpose of trading one off against the other." Finally, the future secretary of state asserted that allies required "an understanding of what should be done jointly and of the limits we should impose on the scope of our autonomy." The speech was littered with specific issues that demanded joint policy making and European concessions—such as European Community regional arrangements with third states, energy problems, the relations of oil-consuming and oil-producing states, and NATO military and burden-sharing issues.

The American proposal to redefine the allied relationship in a new "Atlantic Charter" met with understandable scepticism among European governments, who had been quite unprepared for such a development. Jobert later characterized the Kissinger speech as an "imprudent exposé of American geopolitics" that envisaged an allied camp encircling an American Middle Kingdom, but France did warily join the Atlantic states in the negotiations that ensued.[24] Until discussions bogged down completely because of the Middle East crisis, the initial effect of the American move was to unite the European nine around French notions of the separate European identity that Washington had expected to undermine. The Europeans succeeded in scuttling the pretentious "Atlantic Charter" label and divided it into two sets of negotiations on declarations of principle—one restricted to NATO and focusing on defense issues; the other involving the Community and the United States and dealing with economic and political questions. Community leaders met in Copenhagen on 10-11 September, where British Prime Minister Edward Heath and Jobert induced their colleagues to agree to sever the linkage between economic-political and military issues and, for the former, insist that the United States "welcome the intention of the nine to ensure that the Community establishes its position in world affairs as a distinct entity."[25]

Kissinger was not pleased by the nine's tactics, or by the substance of their economic-political declaration. On 29 September, Assistant Secretary of State J. Walter Stoessel, Jr. presented American amendments, with significant changes in tone and substance, to the EEC draft statement. Washington, for example, inserted references to the "mutually interdependent" character of the American-European "partnership," and brought up the need for advance coordination of policies and joint, harmonious actions on issues connected with East-West détente, foreign investment, world commodity trade, energy, and the like. The nine's claim for a new European role as a "distinct entity" in world affairs was watered down by the American assertion that European union should be "based on partnership" with the United States. Finally, in an attempt to restore the linkage of economic-political and military issues, the American version referred to the indispensable nature of "existing alliance arrangements" and brought up other defense issues, such as MBFR. The net effect of these revisions was to negate Europe's insistence on a separate identity by institutionalizing an American role as a privileged partner across a broad spectrum of issue areas. Similar differences in perspective and interests arose in regard to the NATO declaration under discussion in Brussels, where work had stalled over a stubborn French refusal to include references to trade and financial problems or to agree to the principle of compensating "some" Alliance members for assuming extra defense burdens.[26] The unproductive discussions on defense matters were formally halted at the suggestion of Paris on 26 October, the day after the United States unilaterally put its military forces on a world-wide alert. The other proposals also fell into a limbo because of the Middle East crisis, which cast brutal clarity on the gulf separating American and European policies and conceptions of the future of allied relations.

The October War focused Atlantic attention on an arena where American and European political and economic interests had been historically divergent, a situation that had not abated in the years immediately proceeding 1973. After the Six Day War in 1967, de Gaulle reacted to Israeli expansionism by refusing to recognize the occupation of Arab territory and urging Israel to withdraw as a prerequisite for a peaceful settlement. By 1969, a partial arms embargo to battlefield states was made total as far as Israel was concerned, while Libya, Algeria, and Iraq continued to purchase French weapons freely. The French pro-Arab position was dictated by concrete interests as well as by principles, because in 1971 France was importing 74.1 percent of her oil from members of the Organization of Arab Petroleum Exporting Countries (OAPEC) and was dependent on them for 50 percent of her total energy consumption.[27] By 1973, other West European governments had not adopted such strong pro-Arab policies, but they were acutely aware of their common dependence on

OAPEC for some 75 percent of their total oil supplies and 50 percent of their energy resources.[28] There was also a growing feeling that Israeli intransigency since 1967 had become a primary obstacle to a Middle East settlement, and that the United States was encouraging such an attitude by arming Israel without exerting pressure for more concessions and flexibility. Thus, before the outbreak of hostilities on 6 October, France, Britain, and Italy had, in varying degrees, adopted pro-Arab positions. The Netherlands and Denmark, on the other hand, remained strongly pro-Israel, whereas West Germany was phasing out a "special relationship" with the Jewish state and occupying neutral ground on the Arab-Israeli conflict.

These diverse perspectives made it difficult for the Europeans to arrive at a firm and united position during the war, though their energy interests, and pressures of the oil embargo, eventually pulled them in a pro-Arab direction. To the annoyance of some, Jobert took a particularly realistic view of the conflict, noting that "to try and set your feet back in your own house does not necessarily amount to unforeseen aggression."[29] Initial French and British efforts to formulate a common European policy were not productive, however, and the EEC Council of Ministers barely managed, on 13 October, to issue a weak statement, which called for a cease-fire and negotiations on the basis on U.N. Security Council Resolution 242. This doubtless encouraged the Arabs to press "Europe" for a more definitive stand, and the vehicle chosen by Israel's enemies was a selective embargo on oil deliveries and progressive reductions in oil exports by OAPEC members.

Meeting in Kuwait on 17 October, these governments announced a monthly cut of 5 percent in oil production, based on September figures, to continue until "the international community compels Israel to relinquish [Arab] territories" or until the economies of oil-producing states were suffering.[30] The Arab ministers exempted from the embargo those countries that "actively and effectively" supported the Arabs or damaged Israel, and promised to cut oil supplies further for pro-Israeli states. The United States had already begun airlifting military supplies to Israel on 13 October, and Nixon was requesting massive additional aid from Congress; thus it was no surprise on 19 October when the Arabs announced a total embargo on oil exports to the United States. The next day, the Netherlands was placed in the same category as the United States, whereas friendlier states, such as Britain, France, and Spain (later Japan and Belgium as well), were granted the same level of supplies as of September 1973. By distinguishing among friends, neutrals, and enemies, the Arabs encouraged the Europeans to disassociate themselves from Israel and the United States and to adopt a joint pro-Arab position that would avert major disruptions in oil supplies. Amidst somewhat exaggerated fears of crippling energy shortages, the nine did pull themselves together and on 6 November produced a declaration with major concessions to the Arabs. Clearly intended to placate OAPEC, the statement called on Israel to "end the territorial occupation which it has maintained since the conflict of 1967," declared that peace in the Middle East was incompatible with "the acquisition of territory by force," and asserted that a future peace settlement had to take account of the "legitimate rights" of the Palestinians.[31] Although this declaration was a rather tardy and awkward response to overt blackmail, and did not signify the inauguration of a joint European policy or a more substantial role for Europe in the Middle East, it did at least reflect a minimal Community concern to arrive at a common perspective reflecting some shared political and economic interests.

It seemed especially important that the European perspective was in direct conflict with the American one at the time, as economic interests on one side clashed with the strategic-diplomatic priorities of a global power. One aspect of the Middle East War, then, was its role in clarifying the linkage doctrine espoused by the United States and, in particular, revealing the potential political and economic costs of European dependence on the United States in the security arena. The two security issues that arose were: first, the availability of European territory for American global political-military activities at the expense of European interests; and, second, the consequential risk to Europe, as such American engagements raised the possibility of military clashes between superpowers that might automatically involve their unwilling allies. These quintessentially Gaullist preoccupations seemed, therefore, to acquire a new and more compelling significance for the Alliance after this extended allied conflict over the Middle East.

On the first security issue, divergent energy interests affected Alliance relations most directly by threatening to disrupt American efforts to furnish military supplies to Israel, via Europe, in the midst of the war. The problem was acute because of heavy Israeli losses sustained early in the conflict, partly due to Kissinger's insistence that the Israelis not strike first as the Arabs were preparing for an attack. In competition with Soviet resupply actions for the Arabs, Washington decided to launch a major effort to furnish Israel with aircraft, munitions, and antitank weapons in order to maintain a stable battlefield situation.[32] One immediate consequence of the arrival of American arms was to enable Israel to attack the west bank of the Nile on 15 October and remain ensconced there around the Egyptian Third Army until the time of the cease-fire on 22 October. In shipping supplies to Israel, Washington found that the neutral or overtly pro-Arab policies of American allies prevented the United States from using West European territory as a staging point or fuel stop. The direct delivery of supplies, including military aircraft, from the United States to Israel became a logistics nightmare because the only intermediate landing site was the Lajes airbase in the Azores. Portuguese oil came from Angola at the time, so the Lisbon government was less susceptible to Arab pressures than other allies in Europe. Most European economies were quite vulnerable, however, and direct assistance to American aircraft was banned in Spain, Italy, Greece, and at the British air base of Akotiri on

Cyprus. Greece, for example, declared neutrality in the Middle East War on 13 October, a move that damaged only Israel, as Athens forbad use of its land, air, and sea space for any war-related activities.[33] Other governments took similar measures, forcing American cargo planes to avoid all land areas beyond the Azores, so that Phantom jet fighters reached Israel only by resorting to four air-to-air refuelings.[34] The Sixth Fleet was indispensable to support this kind of mission, and Mediterranean allies at least granted it continued access to fuel supplies.[35]

France's expulsion of American forces and depots in 1966 spared her any direct confrontations over American resupply efforts, but West Germany found itself in a more sensitive position. Early in the war, American depots in West Germany were an important source of stocks to be raided for immediate Israeli needs, and West German and Dutch ports were used to load tanks and other heavy weaponry for transport by sea. Later, the U.S. Air Force base at Ramstein was used as a way station for some American cargo planes headed toward the Middle East. Officially neutral and "unaware" of such activities, Bonn permitted them, without comment, to continue until 23 October. The West German attitude was changed by the intervention of several events—they included the oil embargo and Arab diplomatic pressures; Israeli gains on the West bank of the Nile, in violation of a U.N. Security Council cease-fire resolution; and the publicized loading of an Israeli ship at the U.S. Army dock at Bremerhaven. German protests, and an attempt to halt all such activities, produced an unusually acerbic dispute between Bonn and Washington, leading Secretary of Defense James D. Schlesinger to raise questions about the utility of keeping bases and American military stocks in Europe if they were not available for American activities outside NATO.[36] Washington refused to accept the West German stand that the American military presence there was only for the purpose of deterring or combating Soviet aggression against the NATO area, not for a projection of American military power into contiguous regions heavily engaged in the superpower struggle.[37] The American position, later expressed in a letter from Nixon to Chancellor Brandt, held that, in spite of divergent oil interests between the United States and Europe, the Soviet-American aspect of the competitive intervention in the Middle East meant that "the interests of the Alliance as a whole" were automatically and intrinsically engaged and in such cases the Alliance could not "operate on a double standard," with Europe pursuing a separate policy.[38] Thus, Kissinger's theme that Europe's regional parochialism had to yield to the general interest of a global superpower equilibrium took on concrete significance as a result of the Middle East conflict. Yielding to strong American pressures, the West Germans later agreed that, as a price of American protection, they would in the future permit such resupply activities as long as American carriers were used exclusively.[39] The United States apparently did not place much confidence in such promises, however, and subsequently took a number of measures to avoid dependence on European territory or stockpiles for emergency resupply efforts on behalf of Israel.

The second related security issue (of superpower cooperation and conflict at Western Europe's expense) first arose during this period, as a result of the Nixon-Brezhnev agreement of 22 June on the Prevention of Nuclear War. During the Salt II negotiations and the slow onslaught of the Watergate crisis, Nixon signed this nonbinding declaration of joint superpower intent to avoid military confrontations and to act in such a manner "as to exclude the outbreak of nuclear war between them and between either of the parties and other countries."[40] The United States and the Soviet Union committed themselves to immediate consultations should the risk of nuclear conflict arise, but undertook to reassure their military dependents that the agreement did not impair "obligations undertaken by either party toward its allies." Despite Kissinger's attempts to head off charges that the superpowers were structuring their future conflicts to the disadvantage of their own allies, the agreement was bound to be interpreted in Europe as another incentive to avoid nuclear escalation and weaken the kind of NATO deterrent posture most judged to be essential to West European security.[41] Suspicion and discontent were enhanced by the American failure to consult allied governments before going ahead with the agreement, despite the Year of Europe theme of close and continuous consultations on such issues. Brandt, Pompidou, and Heath were reportedly informed (not consulted) only two or three days in advance, and the NATO council was notified only six and one-half hours before the text was signed.[42] Resulting confusion and anxiety in allied capitals ruffled the already disjointed Year of Europe discussion, and allowed the French to make a convincing case for a separate and distinct European identity. The French position seemed even more compelling after the unilateral American global military alert early in the morning of 25 October, which transformed suspicions of condominium into concern for Europe's involvement in a superpower war.

The alert was a response to Soviet actions and statements that led some analysts in Washington to conclude that only a demonstration of military determination by the United States could prevent a direct Soviet intervention on behalf of Egypt and an ensuing risk of nuclear war between the superpowers. There may also have been considerations, stemming from the Watergate crisis and the firing of the special prosecutor, which convinced some in the administration of the need to display a firm will and mastery of events to the domestic public, foreign allies, the Soviet Union, and governments in the Middle East. The final decision was taken after the breakdown of a ceasefire had produced rapid Israeli gains in Egypt. A terse message from Brezhnev condemned these violations and suggested a joint superpower intervention or, failing that, threatened unspecified unilateral steps by Moscow.[43] American intelligence reports described ominous preparations of Soviet military forces and led a rump NSC meeting (with Nixon in touch only by phone), to agree to call a selective alert of American conventional and nuclear forces on a global basis.

The alert itself affected American forces stationed around the globe, from Panama to Alaska, Guam to the Mediterranean. The Mediterranean-based Sixth Fleet was put on DefCon 2 status, the closest to actual war, and was kept at an enhanced readiness stage of alert into November, even though most units returned to their regular activities as early as 26 October.[44] The alert also involved American forces stationed, on the basis of bilateral or NATO agreements, on the territory of European allies. In Britain, for example, the three USAF strike bases and the Polaris submarine facility in Scotland went on alert status before responsible British authorities were informed.[45] Forces under the American Commander-in-Chief Europe, who doubles as SACEUR, were also placed under alert status in their capacity as American rather than allied troops. It can also be assumed that some of the seven thousand American tactical nuclear weapons, at over one hundred sites in Western Europe, were involved in this exercise, as the TNWs of the Sixth Fleet most certainly were. The land-based TNWs, under the control of the American commander, were linked in American strategy to the possible use of U.S. strategic forces (also alerted), and about one-third of the depots in Europe were earmarked for use by American troops. According to an authoritative report on these weapons, when the alert status changes from normal "quick reaction" to "advanced readiness" level (which probably corresponds to the one on 25 October), the TNWs are moved into readiness position under American custody and more of them are loaded and aimed at priority targets.[46] Despite formal requirements to obtain the consent of the host country before firing such weapons, in a global crisis the use of American strategic weapons is coordinated with theater force actions, and, had the Middle East crisis gotten out of hand, it seems certain that European territory would have been involved in any military confrontation of Soviet-American forces. This linkage had, of course, been Europe's guarantee that American strategic forces would indeed be used to protect the NATO theater. But, in October, the situation seemed capable of turning against Europe, as a bipolar confrontation threatened to spill over onto the territory of reluctant allies.

Because the alert was cancelled for most forces after only one day, when the Soviets immediately agreed to accept a U.N. emergency force in place of superpower intervention, the potentially dangerous crisis quickly deescalated. Many allies were, however, understandably upset because the sudden American decision had caught them unawares and embarrassed when NATO headquarters and individual allied capitals were informed of the alert almost as an afterthought, and only after the news began leaking out to the public.[47] European concerns about Washington's brinksmanship were scarcely allayed as conflicting rationales and motives for the alert gradually emerged from a somewhat incoherent Nixon administration. Whereas Kissinger at one point sought to play down both Soviet actions and the alert itself, terming the latter "certain precautionary measures," his subsequent explanations were more dramatic—and President Nixon described the situation as "potentially explosive" and "the most difficult crisis [the U.S.] had since the Cuban missile crisis of 1962."[48] Different perspectives and shifting interests explain the disjointed explanations about the alert, but the impression of confusion, miscalculation, and even dangerous overreaction was difficult to allay.

As mentioned, France capitalized on allied concern and disunity to convince her European partners to break off negotiations over the Year of Europe's NATO declaration, so talks were not resumed until 14 November. As de Gaulle had done so often, Jobert also attempted to transform European discontent into a joint effort to define a separate European identity with a defense component. After the Nixon-Brezhnev agreement in June, Jobert and Pompidou evidently decided that security issues were bound to figure prominently in the Atlantic negotiations, and, following the Middle East crisis, they saw an opportunity to try and extend European cooperation to include military affairs. Jobert told the National Assembly on 12 November that Europe had been "humiliated" and treated like a "nonperson" during the October conflict.[49] On 21 November he proposed to the Armaments Committee of the Western European Union that the WEU be revived as a forum for defense discussions outside of NATO and as an alternative to "exclusive superpower crisis management."[50] Paris also submitted a new version of the NATO declaration under negotiation. This draft noted that because of the mutual vulnerability of the superpowers and their tenuous equilibrium, Europe remained particularly exposed during conflicts; thus, European defense was "gradually taking on a dimension of its own." Along with some oblique criticism of the June Soviet-American agreement, the draft sought confirmation of American commitments to European security, but acknowledged that EEC progress toward political unity should affect their defense policies as well.[51]

This French initiative received discreet and temporary support from the Heath government, but was diverted and blocked by a West German cabinet that was fearful of expanding the serious rift in Atlantic relations. The Europeans did assemble for the Copenhagen summit in December 1973, and managed to lay some groundwork for future political cooperation. But the more natural European tendency toward disunity in the face of an Atlantic crisis soon prevailed, along with the inclination of most EEC governments to defer to American demands rather than escalate the confrontation, as Jobert seemed willing to do. Thus, the French attempt to solidify the European identity was undermined even before the change in regime in Paris led to a shift in French tactics and priorities.

Another reason for this development was that American policy became unusually direct in its insistence that the Europeans, who were in any case divided, should subordinate their economic and political interests to the formulation of a common Atlantic policy for the energy issues that had suddenly become crucial. After a particularly hostile exchange between Kissinger and Jobert during a North Atlantic Council meeting in December, Washington escalated its efforts to forge a joint American and European approach to energy problems, as part of a strategy of making the United States the fulcrum of Middle East diplomacy and global energy politics. To head off the French effort to create an independent Euro-Arab dialogue, Kissinger insisted that Atlantic consultation on shared problems had to take place before the West Europeans defined their own approaches and then confronted the United States with nonnegotiable *faits accomplis.*[52] The price of European stubbornness was spelled out in subsequent American declarations, which stressed the linkage doctrine with unusual clarity. President Nixon, for example, told American allies gathered for the February energy conference that "security and economic considerations are inevitably linked, and energy cannot be separated from either."[53] A few weeks later, he added that Europeans could not "gang up" against the United States on economic or political issues and still expect to hold on to American forces or, by implication, the security guarantee.[54]

The sometimes brutal language of an administration under seige was probably unnecessary by 1974. American purposes in launching the Year of Europe in the first place were already being fulfilled via the *deus ex machina* of the Middle East War and the drastic rise in oil prices. These events damaged Europe more than the United States and temporarily redistributed relative leverage within the global political economy back in favor of Washington. The United States was thus finally able to prevail over France and a divided EEC, and focus the coordination of Western energy policies within a broad-membership International Energy Agency while the Euro-Arab dialogue never acquired any real significance. France was free to remain aloof from such obviously Atlanticist agencies, devote some attention to the organization of an ineffectual North-South conference, and still ardently pursue the bilateral contacts with oil producers that actually dominated the energy policies of most consumer governments. France could also prevent the final humiliation of a U.S.-EEC declaration, which might have formally ratified the American ascendancy by institutionalizing some sort of veto over European Community decisions. The only tangible result of the Year of Europe was thus a quite inoffensive NATO declaration that Giscard d'Estaing could sign as a first step in repairing Franco-American relations.

Despite the inconclusive outcome of this last major confrontation between the United States and its most obstinate ally, the Year of Europe period does furnish evidence about the new kind of relationship that seems to be emerging between the United States and its European allies. It is based on various factors, including the partial adversary nature of exchanges among members of security alliances; the problematic and often divisive effects for allies of linkages between security and economic issues; and the emergence of more flexible alliance ties characteristic of pluralistic alliance systems at a time when mutual defense and security bonds fluctuate unpredictably in significance. These themes, which indicate that the revival of American domination during 1974 was temporary and incomplete, will be discussed in the concluding chapter, along with an analysis of France's status as a prototype of the new kind of more complex Alliance relationship with the United States.

Giscard d'Estaing and the Diffident Reconciliation.   The sudden death of President Pompidou, and the election in April 1974 of a non-Gaullist successor, seem to have inaugurated a new and remarkable stage in French alliance and security policy. It is notable for a muffling of some cherished Gaullist principles in favor of a pseudoliberal pragmatism characteristic of the French center and evidently cherished by President Giscard d'Estaing.[55] To be sure, the requisite Gaullist vocabulary of "independence," if not "grandeur," and the broad lines of Fifth Republic defense and alliance policy have remained more or less intact as part of an apparent national consensus on the value of the Gaullist security legacy. But there is wide latitude within the parameters of this model, so the thrust of Giscard's policies has been to manage a French accommodation to the prevailing Atlantic order based on a rather modest assessment of France's power and capabilities in the crisis-ridden domestic and international settings of the post-1973 period.

This is an altogether more complex, even baffling, kind of environment, one dominated by economic issues of inflation, unemployment, raw materials resources and prices, export dependency and competition, and the constant threat of protectionism. As Pompidou did to some extent, Giscard and his collaborators have had to scale down traditional French expectations and adjust to a weaker France in the wake of the oil and energy crisis, a partial and uncertain reassertion of American predominance in the West, a shift of political-economic power in the EEC in favor of West Germany, and the increased influence that parts of the Third World have in searching for a radical redistribution of wealth from North to South. To cope with such problems, de Gaulle's successors have used some residual advantages left by a Gaullist design for economic as well as defense independence, in order to reduce France's vulnerability to an unstabled and disruptive international economy and to augment French leverage in the context of mutual dependence.[56] This is clearly no longer a strategy of challenging the prevailing international order, however, which is in any case more amorphous and resists purposeful change from any quarter. Instead, Giscard's regime has tried to manipulate international cooperation, and some privileged French ties to Europe and the Third World, in order to secure the best possible national position within a deteriorating environment for most Western political economies.

One of the most striking aspects of Giscard's foreign policy, especially after the Jobert-Kissinger debacle of the Year of Europe, was a steady rapprochement with the United States and with many American policies, a development that has also affected French attitudes toward NATO. Conciously abandoning the unproductive Jobert approach, Giscard instituted a new international policy under the theme of conciliation, which was transformed into a concerted effort to "soften" (*"déscrispation"*) French relations with the United States. Giscard explained that France's stiff and at times abrasive resistance to the United States over so many issues had proven counterproductive in the long run, and needed to be replaced by an essentially friendly relationship that could survive normal disagreements without the melodrama that had so often plagued Atlantic policies. This seemed particularly necessary in a period of economic uncertainty when, as Prime Minister Jacques Chriac noted in June 1974, "it is clear that [France's] economic development involves close ties with the leading economic power of the world."[57] The first concrete signal of this policy was Giscard's agreement to abandon the Jobert version of a text for the NATO declaration to inter the unfortunate Year of Europe. Thus, formulas implying a future European defense alternative to NATO were scrapped, and, in return, the United States revised one of its long-standing attitudes and recognized the French nuclear force as "capable of playing a deterrent role of its own contributing to the overall strengthening of the deterrence of the Alliance."[58] The détente in relations between Paris and Washington was subsequently transformed into a virtual entente at the unusually friendly Martinique meeting between Presidents Ford and Giscard d'Estaing in December 1974, where they resolved the most outstanding bilateral differences over a future global energy conference. Reconciliation was also the principal theme of Giscard's visit to the United States in May 1976. He made a special effort to reassure the Americans that France, though independent, was still a loyal ally, faithful to her engagements and willing, in Giscard's words, "to contribute to the efficacity of the Atlantic Alliance of which she is a part." The French leader went so far as to reassure the American Congress that France "attaches the greatest value to the American engagement," which, he acknowledged, "protects us from confrontation."[59]

These atypical French references to the value of the American Alliance reflected the generally closer and more cooperative bond between France and NATO itself that was fostered under Giscard. As discussed in the next section, changes in French strategy and defense policy, though somewhat ambivalent, do indicate a new commitment to a more active French role in the conventional defense of West Germany territory. This posture is more compatible with NATO defense plans and implies a greater willingness to participate in the defense of this zone in close cooperation with the allies. Giscard's governments have naturally adhered to the Gaullist principles of maintaining an independent nuclear defense and reserving a basic freedom of decision for France, but they have also stressed France's interest in the Atlantic Alliance as an indispensable factor of security and peace in Europe. As Prime Minister Raymond Barre told the North Atlantic Assembly in September 1977, France is "conscious of collective security, which is why our solidarity and our cooperation with the allies extends to all areas which do not affect our freedom of decision."[60] The practical consequences of this atttiude are somewhat difficult to measure or cite with a number of significant examples, because the change in tone is probably more important than the numerous small and quite discreet instances of collaboration between the military in France and the NATO staffs or commands. It is apparent, however, that Giscard has reinforced the post-1968 trend of rebuilding direct and efficient technical ties between the military organizations of France and NATO. This amounts largely to a more open, and perhaps less hypocritical, relationship on the part of France; it has not signified an obvious repudiation of Gaullist policies.

One reason Giscard has not tried to change the basic France-NATO settlement of 1966 is that he would face resolute domestic opposition from his suspicious Gaullist allies, and from various leftist parties, all of which have become committed to France's status as a nonintegrated and theoretically independent ally.[61] Elected by a bare margin of 50.8 percent, and faced with a sometimes unpredictable parliamentary majority, Giscard has had less independence than his predecessors to pursue policies as controversial and unpopular as a major transformation in France's security ties. This also appears to be an altogether unnecessary development, since the present amicable relationship is generally satisfactory to both France and NATO. Rather than risk a direct collision with the sacrosanct NATO policy, Giscard seems to have decided to grapple with some more peripheral, hence more malleable, aspects of the Gaullist security and foreign policy legacy. Along with recent French European policy, the disarmament and arms control issue is perhaps the best measure of a partial and often problematic French conversion to more extensive cooperation with the United States and other Western powers in arenas where France was once resolutely aloof, isolated, and somewhat impotent.

Under de Gaulle and Pompidou, France had boycotted international arms control agreements and conferences on the grounds that they were dominated by the superpowers and their mutual interest in stabilizing a bipolar equilibrium, or because they would have hampered progress in the development of France's own nuclear force. This policy dictated France's absence from the Geneva Converence after 1962, her refusal to sign the Test-Ban and

Non-Proliferation Treaties, and her absence from regional arms control forums such as the Vienna MBFR talks. Despite this approach and France's abstention from nonproliferation arrangements, it was always French policy to limit the dissemination of nuclear weapons to the natural oligarchy of elite states that had obtained them by the mid-1960s. Thus, France did not sign the Non-Proliferation Treaty, for example, but still declared in 1968 that she would act like a signatory state and support the basic aims of the agreement.

The likelihood of a spread of nuclear weapons to other powers had increased substantially by the mid-1970s, however, and concern about a possibly less stable and more dangerous world of many nuclear-armed governments produced a gradual shift in arms control policy under Giscard d'Estaing. The first indication of a new sensitivity in this area involved a peripheral issue, when Giscard decided, in June 1974, to halt French nuclear testing in the atmosphere as of the summer of 1975 and undertake underground tests at the Polynesian atoll of Fangatuafa.[62] The decision was based on eighteen months of research, initiated by Pompidou, that indicated that underground tests were feasible at this site, although the change was bound to hamper some aspects of French warhead development. Giscard's move also responded to domestic and international opinion, which was increasingly opposed to atmospheric testing and which had led Australia and New Zealand to bring the issue before the International Court of Justice. Because underground testing is essential to the French missile warhead program, Giscard has subsequently shown no interest in efforts to ban all testing and has avoided specific commitments such as adherence to the Test-Ban Treaty itself.

Fear of the potential dissemination of nuclear weapons seems to have prompted more significant steps on the part of France, including some national control measures and more cooperation with the United States and other suppliers of nuclear energy facilities and fuel. Like many Western industrial states, France has invested heavily in nuclear energy as a way of reducing future dependence on oil imports, setting ambitious targets of 23 percent nuclear power by 1985 and 45 percent by 2000.[63] This plan has led Paris to emphasize research in new forms of nuclear energy, including the fast breeder reactor that would free France from dependence on imported uranium from the United States, Canada, and Australia. One way of offsetting the high cost of such programs, of paying for current oil imports, and of enhancing France's position as a world leader in advanced technology has been through exports of current nuclear technology and plant facilities. By 1974, France had preliminary nuclear plant agreements with Iraq, Iran, and Libya. In November 1975, Paris signed a contract to furnish Iraq with an enriched uranium reactor and, in 1976, agreed to provide South Korea and Pakistan with nuclear reprocessing plants that produce enriched uranium suitable for military purposes. The economic, industrial, and political advantages of such arrangements are partially offset, of course, by the danger of furnishing indirect assistance in the spread of nuclear weapons. The Indian bomb test in May 1974 was perhaps the crucial demonstration of the risk of exporting facilities and fuel without imposing stringent controls and safeguards.

In coping with this problem, Giscard's governments have taken a number of national and international measures that reflect the often contradictory nuclear priorities of France and other nuclear export states as well. On the national level, in October 1976, Giscard formed a *Conseil supérieur de politique nucléaire extérieure* to manage nuclear export policy. Shortly thereafter, in December, this committee decided to avoid future bilateral contracts involving the sale of reprocessing plants that produce weapons-grade fuel.[64] By this time, France had also joined the London Suppliers Group (formed in April 1975) and adhered to its "code of good conduct," which set out common standards to govern the sale of nuclear technology, facilities, and fuel. This was an important step, marking the first time France had joined such a cooperative effort, although loose commitments to regulate sensitive sales of nuclear processing plants did not prevent the conclusion of the controversial Pakistan contract in March 1976. French policy has subsequently oscillated between commercial and nonproliferation priorities. On the one hand, Paris has joined most other suppliers and resisted American efforts to tighten up joint controls over sensitive exports, insisting that the guidelines for the London Group of fifteen states should remain loose enough to eschew any suggestion that a supplier cartel is being created.[65] In general, Paris has been unwilling to accept formal restraints on nuclear exports or on the open availability of nuclear energy facilities subject to safeguards. The hope is that current supplier states will be able to fulfill the energy needs of consumer countries and dampen incentives for the latter to develop their own nuclear technologies without any international controls whatsoever.[66] This position is shared by most Europeans, in opposition to the harder line of the Carter administration, which sometimes seemed to turn against nuclear energy altogether. Uncooperative in regard to general principles favored by the United States, France has been more amenable in specific cases; for example, it accepted, under American pressure, South Korea's cancellation of its nuclear purchase contract with France, required more stringent controls for nuclear fuel in Iraq and, after lengthy and embarrassing negotiations, appeared to back out of the risky sale of nuclear installations to Pakistan by the fall of 1978. Despite such efforts, the need to export nuclear facilities and technology was bound to involve Paris in repeated embarrassments over the possible military ambitions of clients, as was the case with Iraq again in 1980. The obvious difficulty in arriving at a clear and manageable nuclear proliferation policy does not, of course, distinguish France from other industrial supplier nations.

Giscard's attempts to seize the initiative and the international spotlight, with respect to other arms control and disarmament issues, have also been shaky, notable more for the symbolic departures from Gaullist precedents than for the substance of the proposals. One major French campaign was announced in January 1978, during the heat of a national election debate and in anticipation of a special U.N. session on disarmament. An evident motive for a conservative government was to counter the left opposition's stress on an ambitious disarmament program as a focal point of a future left government's international security policy. Giscard's own proposals were couched in some standard Gaullist rhetoric as a design to end the superpower domination of the disarmament business by replacing the unproductive Geneva Conference with a new forum, which the United States and the Soviet Union would no longer chair jointly. The French plan also included the idea of a new all-European Conference, which would replace the MBFR talks and deal with both nuclear and conventional arms issues; a proposal for an international satellite monitoring system instead of the current superpower monopoly on such surveillance; and a vague reference to nondiscriminatory regulation of the international conventional arms trade.[67] The French president's personal interest in pursuing these measures led him to address the U.N. special session on disarmament in May 1978.

The typically ambivalent conclusion of that conference, and the general skepticism that greeted the concrete French projects for satellite surveillance and Europeans arms control talks, do not inspire a confident prediction that France will suddenly play a major role in this arena.[68] It does seem, however, that Paris will participate actively in the revived U.N. Committee on Disarmament and may return to the Geneva Conference under a revised format in line with Giscard's proposition.[69] The new arms control tool of French diplomacy remained active (if ineffective) during the international crisis atmosphere of 1980, when Paris advanced ideas for European initiatives in an effort to influence possible East-West theater security negotiations and, more generally, to resuscitate the gravely ill détente regime in Europe. French policy on such issues remained ambivalent, but one arms control problem that seemed altogether unlikely to experience significant concessions from France concerned the conventional arms trade. As the next section points out, arms exports have become quite important to the French economy as a growing source of employment and export earnings, as a means of paying for higher energy import bills, and as a way of sustaining a viable national arms industry.

The generally more accommodating tone of Giscardian diplomacy has also been evident in France's relations with the European Community and its constituent states. A more limited horizon had led Pompidou to stress the European-Mediterranean axis of France's international activities, and this focus continued and flourished under Giscard. The Atlantic rapprochement may even be considered an offspring of Giscard's priority interest in good relations with the European Community, since the new president decided early in his term that pervasive conflict with Washington was an unnecessary source of discord within the European Community. While mending Atlantic fences, Giscard has attempted to foster greater political cooperation and unity within the European Community. One accomplishment was the foundation of a "European Council" of heads of government, which began regular thrice-annual meetings in 1975. This formula, with roots in de Gaulle's confederal vision and Pompidou's own European policy, has proven to be a moderately useful way of resolving some conflicts at the highest level. Giscard also attempted a minor innovation in the Gaullist model by announcing, with great fanfare, that France would abandon the veto right secured after the EEC crisis of 1965. This concession was diluted considerably, however, when it became apparent that the veto was intact for any crucial decisions.

The two other major European initiatives undertaken with French support have been the plans for enlarging the Community to include Portugal, Spain, and Greece, following their conversion to democratic government, and the June 1979 elections for the European parliament. Although Paris's active interest in both these matters testifies to the revived influence of the "European" faction as a power in Giscard d'Estaing's governments, the future impact on European unity is uncertain. The prospect of a European parliament elected by universal suffrage met with some strident criticism from ardent Gaullist and communist defenders of national sovereignty, but the government downplayed the move as mere fulfillment of a commitment in the Treaty of Rome (Article 138)—as an action that would in itself not lead to expanded parliamentary powers. The enlargement of the Community presents an equally ambivalent prospect. Despite the problems that enlargement raises for important sectors of French agriculture and industry, it was strongly supported by the Elysée until some reservations emerged in the prepresidential election year of 1980. Although not the overt reasoning for the tactical and probably short-lived shift in the French position, it can be argued that, whereas the spread of organized European cooperation might represent a certain logical development in geographical and political terms, the lower level of social, economic, and political development of the prospective members seems likely to augur a long period of difficult adjustment for all concerned. At the very least, it seems that enlargement beyond the modern industrial powers of north-central Europe, plus hybrid Italy, will further weaken the tenuous social and political cohesion of the EEC. The entry of a reluctant and perpetually troublesome Britain has already posed numerous obstacles for a stagnating European Community, and the prospect of additional members may hamper the enterprise rather than stimulate it, as supporters obviously hope.

Giscard d'Estaing's proposed insurance against such a development has been the very Gaullist notion of forming an inner circle, or "directorate," to run the vital core of an increasingly amorphous community. This idea was revived by the French in February 1976 and was sometimes presented in the form of a second Council of Ministers reduced to its key members, France, West Germany, Britain, and Italy.[70] A variation of the idea was advanced by then

Chancellor Brandt and found its way into the Tindemans Report on political union, with the suggestion of a two-tiered Community of leaders and laggards. The prospects for this typically French ideal of how to organize political cooperation are uncertain, but it does seem that some such changes in Community institutions will be considered in conjunction with the entry of additional members.

The heart of French European policy has always been the relationship between France and West Germany and the often difficult mixture of cooperation and conflict that has accompanied the postwar rapprochement of these two powers. Giscard's policies necessarily bear the weight of this complicated legacy, but the trend since 1974 has certainly been to reinforce the collaboration aspect of the bond as the nexus of European unity during a period of strain. France and other Western states have had to adjust to a new relationship of equality with the Federal Republic since the Ostopolitik era, which mitigated the dependency status in the West that was always the price of unrealistic West German claims in the East. Also, West Germany has weathered the post-1973 economic crisis better than France and most industrial powers, so it has been natural for Paris to accord more deference to the stronger German partner. In the economic arena, at least, it seems that Giscard's regime is the first since Henri Petain's to accept a German ascendancy in Europe and adjust to a secondary role for France. Unlike Vichy, however, Giscard has the defense and security heritage of the Fourth Republic and of de Gaulle, and he can insist on maintaining an advantage in this area to compensate for West Germany's economic strength. This particular preoccupation of leaders in Paris is a continuous factor of France's policy and has become an immutable feature of the postwar European settlement.

Perhaps a commitment to this special French advantage explains why Giscard's active European policy has been devoid of emphasis on the formation of a separate or identifiable European identity in the defense arena. Despite a minor initiative in regard to European arms standardization, or the potentially more important decision, in early 1980, concerning a joint Franco-German project to develop a new combat tank, the defense dimension of European unity has been conspicuously absent from French policy since 1973. The French government has taken pains, when the issue has been raised publically, to insist that it has no plans to innovate in this arena. This is especially true regarding the prospect of any form of Franco-German nuclear collaboration in the context of a hypothetical European defense arrangement. After the French press and some politicians debated this issue in August and September of 1979, Giscard had an uncharacteristically vehement reaction: "I categorically exclude any proposal for France to create nuclear weapons in the Federal Republic of Germany. I exclude it categorically. It does not conform to the interests of France, of the Federal Republic, of Europe, or of détente."[71] This reflects a traditional and understandable French sensitivity on the subject, especially from an avowedly pro-European leader who must carefully delineate the boundaries of his policies. And, in any case, the more general French reluctance to take initiatives in respect to European defense seems to reflect the judgment that such cooperation would be premature (as it always has been) in the absence of significant political unity. It is also unlikely to develop and flourish outside the Atlantic context or in opposition to it, as de Gaulle's efforts verified. Because the prospects are uncertain, because the issue has only divided Europe in the past, and because France's independent status is an obstacle to European defense cooperation under the aegis of NATO, a European defense initiative is not on Paris's agenda for the time being—although it could be resuscitated by unforeseen developments.

A final and somewhat unexpected development in French security policy under Giscard has been the sporadic and limited expansion of the French political-military role in Africa. The attention given France's military assistance to some conservative and pro-Western African regimes inevitably provokes comparisons with Fourth Republic policies that had supported a more overt French colonialist mission on the continent, as part of a general strategy of thwarting alleged communist schemes to undermine the West. Although the argument was generally dismissed at the time as a pretext for French colonialism, it has since acquired partial credibility in the light of Soviet and Cuban activities in Africa on behalf of radical regimes or revolutionary movements threatening governments with close ties to the West. In the context of a general North-South confrontation over a proposed redistribution of global wealth, it is natural for industrial economies to be uneasy about such activities and the long-range threat they may pose to Western interests. In some ways, France seems the ideal Western state to furnish support to moderate elements in Africa and generally act on behalf of the industrial powers. De Gaulle's decolonization policies salvaged much of France's reputation and many of her interests in Africa. Also, the Gaullist role as an independent Western power aiding a Third World exploited by superpower conflicts always did have an esthetic appeal to new nationalists searching for a suitable ally. Finally, France has been able to supply some practical benefits and has been a sponsor of generous agreements between the European Community and underdeveloped states. Giscard is, therefore, in a position to capitalize on this legacy at a time when French and European interests in Africa may be in jeopardy.

De Gaulle, of course, opposed American interventions in Africa (e.g., the Congo affair) and viewed the continent as a French zone of special responsibility in the wake of the British retreat. Giscard has not had to confront so much American activism in Africa, and instead has usually faced an indecisive American administration unable or unwilling to intervene because of various domestic constraints and reservations. France, on the other hand, has maintained a modest but active military presence in Africa, as part of a network of defense and military assistance agreements with client states in the region. Under de Gaulle, French units acted to support governments in power in

Senegal in 1962, in Gabon in 1964, and in Chad after 1968. Military support of such actions, or to protect other French interests, has been available from six military bases maintained by France in and around Africa: Dakar (Senegal), Djibouti, the island of Réunion, Mayotte, Abidjan (Ivory Coast), and Libreville (Gabon). Although estimates differ, it seems there was a total of 14,000 to 15,000 French military personnel of all kinds on the African continent in 1978. Ten thousand of them were troops rather than mere technical advisers, and the largest combat contingent was the 4,500-man unit stationed in the newly independent and strategically located Djibouti.[72] France was thus the second largest external military presence on the continent, after the Cubans, who had a force of 34,000-35,000 concentrated in Ethiopia and Angola.

Under Giscard, the most prominent French military actions have taken place in Zaïre and in the disputed areas of the Mauritanian Sahara. In April 1977, when the incompetent Mobutu regime was unable to deal with disorders in the mineral-rich Shaba province (formerly Katanga), France furnished thirteen "Transall" military cargo planes and two other aircraft to ferry equipment and Moroccan soldiers to quell the menace of anti-Mobutu guerrillas infiltrating from leftist Angola.[73] This occurred just before the third Franco-African Conference at Dakar and was doubtless intended to reassure Paris's African allies that France could act decisively on their behalf. Giscard made this point at the meeting, adding that such French assistance was preferable to superpower involvement in African affairs.[74] The second and more direct French intervention in Zaïre, in May 1978, did, nevertheless, involve American assistance—for the United States had to furnish C-141 long-range transports for support missions on behalf of the French and Belgian forces flown to the mining city of Kalwezi in Shaba. This intervention, undertaken for both humanitarian and political motives, engaged some thousand French legionnaires and fifteen hundred Belgian troops to save European and American residents from local guerrilla attacks and general disorder.[75]

Giscard's other principle military action in Africa was on behalf of the Mauritanian government and against the Algerian-backed Polisario guerrilla forces fighting for control of this part of the Sahara and its rich phosphate deposits. Following the Polisario's capture, in May and October of 1977, of some French residents working in the area, Paris temporarily increased its military assistance to Mauritania and initiated air reconnaissance and attack missions from the French base at Dakar.[76] The Sahara engagement, in addition to the French presence in Chad—which ended in 1980 and failed to prevent a Libyan-backed victory by Frolinat guerrillas—seemed to represent a commitment in support of a pro-French regime and French commercial investments. This was a more significant military engagement than apparently singular incidents such as the one in the fall of 1979, when Paris had to resort to troops to help remove the embarrassing client regime of Bokassa in the Central African Empire (Republic). Despite the apparent expansion of France's military role in Africa, then, most actions of these kinds were not really a great burden, represented temporary commitments, and probably could be revived or sustained at reasonable, limited levels.

The prospect of an emerging French role as a sort of Western gendarme in Africa does, however, seem remote.[77] It is unlikely in part because of the political reservations of the Gaullists and the left in France, but mostly because France did not have the transport or logistics support to back up large-scale, drawn-out interventions at a great distance. Nor could France hope to sustain alone a major and drawn-out military confrontation against a well-armed and effective opponent. Rather than aspire to a grand imperial role, then, Giscard's African policy has been a characteristic pastiche of pragmatic reactions to situations where identifiable French interests seemed to be at stake and could be protected with minimal risk. This behavior was sometimes justified with grand Gaullist-type allusions, but was more often presented as a limited maneuver for specific and available gains. France's tendency to act in support of a perceived general Western interest in Africa only verifies the region's importance and relatively new role as a contested zone in conflicts involving the superpowers and their allies. The situation also confirms that France's recent rapprochement with the United States and the European-Atlantic system grants her a certain informal status as a Western agent in Africa, a role that eluded both de Gaulle and the Fourth Republic and now ironically seems possible for Giscard, the diffident successor to a series of stubborn and generally antagonistic French leaders.

The picture that emerged of Giscard d'Estaing's security and alliance policies after six years was an elusive and ambivalent one, reflecting often uncertain presidential priorities in the face of difficult internal and international situations. It is clear that security and national defense were, until the international crises of 1979-80, not overriding concerns for a president who had of necessity been preoccupied by economic issues and a hostile or suspicious domestic political environment ill-adapted for the pursuit of grand designs or attempted transformations of international politics. Giscard is obviously unsuited to such exertions by a temperament and outlook that eschew the preoccupation with nationalism and an overriding exertion of state interest (domestic and international), which drove de Gaulle and sometimes even Pompidou. Also, France's relatively weak position in the international context since 1973 reinforced Giscard's own inclination toward a reconciliation with the country's traditional partners in the European and Atlantic arenas.

Although the historical analogy should not be carried to an extreme, Giscard has faced a situation similar, in broadest terms, to the context that shaped French policies in the late 1940s and led then to a partial French accommodation to the emerging Atlantic system. In addition to a national economic crisis featuring the effects of inflation, unemployment, and loss of productive capabilities, the international economy of the 1970s was plagued by a chaotic monetary situation and by disruptions or distortions of international trade that differed specifically from the problems of the early postwar years, but did create a similar climate of widespread concern about the future of the industrial West. Such periods typically produce either a revival of protectionist and nationalist tendencies, as in the 1930s, or greater efforts for cooperation and joint management of problems, as in the postwar period and (with less consistency or success) in the late 1970s.

Another international factor with ominous precedents was the revival of general Western concern about the continuous growth of Soviet military influence and nuclear power, confronting the United States globally and Western Europe locally—a concern that was heightened by the impressive extension of Soviet naval power at a time when assured access to sources of oil and raw materials seemed critical to the developed world. Although an imminent, direct Soviet threat to France's actual physical security has rarely been the determining factor of national security policy, the renewed sense of a generalized and global Soviet menace, after the heyday of Gaullist détente efforts, often did reinforce Giscard's inclination to cooperate with leading Western allies such as the United States and West Germany. There are, naturally, constraints and contradictions in France's more pragmatic approach toward the United States and allied security interests, and the requirement of maintaining a basic posture of independence within the West has been a lasting and compelling one for Paris. In this context, then, Giscard d'Estaing's foreign and security policies probably represent the furthest point of Atlanticism that can reasonably be expected on a French spectrum ranging from full political-military neutrality to a thorough defense integration in NATO with all that it implies. If, for various reasons, neither extreme has been a practical option for France in the entire postwar period, it is unlikely that Giscard will want to move much further toward the Atlanticist pole because of important domestic constraints and because the Atlantic security system itself has turned into a looser, more diversified arrangement that can accommodate a partial ally on the French model of mixed independence and cooperation without subservience.

Defense Strategy and Military Policy

Since 1968, French defense strategy has reflected the evolution in foreign policy and has steadily retreated from the extreme implications of the Ailleret doctrine to adopt a French version of the Alliance concept of graduated response. This trend has accelerated under Giscard d'Estaing, to the point where French strategic doctrines posit an almost certain participation in the defense of West Germany in cooperation with NATO. The precise conditions of this participation remain secret and probably uncertain to planners and decision makers themselves, especially in respect to the guidelines for using France's tactical nuclear weapons over West German territory. The recent emphasis on actual use of military force in Europe and to the south has led the government to place more stress on conventional forces and weapons development, thus slowing down the improvement and expansion of the strategic nuclear force itself. Although Giscard has reversed the post-de Gaulle trend of declining relative defense expenditures within the national budget, his resources are still limited and tend to be spread more evenly among several priorities rather than concentrated on nuclear defense. It is uncertain whether this policy will appreciably augment France's actual military capabilities, just as the French contribution to nuclear deterrence in Europe faces a problematical future.

These trends were initiated shortly after the surfacing in 1967 of the Ailleret concept of *tous azimuts,* which foresaw an ICBM force as the natural outgrowth of France's global strategic role, posited that a military threat to France could come from any direction and not only from the East, and promised virtually exclusive reliance on the doctrine of massive retaliation. At the time of Ailleret's death, in March 1968, this posture was already being reevaluated within the government for its feasibility in terms of financial and technical resources. These and other considerations led to a revision in defense doctrine announced by Ailleret's successor, General Fourquet, in a speech at I.H.E.D.N. on 3 March 1969.[78] There, Fourquet made some modifications in France's nuclear defense strategy and in her plans for the forces and weapons available to implement it. First, the Armed Forces Chief of Staff retreated from Ailleret's exclusive reliance on instantaneous massive retaliation in response to an attack, and he instead adopted a view more closely resembling the Alliance graduated response concept. He said that military victory could only be achieved "by a combination of attitudes, and if need be, 'sub-strategic' actions of all force systems, under the effective threat of this strategic strike." The purpose of defense, according to Fourquet, was to convince the enemy that France still had "the will and capacity to use strategic weapons," but under numerous circumstances "the 'all or nothing' alternative would detract from the plausibility, from the credibility of our attitude." In order to reinforce this credibility, France intended to furnish her armed forces with tactical nuclear weapons, which would demonstrate the will to use the strategic force once a predetermined threshold is reached. This was an important innovation, because Ailleret had refused to admit that TNWs might be employed before recourse to the strategic force, an idea that he considered too close to the American flexible response policy. Thus, Fourquet did move in the direction of NATO concepts, although he specifically denounced a conventional response as economically and politically impossible for France or Europe. Fourquet indicated another modification in the French attitude toward the Alliance by singling out the East as the only likely source of aggression against

France, adding that in the face of such an aggressor, France presumed she would act in "close coordination with the forces of [her] allies."

Paris was once again focusing on security in Europe, especially since the proposed ICBM force had been abandoned, but in the Fourquet strategy there were still significant problems that were to prevent a genuine rapprochement between France and NATO. They were most evident in the role Fourquet assigned to the land-air *Forces de manoeuvre* (or, *Forces d'intervention*), scheduled to be equipped with tactical nuclear weapons. In his 1969 speech, Fourquet envisaged three stages in the escalation process during an attack. The first was the point of initial contact in West Germany between French forces and those of an enemy, which, if the latter did not halt, would lead almost immediately to the political decision to use TNWs. This second stage would occur whether or not the enemy had resorted to atomic weapons; its function was to "test the enemy's intentions" to continue with a thrust toward the national frontier. France's first nuclear response was meant to indicate her resolve to protect her own territory, and, if the enemy did not recoil in the face of this threat, the strategic force was to be employed as the final stage. This strategy retained the crucial distinction between an aggression against West Germany and one directed specifically against France, because TNWs came into use only when the enemy was heading for French territory, and the strategic force was triggered only when this thrust could not be halted. The purpose of tactical arms was thus to avoid a land battle in France and limit it to the "approaches" in West Germany. As before, the allies were expected to meet an attack in the forward zone without direct French assistance. Moreover, as Fourquet admitted, France and NATO could easily fail to agree on the point at which nuclear arms should enter the fray; such a failure would effectively prevent a commitment of French battlefield forces and cause a resort to strategic arms—certainly before the eastern frontier was breached. In this respect, then, the Fourquet revisions did not amount to a convergence with allied strategies and instead created some new problems. For the French version of graduated response remained oriented toward the defense of the hexagon, and it relegated West Germany to the status of a nuclear battlefield where initial engagements would either preclude the necessity of using strategic forces or trigger the deterrent before France herself came under attack.

Until Giscard d'Estaing came into office, developments in French strategic thought did not resolve the ambiguous relationship between national security and the surrounding European territory. On the one hand, there was a further retreat from the rigid adherence to instantaneous nuclear retaliation. Written under the authority of Defense Minister Michel Debré, the 1972 *White Paper on National Defense* seemed to emphasize the first stage of Fourquet's escalation ladder, implying that the conventional nuclear threshold might be as significant as the one separating tactical and strategic nuclear arms:

It is inconceivable to think of retaliating to all hostile action, regardless of where it comes from by nuclear threat. Therefore, the aim is to be able to oppose limited hostile actions, either by counter-acting directly or by reverting to appropriate retaliation. The idea of deterrence is not absent from this viewpoint but when the atomic weapon, due to its very excess, cannot constitute a credible deterrent argument, conventional and easily deployed means should be available. Crossing the threshold of the atomic threat can only be justified in a really critical situation.[79]

Under Debré, then, France adopted a modified version of the flexible response doctrine. It was qualified by her limited ability to provide the armed forces with a large conventional capability and the firm conviction that an attack irresistibly headed for France herself had to trigger the *Force nucléaire stratégique*. This interpretation of the White Paper was confirmed by Debré before he resigned as defense minister. He added that flexible response was a natural doctrine for any nuclear power to embrace in order to avoid a precipitous and suicidal recourse to strategic arms.[80] Such a development did not, on the other hand, augur a substantial modification in the French perspective on the West German battle zone. For the cardinal principle of Gaullist defense was upheld by French officials under Pompidou, namely, that the nuclear deterrent could only be used to protect the "vital national interests," defined as the national territory and its approaches.[81] As in the 1960s, it was contended that the French nuclear force somehow benefited the rest of Europe, even though strategic nuclear deterrence operated only for the national territory itself. The White Paper stated, for example, that "France lives in a network of interests which go beyond her borders. She is not isolated. Therefore Western Europe as a whole cannot fail to benefit indirectly from French strategy which constitutes a stable and determining factor of security in Europe".[82] In his speeches and articles, Debré frequently attempted to dispel the notion of an isolated France and rejected the tendency toward neutralism that others had observed after 1966.[83] Nevertheless, the issue of how to reconcile the autonomous national nature of nuclear deterrence with France's strategic dependence on contiguous West German territory remained unsettled during this period.

French strategists were obviously disturbed by this problem, which was exacerbated by divergent NATO plans for defending Germany and a natural West German reluctance to be branded an "approach" to France and the object of a nuclear bombardment by independent French forces acting on the orders of the Elysée. Although the issue had been debated within French strategic planning offices since the late 1960s, the first significant change in European defense policy was the emergence of a new approach in 1976, under the auspices of Giscard d'Estaing.[84] The principal innovation of the president and his Chief of Staff, General Guy Méry, has been to discard the earlier reliance on a nuclear-protected national sanctuary in favor of an "extended sanctuary" that includes contiguous European territory as well as the Mediterranean basin.[85] This zone, which covers West Germany, is now identified as the "first circle" of a French security perimeter and is a virtual extension of national territory for some purposes. According to Giscard, the new perspective revises the previous Gaullist emphasis on "two battles," one in West Germany and a second distinctive one for France. Instead, in case of a conflict, the president has foreseen that "there will be only a single space, and French space will be from the beginning in the zone of a battle which will be general."[86] Giscard's government has thus abandoned the narrow Gaullist concept of a "total sanctuarization" as impractical in a period of diverse global threats and inappropriate at a time when general French policy stresses "the promotion of a European entity."[87]

The broader implications of this shift for French force doctrines are relatively clear, although some issues, such as the purpose of TNWs, seem unresolved. The role of the strategic nuclear force is still to protect the national territory itself, so it seems that a military attack against French soil would, under most circumstances, bring a strategic retaliation on the aggressor.[88] Only the Soviet hypothesis is seriously considered under this quite unlikely possibility. Rather than the extreme "all or nothing" contingency, it is the extension of French deterrence and military force to cover the neighboring region that actually preoccupies French strategic planners. Thus, in contrast to earlier guidelines, Paris now assumes that France will participate in the "forward battle" of West Germany. As Méry said in 1976:

> I even think that it would be extremely dangerous for our country to deliberately hold herself aloof from such a first battle, in the course of which our own security would in fact be at stake. This does not rule out the idea of a battle on the frontiers; we could still be forced into this if the defense of the forward area crumbled too quickly, or if our decision to intervene came too late, or our movements were hindered by enemy action.[89]

This new policy has naturally led to a reevaluation of the role of France's conventional and tactical nuclear forces in continental European defense. Once designed essentially to test an enemy's intentions to attack France, the role of conventional forces under Giscard has been redefined as one of more active and extensive participation in battlefield actions, both on and off French soil.[90] France's conventional military capabilities are, therefore, being upgraded to give her more weight in a European context. An enhanced conventional capability is deemed particularly important by Giscard's defense planners, who believe that France's own security would immediately be at stake in any military crisis in Western Europe. Thus, they want to ensure a certain French conventional force leverage in determining the outcome of any crisis before it escalates to the nuclear level. Whereas West Germany's predominant conventional strength has now become the crucial factor among West European participants, plans for an increase in French forces are presented as a way of balancing West German influence within the coalition of Western allies.[91] Although de Gaulle evidently felt that France's strategic nuclear weapons provided a sufficient military edge over West German power, the new conventional defense emphasis in Paris has involved a revival of the Fourth Republic's preoccupation that a conventional balance is also the prerequisite for a stable and equal Franco-German partnership.

In this new French strategic environment, the purpose of the national tactical nuclear armory seems ill-defined if one judges by the sometimes contradictory statements of policy makers. In March 1976, for example, General Méry remained within Fourquet's earlier guidelines. He indicated that although the Pluton missile and nuclear warhead (available since 1974) might be considered a battlefield weapon, it was nevertheless intended to serve primarily as the first stage of an escalation process, thereby changing the stakes of a battle and warning the adversary of France's determination to resort to strategic arms.[92] Several weeks later, however, Giscard d'Estaing shifted the emphasis to point out that TNWs were both a stage in graduated deterrence and "an instrument of battle," leaving the impression that the two functions were equal in importance.[93] These diverse indications only confirm that France, like the United States and NATO, has not been able to formulate coherent and precise plans for using TNWs, although it seems that the Pluton's original function—as a trigger for the strategic nuclear force—is somewhat less prominent than in the past. The situation is especially ambiguous because the Pluton missile, allocated to army and air force units, is theoretically to be used only on West German territory in the earlier stages of a European conflict—but Paris has consistently refused to relinquish exclusive national control over this weapon, so the Pluton regiments have had to remain stationed in France.[94] The development and possible production of a neutron bomb, announced by the French government in June 1980, could aggravate these strategic and political problems for Paris. The addition of this tactical nuclear weapon to the French armory would be further confirmation of an intention to participate in the forward battle with significant force and weapons commitments, and without clear linkages for triggering the FNS itself.[95]

In general, then, Paris has pursued the implications of Giscard's strategy and reassured allies of France's "wish to take the part that falls to her in the common defense,"[96] a function that Méry defined as "participation in a support capacity in the first battle, which could ensure, at the same time, indirect cover for our national territory."[97] As indicated earlier, apart from the TNW control issue, the new French strategy is compatible enough with the prevailing NATO concept of a mixed conventional-nuclear battle on the central front for France's allies to assume that joint France-NATO combat plans have been extended and that French participation along agreed guidelines may be expected. This naturally provokes criticism from arch-Gaullist and left circles in France, but the force of such charges is deflected by public indifference and by Giscard's having retained a basic national military decision-making independence intact and, therefore, reserving the political autonomy that de Gaulle acquired in 1966.[98]

The final development of note in recent French strategy reflects France's African involvements and emphasizes that the nation must be prepared to confront the pressing threats reemerging to the south of Europe. Such warnings recall the less extreme interpretations of General Ailleret's statements, in 1967, to the effect that the direct Soviet menace was not the only or even most likely one faced by France. Giscard has noted that whereas the East-West conflict has been characterized by a military equilibrium, the North-South one has generally been fought by other means, but has recently experienced "a regional destabilization of security that revives the military dimension." Such considerations prompt a determination to sustain both France's military presence in Africa as well as her naval capabilities around that continent, in the troubled Indian Ocean-Persian Gulf area, and in the Mediterranean; to reinforce the government's determination to augment its conventional forces on land and sea; and to enhance their operational capacity and mobility for quick action in the event of a crisis.

As far as France's force structure is concerned, the five-year defense program developed under Giscard d'Estaing, as a guideline for military allocations from 1977 through 1982, is characterized by increased budgets for defense in general, especially for conventional forces, and by an apparent slowdown in the development of the strategic nuclear force. Adopted by the National Assembly in May 1976, the plan foresaw that by 1983 total defense spending would rise to 20 percent of the national budget, up from 17 percent in 1977, and reverse the general decline in relative defense expenditures since the late 1960s.[99] Since adopting this program, which was only an indication of intentions, the government has actually increased military spending at a faster pace than originally planned. The 1980 defense budget of 88.6 billion francs (excluding pensions) was 1.3 billion over the sum foreseen in 1976. It represented an increase of 14.9 percent over the 1979 defense budget, whereas the entire state budget grew by only 14.4 percent. The projected 1981 budget figure amounted to 104.4 billion francs, an increase of 17.9 percent over 1980, while the whole budget rose by only 14.8 percent. In spite of a planned increase in spending on the FNS, rising upkeep costs and other factors meant that in constant francs the FNS budget line actually was reduced slightly from 1969 to 1979.[100] For example, the favored sector of conventional programs increased 20.3 percent in 1978 over 1977, while the nuclear weapons section rose only 16.6 percent—confirming that the general orientation of the original program was being fulfilled.

According to defense ministry plans, then, France's conventional forces were undergoing a major restructuring and modernization effort that should have increased operational capabilities and mobility in this area. The land army was the major beneficiary of the effort, reversing the relative neglect it suffered before and at least halting the debilitating trend of increased spending on personnel and general functioning at the expense of training and new equipment. The Gaullist organization for the army was based on a structure of five active combat divisions for the *Forces de manoeuvre,* each with 15,000 men and a planned (but unfulfilled) armory including 1,500 AMX-30 tanks.[101] Under Giscard's 1982 project, the army was being restructured into a core of eight lighter armored combat divisions, with a total of between 1,000 and 1,200 AMX-30 tanks and 8,200 men per division.[102] In addition, the forces of the territorial defense force (*Défense opérationnelle du territoire,* or D.O.T.) were being merged with the battle corps of the *Forces de manoeuvre,* so that a fully mobilized French army will amount to about fifteen light divisions backed up by fourteen reserve divisions.[103] These plans involve a unification of the operational and territorial command structures and a more even dispersion of the new units around French national territory. The policy has led to the withdrawal of some 5,000 men from the units stationed in West Germany,[104] as well as a new diversion of forces away from the eastern frontier—developments that are somewhat puzzling in light of new French emphasis on a strong future participation in conflict on West German soil. Finally, for military interventions outside of Europe, France depends on the Eleventh Parachutist Division (15,000 men) and the Ninth Marine Infantry Division (6,000 men), although available professional (nonconscription) forces for service in Africa or elsewhere are limited to five regiments with around 1,000 men each. One principal material restriction on these interventions has been a weak long-distance transport and supply capability, which through 1978 was limited to thirty-eight Transall planes and four intercontinental DC-8s. This weakness may soon be partially overcome, however, since the Transall production lines are scheduled to be reopened, and a planned new production of twenty-five planes will include a modification to allow for air-to-air refueling when necessary.[105]

The new army organization was to result in a net decrease of about 20,000 men by 1980, from a total of 330,000 men in 1976.[106] Although the trend of decreasing manpower needs for a more modern army might lead decision makers to reevaluate the present universal conscription policy in France, it is a controversial political issue, and there are few prominent partisans of abolishing this expensive and often unsatisfactory way of securing manpower. The issue is bound to be revived periodically by unrest among draftees and financial considerations, but the government has been reluctant to attack the principle of the nation-in-arms.[107] Along with a more efficient and combat-oriented structure, France's conventional forces were scheduled to receive more modern equipment to bring them closer to the capability levels of the most advanced NATO units. Thus, for example, the twenty-year-old Mirage III fighter planes will be replaced by the Mirage 2,000 during the mid-

1980s, and, in the interim, the air force would have to be content with some new Mirage F-1 interceptors, despite qualms about the capabilities of this series. The army may also finally receive a modern combat rifle by the 1980s, and the navy's increased responsibilities in the Mediterranean and Indian oceans have focused more official attention on the problem of replacing or modernizing France's aging fleet.[108] The long lead time in ship construction and weapons development means that the results of programs developed now will not be visible before the mid-1980s, however, and it is unclear whether France's limited financial and technological resources will be able to produce a first-rate capability in many categories, despite the prospect of an overall improvement in conventional defense posture.

An additional factor affecting France's conventional army has been the growing dependence of the arms industry on export sales and the increasing importance of such arms production for the domestic economy and for national export capability. In relative terms, France's conventional arms exports have now returned to the status they held in the mid-1960s and by 1976 amounted to 4.3 percent of all exports (versus 4.2 percent in 1967). In the context of slowed economic growth, a loss of some traditional markets in the consumer goods sectors, and a generally weakened position in international trade competition, arms exports and expectations of future arms orders have assumed an increased economic and political importance. For example, the oil import bill, which grew after 1973 and left a 60 billion franc energy deficit by 1976 (versus an 18 billion franc deficit in 1973), is partially offset by arms contracts with Middle East states. About one-fifth of France's oil imports are currently covered by arms exports to OAPEC states and clients such as Egypt and Yemen, who have been financed with Saudi Arabian funds. The Middle East purchased 54 percent of French exported arms in 1974, up from 37 percent in 1970. France's total arms exports leaped from 2,081 million francs in 1965 to 11,640 million by 1976. Actual exports, as opposed to orders, amounted to $1,245 million by 1977, two-thirds of which were in the aeronautics sector, making France the third-ranking international arms supplier, surpassed only by the United States and the Soviet Union.[109] Finally, as a measure of the arms industry's domestic economic importance, it employs a total of nearly 300,000 workers, 110,000 to 120,000 of whom are estimated to handle export orders.

Apart from the general economic importance of the arms industry and its export capability, it is clear that foreign orders for some kinds of weapons have become essential to cover the research and development costs of weapons and aircraft series, as well as the cost of setting up or maintaining production lines that could not economically supply the limited needs of the French armed forces. Thus, although an advanced and internationally competitive arms industry has been an additional source of leverage against excessive dependence in the international economic arena, the situation does indicate that France's own "independent" military capabilities are increasingly dependent on export orders and specifications. The Mirage series, for example, was kept alive by 497 foreign orders from 1974 to 1978, while the French air force took only forty-one planes during the same period.[110] Of the 318 military helicopters produced by SNIAS between 1975 and 1978, 80 percent went to foreign clients, along with 50 percent of the company's antitank missiles. The AMX-30 tank series has also become an important export item; foreign orders rose from 25 percent of business in 1971 to 45-50 percent in 1977.[111] Export dependence increased to the point where Arab specifications for a revised tank and its gun almost had to be accepted by a reluctant French army as well.[112] Despite some disadvantages, however, it seems that France's economy and armed forces have benefited from the long-term Gaullist promotion of a national arms industry. It has allowed the country to meet most French requirements and still offset some of the consequences of a more open economy exposed to the consequences of international competition and penetration.

The centerpiece of the Gaullist security system has been the strategic nuclear deterrent force, and, in the light of Giscard's policies, the future of this key element of national and European security is somewhat uncertain. At present, the FNS still consists of the three basic components of the Gaullist structure. The oldest are the thirty-six Mirage IV aircraft in service, which are dispersed over seven bases. Each plane carries a seventeen-kiloton nuclear weapon. These planes are scheduled to be phased out of service between 1985 and 1990, although their present vulnerability to improved radar detection, and to defense systems effective against low altitude penetration, makes them a weapon of dubious value even today. France was studying the option of developing a cruise missile of her own, which might lead officials to reconsider the desirability of retaining some kind of strategic bomber force after 1985. The second component of the FNS consists of the eighteen S-2 ballistic missiles grouped in the two squadrons at hardened sites on the Plateau d'Albion in Haute-Provence. The existing missiles have a range of 2,800 kilometers and carry warheads of 150 kilotons each, but this system is being replaced by S-3 thermonuclear weapons, which can travel about 3,500 kilometers, with warheads of over one megaton. By 1980, defense officials were studying the possibility of installing a third-generation warhead such as the M-4 (a MRV device). The most important innovation for the land-based missile force was, however, the decision taken by Giscard d'Estaing in June 1980, to order development of a mobile missile-launching system for installation after 1992.[113]

Grouped under the *Force océanique stratégique* (FOST), the missile-launching nuclear submarines continue to be the most important part of France's strategic nuclear triad. There are five such submarines in service. Each has been equipped with sixteen missiles; each missile has a range of 2,500 kilometers and a "doped" warhead of 500 kilotons. Since early 1976, the submarines have been receiving new M-20 missiles, with a 3,000 kilometer range and one-megaton thermonuclear warheads.[114] The fifth submarine, *le Tonnant,* was launched in September 1977 and entered service in May 1980. Plans call for all but one of the submarines to receive the MRV-type missiles after 1985. This three-stage missile, which has evidently run into some testing and development problems, should have a range of 4,000 kilometers and carry six warheads of 150 kilotons each. Apart from a rather slow pace in upgrading these systems, the most controversial of Giscard's decisions regarding the FNS was a long internment of the scheduled sixth nuclear submarine, *l'Inflexible,* due to enter service in 1985. It was planned to represent an improved generation of technology over its predecessors. A total of six submarines has generally been considered necessary to ensure that two would be on duty at all times, while two others would likely be in port for refitting and the remaining two in drydock for major overhauls.[115] Giscard d'Estaing had originally agreed, in October 1974, to the future construction of a sixth submarine, but in 1977 plans for construction were set aside until a new commitment was made in September 1978.[116] The explanation given to Gaullist and other critics of this delay was that more time was needed to develop an entirely new submarine type that would be viable in the face of anticipated improvements in antisubmarine warfare technology. This generation will probably not be born until the mid-1990s, however, when it will have to replace, not supplement, the existing fleet.[117]

Given the unimpressive budget resources now being allocated to research in this area, it is not certain that France will be able to sustain the minimum level of sophisticated technology that will be required to maintain a small but viable nuclear deterrent toward the end of this century. France does not, of course, have to match either the gross destructive power or the technological resources of superpower nuclear forces, but she does have to maintain a credible retaliatory capability in the face of ongoing refinements in superpower strategic or theater weapons and defense systems. France's national security, and her acknowledged contribution to the overall Alliance deterrent posture in Western Europe, have always rested on the additional element of unpredictability posed by a semiindependent nuclear force in an environment of uncertainty about the American nuclear guarantee. Once the object of skepticism and incredulity, in the 1970s the French nuclear deterrent acquired more significance and emerged as a useful compensation for the erosion of American strategic superiority over the Soviet Union. Superpower parity has certainly been a factor undermining the authority and credibility of the American guarantee to Western Europe, and additional dilemmas are posed by the possibility (or even likelihood) of a Soviet drive for strategic advantages in the context of an erosion of détente and an expanding global military capability for the Soviet Union. In the light of such developments, a possible deterioration in France's strategic capabilities is unsettling and dangerous, despite the obvious utility of the stronger conventional and theater forces planned by

Giscard's budget priorities. Such forces are incapable of compensating for any overall degradation in the complex multiple nuclear deterrent structure that emerged as one foundation of East-West stability in Europe during the 1970s. France's contribution to this fragile equilibrium has become indispensable to Atlantic as well as national security. It should be maintained and reinforced—largely because it is such an important component of the East-West balance today, but also because it might play a crucial role in the emergence of a West European entity that may eventually acquire a political-military dimension to the general benefit of the West.

Opposition Politics and Fifth Republic Security Policy[118]

The Gaullist Legacy and a Pluralist Opposition. The essential elements of Gaullist security policy have been to restore a certain autonomy of decision in the defense arena, primarily through an independent military system based on a nuclear force, a semiautonomous national defense strategy, and a restrained and carefully controlled set of relations with France's allies. Whichever aspect of this quite flexible policy is emphasized for domestic or international reasons, the basic premise is that a state or government without maximum feasible independence in defense affairs will be unable to define its priorities in other arenas of importance to the national interest. It will consequently be incapable of coherent national action and international cooperation to promote the state's interests. Although this perspective can be distorted or interpreted narrowly and unrealistically, it amounts primarily to a reasonable emphasis on the integrity of national decision making as one means of guaranteeing maximum leverage in the context of an interdependent and often hazardous international order.

One of the most significant developments under the Fifth Republic has been the emergence of a broad national consensus around the Gaullist security model on the part of opposition political parties with otherwise diverse interests and views. Once subject to acrimonious disputes within France, the premises of the model seem to have been generally accepted and now set the terms and parameters of internal debates over contemporary security issues. Thus, the Gaullist security legacy commands the respect of Giscard d'Estaing and the neo-Atlanticists of the center, as well as the more or less enthusiastic allegiance of those closer to the extremes of the French political spectrum—socialists, Gaullists, and communists. Although Giscard and his centrist allies might be willing to make excessive compromises with Atlantic allies and risk fatally undermining the Gaullist legacy, the attachment of most other parties and elites to an independent defense force seems to constitute a significant restraint on the government. Such restraints increase in importance as the Fifth Republic political system becomes more pluralistic and less executive-centered, so that national policy depends more on coalitions of political parties that can undermine or block initiatives from the president. Although security policy is still largely a presidential domain, and Giscard has been able to innovate to some extent, it does seem that a major deviation from the Gaullist model would arouse a very hostile majority against him.

The French left's gradual and somewhat disjointed embrace of the Gaullist model represents a particularly striking evolution in the perspectives and policies of socialists and even communists. For, just as the left appears to have finally rallied to the constitutional and institutional framework of the Fifth Republic, it has embraced the symbols, rhetoric, and instruments of Gaullist security policy as potentially useful vehicles for achieving the aims of socialism. Both major left-wing parties have thus abandoned their rigid opposition to a French nuclear force, have rallied to Gaullist strategic concepts as a flexible basis for their own defense interests, and have accepted (with numerous reservations, discussed below) France's status as a special kind of independent Atlantic ally as a tolerable one from their own perspectives. On the other hand, despite the common Gaullist approach of these parties, the more practical implications of the model are sources of unresolved conflicts within the left and have often surfaced to reveal starkly divergent perspectives on France's international role, her alignments, and her status within an interdependent Western capitalist order.

The Gaullist model was not a point of common reference to the opposition during the 1960s, when ad hoc alliances within the left were first developing, but security policy was an issue that divided socialists from communists and instead tended to unite the noncommunist left and the center in opposition to de Gaulle. During that period, although the communists condemned nuclear weapons in general, and especially the French national force, they perceived advantages in de Gaulle's opposition to an American-dominated West, in his resistance to the supranational aspects of European cooperation, and in his policy of seeking a détente with the Soviet Union and the East bloc as one element of a new order in Europe. Thus, the principle of independence from debilitating international constraints, and the characteristic Gaullist challenge to a hegemonic Western bloc, were appealing to communists who supported the withdrawal from NATO and hoped it would lead to a denunciation of the Atlantic Treaty and to complete neutrality. On the other hand, France's weak socialist party, the *Section française de l'internationale ouvrière* (SFIO)—and its allied group of left-wing cadre parties and clubs, including François Mitterrand's *Convention des indépendants républicains* (CIR)—and various centrist groups, had not only opposed the construction of a national nuclear force but also generally criticized de Gaulle's isolationist defense policies as unrealistic and dangerous for European unity. Reflecting their roots in the perspectives of the Fourth Republic, centrist parties and most of the Federation of Left coalition preferred to accept the inconveniences of full NATO membership, while they looked to European cooperation and unity as a basis for ultimate independence from the United States.

At the time of the 1966 NATO withdrawal, centrists and socialists expended a great deal of energy attacking the Gaullist move—sometimes on the grounds that it would only reinforce a German-American duopoly over Western affairs, sometimes on the assumption that European defense cooperation was an available option despite the Atlantic hegemony of the United States, and sometimes by attacking de Gaulle's haughty security decisions as abuses of his "personal power" under a semiauthoritarian regime.[119] Despite these standard criticisms, the main impression left by opposition reactions to the 1966 Atlantic crisis was one of sterile viewpoints and a general inability to muster a coherent and persuasive critique of Gaullist security policy. Rather than unifying parties opposed to de Gaulle's defense and alliance policies, then, the political debate over the NATO withdrawal served primarily as an occasion to vent internal quarrels and mark another stage in the fluctuating political ties among various opposition parties. The left found itself divided between the PCF and the *Parti socialiste unifié* (PSU), who supported the withdrawal, and the alliance of the SFIO, Radicals, CIR, and club groups, who were cautiously critical of the unilateral denunciation of some NATO ties. This coalition was most in tune with the centrists on the NATO issue, but was largely unwilling to revive the discredited cooperation with the center, which had been abandoned during the presidential campaign the previous year, in favor of collaboration with communists on behalf of Mitterrand's candidacy. The censure motion, proposed as a response to the NATO withdrawal, was finally sponsored by only part of the SFIO and some Radicals, and was remarkable mainly for its failure to take a strong stand on behalf of NATO despite the ostensible occasion for the debate.[120] This twelfth censure motion of the Fifth Republic was the first to lose communist votes and received only mixed support from the rest of the opposition, because of the weak substance of the text or the political tactics of the sponsors. The Gaullist majority in the Assembly guaranteed defeat of the motion, which received only 137 of the necessary 242 votes.[121] The impression of feeble opposition to the NATO withdrawal was confirmed during the legislative elections the following year, when no party was willing to advocate a return to NATO and this aspect of Gaullist policy already seemed secure.

During the 1970s, perhaps the most important domestic political development, apart from the center's revival under Giscard d'Estaing's patronage, was the even more astounding resuscitation of a transformed Socialist Party and the emergence of a coalition of socialists and communists, the Union of the Left, which lasted from 1972 to 1978 and mounted a persuasive threat to both the domestic status quo and France's general attachment to a Western capitalist order. As noted earlier, one aspect of the socialist-communist alliance was its growing mutual attachment to the Gaullist security model as a useful tool for achieving their domestic aims and as the basis of a common left-wing security policy. Nevertheless, a gradual reconciliation to the Gaullist legacy proved to be difficult and awkward for a left long accustomed to simplistic criticism and a posturing that usually betrayed an unwillingness to confront its own confused priorities. This congenital problem was doubtless exacerbated by intraparty conflicts and sometimes radical fluctuations in socialist and communist assessments of the domestic and international situations. Abrupt shifts in the views of the PCF may reflect uncertainties inherent in a recent and uncertain independence within the international communist movement, and an inability to find a comfortable relationship with the Soviet Union that is also compatible with the sometimes ambiguous priorities of national communism.[122] Despite its awkward handling of many issues, the PCF does seem, in defense affairs, to be guided by a consistent antagonism toward French association with Atlantic or West European security institutions—a stand that is perfectly compatible with general communist hostility to economic and political dependence on the West. Because the communists often cannot directly attack all the instruments of Western capitalist interdependence, they have sometimes focused on defense and security issues as a metaphorical arena for exposing the party's most congenial international choices. Thus, for example, the particular French communist ideological paradigm and habit of relying on Soviet analyses of the international situation often leads the PCF to embrace Soviet security perspectives and endorse deplorable Soviet practices (such as the occupation of Afghanistan), even though these actions seem to be at odds with the party's commitment to defining its own domestic and international priorities.

Although communists and socialists have both provided evidence of ill-defined or contradictory perspectives on West European security in the context of East-West détente, the *Parti socialiste* (PS) faces the more distinctive problem of also managing diverse and often combative factions within its organization. It has thus been difficult for PS elites to produce coherent policy because, on defense and most other issues, the party is awash with different viewpoints and postures, which only sometimes coincide with the "official" majority-minority divisions that emerged after the new party was formed in 1971.[123] Mitterrand's leadership has doubtless compounded this particular problem, because he has held the party and, until 1977-78, the left alliance together through a cultivated talent for ambiguity, indecision, vacillation, and dissimulation. In security matters, at any rate, Mitterrand often appears uncertain of his own attitudes and interests, and this state of mind has only stimulated the contradictions that characterize Socialist Party policy.

Elusive Threats and Hostile Allies for the Left. The stormy alliance between socialists and communists in France was based on the Socialist Party's post-1971 commitment to an anticapitalist philosophy assigning priority attention to socioeconomic factors of domestic and international politics. Socialist security perspectives shifted closer to a communist framework as traditional diplomatic and military interpretations of international threats were superceded (but not entirely replaced) by a neo-Marxist analysis asserting that the structure of international politics is primarily a product of economic relations and the international division of labor.[124] Estimates of political-military intentions were inevitably accorded less weight in this analysis than factors of political economy that determine imperialist activities and the structure of international dominance and dependence. Given their values, and this analytical framework, socialist elites could easier sympathize with communist sensitivities to the potential costs of international economic interdependence and the severe restraints it might impose on an audacious program deemed incompatible with the structure and logic of the Western system.

Profound communist distrust of the socialists' intentions and commitments was overcome or set aside in 1972, partly because the PS's international perspective seemed radical enough to give grounds for hope that the minimalist Common Program could be transformed into a maximalist communist strategy of rupture with the West.[125] This perspective was indeed a prominent feature of the new PS, where the extremist and anti-Atlanticist views of the *Centre d'études, de recherches, et d'education socialiste* (CERES) group were influential until 1975 and lent support to communist expectations. It is difficult to determine precisely when the Socialist Party's views began to shift away from this pervasive antagonism toward France's major Western partners. The influence of CERES over party policy declined after the Congress of Pau in February 1975, when the abrasive minority was barred from positions on the secretariat (until the spring of 1979) and Mitterrand's own pragmatic cadres and their more moderate allies began consolidating their domination. A number of other factors doubtless contributed to a partial (and erratic) moderation of PS views and an estrangement from the more inflexible communist position. They include the influence of anticommunist elements, such as Michel Rocard and Christian militants, after 1975; the failure of radical experiments in Portugal; the accommodation of the Italian Communist Party to Western economic and security institutions; a declining American interest in overt or covert intervention abroad; the growing strength and confidence of the PS itself; the party's closer ties with other European socialists—especially the reformist *Sozialdemokratische Partei Deutschlands* (SPD)—in the context of the Socialist International; and revived concern over Soviet intentions and behavior.

By 1977, one of the most significant socialist-communist divergences arose over assessments of the international economic crisis and a preferred leftist strategy for coping with its effects on France. The communists continued to rely essentially on their "socialism in one country" perspective, which stressed a rupture with some key international capitalist restraints and a rigid control of others by a centralized, state-dominated socialist system.[126] On the other hand, with some strong dissent from CERES, the majority of the PS shifted toward a mixed national and international solution, while it retained the party's commitment to the autogestion socioeconomic model that seems to be the antithesis of PCF ideals. By 1977, PS international policy was based on the assumption that a socialist-dominated left government in France could secure the international concessions necessary for a domestic transition to socialism. Thus, such a government might avoid the drastic ruptures judged by most to be dangerous and counterproductive in a period of serious economic disruption and decay. The communist preference for national economic self-reliance was accompanied by a stress on defense autonomy compatible with relative isolation from the West, just as the socialist refusal to countenance a rupture with the Western international economy was complemented by a stronger insistence on maintaining basic French ties to the Western allies and avoiding moves in any sphere that could jeopardize a fragile Western system. In the environment of an intense preelectoral debate in France, these divergent assessments of leftist international policies also reflected the distinctive electorates of the socialist and communist parties, and especially socialist sensitivity to the important part of its public that was leery of dramatic and risky policy initiatives.[127]

In a decade dominated by economic issues—national and international, actual and hypothetical—military threats did not usually preoccupy leftist leaders. A focus on the inconveniences of Western economic interdependence did, however, sometimes evoke public discussion of military interventions or pressures from France's ostensible allies. For the PCF, there has never been any doubt whatsoever that the only significant imperialist threats to France emanate from the United States and West Germany, the latter having become "the heir to German militarism."[128] Socialist Party defense experts also cited an independent national defense as the best guarantee against such pressures, and the argument sometimes extended to indulgent speculation about how to ward off American or West German armed forces.[129] Although the idea of Western military pressures was perhaps useful to the Socialist Party in convincing antinuclear militants to tolerate a French nuclear force, or in competing with the supernationalist rhetoric of the Communist Party, it is difficult to believe that such extreme notions were ever taken very seriously by socialist elites—who realized that their most pressing problems were bound to arise in the context of mutual Western economic dependencies relatively unsusceptible to direct military pressures.

Until the rupture of the leftist alliance, the corresponding issue of a Soviet political-military threat to France and Western Europe was treated gingerly by Socialist Party leaders. This was partly in deference to communist sensitivities; it was also a consequence of socialist preoccupation with instruments of economic intervention, which naturally diverted attention from the East.

Thus, the dominant opinion in the PS seemed to be that the Soviet Union was essentially a defensive state, compensating for an inefficient economic system by building up exaggerated military power in Europe and on the seas. The leftist wing of the PS was especially determined that the specter of Soviet military imperialism should not again be manipulated to divert the socialists from their ideological goals and induce them to compromise with Western capitalism. As long as the Union of the Left was intact, the PS also had an intrinsic interest in minimizing East-West tensions, which might jeopardize a détente environment conducive to the political success of the left in France and elsewhere, and constituting a broad but important condition for the socialist-communist alliance itself.

This perspective gradually changed as a result of mounting tensions within the Union of the Left, and a generally cloudy atmosphere of East-West détente in the context of continuing Soviet internal repression and the remarkable expansion of Soviet military power. The Socialist Party thus became more sensitive to the arguments of its own right wing and particularly of Robert Pontillon, the secretariat's expert on international affairs until 1979. Pontillon had long insisted that Soviet inability to use sophisticated political-economic instruments of hegemony made crude military power a more attractive weapon for Soviet leaders. By November 1977, the PS *bureau exécutif* was able to agree on a defense platform singling out the Soviet Union as the only power to conduct military actions in Europe since the end of World War II, against Hungary and Czechoslovakia. This was given as the principal reason for continuing to adhere to the Atlantic Alliance, a rationale bound to antagonize the French communists. Although PCF relations with Moscow were deteriorating significantly during this period, communist party leaders still seemed unable to imagine a Soviet threat to a democratic and socialist France; nor could they contemplate the use of military force or even instruments of deterrence against the homeland of the communist revolution.

These divergent perspectives emerged most clearly in debates over French nuclear strategy, but they were also readily apparent in different and often fluctuating socialist and communist approaches to France's formal alliance commitments, especially the Atlantic Alliance. After abandoning the SFIO's basically pro-NATO views of the 1960s, the new Socialist Party originally adopted the position of its young radicals and Mitterrand's ambitious cadres, who asserted that "for France, membership in the bloc of the Atlantic Alliance does not signify a guarantee of security, but offers an additional facility for her economic colonization by the United States."[130] The Socialist Party program of 1972 accepted the Gaullist solution to Alliance membership and did not urge an outright withdrawal, pending the simultaneous dissolution of both military blocs. It did, however, note that membership was still a substantial inconvenience because the Atlantic Treaty "ties all signatories to American imperialism and in the case of war involving the United States exposes them to preventive attacks."[131]

This rather sour tolerance for the Atlantic Alliance prevailed only after the defeat of a CERES proposal branding the North Atlantic Treaty as "an alliance which, having no military purpose, appears only as a mark of complacency in respect to an imperialism which endangers our very substance more than any other, and which oppresses two-thirds of humanity."[132] When it came time to negotiate the Common Program with the communists, the reluctant pragmatism of the PS prevailed over the communist stand in favor of a full withdrawal from the Alliance. This major communist concession was concealed in a vague statement that committed a government of the united left to "respect for France's existing alliances."[133] Greater emphasis was placed, however, on a left government's determination to pursue a resolutely independent policy toward all political-military blocs, and to work for a European collective security system that would render such alliances obsolete.

Later, reflecting new domestic and international conditions, the Socialist Party defense convention in January 1978 reaffirmed this commitment to the Atlantic Alliance in much more positive terms and seemed to offer it as a guarantee against irresponsible leftist ruptures with the Western international order. Thus, the socialists rejected the persistent communist preference for *"la France seule"* and asserted that, in the event of a clear aggression against her allies, a socialist France would fulfill her obligations under both the Brussels and Atlantic treaties.[134] Voicing a new enthusiasm for the Atlantic security connection, Mitterrand cited approvingly the Gaullist precedent of maintaining basic Atlantic ties and even insisted that "the Americans ought to know that we will be loyal allies, if there is a war and if this war is provoked by the desires of outside powers."[135] This accommodation to the Atlantic Alliance was doubtless prompted by an inclination to avoid unnecessary international confrontations, particularly during a vulnerable transition to socialism under a (hypothetical) future left regime. Another factor favoring "detachment without disengagement"[136] is the flexible kind of Alliance membership de Gaulle carved out for France after 1966—one that permits closer or more distant political-military relations with the United States and NATO according to both government composition and the course of substantive disagreements over issues. Charles Hernu, the leading PS defense expert, has commented favorably on the NATO trend toward a looser structure, noting that allied governments can now engage in dialogues over security issues without facing the constant threat of submission to an American-dominated military institution.[137] Despite a more favorable position on the Western Alliance, the Socialist Party still constantly reaffirms its anti-American and Gaullist credentials by resolutely opposing any form of French reintegration into the NATO military structure that might compromise the independence of France's defense system. The PS has thus been careful to follow the Gaullist precept that France must retain her essential autonomy of decision in military affairs in order to avoid being dragged into a conflict in which French interests or responsibilities are not at stake.

Although the leftist parties were able to sustain agreement on the issue of NATO integration, it does seem that their original pact in favor of Alliance membership was tainted by communist reservations, which cast a shadow over the 1972 agreement in the Common Program. According to Georges Marchais's report to the Central Committee on 27 June 1972, the PCF had not really revised its basic judgment that the Atlantic Alliance (and the EEC) was a vehicle for "imprisoning [France] in the imperialist system under the direction of the United States." It was, he said, a fundamental communist goal to use both foreign and military policy to liberate France from "the class imperatives of the world imperialist system," adding that the Common Program should be seen as a first step in fulfilling the PCF aim of gradual French disengagement from the Atlantic Alliance.[138] After the signing of the Common Program, then, the Communist Party did not lose an opportunity to bemoan the alliance provisions and to suggest that French interests would be served by renegotiating the Atlantic Treaty's provisions as they apply to France, in order to minimize all contacts with Western allies.[139]

For some time, socialists and communists did manage to paper over their basic disagreement on the Alliance issue with their common commitment to work for the eventual dissolution of both military blocs. This perspective was compatible with traditional French hostility to a bipolar order that limits the independence of middle-range powers and subjects all states to the twin dangers of superpower conflict or condominium. Socialist leaders often exhortated France to combat the hegemonic tendencies of the superpowers and work for the disappearance of the blocs.[140] Reflecting the strong Gaullist influence on their thinking, the socialists' long-range and largely rhetorical goal has been twofold: to secure national independence from bloc military systems and to encourage the evolution of a more pluralist international framework. Despite a superficial agreement on this perspective, it seems that the communists went much further than the socialists and interpreted their bloc position as a tactic for chipping away at French alignment with the West while establishing new and eventually decisive ties to the East and the radical Third World. The 1972 Marchais report, for example, cites the Communist Party's policy of "independence towards any political-military bloc" as simply another version of the basic communist position in favor of disengagement from the Atlantic Alliance.[141] Later, during the 1977 negotiations on updating the Common Program, the communists proposed a nonalignment policy involving treaties of nonaggression and renunciation of force with the East, a move that Mitterrand and the PS rejected outright because it implied the sanctioning of a neutral status for France.[142] Marchais and his party apparently still adhered to this strategy in March 1978, when the secretary-general insisted that "France ought to practice a policy founded on the rejection of alignment —of any alignment with anyone whatsoever."[143] The PCF's abandonment of political ties to the socialists after the 1978 elections was accompanied by the reemergence of intensely nationalist and pseudoneutralist policies within the party and even the revival of an overt and crude pro-Soviet line on European security issues and the Afghanistan crisis. For all practical purposes, then, by 1980 the PCF had renounced its previous concessions regarding the Atlantic Alliance and was returning to an obviously more congenial stand that betrayed its pervasive and fundamental antagonism toward the status of independent ally and partner in the framework of the West.

The communists have been able to include a perspective of neutrality within the Gaullist security model, because of some interpretations of the *tous azimuts* position adopted by de Gaulle for a brief time at the end of 1967. But neutrality or a more drastic reversal of alliances was not part of de Gaulle's security repertory, even though by the mid-1960s he may have perceived the need to combat a nascent American global hegemony by offering some support to the Soviet Union and the Third World. De Gaulle's most charac- teristic formula for an ambitious transformation of the international system involved the construction of a French-led European bloc, united and inde- pendent of the superpowers. The left has been unable to agree on this matter. The communists are fundamentally opposed to any West European coopera- tion with a political or military dimension, and suspicion of Socialist Party toleration for some future EDC evidently contributed to communist intransi- gence during the 1977 Common Program negotiations.[144] There is indeed a pro-European bias within the Socialist Party, where the right wing has empha- sized a formal PS commitment to European unity and can even envisage a military dimension to this cooperation.[145] The party's other flank, concentrated around CERES, has resisted this commitment because it sees that the Com- munity is unlikely to foster socialist goals, may sabotage a socialist program in France, and is incapable of becoming an economic or political-military counterweight to the United States. Hence, Jean-Pierre Chevènement and his supporters have implicitly argued that the leftist government in France cannot expect to construct an international alternative to the bloc system and should temporarily secede from it alone and adopt a posture of semiautonomy re- sembling the communist model.[146]

The Socialist Party as a whole has rejected such stark pessimism and clings to more ambivalent views, which include the strong rhetorical commit- ment to European cooperation along with a reluctance to favor the kind of political-military collaboration that might encourage the emergence of a new West European bloc. The argument, often repeated, has been that such an entity "would only reinforce existing blocs and would maintain states of tension dangerous for peace."[147] Instead, the dominant group of PS policy makers has preferred to speculate on vague and certainly remote prospects for general disarmament, collective security, denuclearized zones in Central Europe, and the eventual dissolution of opposing military alliances in Europe. Perhaps the only conclusion one can draw from these diverse and contradictory attitudes is that the Socialist Party, at least, has no grand alternative to propose to the contemporary international security structure—other than somewhat worn rhetoric about how an avant-garde socialist France is bound to serve as a stimulus for renovating the international system.

Nuclear Weapons and Deterrence. De Gaulle's most concrete legacy and guarantee of French independence has been the *Force nucléaire stratégique* (FNS). Whereas the status of the most visible symbol of France's grandeur was once likely to be jeopardized by a leftist regime, this no longer seems to be the case, because of shifts in perspectives on the part of both major left-wing parties. This is an important change of attitude for both communists and socialists, who had each previously condemned national nuclear forces and threatened to dismantle, renounce, or at least not promote any development of the French force. In 1965, for example, Mitterrand's presidential program condemned the notion that France could have a full defense system of her own, particularly one based on a small nuclear force that was "ineffectual, costly, and dangerous." The force, he said categorically, should be dismantled.[148] By 1972, however, the program of the radicalized Socialist Party had become more ambiguous—it mentions "renouncing" the nuclear force along with a "reconversion of atomic industry," but the only genuine commitment was to "interrupt the construction of the *force de frappe*" by halting atmospheric nuclear tests.[149] Socialist reservations about the wisdom of immediately jettisoning France's nuclear deterrent system nearly broke up negotiations with the communists on the Common Program that same year, until a compromise was reached in which the nuclear force was to be "renounced" and all construction halted, but no precise schedule or commitment to dismantle was made. By 1974, the united left's position had become sufficiently muddled for Mitterrand to state that his first priority was not to promote the development of the nuclear force, but he had no intention of liquidating existing armaments without international guarantees.[150] These subtle and glacial changes in socialist attitudes were the result of patient work by Hernu and his defense experts, who since 1971 were urging Mitterrand and the party leadership to accept at least a "minimum deterrent force" as protection against unknown future threats and particularly "to ward off any risk of aggression against the construction of a socialist society as long as the blocs have not disarmed."[151] Hernu's position gradually gained acceptance among the elite, so that by November 1976 a discussion at a meeting of the *Comité directeur* reflected a consensus that the nuclear force was indeed an indispensable means of protecting the independence of a socialist France.[152]

The evolution in socialist thinking was also characteristic of the Communist Party, which abandoned its once-fervent opposition to French nuclear weapons. The somewhat abrupt change in policy, envisaged by some communist defense experts since at least early 1976,[153] came in May 1977 in the form of a report to the Central Committee. It was presented by Jean Kanapa and argued that only the nuclear deterrent protects France against external aggression, owing to the weakness of her conventional forces.[154] After long and abrasive criticism of the *Force nucléaire stratégique,* the communists rallied to these weapons in the apparent belief that they could be useful in convincing the socialists to sever ties with NATO military organs and redirect France's entire defense system away from its preferred targeting on the Soviet Union. Both socialists and communists must also have perceived that public accommodation to the FNS was a politically astute means of placating and even seducing a French bourgeoisie attracted to Gaullist symbols of independence. It could also reassure the most sophisticated and technologically oriented military cadres that the foundation of France's defense network would not be summarily discarded by a leftist regime.

Many of the advantages of the new position were, however, undermined by the left's inability to come to terms honestly and directly with the conclusions and recommendations of its own experts. The Socialist Party bore great responsibility, partly because Francois Mitterrand continued to be troubled by a profound moral reservation about nuclear weapons, which reinforced his natural political prudence. It is also true that Socialist Party militants had strong pacifist, antimilitarist, and antinuclear sentiments that became more vocal and complicated decision making for party elites.[155] These factors played a prominent role in the 1977 renegotiation of the Common Program, in which the parties at times seemed able to agree to maintain the FNS in working order pending the outcome of a major French initiative in favor of general nuclear disarmament. The Socialist Party, however, could not take a definitive position and fed communist suspicions by insisting that a clear commitment would have to await a socialist convention on defense then scheduled for late 1977. Also, Mitterrand's last-minute proposal for an eventual referendum on the nuclear force was interpreted as yet another example of PS indecision and evasion. It confirmed fears that the PS would be an unreliable government partner, constantly inclined to undermine the Common Program and the PCF with Gaullist-type public appeals.[156] A relatively minor issue in relation to the FNS itself, the ill-considered referendum proposal evidently made an important contribution to the breakdown of the leftist alliance by the fall of 1977.

All along, the communists were understandably annoyed that the Union of the Left's policy on such an important issue was left up in the air until the

Socialist Party could sort out its internal disagreements on nuclear weapons. Socialist discussions continued to betray a rather uncertain commitment to the FNS and the principal of national deterrence. On the one hand, the CERES position resembled that of the PCF and insisted on firm support for the strategic force as a basis for relative autonomy from the United States. But the party's strong antinuclear element, which cut across the major factions, resisted an unqualified commitment and insisted that at least the national territory be denuclearized by relying solely on the submarine part of the deterrent. This group remained quite hostile to even the concept of an independent nuclear force and seemed to prefer a stronger French dependence on the Atlantic Alliance and the American nuclear guarantee.[157] Mitterrand himself, while criticizing the CERES position and sometimes seeming partial to the antinuclear arguments, did, nevertheless, support a basic decision in favor of maintaining the FNS pending the outcome of a major socialist campaign in favor of international disarmament. Approved by the party national convention in January 1978, this reversal of previous socialist positions finally brought the left around to a minimum consensus on the nuclear issue.[158]

Leftist mores require that such a radical departure from the ideological aversion to nuclear weapons be presented as a temporary aberration until the world agrees to a general disarmament program inducing all states to abandon their arsenals. Communist and socialist elites are perhaps genuinely committed to this viewpoint, which has also helped them to justify their new policies to suspicious and even hostile militant opinion. The Socialist Party could thus "solemnly" announce "that it is ready to renounce nuclear arms" and seek "a world conference on disarmament or, failing that, a conference of nuclear powers."[159] Among the other measures proposed by the socialists were severe restraints on French arms sales, measures against the dissemination of nuclear technology, termination of the French nuclear testing program, and French participation in existing arms control forums such as the Geneva and MBFR talks. Although there were differences between particular communist and socialist positions, a strong mutual interest in this theme was perhaps the most coherent element of left defense policy and naturally received priority attention by both parties.[160]

Although the French left was able to achieve a certain consensus on arms control and disarmament because of its predilection for utopian projects, on more practical and immediate issues, such as the structure and strategic orientation of French national defense, communists and socialists have had trouble finding a basis for agreement or eventual government policy. The structure and development of the FNS itself has posed a lesser problem, because the Gaullist inheritance of a triad of strategic forces could be altered without fatal damage to its deterrent value. Socialist plans for developing this weapons system have been marked by some prudence and hesitation because, until early 1978, the party as a whole had not actually reversed its original position on renouncing the FNS. The PS Commission on National Defense had, however, indicated a preference for modernizing the submarine fleet and furnishing it with an independent satellite alert system in place of dependence on the NATO network.[161]

In January 1978, the party agreed that a leftist government would "renounce" the Mirage force and consider abandoning the land-based missiles if there were any significant developments in reciprocal disarmament projects. The socialist decision to give up the Mirage component of the FNS was singled out by Mitterrand as an example of the party's willingness even to engage "in a form of unilateral disarmament" and induce other powers to follow the French example.[162] Mitterrand did, nevertheless, insist that the party would "not destroy the atomic arsenal and, by maintaining it intact, and not only intact," would "carry out the technical modifications required by the advance or progress of technology."[163] For its part, the PCF Central Committee accepted the full French triad and also urged technological innovations such as satellite and air-borne radar systems.[164] During negotiations with the socialists in 1977, the PCF argued for the goal of full independence from NATO detection systems, while the socialists maintained that, for the time being, the situation was one of reciprocal dependence, which would not interfere with the autonomy of French military decisions in a crisis.[165] The discussions did, however, indicate agreement on eventually finding a means of independent warning against aggression.

The complexities of finding a nuclear deterrence strategy for a left-wing medium-sized power posed one of the most vexing problems for the Union of the Left, not so much because of technical issues of appropriate weapons systems and targeting requirements, but because of the political implications of a particular strategic emphasis. Leftist parties may, however, find some comfort in the ample precedent for contradiction, confusion, and inspired ambiguity in strategic thinking under the Fifth Republic—even though a certain degree of evasiveness is justified in deterrence strategy and has probably enhanced the value of the FNS. Socialist and communist thinking on strategic issues is largely derived from various Gaullist concepts, which can be emphasized selectively according to their convenience for the broader political and security goals of each party. Recourse to often narrow interpretation of Gaullist security policy has also been useful fodder for attacks on Giscard d'Estaing's modifications in this area, which deemphasize a rigid national deterrence in favor of defense collaboration with Atlantic allies. The principal concern of the socialists has seemed to be to return to a posture of absolute deterrence, eliminating or at least restricting plans for preliminary engagements of nonstrategic forces and restoring the FNS deterrent function of ensuring that a European conflict involving France would escalate rapidly. The corollary Gaullist theory is also stressed, namely, that the FNS may serve to protect France against unwilling involvement in a European conflict, because "it is an arm of neutrality."[166] This position is reconcilable with previous defense policy. Nevertheless, the concept of neutrality is flexible enough to set the stage for a shift from merely preserving a capacity for noninvolvement in a crisis to a more ominous political definition of armed neutrality sometimes attributed to the Ailleret strategy of *tous azimuts*.

This issue blossomed during 1977 and contributed to the escalation of conflict between socialists and communists. For the PCF interpreted the Common Program agreement on military strategy, which mentioned a capacity "to oppose any aggressor whatsoever," as the equivalent of a neutral position with no predesignated enemy target. The communists were essentially pursuing their interest in adjusting targeting plans and strategy away from the Soviet bloc, whereas the socialists proved unwilling to jeopardize the Atlantic Alliance tie by giving the West "equal time" along these lines. As Mitterrand said, he did "not perceive the necessity of pointing [France's] missiles at [her] own allies."[167] Although it revealed significant differences in the bloc perspectives and alliance interests of the leftist parties, the argument ended inconclusively in a mutual willingness to consider the feasibility of abandoning all predesignated targeting for the nuclear force.[168] The socialists later seemed unwilling to go even this far, probably because a truly neutral FNS in the hands of a leftist government seemed incompatible with membership in the Atlantic Alliance, which, by its nature, commits allies to a priority military engagement against the Warsaw Pact. In general, it seems that the French left's internal contradictions and indecisiveness would have undermined the credibility of a small nuclear deterrent. As if to confirm such an assessment, the left also focused on raising the rather artificial and demogogic issue of how to control the triggering of the nuclear force. Of course, both communists and socialists have often insisted on restoring parliamentary and cabinet influence over an imperial or arbitrary presidential office, and, specifically, they have refuted the Gaullist notion of a *"domaine réservé"* in defense affairs. In addition to a greater parliamentary and cabinet role in the making of defense policy, the left began to insist that an exclusive presidential decision to trigger the FNS was ideologically distasteful and perhaps dangerous. The communists proposed that any decision be made instead by a National Defense Committee, composed of the president, prime minister, chief of the general staff, and other members approved by parliament—although the president would retain responsibility for executing the decision.[169] Despite some typical and tiresome quarreling over wording and intentions, the socialists could only agree that the FNS should be subject to broader, more stringent, and more democratic controls than in the past.

Another dilemma for the left has been France's strategic ties to her European neighbors and, by implication, to the NATO system, which would direct the course of a conflict on the Central Front. The issue has become prominent recently because of the changes in government policy that favor an early French participation in the forward "battle of Germany," to be fought along NATO guidelines, which stress conventional defense and relatively late escalation to selective use of tactical nuclear weapons on the battlefield. The left has been most troubled by the prospect of French collaboration in large-scale conventional and tactical nuclear warfare in Europe, a possibility that grows stronger with every French accommodation to NATO flexible response plans. The TNW issue is a particularly sensitive one because almost any plans for TNW use are bound to extend the escalation process, detract from absolute national deterrence, and involve France in allied defense plans.

Whatever their current status, the propensity of the army's tactical arms to engage France in European defense cooperation, and in the controversial "forward battle," has made the left extremely reserved and pessimistic about this weapon's future utility to a socialist government. The communists have naturally wanted the TNWs to remain on national territory and uncoordinated with NATO planning. Socialist Hernu has branded the Pluton a "dangerous toy" of desanctuarization that could turn Europe into a nuclear battlefield.[170] At their 1978 convention on defense policy, however, the socialists seemed unable to arrive at a clear position on this issue. Despite an insistence on maintaining the Gaullist heritage of defense autonomy and absolute deterrence, the party rejected amendments warning France against a "harmonization of her strategy with that of the United States in Europe."[171] Given the confusion that often surrounds leftist defense debates, as well as upheavals in the Socialist Party after 1978, it was impossible to say whether or not such actions indicated an actual PS shift in favor of forward defense and more European military cooperation. Socialist policy makers seemed inclined to leave their options open at the outset of the 1980s, to the extent of sanctioning the French government's decision to develop a neutron bomb capability. The PS's unwillingness to support actual production and deployment of the weapon was also in line with official policy.[172] A growing socialist pragmatism in security affairs was doubtless tied to Mitterrand's own inclination to appear as a responsible and "presidential" leader in anticipation of his eventual candidacy in the 1981 race for head of state. Stressing a growing Soviet threat to global stability and security in Europe, Mitterrand even found kind words for a French policy of "solidarity with allies," rather than an excessive self-reliance that might tempt France to slip into a brand of neutralism more suited to communist aims and interests.[173]

Conclusion.   This analysis has suggested that the thrust of opposition defense and security policy in France has been to adapt to the Gaullist model established under the Fifth Republic, a model that is flexible and ambiguous enough to appeal to a variety of groups and interests that are able to select the aspects which best serve their purposes. Particularly for the left, it is clear that the cornucopia of Gaullist policies and postures furnishes ample material to suit the often divergent and clashing interests of the various actors. Intra-left disagreements on defense do reflect contradictory goals or interpretations of domestic and international issues, but it is revealing that explanations or justifications have increasingly resorted to the Gaullist security model as a guideline or natural point of reference.

The left's embrace of Fifth Republic security policy is not surprising, because in this arena de Gaulle represented attitudes and views widely shared by French elites and generally appealing to the nation as a whole. He was thus able to synthesize and organize the incoherent security policies of the Fourth Republic and present a compelling but flexible vision of independence. This accomplishment lay the foundation for a national consensus on defense, which had eluded previous regimes. The achievement described here suggests that de Gaulle was not the idiosyncratic leader he is sometimes made to appear. Nor was he an anachronism focusing on outmoded and irrelevant security issues while neglecting the more important developments of national or international political economy. Apart from a clear Fifth Republic attention to such matters, it is of course true that de Gaulle was preoccupied with the potential costs of military dependence and subordination in a nuclear age that could extract terrible penalties. He also saw that nuclear weapons were an available and relatively inexpensive means of minimizing dependence and acquiring some leverage over the international security system. Precisely because France's influence in nonsecurity arenas seemed weaker than her potential leverage over European regional defense, de Gaulle doubtless seized upon military power as a compensating factor. A strong defense system could thus increase French status and prestige, traditional elements of power. They could also be a source of leverage in a newly complex international system in which states are not only mutually dependent, but find that dominant influence in the context of one arena can be manipulated to compensate for weaknesses elsewhere. De Gaulle, it seems, perceived a key relationship, or linkage, between economic and security arenas and judged that a strong national defense could help minimize the potential costs of dependence across a spectrum of issues.

The left in France has been particularly concerned with the consequences of international economic interdependence, and it has seized on the Gaullist defense legacy as one tool for limiting and managing the many constraints of the international system. This is certainly in accord with the intentions of de Gaulle. On the other hand, while the search for independence in the 1960s entailed a certain autonomy and distance from the American-dominated Western security system, this autonomy was always partial and carefully controlled to avoid irresponsible damage to the West or France's own interests. Nor was the Gaullist challenge distorted and exaggerated by ideological attachment to an alternative model of socioeconomic organization on the domestic or international levels. In many respects, the French left has offered this kind of challenge and has, therefore, posed a more serious risk of eventual disruption and fragmentation than de Gaulle did. But one of de Gaulle's other accomplishments was to help establish a more flexible and pluralist order in the West, one that may be able to accommodate and even thrive on the radical and often innovative ideas offered by the left in France and elsewhere. This challenge has not materialized into a mature and irrefutable critique of the Western system, but it may yet emerge as a crucial test for national and international politics in the postwar period.

6 Conclusions: Transformations in Atlantic Politics

This study has singled out a number of themes that seem to be the best explanations for the characteristics and development of France's postwar security policies, with a particular emphasis on the relationship with the Atlantic Alliance and the United States. The most significant sources of these policies have been found in French images of a certain national role, status, and security that were usually at odds with the prevailing Alliance structures and preferences of other actors, who were, nevertheless, more influential and able to prevail in frustrating French attempts to alter the international milieu. French decision makers themselves, however, found that the Western system was usually pliable enough to allow them to resist accommodation and compliance under the Fourth Republic and to carve out a distinctive and even privileged position under the Fifth Republic. The reconciliation to the Atlantic order, which has been a notable feature of Giscard d'Estaing's policies, is feasible primarily because it is based on a general acceptance of France's independent status and because the Atlantic system of the 1970s became a more pluralistic and even less hierarchical one that was more compatible with general French conceptions and expectations. Satisfied with this form of independence, France has in return accepted the European status quo based on détente and improved East-West relations in the context of two bloc systems, the loose Western one and an enduring Soviet hegemony in the East.[1]

The pragmatism and cooperation that have characterized France's international behavior since 1974 are probably also a result of the modernization of the French economy and an increasing dependence in the context of an entangling international economic order. In terms of security policy, however, France's postwar policies have usually not been determined by the international system and its overall structure of threat and dependence, unlike the attitudes and actions of a state such as West Germany.[2] Instead, French perspectives have been notable for the persistence of a set of nationally generated images and policies most clearly assembled and articulated by de Gaulle, which tended to resist subordination within a bipolar structure and the domination, however benevolent, of the United States over the West. The Fourth Republic was thus reluctant to adapt to the international bloc structure and, instead, limited its active participation in NATO; sought to create an oligarchical Western system to enhance French privileges and to control the United States; refused to have its policies determined by reactions to a direct Soviet threat to the West; resisted decolonization and the abandonment of extra-European political-military interests; and did not accept the American allocation of a nonnuclear military role for continental allies.

De Gaulle transformed many of these perspectives into a more active and coherent challenge to the Atlantic order. He also perpetuated the characteristic French preoccupation with national defense interests at the expense of NATO or a more consolidated European effort. The Fourth Republic had refused European defense cooperation because it would have weakened overseas efforts and might have led to West German preeminence within Western Europe. Armed with a growing nuclear force, de Gaulle had less fear of the political consequences of a German military superiority. But he finally perceived that European political-military cooperation in the 1960s would only have reinforced Atlanticism and an American preponderance that was less and less justified from the point of view of security or changes in the structure of international politics. The General's contention that many West European and American interests were not basically compatible or congruent struck at the heart of the Atlantic system and was the most prominent sign that its ideological and practical foundations were eroding.

French leaders, who have assumed a negative and critical role that has often been useful and illuminating, have also envisaged alternative structures and principles for organizing Atlantic and international politics, in order to increase France's influence or at least to reduce her dependence on more powerful actors across a number of issue areas. These conceptions have acquired an attraction and significance that extend beyond their relationship to one particular national interest. This is in part because of a characteristic penchant for universalizing national concerns that has led France's elites to formulate their designs specifically to enhance an appeal to other states, and to have them reflect general conceptions of a more just, efficacious, and stable international order. Also, whereas many of these concepts have often been considered products of a special set of national or even personal images, they do seem more interesting and instructive now because many aspects of France's own experiences and past policies seem especially relevant to the contemporary Atlantic system and to the changing relationships among key actors.

Thus, for example, the French search for inner directorates in the context of Atlantic, and sometimes European, decision making has met with more widespread approval in recent years as economic summits among leading industrial powers have been institutionalized as one method for slowing the decay of a complex and increasingly unmanageable Western international economy. The Fourth Republic and de Gaulle pursued this oligarchical vision as a means of securing an artifically high status for France and for restraining the United States. But they also wanted to foster a practical coordination of policies and interests among mutually dependent states with greater responsibility for managing issues on behalf of many allies and partners.[3] This conception seems now to offer a mechanism for adjusting to and compensating for the disorder accompanying the United States' decline as the dominant Western economic power. It is a middle way between the stability offered by a single leading power's hegemony, which can also be dangerous, and a chaotic pluralism amounting to anarchy. In a similar vein, French proposals for limited membership councils may prove to be an effective way of facilitating an expansion of the European Community and still retaining political coherence at the core of an increasingly amorphous enterprise.

In general, changes in the Atlantic system during the 1970s reinforced certain traits that sometimes created the impression that Atlantic politics were indeed oscillating dangerously between a healthy, organized pluralism encouraged by Gaullist policy and a more ominous state of anarchy. Despite the inconclusive outcome of the confrontation between the United States and its allies during the Year of Europe, that period and subsequent trends in interallied relations furnish evidence of the new kind of relationship that emerged and dominated the Atlantic system until a possible crossroads was reached at the beginning of the 1980s. Its principal features were, first, a declining relative salience of alliance and defense relationships that made them less capable of shaping the overall pattern of international or domestic politics; second, the "spill over" or linkage of many policies and perceptions between the arenas of military security and political economy so conflicts and shifting interests or relations in one arena had direct ramifications on ties in the other; and, finally, a general tendency for allies to behave more often as adversaries because of the emergence of these newer and quite divisive issues, which were not easily settled in the more complex setting of contemporary Atlantic and global politics. These developments were certainly not separate and distinct aspects of Atlantic relations and, instead, tended to coincide and reinforce each other with often unfortunate results.

The significance of the Atlantic Alliance as an instrument for structuring Western politics and maintaining a minimum of political cohesion and cooperation among member states has been declining since at least the late 1960s, although the history of French security policy is testimony to the resilience of some independent national roles throughout the postwar period. More readily apparent at some times than others, one trend dominating the 1970s and encouraging the debilitation of Alliance ties was the reduced sense of direct military threat from the Soviet Union, or even an indirect political threat backed by military power. Allies other than France were thus less and less susceptible to aligning or coordinating their policies on the basis of mutual security requirements that no longer seemed so pressing. The precise effect of this trend differed from government to government and from time to time. Although the United States remained sensitive to a Soviet global challenge and resisted encursions in pro-Western or neutral regions, Washington tended to accord priority to confidence-building measures and bipolar cooperation on behalf of a superpower equilibrium. This priority could often be at odds with the desire to sustain the confidence of allies in the American commitment to their own security interests, just as American goals at stake in superpower confrontations might not be shared by West European states. The European allies had diverse perceptions of the Soviet Union and its threat potential. In the wake of détente and Ostopolitik, however, they followed the French precedent and usually behaved as if the threat were low enough to permit greater individual autonomy and substantial conflict with the United States when required by their individual or collective interests.

Whereas residual interest in common security problems might still have induced allies to place great priority on mutual accommodation, this factor was offset by a perceived incompatibility in security perspectives that had been accumulating since the late 1950s and was most clearly articulated by de Gaulle during the 1960s. The European members of NATO became unwilling victims of a situation of superpower nuclear parity, in which the United States had an obvious interest in qualifying its military commitments to allies and selectively disengaging from some guarantees, or at least ensuring that it could manage confrontations for its own benefit. This applied both to the regions covered by alliance agreements and to contiguous zones of superpower conflict where Soviet and American interests have been heavily engaged, such as the Middle East. Under the Nixon-Kissinger leadership, the American priority was one of maintaining maximum freedom and flexibility, which only encouraged similar behavior on the part of European allies to the extent that they were less conditioned by a sense of Soviet threat or by the expectation that American aims were compatible with their own. The conflicts and frustrations endemic to this aspect of Atlantic pluralism have been compounded by the fact that, however great the divergence in interests, the European allies are still unable to provide for their own security individually or collectively. They must thus calculate the degree of opposition to the United States according to rough and uncertain estimates of the present and future relevance of their military dependence, and the residual benefits of an eroding security guarantee.

A second major development in Atlantic politics was that conflicts among allies over political, economic, and military issues were increasingly interrelated so that discord over one problem often "spilled over" into another and reinforced adversary perceptions and behavior across all issue areas. Economic and welfare matters tend to be the most contentious and because of a (perhaps temporary) reduced attention paid to defense issues and the rising importance of economic issues of all kinds, the latter dominated interallied relations and crises during the 1970s.[4] This was often to the detriment of their military security ties, which were already frayed for reasons just described. Transnational in scope and effect, and less susceptible to control by existing national or international institutions, economic issues involve different interests and power resources than those in the security arena and are more dominated by domestic pressures and various "national interest" or protectionist considerations. They are, therefore, more likely to produce adversary situations among governments whose willingness to accommodate allies has already been strained for other reasons. Conflictual behavior because of incompatible economic policies among allies is doubtless enhanced by a growing inclination for governments to accord priority to protecting the national political economy at a time when domestic politics have seemed more autonomous from, or even in contradiction with, the restraints of bloc politics. One of the most visible examples of this phenomenon has been the rising (but uncertain) prospects of left-wing parties and coalitions in some West European countries, in spite of allied pressures.

As a consequence of the partial disaggregation of the Atlantic system, there was a growing temptation for policy makers to resort to overt and sometimes brutal linkages between issues and issue areas, to control the spill-over tendency or capitalize on it and ensure that international trade-offs were finally advantageous. This is the more vicious side of the interdependence phenomenon, which can just as easily stimulate such conflicts as it can induce states to cooperate and reconcile themselves to adjusting advantages and weaknesses for the general welfare. Trade-offs between one economic issue and another have been difficult enough to manage and produce mutually satisfactory benefits. But when divergent economic and security interests are either focused in one issue, such as nuclear energy and proliferation, or linked in a crisis situation, such as during the 1973 Middle East conflict and its aftermath, it has seemed that some allied governments are likely to make explicit linkages while others insist on the autonomy of economic and security arenas. The former case was evident during the 1973-74 Alliance crisis, when the ally dominant in the security arena attempted to reassert its waning authority by employing threats to secure trade-offs between military protection and economic or political concessions. The latter was also at work as military dependents refused direct assistance to their protector, or even support for its political aims during and after a military confrontation, because such actions might have jeopardized their access to energy supplies or otherwise have damaged their domestic economies.

Judging from such examples of behavior among governments in the Atlantic Alliance, then, there has been a tendency among key policy makers to perceive alliance structures and relationships as less significant factors conditioning or restraining the pursuit of many policy goals. Thus, the distinction between allies and adversaries becomes less compelling in the formulation and conduct of more aspects of foreign policy, as allies are treated as partial or potential adversaries across a broader spectrum of issues. The frequency and intensity of adversary behavior usually increases the further issues are removed from the security functions of an alliance that is still valued, but it is characteristic of international relations today that issues tend not to be contained and, instead, conflicts easily spread and reinforce the partial adversary nature of interallied diplomacy. This feature is exacerbated when governments with more power in the security or alliance arena attempt to manipulate alliance ties for leverage over issues less directly tied to core political-military affairs. Linkage doctrines and a policy of explicit trade-offs seem especially dangerous because they intensify these conflicts and further weaken bonds among governments.

According to the literature on alliance cohesion, this development alone might be grounds for questioning the viability of the Atlantic Alliance in its present form, and for asking whether its once characteristic mixture of limited pluralism and usually self-restrained American hegemony could be restored as the basis for stability. Such alliances have been considered to be more cohesive and less prone to disintegration than monolithic ones, precisely because of the narrower scope and the lower intensity of conflict among their members.[5] Specific conflicts are supposed to remain "capsulized" rather than spread and "spill over" into other issue areas, and the bloc leader is, therefore, less likely to try and assert its dominance in all arenas. But, from trends in the 1970s, we have seen that issue areas are becoming more interdependent and diverse economic and political interests may only reinforce incipient allied conflicts over security goals and obligations. Moreover, they are more susceptible to manipulation by the dominant ally, which is tempted to try to enforce an artificial consensus in all issue areas. Some of the distinctions between monolithic and looser Western alliance processes have thus become less compelling in Atlantic affairs, even though a restored partial hegemony could not be a stable outcome because it would rest on very shaky, almost atavistic, foundations.

Conflicts among allies may, then, even be exacerbated by some rigidities in the Atlantic Alliance structure, or by outmoded behavior patterns that have not fully adapted to the new pluralism and, instead, can still tempt American policy makers to resort to superior leverage over security affairs as a means of imposing their perceived interests on allies. But this currency is always of decreasing value because, in terms of individual policies and behavior, allied governments have become more independent and tend to adopt French standards of mixed allied-adversary behavior to enhance their own leverage. A semiautonomous military power such as France has usually been most capable of resisting exertions of American power, but many allies find the model appealing and often feasible. Thus, the looser alliance system foreseen by Gaullist policy became more of a reality during the 1970s, as the French pattern was to some extent generalized and as the Atlantic Alliance evolved into a flexible umbrella organization that structured bilateral and multilateral arrangements according to diverse and shifting concepts of national interest. Although this development posed the risk of an unwelcome balkanization of the Alliance, it does seem that the most serious crises and tensions have resulted from attempts by the United States to restore the old pattern of American predominance, rather than adjust to a more flexible system capable of embracing a wider diversity of allied policies.

Apart from the Year of Europe example, the evidence since 1973 suggests that the pattern varies according to the particular ally and set of issues. In some instances, the French precedent has served as a striking model for policies of other allies. Greece provides the most notable example. Greek antagonism for both the United States and NATO arose in reaction to the Turkish occupation of most of Cyprus in the summer of 1974, and after American toleration of or support for the colonels' dictatorship until it fell in the wake of the Cyprus affair.[6] The Caramanlis government of democratic Greece responded to popular and nationalist opinion and to pressures from the left to redefine ties with NATO and Washington, both of which had proven incapable of restraining Turkish military action in the Eastern Mediterranean. Consciously following French precedents, the Greek government announced its withdrawal from the NATO military organization in August 1974. Athens recovered direct control over the 80 percent of its armed forces earmarked to NATO, ceased to participate in the Defense Planning Committee, and revised the status of its officers assigned to SHAPE and other NATO commands. The NATO communications system in Greece reverted to national authority, no NATO maneuvers were allowed in the country, and Greece did not participate in other joint allied exercises until special arrangements were reached in September 1977.[7] Although American forces were not expelled from Greece, home port plans had to be cancelled, some bases were closed, and the status of American forces was revised along less permissive lines. Greece's relations with NATO and the United States had improved by late 1980, but it was likely that Athens would retain a more independent status in the Alliance corresponding to the requirements of domestic politics and the tensions of Greco-Turkish relations.

Other examples of Atlantic pluralism and fluctuating allied relationships in recent years can readily be cited. The Cyprus conflict also produced a change in Turkey's NATO status between 1974 and 1980, when the use of American-NATO military installations in Turkey was restricted in reaction to a congressional ban on most military aid to Ankara.[8] There was a notable, if temporary, alteration in Portugal's status in NATO during the period of communist participation in the government, whereas Iceland's position on the issue of American base rights shifted according to the communist presence in coalition governments. In the case of Spain, it was possible that new trends in domestic politics and foreign policy might lead to closer association with NATO, or even membership in the Alliance. For Italy, however, an eventual communist participation in national government has seemed likely to lead Rome or NATO, or both, to seek a redefinition of Italy's membership status as a way of resolving problems such as Italian access to nuclear strategic plans and the presence of American nuclear strike bases on Italian soil. Italy is an example of a dependent and in many ways weak regime that could nevertheless resist pressures of stronger allies and international financial forces while forming original kinds of popular front governments in response to domestic political requirements. Because of the Gaullist accomplishment, a leftist regime in France would not present the same kind of dilemma for the Alliance as has been the case for Italy, although aspects of French-NATO military ties would doubtless be altered along lines discussed earlier.[9]

Thus, the pattern of alliance relationships described here provides further evidence that the Atlantic Alliance has been evolving into a more flexible and untidy coalition subject to shifting membership arrangements within NATO and with the leading ally, according to changing conditions of national, regional, interbloc, and global politics. At the very onset of the 1980s, however, new and still fluid developments in international politics and East-West relations had arisen that, initially at least, seemed to reinforce trends stressed in this analysis but, in the long run, might well undermine them by stimulating the revival of more rigid structures of mutual threat and bloc politics. A new sense of alarm sprang principally (but not solely) from the unprecedented Soviet military occupation of Afghanistan, a country outside the accepted spheres of political-military bloc politics. The expanded Soviet presence in this region seemed especially ominous for the West in the context of a highly unstable Middle East, where, with the unpredictable and dangerous theatrics of the Iranian revolution, the number and kinds of menaces to critical oil supplies for industrial countries were multiplying dramatically.

Members of the Western Alliance were troubled, not only by the issue of security in this volatile region, but also by the implications of an apparent Soviet willingness to capitalize on the neutralizing effect of superpower parity and its own regional superiority, and resort to overt military force to determine political developments in a weak state along its periphery. It was uncertain whether the occupation of Afghanistan was only a one-time measure to secure control of an unstable border country, or if there was an emerging Soviet intention, matched or propelled by new military capabilities, to extend a sphere of influence into the Persian Gulf zone itself. Despite obvious and important differences between this area and those regions of Europe for which the Alliance was directly responsible, the allies were forced to weigh

the consequences of a possible fundamental alteration in the normally conservative and restrained military behavior of the Soviet Union. The allies also
had to adjust their own reactions to take account of a number of disad-
vantageous international factors, including a milieu characterized by a
weakened and often inconsistent U.S. leadership; superpower parity and an
increasingly devalued American guarantee; strong, but perhaps misguided,
allied interests in preserving a beleaguered détente in Europe; and a pluralistic
Alliance system with independent-minded members who were traditionally
unable to agree on common assessments of or reactions to conflicts in
peripheral regions.

It would be precipitate and unwise to assert firm judgments about long-
range trends in international politics and interallied relations on the basis of
initial reactions to what may or may not be a genuine crossroads in global
politics and East-West relations. In a more modest vein, however, it was true
that until the close of 1980 reactions to the Afghanistan and Iranian crises
tended to reinforce the characteristics of allied behavior already noted in this
analysis. There was thus a predictable pluralism of policies ranging from the
bluster of an archconservative government in Britain to the cultivated mantle
of independence, restraint, and moderation assumed by Giscardian France,
as her rulers adapted the Gaullist legacy to new circumstances and tailored
foreign policy in anticipation of the 1981 presidential election. Although the
reaction of French leaders, especially the president, at times betrayed an
astonishing incoherence and inability to articulate a clear and defensible
policy,[10] the position that gradually emerged in Paris was one that firmly condemned the Soviet move in Afghanistan and called for a withdrawal of
troops; warned that further such actions would be fatal to an already gravely
wounded détente in Europe; and in the meantime sought to preserve existing
East-West ties and use them to reduce tensions and induce positive changes
in Soviet behavior.[11]

Although the French government was generally critical of the American
policy of punishing Moscow with a variety of reprisals, one of its goals was to
avoid (or at least defer) the threatening revival of a classic bipolar bloc structure in Europe. Under the circumstances, this priority amounted to a French
refusal to endorse, in word or deed, what Paris considered to be an excessive
and ill-considered Carter administration reaction, one that posed the risk of
forcing Soviet policy into a mold that would indeed confirm the worst Western
fears. While working to prevent this development, and awaiting clarification
of basic Soviet intentions in a period of uncertain leadership in Moscow, the
French were considering a number of long-range military commitments, including expansion of the strategic nuclear force. These commitments signified
that an independent policy at a time of rising East-West tensions was not
synonymous with a complacent one.[12] Although the official government
position in this crisis was subject to some domestic criticism, ranging from

the overtly pro-Soviet view of the communists to the usual cries for Western unity from Atlanticist and Europeanist circles, a policy stressing détente and independence from the blocs gathered a wide margin of basic support from groups as diverse as Gaullists and socialists.[13]

In addition to restraining the impulsive Americans, a key French goal was to preserve the complementarity of Franco-German policies, which was the fulcrum of West European cooperation and seemed particularly indispensable during a period of rising tensions in Europe and the world. Because of West Germany's substantial commitment to détente in human, economic, and political terms, Bonn and Paris had similar general interests and found that many of their priorities in the evolving crisis were indeed complementary. President Giscard d'Estaing and Chancellor Helmut Schmidt could thus agree that in the crisis Europe had a "special position," which required a certain solidarity with the United States and the Atlantic Alliance, yet accorded a priority to maintaining détente and the freedom of decision among allies,.[14] The West German theme of a "division of labor" in allied responses to the Afghanistan affair sometimes appeared as a disguise for a business-as-usual approach to the East, sometimes as a genuine attempt to sort out appropriate and effective allied roles, often as a vehicle for maintaining independence and flexibility in allied policies while controlling American impetuosity until Soviet intentions were clearer. Thus, France and West Germany seemed, in the early stages of the crisis, to be developing an informal allocation of responsibilities in which France assumed the traditional role of opposing the United States on many matters of principle, while West Germany presented the correct posture of loyal ally yet worked to salvage a European status quo that directly benefited the Federal Republic more than any other Western state.

It was not, however, clear that such attempts by West Europeans to manage and contain the superpower confrontation would be successful, or that they could sustain the privileges European allies had enjoyed under the détente regime of the 1970s. For their effort was predicated on the hope that a new and much more ominous Soviet threat to the West was not a firm development and, instead, could be deferred or derailed altogether. This was perhaps an optimistic assessment of Soviet behavior and might prove to be unrealistic. And, in the event that a clearer Soviet threat does emerge in tandem with efforts to divide Western Europe from the United States for Moscow's benefit, a revival, in some form, of Western political-military solidarity would become more feasible and perhaps essential. In this case, in the short run at least, the convenient ambiguity of Bonn's policy would be untenable and a dependent West Germany might feel compelled to move more closely to the U.S. side during the escalation of East-West tension. France's independent policy would then be isolated in Western Europe; it would be more difficult to sustain than de Gaulle's own brief flirtation with aloof independence after 1965—which was founded on the very different international environment of declining East-West tensions. Fired by Middle Eastern and Southwest Asian crises and by growing Soviet military capabilities partly aimed at Western Europe itself, the circumstances at the outset of the 1980s were not propitious for a sustained revival of this kind of French role.[15]

The future evolution of the Alliance itself, and the broader context of allied relations, were therefore essentially unpredictable at a time when multiple dangers—ranging from Soviet aggression to the Iranian revolution's defiance of the United States and the West—were placing allied ties under great strain. The network of security interests, economic well-being, and national prestige at stake in several arenas of conflict highlighted the reduced significance of such an alliance for structuring government policies in crisis situations—as EEC mechanisms and even national Olympic committees became key actors in Western politics. The "spill over" and linkage phenomena further complicated the situation, as various national economic, military, and political interests came into conflict or were manipulated by governments for leverage and advantage. In their diverse and confusing reactions to these grave events, the Western allies sustained the image of a pluralistic bloc once again in disarray, as the interplay of ally and adversary roles proved difficult to manage. The apparent revival of concern for military security in the European and key peripheral regions was also an awkward phenomenon, as allied governments struggled to reconcile conflicting priorities at a time when future needs, interests, and responsibilities were altogether uncertain.

As often in the past, much of the disarray so characteristic of the Western Alliance could be ascribed to problems of erratic American policy on a number of fronts. Thus, the impulsive Carter administration reaction to the Soviet invasion of Afghanistan could, in part, be explained by a foreign policy strategy that had unduly hastened the decline of American power and leverage in the world without constructing or encouraging a stable or feasible alternative system of order that might have benefited the United States and the West. A feeling of self-betrayal and even debasement was evident in the national debate over SALT II, and the mood of angry resentment was reinforced by President Carter's hesitant handling of the Iranian hostage affair. The often ill-considered behavior of a besieged and indecisive administration in a presidential election year was bound to create problems in interallied relations, and Washington confirmed apprehensions with a display of erratic and seemingly ineffective actions against Iran and the Soviet Union. Although allied cooperation in most measures was expected, in conception and execution the American actions strongly reinforced the established pattern of failure to consult and coordinate with Atlantic partners. Most allies could and did welcome the prospect that one therapeutic effect of these unwelcome international developments might be to revive American attention to global security problems and defense capabilities, which, to the general disadvantage of the West, had been neglected. Yet the likelihood of a complementary revival of

American "leadership" over a consolidated West inspired skepticism or outright resistance for reasons that go beyond the failings of a particular administration in Washington and, instead, are derived from the structural changes in Atlantic and global politics already discussed here.

Thus, it seems improbable that the resurgence of concern over Western security will for long restore even a galvanized United States to a position of primacy and leadership or that the Alliance role as a centerpiece of Western politics can be revived and solidified. This is, at least, no more likely than the possibility that more attention to problems of European security in the face of military developments in the Soviet bloc and on Europe's southern periphery will actually exacerbate tensions and conflicting interests between the United States and its allies, and once again focus attention on the need for more drastic, hence more problematic, reconstruction efforts by the major Western powers. One appropriate response for the 1980s would be a revival of interest in the 1958 Gaullist proposal for the Alliance's leading members, with worldwide economic, political, and military interests to coordinate their Atlantic and global security policies for the overall benefit of the West. Thus, the United States, France, a weakened Britain, and a stronger, more mature West Germany are obvious candidates for a quadripartite group, which would contribute resources and jointly manage efforts to exert Western power and leverage in troubled regions, such as Africa, the Middle East, and the Indian Ocean. The wide diversity of problems, interests, and sources of influence in these areas calls for an equivalent diversity of allied actions—military, economic, political—which can be coordinated among those states with appropriate means at their disposal, although they might initially concentrate on the crucial military dimension essential to deterring or containing Soviet expansionism. Because formal "directorates" over NATO and issues of controlling allied nuclear forces are no longer so salient, a revived interest in the global policy aspects of de Gaulle's memorandum initiative would meet less skepticism or resistance within the Alliance. A Gaullist approach could even be linked and coordinated with efforts to enhance the Atlantic Alliance's military strength in Europe itself, in the context of a reallocation of resources among the various allies and between the Atlantic and key peripheral regions.

In addition to this kind of development, the new dilemmas confronting the security of Western Europe itself may revive the prospects for European defense cooperation. A renewed interest in the political-military dimension of European unity might, in the context just described, provide a constructive and manageable long-run alternative to a heterogenous and asymmetrical Atlantic system with its attendant problems. It might also offer a creative way to manage a redistribution of Western defense tasks and resources at a time when the United States needs to devote major conventional defense efforts to critical regions outside of the Atlantic arena while simultaneously straining to prevent a clear and decisive loss of global nuclear parity. In such circumstances, enhanced West European attention to problems of defense in Europe itself should be beneficial to the West as a whole, even if the political and military efforts are undertaken outside of or on the margins of the Atlantic framework.

In one form or another, some European alternative of this nature has both plagued and seduced the West since France proposed a first version in 1950. At various times, France and the United States have continued to suggest or represent different arrangements for the American-European security tie and have managed to deny or defer each other's grand designs. The issue of a European defense, integrated or not, as an Atlantic partnership or as a more independent Europe, has not yet crystallized in its newest guise. It faces formidable political, economic, and technological problems that can scarcely be underestimated. But it is certain that this issue, as phoenix or chimera, will revive during the precarious 1980s and once again tax the imagination and versatility of the Alliance's leading powers.

Awaiting such compelling but problematic developments, the Western allies, including France, have an undoubted interest in maintaining and even reinforcing, directly or indirectly, their Atlantic coalition as an indispensible framework of mutual security among an otherwise diverse group of states and regimes. This assessment and prognosis assume that the international system will not suffer a prolonged and unwelcome return to the politics of escalating threats and rigid bipolarity, but instead will be dominated by the volatile but manageable mixture of détente (in a new form and phase) and competition between alliance systems. This has long been the state of affairs that requires the Atlantic Alliance to retain a significant role on behalf of the West, but one that has in many ways become less pervasive and constraining for allied states. Pragmatic toleration of a diffuse and often vexing alliance system implies a restraint and flexibility unusual for governments, and especially for large powers with complicated and sometimes debilitating political and bureaucratic systems. It also calls for remarkable maturity and steadfastness on the part of policy makers in times when such qualities seem as rare as self-confidence and simple good judgment. Nevertheless, in an unstable international environment that afflicts allies with a growing sense of military and economic insecurity, the relative cohesion of a pluralist and tolerant alliance network stands out as a welcome factor of cohesion, equilibrium, and perhaps even creativity for the West.

Notes

Introduction

1. For discussions of these perspectives, see: Ronald Inglehart, *The Silent Revolution: Changing Values and Political Styles among Western Publics* (Princeton, N.J.: Princeton University Press, 1977); Robert S. Keohane and Joseph S. Nye, *Power and Interdependence: World Politics in Transition* (Boston: Little, Brown & Co., 1977), esp. chaps. 1-3; and Edward L. Morse, "The Transformation of Foreign Policies: Modernization, Interdependence, and Externalization," *World Politics* 22 (April 1970): 371-92.

2. These different approaches are discussed at various points in this study. See Chapter 2, in particular.

Chapter 1

1. On de Gaulle's late wartime and early postwar diplomacy, see Anton W. DePorte's work, *De Gaulle's Foreign Policy, 1944-1946* (Cambridge, Mass.: Harvard University Press, 1968).

2. The Moscow Conference of March-April 1947 and Soviet refusal to agree to French demands to separate the Saar from Germany are considered by most authorities to be the key to subsequent French policies. See, for example, Jean-Baptist Duroselle, "The Turning Point in French Politics: 1947," *Review of Politics* 13, no. 3 (July 1951): 302-28; Raymond Aron, "France in the Cold War," *Political Quarterly* 22, no. 1 (January-March 1951): 57-66; and Guy de Carmoy, *The Foreign Policies of France: 1948-1968* (Chicago: University of Chicago Press, 1970), p. 23. For Bidault's recollections (though not always reliable) on this and other matters, see his memoirs, *Resistance: The Political Autobiography of Georges Bidault* (New York: Praeger, 1967).

3. Georges Bidault and Edmond Michelet, *Ministre des Armées,* had decided to send General Billotte (adjunct chief of the general staff) to the United States to discuss the problem of a common European defense against the Russians. Premier Félix Gouin intervened and stopped the project. See Georgette Elgey, *Histoire de la IVe République,* vol. 1, *La République des illusions, 1945-1951* (Paris: Fayard, 1965), p. 118.

4. Ibid., 1: 381.

5. For the text of the Brussels Treaty, see North Atlantic Treaty Organization, *NATO: Facts and Figures* (Brussels: NATO Information Service, 1971), pp. 266-67.

6. One of the first acts of the Brussels Military Committee was to fill out American questionnaires on the Brussels Treaty Organization's armaments requirements. See Paul Stehlin, *Retour à zéro: L'Europe et sa défense dans le compte à rebours* (Paris: Robert Laffont, 1965), p. 50.

7. On these negotiations, see Dean Acheson's memoirs, *Present at the Creation: My Years at the State Department* (New York: W. W. Norton & Co., 1969). See also the records in the State Department series of documents: U.S., Department of State, *Foreign Relations of the United States, 1948*, vol. 3, *Western Europe* (Washington, D.C.: Government Printing Office, 1974); and U.S., Department of State, *Foreign Relations of the United States, 1949*, vol. 4, *Western Europe* (Washington, D. C.: Government Printing Office, 1975). This series is cited below as *FRUS* with the year covered and volume number, along with appropriate information for each document.

8. See Duroselle, "Turning Point," pp. 316-18; and Alfred Grosser's indispensable work, *La IVe République et sa politique extérieure* (Paris: Librarie Armand Colin, 1961), pp. 105-6.

9. For example, party Secretary General Thorez said in February 1949 that if France were dragged into war against the Soviet Union, and if the Soviets pursued the aggressor onto French soil, then (rhetorically) he wondered how French workers and the population could behave differently from those of Poland, Rumania, and Yugoslavia. This ill-timed statement helped the French government obtain public approval for the Atlantic Treaty. It appeared in *L'Humanité* on 23 February 1949, and is cited in Ronald Tiersky, *French Communism, 1920-1972* (New York: Columbia University Press, 1974), pp. 207-8.

10. In U.S. Congress, Senate, Committee on Foreign Relations, *North Atlantic Treaty, Documents Relating to the North Atlantic Treaty*, 81st Cong., 1st sess., 1949, p. 6.

11. See Acheson, *Present at the Creation*, pp. 280-82; and Robert E. Osgood, *NATO: The Entangling Alliance* (Chicago: University of Chicago Press, 1962).

12. Senate, Foreign Relations Committee, *Documents Relating to the North Atlantic Treaty*, p. 10.

13. See, for example, the resumé of a telegram from Foreign Minister Bidault to French Ambassador Bonnet in Washington, made by the U.S. embassy in Paris: *FRUS, 1948*, vol. 3, document #840.00/6-2048, dated 29 June 1948, pp. 142-43.

14. For example, Premier Henry Queuille noted in February 1949 that the United States had to help Europe prepare for a possible Soviet invasion. See the statement quoted in Stehlin, *Retour à zéro*, pp. 55-56.

15. François Quilici, in *Journal officiel de la république française*, Débats parlementaires, Assemblée nationale, 1e Législature, session de 1949; Compte rendu in extenso, 26 July 1949, p. 5325. On the other hand, Robert Schuman reminded the deputies that the French constitution, like the American one, prohibited entry into war without parliamentary consent (Article VII); he added that a certain freedom for each signatory under Article V of the Atlantic Treaty could also be advantageous for France in the future. See *Journal officiel*, 25 July 1949, p. 5230.

16. Article IX establishes the council and empowers it to "set up such subsidiary bodies as may be necessary; in particular it shall establish immediately a defense committee which shall recommend measures for the implementation of Articles III and V."

17. See Senate Foreign Relations Committee, *Documents Relating to the North Atlantic Treaty*, p. 6.

18. *Journal officiel*, 29 July 1949, p. 5069. For another discussion of these important debates in the National Assembly, see Simon Serfaty's *France, de Gaulle, and Europe: The Policy of the Fourth and Fifth Republics toward the Continent* (Baltimore: Johns Hopkins University Press, 1968).

19. See the Gaullist scheme in the *Journal officiel*, 26 July 1949, pp. 5272-73.

20. See the British memorandum of a conversation between Secretary of State Marshall and British Foreign Secretary Ernest Bevin, held on 17 December 1947. Although the French Chief of Staff (General Revers) was to come to the United Kingdom for talks early in 1948, Marshall and Bevin agreed to exclude the French from their bilateral discussion (*FRUS, 1947*, vol. 3, CFM Files of Anglo-French Conversations, pp. 818-19).

21. French dissatisfaction with the Brussels Treaty Organization is discussed in Stehlin,

(*Retour à zero,* pp. 53-54) and in General André Beaufre's useful work, *NATO and Europe,* trans. Joseph Green (New York: Alfred A. Knopf, 1966), pp. 20-27. On the BTO, see William A. Knowlton, "Early Stages in the Organization of SHAPE," *International Organization* 13, no. 1 (Winter 1959): 3-5.

22. See the summary of a Bidault communiqué to Ambassador Bonnet, in *FRUS, 1948,* vol. 3, p. 142 (dated 29 June 1948).

23. State Department memorandum of a meeting between Acheson and Ambassador Bonnet on 14 February 1949 (*FRUS, 1949,* vol. 4, document #840.20/2-1449, pp. 107-8).

24. See a memorandum by State Department Counselor Charles E. Bohlen, dated 31 March 1949 (*FRUS, 1949,* vol. 4, document #820.20/3-3149, pp. 255-57).

25. Memorandum from the director of the Office of European Affairs to the secretary of state, reporting the attitude of Joint Chiefs of Staff toward issues raised by Bonnet (*FRUS, 1949,* vol. 4, document #840.20/2-1749, dated 14 February 1949, pp. 120-21).

26. See F. Roy Willis, *France, Germany, and the New Europe: 1945-1967,* rev. ed. (New York: Oxford University Press, 1968), esp. p. 29.

27. See, for example, a memorandum by John Foster Dulles to the undersecretary of state reporting on a conversation with French Foreign Minister Schuman in June 1949 (*FRUS, 1950,* vol. 3, document #740.5/4-2150, p. 60).

28. *Journal officiel,* 25 July 1949, p. 5277.

29. See Mayer's speech, *ibid.,* 22 July 1949, p. 5068, and the text of the amendment in proceedings for 26 July 1949, p. 5330. According to Pierre Gerbet, this procedure was improper, since Article 69 of the *Règlement de l'Assemblée nationale* stated that the French Assembly could only accept or reject the entire text of a treaty and not modify or amend it. See his article, "L'Influence de l'opinion publique et des partis sur la politique étrangère de la France," in *La Politique étrangère et ses fondements,* ed. Jean-Baptist Duroselle (Paris: Librarie Armand Colin, 1954), p. 98.

30. See early American allocations plans in a JCS memo to Secretary Forrestal, dated 13 September 1948 (*FRUS, 1948,* vol. 3, NSC files, pp. 641-49).

31. See the excellent analysis by Raoul Girardet, *L'Idée coloniale en France, 1871-1962* (Paris: La Table ronde, 1972).

32. The reference is from Léon Blum's investiture speech on 21 November 1946, quoted in Grosser, *La IVe République,* p. 116.

33. The inclusion of Algeria was decided along with Italy's adherence to the treaty, but only after overcoming Pentagon and Senate reservations about a Mediterranean-southern orientation for the Alliance. On the negotiations, see the reports of the ambassadorial negotiating groups in *FRUS, 1949,* vol. 4, specifically, minutes of the meeting of 14 January 1949 (Document #840.20/1-1449, pp. 27-34). The provisions on Algeria were attacked by left-wing Algerian deputies, who feared that the Alliance would be used to sustain France's presence in North Africa (*Journal officiel,* 26 July 1949, pp. 5218, 5321).

34. See the discussion in Elgey, *La IVe République,* 1: 442. The idea was apparently suggested to Bidault by Jean-Jacques Servan-Schreiber.

35. See the memorandum summarizing U.S.-French bilateral talks in preparation for the conference (*FRUS, 1950,* vol. 3, document #396.1-LO/4-2750, dated 27 April 1950, pp. 894-95).

36. American policy is summarized in a memorandum from Secretary Acheson to the U.S. Embassy in Paris, dated 21 April 1950 (*FRUS, 1950,* vol. 3, document #740-5/4-2050, pp. 59-60).

37. They also indicated that the three representatives to the North Atlantic Council would consult among themselves. See a State Department memorandum dated 11 May 1950 in *FRUS, 1950,* vol. 3, document #396.1-LO/3-1150, pp. 1033-40.

38. From a summary Ambassador Bruce made of a discussion with Hervé Alphand, sent to Secretary Acheson on 20 July 1950 (*FRUS, 1950,* vol. 3, document #740.5/7-2050, pp. 134-35).

39. Acheson noted: "We have consistently made clear to the French our strong objection to any 'political standing group'" (memorandum dated 20 July 1950, *FRUS, 1950*, vol. 3, document #740.5/7-2050, p. 135).

40. From the important French memorandum to the United States dated 17 August 1950, which summarized Paris's NATO goals during this period (translation in *FRUS, 1950*, vol. 3, p. 223).

41. For a thorough and balanced discussion of the U.S. conception of its role in NATO, see William T. R. Fox and Annette B. Fox, *NATO and the Range of American Choice* (New York: Columbia University Press, 1967).

42. See the State Department policy paper entitled "Essential Elements of US-UK Relations," dated 19 April 1950 (*FRUS, 1950*, vol. 3, CFM files, lot M-88, box 149, esp. p. 875).

43. See the discussion between American and British representatives in preparation for the May 1950 Foreign Ministers Conference, especially remarks by Ambassador Philip Jessup on 27 April 1950 (*FRUS, 1950*, vol. 3, document #396.1-LO/4-2750, esp. p. 885).

44. From the State Department policy paper, "US-UK Relations," p. 871.

45. See the report of the Working Group on Organization, made to the North Atlantic Council and dated 17 September 1949 (*FRUS, 1949*, vo. 4, document #740.5/2-1951, pp. 330-37).

46. From the French memorandum of 17 August 1950, pp. 221-22.

47. Ibid., p. 221.

48. See the North Atlantic Council Resolution of 26 September 1950 (*FRUS, 1950*, vol. 3, pp. 350-52). See also the "treaty" between the U.S. departments of Defense and State that made this possible, dated 8 September 1950 (*FRUS, 1950*, vol. 3, document #740.5/9-850, esp. p. 277); and the agreement reached at the New York Foreign Ministers meeting on 14 September 1950 (*FRUS, 1950*, vol. 3, CFM files, lot M-88, box 152, SEM document I-40, p. 1281).

49. On the problems of the Standing Group, see E. Vandevanter, Jr., *Some Fundamentals of NATO Organization*, memorandum RM-3559-PR (Santa Monica, Calif.: Rand Corporation, April 1963), esp. p. 43. See also Jean Valluy, *Se Défendre? Contre Qui? Pourquoi? Et Comment?* (Paris: Plon, 1960), esp. pp. 182-85; and Francis A. Beer, *Integration and Disintegration in NATO: Processes of Alliance Cohesion and Prospects for Atlantic Community* (Columbus, Ohio: Ohio State University Press, 1969), esp. p. 119.

50. See Elgey, *La IVe République*, 1: 459.

51. The policy in favor of a major effort to strengthen the West's military position in the face of a Communist threat had already been approved by Truman on 25 April 1950 in NSC-68.

52. Truman quoted in Osgood, *NATO*, p. 69.

53. On the early history of SHAPE, see Robert K. Sawyer, "SHAPE: Bulwark of Defense—A Lesson in Cooperation," in North Atlantic Treaty Organization, *SHAPE and Allied Command Europe: Twenty Years in the Service of Peace and Security, 1951-1971* (Brussels: SHAPE, 1971); Andrew J. Goodpaster, "The Development of SHAPE, 1950-1953," *International Organization* 9, no. 2 (May 1955): 257-62; Knowlton, "Organization of SHAPE"; and the informative French narrative, Robert Lefranc's *Aux Premier Temps de l'OTAN: D'Eisenhower à Ridgeway* (Paris: Editions municipales, 1966).

54. See the favorable comments on the staff experience from a French source: André Fontaine, *L'Alliance atlantique à l'heure du dégât* (Paris: Calmann-Levy, 1959), p. 30.

55. See the comments by an American officer writing under the pseudonym of Colonel Fontainebleau, in "NATO Handicap: The Integrated Staff," *NATO Letter* 11, no. 5 (October-November 1966): 30-35.

56. Fox and Fox, *American Choice*, p. 278.

57. Beaufre, *NATO and Europe*, p. 41.

58. Ibid., and Contre-Amiral Lepotier, "Pourquoi la 'force de frappe'?," *Revue de défense nationale* 16 (March 1960): 411-29.

59. "Letter from Dwight D. Eisenhower to Senator Henry M. Jackson," in *The Atlantic*

Alliance, Hearings before the Subcommittee on National Security and International Operations of the Committee on Government Operations, U.S., Congress, Senate, 89th Cong., 2nd sess., 1966, pp. 224-25.

60. North Atlantic Treaty Organization, *NATO: Facts and Figures,* p. 29.

61. See, for example, "Accord entre la France et les Etats-Unis d'Amérique relatif à l'aide pour la défense mutuelle," in France, Ministère de la Guerre, *L'Organisation militaire atlantique: O.T.A.N.,* Bulletin officiel du Ministère de la Guerre, no. 110-1 (Paris: Charles-Lavauzelle et Cie., 1956), pp. 11-112. Most agreements concerning France and NATO, including bilateral Franco-American ones (through September 1956), are included in this bulletin.

62. See, for example, Protocol II of the Paris Agreements on Forces of the Western European Union, in North Atlantic Treaty Organization, *NATO: Facts and Figures,* p. 316.

63. Beaufre, *NATO and Europe,* p. 44.

64. For some discussion of this complex subject, see Raymond H. Dawson and George E. Nicholson, Jr., "NATO and the SHAPE Technical Center," *International Organization* 21, no. 3 (Summer 1967): pp. 565-91; and Joannes H. Knoop, "The Evolution of Air Defense in Allied Command Europe," in North Atlantic Treaty Organization, *SHAPE and Allied Command Europe,* pp. 99-112. Beer's study, *Integration and Disintegration in NATO,* emphasized the failure of NATO to foster integration in supranational terms, although this aim was probably not an intention of most members in any case.

65. See below, pp. 34-35.

66. North Atlantic Council, "Resolution to Implement Section IV of the Final Act of the London Conference" (paragraph 4), in North Atlantic Treaty Organization, *NATO: Facts and Figures,* p. 330. Paragraph 5 of this resolution did require "a broad statement" to justify keeping forces in Europe under national jurisdiction. Thereafter, the NAC was to be kept informed of changes through the annual review process.

67. For additional details about U.S. facilities, see *New York Times,* 10 November 1964, and *Le Monde* 9 March 1966; see also chapter 4, below.

68. See "Agreement between the United States of America and the Republic of France Regarding the Construction, Operation, and Maintenance of a Pipeline (Donges-Metz)," 30 June 1953, in Western European Union, Assembly, Committee on Defense Questions and Armaments, 13th ordinary sess., *France and NATO,* ed. L. Radoux (Paris, June 1967), pp. 17-19.

69. "Accord entre le gouvernement de la république française et le commandant suprême allié en Europe au sujet des conditions particulières d'installation et de fonctionnement, en territoire français métropolitain, du quartier général suprême des forces alliées en Europe et des quartiers généraux interalliés qui lui sont subordonnés," in France, Ministère de la Guerre, *L'Organisation militaire atlantique,* pp. 46-55.

70. "Agreement between the United States of America and the Republic of France regarding Certain Air Bases and Facilities in Metropolitan France Placed at the Disposition of the United States Air Force," 4 October 1952, in Western European Union, *France and NATO,* pp. 13-14. There was also a Status of Forces Agreement concerned with the rights and obligations of foreign military personnel and legal jurisdiction over their activities in the host state. An exhaustive and legalistic study of its application in France is available: Serge Lazareff, *Le Statut des forces de l'O.T.A.N. et son application en France* (Paris: Editions A. Pedone, 1964). In the light of de Gaulle's actions in 1966, it is interesting to note that bilateral Franco-American agreements were to remain in effect for the duration of the North Atlantic Treaty and could be terminated only by mutual agreement. The one bilateral agreement of this nature negotiated under de Gaulle, however, provided for revision by mutual accord or unilateral denunciation after specified periods. See "Agreement between the Government of the United States of America and the Government of the French Republic concerning the System of Communications and Depots of the United States Army in Metropolitan France," 8 December 1959, in Western European Union, *France and NATO,* pp. 24-26.

71. *Le Monde,* 12-13 July 1959.

72. De Gaulle, speech at Bar-le-Duc, 28 July 1946, in *Discours et messages,* (Paris: Plon, 1970), 2: 12-17. See also, in the same volume, his speech at Strasbourg on 7 April 1947 (pp. 48-55).

73. This was an explicit aspect of Jean Monnet's approach to Schuman with the EDC idea. See the text of Monnet's note of 23 September 1950 in Georgette Elgey, *Histoire de la IVe République,* vol. 2, *La République des contradictions, 1951-1954* (Paris: Fayard, 1968), pp. 234-35. See also Grosser, *La IVe République,* p. 236, and Thierry de Clermont-Tonnere, "L'Armée européenne: Une Analyse sans passion," *Politique étrangère* 19, no. 2 (April-May 1954): 169-94; and Olivier Manet, "La Communauté européenne de défense: II. Les Données politiques," *Politique étrangère* 18, nos. 2-3 (May-July 1953): 160-68.

74. For a discussion of French neutralism in this period, see John T. Marcus, "Neutralism in France," *Review of Politics* 17, no. 3 (July 1955): 295-328; and, by the same author, *Neutralism and Nationalism in France: A Case Study* (New York: Bookman Associates, 1958).

75. Roger Morgan, *The United States and West Germany, 1945-1973: A Study in Alliance Politics* (London: Oxford University Press, 1974), pp. 43-44.

76. See the agreement between the departments of State and Defense, dated 8 September 1950 (*FRUS, 1950*).

77. The first public statement was made in an interview with Adenauer published in the *Cleveland Plain Dealer* on 4 December 1949.

78. American pressure included notice that blocking West German rearmament could result in a cut-off of U.S. funds for European defense. See the memorandum of a discussion between Secretary of Defense Marshall and French Defense Minister Jules Moch on 16 October 1950: Memorandum dated 17 October 1950, *FRUS, 1950,* vol. 3, document #762A.5/10-1750, p. 384.

79. For descriptions of the treaty and EDC institutions, see Jean Legaret and E. Martin-Dumesnil, *La Communauté européene de défense: Etude analytique du traité du 27 mai 1952* (Paris: Librarie J. Vrin, 1953); and Gerhard Bebr, "The European Defense Community and the Western European Union: An Agonizing Dilemma," *Stanford Law Review* 7, no. 2 (March 1955).

80. With no apparent illusions about French motives, Secretary of State Acheson had labled the initial Pleven formula as a device for France to achieve the status of Western Europe's representative in NATO and also to control the integrated military force. He noted that "we do not believe other countries and especially Germany have sufficient confidence in France to accord her this primacy" (telegram from Acheson to Ambassador Bruce in Paris, dated 28 October 1950, *FRUS, 1950,* vol. 3, document #740.5/0-2750, p. 411).

81. These and other arguments in support of EDC were expressed in innumerable articles and speeches. See, for example, Clermont-Tonnere, "L'Armée européene"; Alfred Coste-Floret, "Bilan et perspectives de la politique européene," *Politique étrangère* 17, no. 5 (November 1952): 321-34; and Guy Mollet, "France and the Defense of Europe: A Socialist View," *Foreign Affairs* 32, no. 3 (April 1954): 365-73. Arguments pro and con are discussed in the collection edited by Daniel Lerner and Raymond Aron, *France Defeats EDC* (New York: Frederick A. Praeger, Inc., 1957).

82. See Michel Debré, "Contre l'armée européenne," *Politique étrangère* 18, no. 4 (September-October 1953): 275.

83. British policy is discussed in Clarence C. Walton's "Background for the European Defense Community," *Political Science Quarterly* 68, no. 1 (1953): 42-69.

84. XXX, "Union française et institutions européennes," *Politique étrangère* 18, no. 4 (September-October 1953): 275.

85. See the text in North Atlantic Treaty Organization, *NATO: Facts and Figures,* p. 316.

86. Protocol no. IV on the Agency of the Western European Union for the Control of

Armaments provided control functions only for forces in Europe *and* under NATO authority, although all ABC weapons were subject to inspection. Article VI of the protocol put "forces remaining under national control" virtually outside the purview of WEU. See ibid., pp. 322-27.

87. "Convention on the Presence of Foreign Forces in the Federal Republic of Germany," Article I, text in ibid., p. 311.

88. See ibid., pp. 317-22. With the important exception of ABC and actual strategic weapons, these restrictions were not strongly enforced and, in any case, a coalition of SACEUR and two-thirds of the WEU Council could and did make exceptions. Nor did the WEU Agency for the Control of Armaments function effectively, because of reluctance on the part of certain members, especially France and Britain. See the discussion in Armand Imbert's *L'Union de l'Europe occidentale* (Paris: Bibliothèque de droit international, 1968), esp. pp. 53-77.

89. The American image of France as a trouble maker and a weak link in the Alliance was evident in Dulles's reaction to the defeat of the EDC in the National Assembly, when he said, "It is a tragedy that in òne country, nationalism, abetted by Communism, has asserted itself so as to endanger the whole of Europe" (statement of 31 August 1954, *NATO Letter* 2, no. 3 [1 September 1954], p. 13).

90. Morgan, *United States and West Germany,* p. 45.

91. See the bilateral Franco-American agreement of January 1950 in France, Ministère de la Guerre, *L'Organisation militaire atlantique* pp. 109-19.

92. See the policy statement of the (U.S.) interdepartmental Foreign Assistance Correlation Committee, entitled "Basic Policies of the Military Assistance Program," in *FRUS, 1949,* vol. 1, dated 7 February 1949; FACC files, esp. p. 256.

93. For an analysis of the role of American military aid in France's defense spending, see Jean Godard, "La Contribution alliée aux charges militaires de la France," *Revue de défense nationale* 12 (April 1956): 436-45. The overall contribution of American financial and material assistance to France's public expenditures and shaky balance of payments position is discussed in another article by the same author, "L'Aide américaine à la France," *Revue de science financière* 48, no. 3 (July-September 1956), 438-54.

94. These sums include $368 million in Special Military Support (for Indochina War expenses) allocated to France. By comparison, the United Kingdom received $410 million and Italy $385 million. See Lord Ismay, *NATO: The First Five Years, 1949-1954* (n.p., n.d.), pp. 137-38.

95. Excluding Greece and Turkey. By comparison (in millions of dollars), Italy had received $2,301, Belgium $1,236, the Netherlands $1,035, Britain $1,025, and West Germany $901. The figures include only direct bilateral aid for military purposes and do not cover either ERP counterpart funds that may have been channeled into military spending or grants to NATO for infrastructure construction. Source: Harold A. Hovey, *United States Military Assistance: A Study of Policy and Practices* (New York: Frederick A. Praeger, 1965), p. 81.

96. Paul-Marie de la Gorce, *The French Army: A Military-Political History* (New York: George Braziller, 1963), p. 373. De la Gorce notes that France was the first NATO ally to create this type of division, which the United States did not have before 1957. In 1954, a French division at full strength would have comprised 16,500 men plus support elements.

97. Compared to 10 percent in the United States, 13 percent in Britain, and 14 percent in Belgium during the same period. See Jean Autin, *20 Ans de politique financière* (Paris: Editions du Seuil, 1972), p. 13. Also, Paul Legatte, "Economie d'armement et économie française," *Politique étrangère* 17, no. 2 (April-May 1952): 83-85, esp.

98. Jean Planchais, *Une Histoire politique de l'armée: De de Gaulle à de Gaulle, 1940-1967* (Paris: Editions du Seuil, 1967), p. 233.

99. Since, by law, conscripts could not be sent to Southeast Asia except as volunteers, of the 175,000 regular troops in Indochina only 54,000 were Frenchmen from the metropolitan

army, and most of these were officers. The remainder included 30,000 North African forces, 18,000 from sub-Saharan Africa, 30,000 Legionnaires, and 53,000 natives from Indochina (de la Gorce, *French Army*, pp. 376-77).

100. XXX, "Chronique militaire: L'Armée de terre en 1956," *Revue de défense nationale* 13 (January 1957): 141-42.

101. This action led to the resignations of General Guillaume (Chief of Staff of National Defense) and General Zeller (Army Chief of Staff), both of whom opposed the action. The former had served as CINCENT and favored maintaining a major French presence in NATO (Planchais, *Histoire politique de l'armée*, pp. 289-90, and de la Gorce, *French Army*, p. 374).

102. For example, whereas the Lisbon goal of a 540,000-ton navy would have required 30,000 tons of naval construction annually, the rate in 1958 was only 3,600 tons and in 1959 only 2,200, due mainly to Algeria. See G. Cabanier, "L'Evolution de la marine française," *Revue de défense nationale* 21 (July 1965): 1128-46.

103. Fontaine, *L'Alliance atlantique*, p. 85.

104. The evolution of this strategy is described by Samuel P. Huntington in *The Common Defense: Strategic Programs in National Politics* (New York: Columbia University Press, 1961), pp. 64-68.

105. Declaration of 6 June 1952, in *Discours et Messages* 2: 525.

106. Quoted in Pierre Rouanet, *Mendès-France au pouvoir (18 juin 1954-6 fevrier 1955)* (Paris: Robert Laffont, 1965), p. 433.

107. Ibid., pp. 425-26.

108. Quoted in ibid., p. 433.

109. The government itself was divided, but its fall on 6 February 1955 meant that no final decision was taken at all and officials responsible for nuclear energy simply carried on with research on nuclear explosions. See the account in Lothar Rühl's *La Politique militaire de la Ve république* (Paris: Presses de la Fondation nationale des sciences politiques, 1976), pp. 244-48. See also Wilfrid L. Kohl's *French Nuclear Diplomacy* (Princeton, N.J.: Princeton University Press, 1971), pp. 15-47.

110. On these different traditions, see Girardet, *L'Idée coloniale*, esp. p. 62. For an example of Mendès-France's arguments, see the discussion in R.E.M. Irving, *The First Indochina War: French and American Policy, 1945-54* (London: Croom Helm, 1975), p. 81.

111. Much of this discussion is based on Irving, *First Indochina War, passim.*

112. Claude de Lagarde, "The Meaning of NATO for France and Europe," *Annals of the American Academy of Political and Social Science*, vol. 288, *NATO and World Peace*, ed. Ernest Minor Patterson (July 1953): 65. The case for world-wide application of the Alliance is persuasively stated by Jacques Soustelle in "France and Europe: A Gaullist View," *Foreign Affairs* 30, no. 4 (July 1952), pp. 545-53.

113. See, for example, the conclusion of the State Department Policy Planning Staff dated 8 February 1950 in *FRUS, 1950*, vol. 1, document #661.00/2-850, pp. 145-47.

114. Britain claimed to be hamstrung by the commonwealth's neutral bias regarding this conflict. See the record of Anglo-American discussions dated 1 May 1950 in *FRUS, 1950*, vol. 3, document #396.1 LO/5-150, pp. 935-38.

115. Irving, *First Indochina War*, p. 104. Osgood (*NATO*, p. 27) estimated that in 1952 Indochina was costing some $2.25 billion a year, of which about one-third was being paid by the United States.

116. Resolution 2, "Indochina," 17 December 1952. The text is given in Ismay, *NATO*, p. 194.

117. "Policy Statement by U.S. on Goals in Southeast Asia," in *New York Times, The Pentagon Papers As Published by the New York Times* (New York: Bantam Books, Inc., 1971), pp. 27-32. Donald Heath, the American representative to the Associated States of Indochina, often bypassed French authorities and dealt directly with local officials. This behavior led Premier Pleven to give the American ambassador in Paris a note on 8 October

1950 that criticized the way the United States was applying its aid and contended it constituted an inadmissable interference in French domestic affairs. See Grosser, *La IVᵉ République,* pp. 282-84.

118. NSC document #5405 as summarized in "'54 Report by Special Committee on the Threat of Communism," in *New York Times, Pentagon Papers,* p. 36.

119. Rouanet, *Mendès-France au pouvoir,* pp. 67-68, and Irving, *First Indochina War,* pp. 120-21. It was Admiral Radford, Chairman of the JCS, who replied favorably.

120. George A. Kelly, *Lost Soldiers: The French Army and Empire in Crisis, 1947-1962* (Cambridge, Mass.: M.I.T. Press, 1965), p. 123.

121. See, for example: L. M. Chassin, "Vers un encerclement de l'occident," *Revue de défense nationale* 12 (May 1956): 531-53; and Georges R. Manue, "La Leçon de Suez," *Revue de défense nationale* 12 (October 1956): 1155-64.

122. See: General de Monsabert, "North Africa in Atlantic Strategy," *Foreign Affairs* 31, no. 3 (April 1953): 418-26; E. J. Debau, "La France vue de Washington à travers l'O.T.A.N.," *Revue de défense nationale* 12 (March 1956): 332-36; Colonel Parisot, "Valeur stratégique de l'Afrique pour l'O.T.A.N.," *Revue de défense nationale* 14 (March 1958): 430-35; Jacques Allard, "Vérités sur l'affaire algérienne," *Revue de défense nationale* 14 (January 1958): 5-41.

123. "Notre Politique militaire," *Revue de défense nationale* 13 (July 1957): 1040. This article by the Armed Forces Chief of Staff is an authoritative statement of the general strategic implications of the *guerre révolutionnaire* doctrine. See also Ely's "Les Problèmes français et l'équilibre mondial," *Revue de défense nationale* 15 (November 1959): 1709-25.

124. Manue, "La Leçon de Suez," p. 1163 (italics removed).

125. See Ely's recollections in *Memoirs, Suez . . . Le 13 Mai* (Paris: Plon, 1969), p. 225; see also the SHAPE lecture of November 1957, delivered by General Jacques Allard, the text of which was printed as "Verités sur l'affaire algérienne."

126. Ely, *Memoirs,* p. 22.

127. Grosser, *La IVᵉ République,* pp. 390-91.

128. American intelligence apparently did know of the invasion plans in advance, but either did not take them seriously or decided that premature American opposition would have been ineffective. See André Fontaine, *History of the Cold War: From the Korean War to the Present* (New York: Vintage Books, 1970), p. 240.

129. For an illuminating discussion of American and British perspectives and interests in this affair, see Richard E. Neustadt, *Alliance Politics* (New York: Columbia University Press, 1970).

130. Claude Delmas, "Quel est l'avenir du pacte atlantique?," *Revue de défense nationale* 14 (July 1958): 1111. For a similar point of view expressed by General Ely as late as 1961, see his *L'Armée dans la nation* (Paris: Librarie Arthème Fayard, 1961), esp. p. 93.

131. For the text of Premier Bulganin's warning to Mollet on 6 November, see Grosser, *La IVᵉ République,* p. 372.

132. For an example of this point of view, based on the Suez experience, see General Gazin's "Réplique ou représailles," *Revue de défense nationale* 14 (October 1958): 1488-95. Gazin's claim that Paris and London had been threatened and found themselves temporarily unprotected by the American nuclear umbrella was apparently incorrect on both counts. The Soviet threats were most likely a bluff, and, in any case, American Ambassador Douglas Dillon immediately informed Mollet that the United States would carry out its defense commitments in the event of a Soviet attack on European territory (Fontaine, *L'Alliance atlantique,* pp. 248-49).

133. Speech to the American Club of Paris on 12 April 1956, in *NATO Letter* 4, no. 5 (1 May 1956): 12.

134. For example, a council communiqué of 27 March 1956 was carefully worded to avoid direct support of the French position in Algeria: "It [the council] has noted that France has found it necessary, *in the interest of her own security,* to reinforce the French forces in

Algeria, which is a part of the North Atlantic Treaty area. The Council recognizes the importance to NATO of security in this area. Expressing the hope of an early and lasting settlement, the Council noted the determination of the French Government to restore, as soon as possible, its full contribution towards the common defense in Europe" (*NATO Letter* 4, no. 4 [1 April 1956]: 2, emphasis added).

135. See Claude Delmas's interview with Spaak, "Nous devons passer de l'alliance à la communauté atlantique," *Revue de défense nationale* 13 (November 1957): 1617-25.

136. Gaillard was premier from 11 November 1957 until 14 May 1958, followed by Pierre Pflimlin until de Gaulle became the Fourth Republic's last premier on 1 June 1958.

137. For an analysis of this conflict, see Jacques Vernant, "France-Tunisie-Maroc," *Revue de défense nationale* 14 (August-September 1958): 1398-1405.

138. *Le Monde,* 6 December 1957.

139. *Le Monde,* 24 December 1957.

140. Morgan, *United States and West Germany,* p. 67. On West German nuclear weapons policy in general, see Catherine Kelleher, *Germany and the Politics of Nuclear Weapons* (New York: Columbia University Press, 1975).

141. On the Mediterranean community project, see Lothar Rühl's account of his interview with Gaillard in "La Politique militaire du gouvernement français, 1958-1970" (Ph.D. diss., Fondation nationale des sciences politiques, Cycle supérieure d'études politiques, 1971), p. 51; and Henry Marchat, "A Propos d'un plan de communauté méditerranéenne," *Revue de défense nationale* 14 (August-September 1958): 1339-53.

142. The team was headed by Harold Beeley of the United Kingdom and Robert Murphy of the United States. The latter had been Roosevelt's contact with Vichy and was a *bête noire* of the Gaullists.

143. On this, see Kohl, *French Nuclear Diplomacy,* p. 47.

144. "General de Gaulle and the Foreign Policy of the Fifth Republic," *International Affairs* (London) 39, no. 2 (April 1963): 199.

Chapter 2

1. 28 October 1966 (press conference), in France, Ambassade de France, *French Foreign Policy: Official Statements, Speeches and Communiqués, 1966* (New York: Service de presse et d'information, 1967), p. 157. (This series is cited below as *French Foreign Policy,* with the appropriate date.)

2. See Stanley Hoffmann's *Decline or Renewal? France since the 1930s* (New York: Viking Press, 1974), esp. pp. 259-60. For much of the discussion in this chapter, I am indebted to Hoffmann's profound analysis of de Gaulle's ideas and statecraft.

3. France, Assemblée nationale, *Compte rendu analytique,* séance du 10 Mars 1960, p. 8.

4. *Une Politique étrangère, 1958-1969* (Paris: Librarie Plon, 1971), p. 481.

5. Ibid., p. 478.

6. See, for example, the statement on p. 116 of Morse's *Foreign Policy and Interdependence in Gaullist France* (Princeton, N.J.: Princeton University Press, 1972).

7. Hoffmann, *Decline or Renewal,* p. 283.

8. John Zysman, "The French State in the International Economy," *International Organization* 31, no. 4 (Autumn 1977): 839. See also Zysman's full study, *Political Strategies for Industrial Order: Market, State, and Industry in France* (Berkeley, Calif.: University of California Press, 1977).

9. Charles de Gaulle, *The Complete War Memoirs of Charles de Gaulle* (New York: Simon & Shuster, 1968), p. 575.

10. Couve de Murville, *Politique étrangère,* pp. 482-83.

11. Charles de Gaulle, *Le Fil de l'épé* (May 1932; reprint ed. Paris: Editions Berger-Levrault, 1961), p. 77.

12. Idem, *The Army of the Future* (Philadelphia: J. B. Lippincott, 1941), p. 174.

13. Idem, *Le Fil de l'épé*, p. 78.

14. Stanley Hoffmann, "The Will to Grandeur: De Gaulle As Political Artist," *Daedalus* 97, no. 3 (Summer 1968): 283.

15. Couve de Murville, *Une Politique étrangère*, pp. 482-83.

16. *Leviathan*, ed. Michael Oakeshott (New York: Collier Books, 1962), p. 72.

17. Raymond Aron, *Peace and War: A Theory of International Relations*, trans. Richard Howard and Annette Baker Fox (Garden City, N.Y.: Doubleday & Co., 1966), p. 73.

18. J. R. Tournoux, *La Tragédie du général* (Paris: Plon, 1967), p. 310.

19. Radio-television speech of 26 March 1962, in France, Ambassade de France, *Major Addresses, Statements, and Press Conferences of General Charles de Gaulle, May 19, 1958-January 31, 1964* (New York: Service de presse et d'information, 1964), p. 168.

20. Speech of 18 June 1959 at the Hôtel de Ville, Paris, in André Passeron, *De Gaulle parle: Des institutions, de l'Algérie, de l'armée, des affaires étrangères, de la communauté, de l'économie et des questions sociales* (Paris: Plon, 1962), p. 535.

21. Press conference of 28 October 1966, in *French Foreign Policy, 1966*, p. 199.

22. Ibid.

23. See the collected essays in *In Search of France* (New York: Harper Torchbooks, 1963), especially those by Stanley Hoffmann and Jesse R. Pitts; and Michel Crozier's *The Bureaucratic Phenomenon* (Chicago: University of Chicago Press, 1964), pp. 213-69. Hoffmann applies Crozier's analysis of French behavior to explain de Gaulle's appeal as a charismatic and crisis leader in "Heroic Leadership: The Case of Modern France," in *Political Leadership in Industrialized Societies: Studies in Comparative Analysis*, ed. Lewis J. Edinger (New York: John Wiley & Sons, Inc., 1967), pp. 108-54.

24. *Peace and War*, p. 468.

25. For a discussion of normal rules of accommodation among friendly countries and allies, see Fred Charles Iklé's *How Nations Negotiate* (New York: Frederick A. Praeger, 1964), pp. 97-121.

26. Speech at Lille, 29 June 1947, in Charles de Gaulle, *Discours et messages* (Paris: Plon, 1970), 2: 87.

27. On this theme see, for example, de Gaulle's speech at La Pelouse de Bagatelle on 1 May 1949, *Discours et Messages*, 2: 294.

28. *Army of the Future*, p. 37.

29. Press Conference of 30 June 1955, *Discours et Messages*, 2: 645.

30. Ibid., 3: 126.

31. See Morse, *Gaullist France*, esp. statements on pp. xi and 148. This is also a view permeating the unsympathetic and uncomprehending polemic by John Newhouse, *De Gaulle and the Anglo-Saxons* (New York: Viking Press, 1970). Skepticism also predominates in David Schoenbrun's *The Three Lives of Charles de Gaulle* (New York: Atheneum, 1966).

32. Speech at Nîmes on 7 January 1951, in *Discours et messages*, 3: 405.

33. Press Conference of 5 September 1960, in France, Ambassade de France, *Major Addresses, 1958-1964*, p. 96.

34. 3 November 1959, *Discours et Messages*, 3: 126-27.

35. For general analyses of alliances and NATO that tend to confirm de Gaulle's views, see George Liska, *Nations in Alliance: The Limits of Interdependence* (Baltimore: Johns Hopkins Press, 1962). David P. Calleo's *The Atlantic Fantasy: The U.S., NATO, and Europe* (Baltimore: Johns Hopkins Press, 1970); and Edwin H. Fedder's *NATO: The Dynamics of Alliance in the Postwar World* (New York: Dodd, Mead, & Co., 1973).

36. *Complete War Memoirs*, p. 817.

37. Ibid., p. 818.

38. Ibid.

39. Ibid., esp. p. 831.

40. Ibid., pp. 831-32.

41. See his speeches at Compiègne, 7 March 1948, and at Marseilles on 17 April 1948, in *Discours et messages,* 2: 173-74, 179-80.

42. Speech at Marseilles, 17 April 1948, ibid., p. 180.

43. Speech at Reims, 15 April 1951, ibid., p. 416.

44. Citations are from de Gaulle's press conference in Paris on 12 November 1953, ibid., p. 589.

45. See the speech at Paris on 11 November 1952 (ibid., p. 553) and an interview with a United Press correspondent on 10 July 1950 (ibid., pp. 376-77); see also de Gaulle's press conference on 17 November 1948 (ibid., p. 238). Many aspects of de Gaulle's proposals are contained in an RPF plan submitted to the National Assembly during the Atlantic Treaty ratifications debates (*Journal officiel,* 26 July 1949, pp. 5272-273).

46. Paris speech, 11 November 1952, *Discours et messages,* 2: 553.

47. Speech to the RPF in Paris, 4 December 1954 (ibid., pp. 625-26).

48. See his Paris press conference, 25 February 1953 (ibid., pp. 567-69).

49. Press conference of 10 March 1952 (ibid., p. 511), which was the first time de Gaulle publicly and specifically called for a "reorganization" of the Atlantic Alliance.

50. De Gaulle's most thorough description of the revised alliance is found in his press conference of 25 February 1953 (ibid., pp. 573-74).

51. Press conference of 17 November 1948 (ibid., p. 237).

52. See his speeches at La Pelouse de Bagatelle on 1 May 1951 (ibid., p. 426) and at Nancy, 25 November 1951 (ibid., p. 479).

53. See the speech at Nancy (ibid., p. 479). Britain's position is even more ambiguous, although in the November 1948 speech (ibid., 2: 238) London was assigned responsibility for Europe north of the channel, for the Baltic, and for the Middle East.

54. The proposal is discussed in Paul Stehlin, *Retour à zero: L'Europe et sa défense dans le compte à rebours* (Paris: Robert Laffont, 1968), pp. 103-6.

55. De Gaulle mentions acquiring a nuclear force in the press conference of 7 April 1954 (*Discours et messages,* 2: 606-7) and again in a speech on 4 December 1954 (ibid., p. 626).

56. Ibid., p. 238.

57. Press conference in Paris on 10 March 1952, ibid., p. 510.

58. See the press conference of 30 June 1955, ibid., p. 656.

59. This chronology coincides roughly with Wilfrid L. Kohl's analysis of trends in de Gaulle's political and strategic policies: *French Nuclear Diplomacy* (Princeton, N.J.: Princeton University Press, 1971), pp. 132-45.

60. No attempt is made to describe or analyze de Gaulle's foreign policies in great detail here, only to highlight certain aspects of them. For a lengthy discussion and analysis of Fifth Republic foreign policy, see Edward A. Kolodziej, *French International Policy under de Gaulle and Pompidou* (Ithaca: Cornell University Press, 1974).

61. For a discussion of presidential power over the making of foreign policy in France, see Elijah Ben-Zion Kaminsky, "The French Chief Executive and Foreign Policy," in *Sage International Yearbook of Foreign Policy Studies,* ed. Patrick McGowan, (Beverly Hills: Sage, 1973), vol. 1.

62. Press conference of 29 July 1963, *Discours et messages,* 4: 121.

63. The third volume, *Le Salut,* was not published until October 1959.

64. *Complete War Memoirs,* pp. 872-73.

65. See, for example, the speech at Bar-le Duc, 28 July 1946 (*Discours et messages,* 2: 12-17); see also a speech at Strasbourg on 7 April 1947 (ibid., pp. 84-55).

66. The best analysis of these divergent approaches to European unity is found in David P. Calleo's *Europe's Future: The Grand Alternatives* (New York: W. W. Norton & Co., 1967).

67. In 1957, Michel Debré denounced the Treaty of Rome as an illegitimate renunciation of sovereignty and predicted that it would eventually be abandoned by a regime conscious of France's real interests. See Roger Massip, *De Gaulle et l'Europe* (Paris: Flammarion, 1963), p. 26.

68. Ibid., pp. 27-28.

69. Press Conference of 5 September 1960 (France, Ambassade de France, *Major Addresses 1958-1964*, pp. 92-93).

70. Ibid.

71. This is a major theme and conclusion of Kolodziej's study, *French International Policy*.

72. "Revolt and Revisionism in the Gaullist Global Vision: An Analysis of French Strategic Policy," *Journal of Politics* 33, no. 2 (May 1971): 456.

73. These were constant themes of Gaullist speeches and press conferences by the mid-1960s. See, for example, the press conference of 23 July 1964, *Discours et messages*, 4, esp. p. 227.

74. *Atlantic Fantasy*, pp. 70-71.

75. *Memoirs of Hope: Renewal and Endeavor* (New York: Simon & Schuster, 1971), p. 48.

76. This is the view of Paul-Marie de la Gorce, in *La France contre les empires* (Paris: Grasset, 1969), p. 207.

77. Speech of 27 April 1965 in France, Ambassade de France, *Major Addresses, Statements, and Press Conferences of General Charles de Gaulle, March 17, 1964-May 16, 1967* (New York, Service de presse et d'information, 1967), p. 89.

Chapter 3

1. William W. Kaufmann indicates that the doctrine was often toned down by American officials, and that there were serious dissents over it within the Joint Chiefs of Staff (*The McNamara Strategy* [New York: Harper & Row, 1964], esp. pp. 1-46).

2. See Kissinger's *Nuclear Weapons and Foreign Policy* (New York: Harper & Brothers, 1957). For an incisive French criticism of massive retaliation, see Edmond Combaux, "La Défense de l'Eurafrique," *Revue de défense nationale* 14 (January 1958): 59-71.

3. See the useful summary of Wohlstetter's views in John D. Steinbrunner's *The Cybernetic Theory of Decision: New Dimensions of Political Analysis* (Princeton, N.J.: Princeton University Press, 1974), pp. 201-3.

4. This information is from Steinbrunner's account, ibid., pp. 202-3.

5. See McNamara's speech at Ann Arbor on 16 June 1962, quoted extensively in Kaufmann, *McNamara Strategy*, p. 115. Kissinger points out that by 1965 McNamara had grown more skeptical of a strictly counterforce doctrine (*The Troubled Partnership: A Re-appraisal of the Atlantic Alliance* [New York: Anchor Books, 1966], p. 112).

6. McNamara, "Address before the Fellows of the American Bar Foundation," Chicago, Ill., 17 February 1962, in Kaufmann, *McNamara Strategy*, p. 161.

7. Deputy Assistant Secretary of Defense Alain C. Enthoven, statement of 10 February 1963 before U.S. Senate Committee on Armed Services, reprinted as "American Deterrent Policy," in *Problems of National Strategy: A Book of Readings*, ed. Henry A. Kissinger (New York: Frederick A. Praeger, 1965), p. 124.

8. Kaufmann, *McNamara Strategy*, p. 44.

9. Enthoven, "American Deterrent Policy," p. 121.

10. See, for example, General Gallois's reaction to the landmark Wohlstetter article of 1958 ("The Delicate Balance of Terror," *Foreign Affairs* 37, no. 1 [January 1959]): "L'Alliance atlantique et l'évolution de l'armement," *Politique étrangère* 23, no. 2 (1959): 179-203.

11. See, for example, Edmond Combaux, "Au delà de Clausewitz: Une Nouvelle Doctrine de la guerre," *Revue de défense nationale* 13 (April 1957): 518-32.

12. Made on 21 April 1959, during Senate hearings on his confirmation as secretary of state. Harald von Riekhoff comments that, in context, Herter was referring to limited probing actions and had added that the United States would enter such a war if it judged a local attack to be a prelude to one against the United States itself, or the beginning of an escalation that

would have the same result. See Harald von Riekhoff, *NATO: Issues and Prospects,* Contemporary Affairs, no. 38 (Toronto, Ont.: Canadian Institute of International Affairs, 1967), citation from p. 25.

13. Cited in Kaufmann, *McNamara Strategy,* p. 117.

14. For examples of these views, see: George Ball, "U.S. Policy toward NATO" in *NATO in Quest of Cohesion,* ed. Karl H. Cerny and Henry W. Briefs (New York: Frederick A. Praeger, 1965), pp. 11-19; Malcolm W. Hoag, "Nuclear Policy and French Intransigence," *Foreign Affairs* 41, no. 2 (January 1963): 286-98; the important article by Albert Wohlstetter, "Nuclear Sharing: NATO and the N+1 Country," *Foreign Affairs* 39, no. 3 (April 1961): 355-87; and Robert R. Bowie, "Strategy and the Atlantic Alliance," *International Organization* 17, no. 3 (Summer 1963): 709-32.

15. Reportedly reached by Eisenhower and Macmillan at Bermuda in March 1957. See John Newhouse, *De Gaulle and the Anglo-Saxons* (New York: Viking Press, 1970), pp. 14-15.

16. *New York Times,* 8 February 1958.

17. *Memoirs of Hope: Renewal and Endeavor* (New York: Simon & Shuster, 1971), p. 203.

18. Wilfrid L. Kohl, *French Nuclear Diplomacy* (Princeton, N.J.: Princeton University Press, 1971), pp. 65-67.

19. Newhouse reports that Dulles and most of the State Department were also opposed to substantial aid (*De Gaulle and the Anglo-Saxons,* pp. 21-24).

20. See *New York Times,* 16 March 1959; and *New York Herald Tribune,* 18 March 1959, which noted that the U.S. Atomic Energy Act required that a state receiving aid should be making a substantial contribution to the mutual defense and security of the free world.

21. "A force capable of acting on our behalf . . . which ought to belong to us," 3 November 1959, text in Charles de Gaulle, *Discours et messages* (Paris: Plon, 1970), 3: 127.

22. Speech of 3 December 1959; text in "Chronique aéronautique," *Revue de défense nationale* 16 (February 1960): 363.

23. The British nuclear force was certainly not exempt from criticism; see Robert Bowie, "Tensions within the Alliance," *Foreign Affairs* 43, no. 1 (October 1963), esp. p. 66. In *The Discipline of Power: Essentials of a Modern World Structure* (Boston: Little, Brown & Co., 1968), pp. 96-108, George Ball later contended that the Eisenhower and Kennedy policies of keeping the British nuclear force alive had been a mistake.

24. For details, see Newhouse, *De Gaulle and the Anglo-Saxons,* p. 156.

25. This group included General Maxwell Taylor, the Joint Chiefs of Staff and most of the Pentagon, Secretary of the Treasury Douglas Dillon (motivated by the balance of payments), John McCone of the CIA, Ambassador Gavin, and NATO Ambassador Finletter.

26. In this camp were Secretary Rusk and the European Bureau at State, Presidential Assistant McGeorge Bundy, the JCAE, and General Norstad.

27. For accounts of this decision and related intraadministration discussion, see Robert Kleiman's *Atlantic Crisis: American Diplomacy Confronts a Resurgent Europe* (New York: W. W. Norton & Co., Inc., 1964), pp. 56-57; Newhouse, *De Gaulle and the Anglo-Saxons,* pp. 153-61; Kohl, *French Nuclear Diplomacy,* pp. 217-19.

28. There had been a NATO ministerial meeting from 12 to 15 December, and Macmillan had seen de Gaulle at Rambouillet on 15 December, but apparently did not bring up the issues scheduled for discussion at Nassau.

29. Paragraphs 6 and 8 of the Nassau communiqué.

30. Kleiman, *Atlantic Crisis,* p. 51.

31. De Gaulle's pique came out during his press conference on 14 January 1963; see *Discours et messages,* vol. 4, esp. p. 74.

32. Kleiman, *Atlantic Crisis,* p. 45. Newhouse (*De Gaulle and the Anglo-Saxons,* p. 231) claims that Kennedy meant to indicate flexibility, but there is no substantial evidence that he or his staff intended to include warheads in the offer.

33. See Kleiman, *Atlantic Crisis,* p. 54, and Newhouse's slightly different account of this meeting, *De Gaulle and the Anglo-Saxons,* p. 335.

34. See the press conference text, *Discours et messages,* vol. 4.

35. The agreement had provided for deliveries over a period of ten years. This American action was made public by the French only in April 1966. See the *New York Times,* 18 April 1966.

36. For details, see Kohl, *French Nuclear Diplomacy,* pp. 245-51.

37. See pp. 86-95.

38. This was Kissinger's view then; see *Troubled Partnership,* pp. 168-69.

39. The quote is from Kohl, *French Nuclear Diplomacy,* p. 233.

40. In 1959, Italy accepted thirty Jupiters and Turkey took fifteen under these restrictions. Under the March 1957 agreement, Britain took sixty Thors in four squadrons, but they were not directly linked to NATO.

41. SACEUR also served as the commander of American forces in Europe, who authorized release of warheads upon the orders of the president.

42. See the conclusion of Lothar Rühl in "La Politique militaire du gouvernement français, 1958-1970" (Ph.D. thesis, Fondation national des sciences politiques, Cycle supérieure d'études politiques, 1971), p. 40.

43. Quoted in Guy de Carmoy, *The Foreign Policies of France: 1944-1968* (Chicago: University of Chicago Press, 1970), p. 55.

44. See Kohl, *French Nuclear Diplomacy,* pp. 65-67.

45. See Claude Delmas's interview of Norstad, "Entretien avec le Général Norstad, Commandant suprême des forces alliées en Europe," *Revue de défense nationale* 13 (December 1957): 1803-13; Norstad's speech of 2 March 1960 in "Chronique de l'OTAN," *Revue de défense nationale* 16 (April 1960): 740; other speeches of his in New York and Washington reported in *Le Monde,* 9 and 16 January 1963; and Norstad's presentation before the Jackson Committee in 1966, "Testimony of General Lauris Norstad," 6 May 1966, in U.S., Congress, Senate Committee on Government Operations, Subcommittee on National Security and International Operations, *The Atlantic Alliance: Hearings,* 89th Cong., 2nd sess., 1966, esp. pp. 70-74.

46. See Robert E. Osgood, *NATO: The Entangling Alliance* (Chicago: University of Chicago Press, 1962), p. 232; and Steinbrunner, *Cybernetic Theory of Decision,* p. 185.

47. See NATO Secretary General Paul-Henri Spaak's record of his discussion with de Gaulle, in *The Continuing Battle: Memoirs of A European, 1936-1966* (Boston: Little, Brown & Co., 1969), pp. 324-30; and de Gaulle's press conference of 5 September 1960 in *Discours et messages,* vol. 3, esp. p. 149.

48. See the account of Adenauer's discussions with Couve de Murville and Michel Debré on 7 and 8 October 1960, in Kohl, *French Nuclear Diplomacy,* pp. 274-75, and Rühl, "Politique militaire," pp. 128-31.

49. See *New York Times,* 9 December 1960.

50. Much of the following discussion is drawn from Steinbrunner's interesting account in *Cybernetic Theory of Decision.* Other descriptions of the MLF affair include: Wilfrid L. Kohl, "Nuclear Sharing in NATO and the Multilateral Force," *Political Science Quarterly* 80, no. 1 (March 1965): 88-109; the more negative critique by Alastair Buchan, "The Multilateral Force: An Historical Perspective," in *Problems of National Strategy,* ed. Kissinger, pp. 264-87; and Kissinger, *Troubled Partnership,* pp. 129-61.

51. The Kennedy ideal is presented in Joseph Kraft's *The Grand Design: From Common Market to Atlantic Partnership* (New York: Harper & Brothers, 1962). For contrasting treatments of American and French ideas, see Harold van B. Cleveland's *The Atlantic Idea and Its European Rivals* (New York: McGraw-Hill, 1966) and, more sympathetic to the Gaullist design, David P. Calleo's *Europe's Future: The Grand Alternatives* (New York: W. W. Norton & Co., 1967).

52. See Steinbrunner, *Cybernetic Theory of Decision,* p. 233.

53. Nevertheless, it seems American policy makers did not seriously consider withdrawing the veto the United States would have had under the plan.

54. See Couve de Murville, *Une Politique étrangère, 1958-1969* (Paris: Librarie Plon, 1971), p. 97.

55. *Le Monde,* 7 November 1964. For other French criticism, see Pierre M. Gallois, "This Is a Policy Move by Washington," *NATO's Fifteen Nations* 8, no. 6 (December, 1963-January, 1964): 18-21; André Fontaine, "The ABC of MLF," *Reporter,* 31 December 1964; and Maurice Duverger in *Le Monde,* 10 December 1964.

56. 24 November 1964. For similar leaks from the government, see *France-Observateur,* 12 November 1964.

57. James Reston, after seeing Johnson, made this clear in his *New York Times* report of 21 December 1964 (see Steinbrunner, *Cybernetic Theory of Decision,* esp. p. 309).

58. For criticism of American methods, see Alastair Buchan, "Partners and Allies," *Foreign Affairs* 42, no. 4 (July 1963), esp. p. 632; and Henry Kissinger, "Strains on the Alliance," *Foreign Affairs,* 41, no. 2 (January 1963): 261-85.

59. William T. R. Fox and Annette B. Fox, *NATO and the Range of American Choice* (New York: Columbia University Press, 1967), p. 134.

60. McNamara said at Ann Arbor, "We want and need a greater degree of Alliance participation in formulating nuclear weapons policy to the greatest extent possible" (Kaufmann, *McNamara Strategy,* p. 118).

61. See, for example, the conclusions of Riekhoff, *NATO,* p. 75.

62. Newhouse, *De Gaulle and the Anglo-Saxons,* pp. 53-54.

63. The description is from his memoirs, *Politique étrangère,* p. 30.

64. Ibid.

65. David Schoenbrun, *The Three Lives of Charles de Gaulle* (New York: Atheneum, 1966), p. 293.

66. Ibid. According to George Ball, Dulles was doubtless well aware of the General's views—not only from the Macmillan talks, but also from a meeting with an American official earlier in June, when de Gaulle said that "France wished to play a central role in the development of Western Strategy around the world" (*Discipline of Power,* pp. 128-29). Newhouse (*De Gaulle and the Anglo-Saxons,* p. 56) identifies the official as General Norstad.

67. Couve de Murville (*Politique étrangère,* p. 33) states that "it was understood that consultations would follow."

68. De Gaulle's own recollection claims that "we held aloof from their joint expedition and sent a cruiser to Beirut to establish our separate presence" (*Memoirs of Hope,* p. 204). De Gaulle even seems to place the incident after his Ecole Militaire speech in November 1959 as an example of French independence.

69. Quoted in André Fontaine, *History of the Cold War: From the Korean War to the Present* (New York: Vintage Books, 1970), p. 300.

70. The memorandum was the subject of wide speculation and rumor, because the text was not officially revealed until the copy deposited in the Eisenhower library was published in the review *Espoir* and in *Le Monde* on 26 June 1976. For earlier and often inaccurate accounts, see articles in *Le Monde,* 11 and 13 November 1958, 2 and 3 April 1959, and 28 October 1969; Schoenbrun, *Three Lives of de Gaulle,* pp. 298-99; Kohl, *French Nuclear Diplomacy,* pp. 70-71; and a State Department summary, "Department of State Statement. . .," appended to Senate, Subcommittee on National Security, *Atlantic Alliance: Hearings,* p. 228. See also a partial text in Newhouse, *De Gaulle and the Anglo-Saxons,* pp. 70-71, and a nearly correct version in J.-R. Tournoux's *Jamais dit* (Paris: Plon, 1971), pp. 191-92.

71. I am indebted to John Newhouse for this information.

72. J.-R. Tournoux, *La Tragédie du général* (Paris: Plon, 1967), pp. 316-33. This and other incidents led to Antoine Pinay's resignation as minister of finance in January 1960.

73. Quotations and references are from the text published in *Le Monde.* The term *directorate* does not occur in the memorandum, although it was subsequently used in many analyses of the proposal.

74. "Letter from President Eisenhower to General de Gaulle," appended to Senate, Subcommittee on National Security, *Atlantic Alliance: Hearings,* pp. 230-31.

75. *Memoirs of Hope*, p. 203.

76. It was probably a mistake to involve Murphy in these proceedings, since he had represented Roosevelt in dealings with Vichy France and Admiral Darlan and, according to Schoenbrun, "was one of the few men whom de Gaulle despised personally to the point of hatred" (*Three Lives of de Gaulle*, pp. 124-25.) Nor was the French ambassador, Hervé Alphand, particularly well suited to deal with an Anglophile State Department, where he was personally disliked by many high officials, Murphy among them. Britain's representative was Sir Harold Caccia.

77. *New York times*, 29 August 1966.

78. Ibid. This report is from a secret State Department summary of the course of the negotiations. If often conflicts with the public version issued in Senate, Subcommittee on National Security, *Atlantic Alliance: Hearings*.

79. James Reston, *New York Times*, 4 May 1964.

80. According to the public State Department version, "The United States and the United Kingdom indicated that they were willing to continue these meetings with discussions among military experts of our respective views on African military questions. The French Government did not respond to this proposal and no further talks along these lines took place" (Senate, Subcommittee on National Security, *Atlantic Alliance: Hearings*, p. 229) Eisenhower, however, indicated that he had something more extensive than regional issues in mind.

81. All citations are from a translation of the original letter furnished me by the Dwight D. Eisenhower Library in Abilene, Kansas. I am grateful for the kind assistance of its staff.

82. See his letter dated 11 September 1959 and quoted in Harold Macmillan, *Pointing the Way, 1959-1961* (New York: Harper & Row, 1969), p. 88. Cf. de Gaulle's recounting in *Memoirs of Hope*, p. 214.

83. Macmillan, *Pointing the Way*, p. 106.

84. See the memorandum to Foreign Secretary Selwyn Lloyd, dated 22 December 1959, in which Macmillan stated that he was willing to push Washington into accepting the French design in order to improve Britain's relations with Paris (ibid., pp. 112-13).

85. Ibid., pp. 241-43.

86. See the Eisenhower letter dated 4 June in ibid., pp. 243-44.

87. Radio-television speech of 31 May 1960, *Discours et messages* 3: 220 (emphasis added).

88. Macmillan, *Pointing the Way*, p. 245.

89. From Schoenbrun's account of the letter, *Three Lives of de Gaulle*, p. 309.

90. From a 30 June letter to Macmillan, in which Eisenhower summarizes his message to de Gaulle (Macmillan, *Pointing the Way*, p. 246).

91. Ibid.

92. See Schoenbrun, *Three Lives of de Gaulle*, p. 309, and Macmillan, *Pointing the Way*, p. 247.

93. Newhouse, *De Gaulle and the Anglo-Saxons*, p. 132.

94. Schoenbrun, *Three Lives of de Gaulle*, pp. 316-17.

95. See Debré's April 1959 speech to the Diplomatic Press Association (France, Ambassade de France, *Speeches and Press Conferences*, no. 130, 1959); his speech of 7 June before the National Assembly, reported in *Le Monde* of 8 June 1959; and reports of a meeting with Christian Herter in *Le Monde* on 16 June 1959.

96. See Ely's article, "Perspectives stratégiques d'avenir," *Revue de défense nationale* 14 (November 1958), esp. p. 1640. For a similar position, see also General Bouvard's "Force et faiblesses de l'alliance atlantique," *Politique étrangère* 23, no. 2 (1959): 241-47.

97. For a representative argument, see René Pleven's article, "France in the Atlantic Community," *Foreign Affairs* 38, no. 1 (October 1959): 19-30.

98. Alfred Grosser, *French Foreign Policy under de Gaulle* (Boston: Little, Brown & Co., 1967), p. 31.

99. See remarks de Gaulle made to RPF deputy Henri Ulver, quoted in Tournoux, *Tragédie du général*, p. 308.

100. *Le Monde*, 16 June 1959, and an interview Couve de Murville granted me in 1972.

101. Newhouse, *De Gaulle and the Anglo-Saxons,* pp. 74-75.

102. See de Gaulle's recollection of the discussion in *Memoirs of Hope,* p. 214.

103. See de Gaulle's remarks to the Council of Ministers at the end of 1959, recounted by Maurice Schumann in "De la continuité du gaullisme," *Revue de défense nationale* 16 (January 1960): 201-16.

104. "Aspects politiques posés par l'armement nucléaire français," no. 1053 (Paris: Institut des hautes études de défense nationale, 18 November 1958), p. 8 (quoted in Kohl, *French Nuclear Diplomacy,* p. 79).

105. Assemblée nationale, *Compte rendu analytique officiel,* séance du 10 octobre 1960, p. 9.

106. Quoted in André Passeron, *De Gaulle parle: Des institutions, de l'Algérie, de l'armée, des affaires étrangères, de la communauté, de l'économie et des questions sociales* (Paris: Plon, 1962), p. 373.

107. Press conference in France, Ambassade de France, *Major Addresses, Statements and Press Conferences of General Charles de Gaulle, May 19, 1958-January 31, 1964* (New York: Service de presse et d'information, 1964), p. 124.

108. Couve de Murville gives somewhat contradictory accounts of this meeting in his memoirs, *Politique étrangère,* pp. 56-57 and 98-99. The result, however, is not in doubt.

109. Interview on Europe no. 1, 7 April 1966, in La Documentation française, "Interviews de M. Couve de Murville, ministre des affaires étrangères, concernant l'O.T.A.N.," *Textes et Notes,* 31 May 1966, no. 170/1P.

110. Press conference in France, Ambassade de France, *Major Addresses, 1958-1964,* p. 123.

111. See André Beaufre, *NATO and Europe* (New York: Alfred A. Knopf, 1966), p. 33; and Admiral M. Douguet's revealing speech of 10 June 1964 to the NATO Defense College, "Considération sur la structure de l'alliance atlantique," *Revue de défense nationale* 20 November 1964): 1705-19.

112. *Memoirs of Hope,* p. 202.

113. See, for example, de Gaulle's press conference of 5 September 1960, where he linked such a development to his tripartite design (*Discours et messages,* 3: 248-49).

114. As a confirmation of this interpretation, see Macmillan's recollection of a conversation with de Gaulle on 13 March 1960, in which the General discusses his long-range aims and alludes to the conception outlined here. (Macmillan, *Pointing the Way,* p. 192.)

115. *Memoirs of Hope,* pp. 202-3.

116. Kohl, *French Nuclear Diplomacy,* p. 75.

117. Ibid., p. 78. For a view with a stronger emphasis on de Gaulle's Machiavellianism, see Newhouse, *De Gaulle and the Anglo-Saxons,* p. 51.

118. De Carmoy, *Foreign Policies of France,* p. 276.

119. However, this phrase was Debré's and not de Gaulle's. The General preferred to speak of "the cooperation of states." See his remarks quoted in Passeron, *De Gaulle parle,* p. 74.

120. Speech of 22 November 1964, in France, Ambassade de France, *Major Addresses, Statements, and Press Conferences of General Charles de Gaulle, March 17, 1964-May 16, 1967* (New York: Service de presse et d'information, 1967), p. 72.

121. Press conference of 15 May 1962, *Discours et messages,* 3: 413.

122. See de Gaulle's speech at the Ecole militaire on 15 February 1963, ibid., 4: 84-87.

123. Press conference of 14 January 1963, ibid., pp. 72-73.

124. See especially the press conference of 23 July 1964 (ibid., p. 227); and de Gaulle's Elysée broadcast of 27 April 1965 (ibid., pp. 357-358).

125. During a June 1959 visit to Italy, de Gaulle proposed to Premier Antonio Segni that the Foreign Ministers of the Six begin holding periodic meetings and set up a permanent secretariat. This was resisted by France's partners, and instead the seven-member council of the WEU (including Britain) was revived, with the provision that all relevant discussions would be reported to the Atlantic Council (Couve de Murville, *Politique étrangère*, pp. 356-58).

126. Ibid.

127. For an extensive analysis, see Susanne J. Bodenheimer, *Political Union: A Microcosm of European Politics, 1960-1966* (Leyden: A. W. Sijthoff, 1967), esp. pp. 53-102.

128. See Roger Massip, *De Gaulle et l'Europe* (Paris: Flammarion, 1963) pp. 75-76.

129. Negotiations on British entry into the EEC had begun in Brussels on 10 October 1961 and were still in progress. See Spaak's memoirs (*Continuing Battle,* p. 436-56) for his motives in ending the Fouchet talks.

130. Press conference of 16 May 1967, *Discours et messages*, 5: 167.

131. De Gaulle makes this point in his *Memoirs of Hope*, p. 200.

132. This was de Gaulle's claim to a group of deputies on 6 February 1963; see document #20 in Western European Union, Assembly, Committee on Defense Questions and Armaments, 13th ordinary sess., *France and NATO* ed. L. Radoux (Paris, June 1967), p. 31.

133. See Newhouse on Rambouillet, *De Gaulle and the Anglo-Saxons*, pp. 207-11.

134. *Politique étrangère*, p. 411.

135. Press conference of 14 January 1963 in France, Ambassade de France, *Major Addresses, 1958-1964*, pp. 214-15.

136. On West German policy, see: James L. Richardson, *Germany and the Atlantic Alliance: The Interaction of Strategy and Politics* (Cambridge, Mass.: Harvard University Press, 1966), pp. 245-336; and Roger Morgan, *The United States and West Germany, 1945-1973: A Study in Alliance Politics* (London: Oxford University Press, 1974), chap. 6.

137. The treaty was based on French proposals submitted to the West German government on 19 September 1962. Only a protocol was envisaged then, but at the last minute Bonn insisted on a formal treaty for constitutional reasons. See the text of the treaty in *Le Monde*, 24 January 1963 and the discussion in F. Roy Willis's *France, Germany, and the New Europe: 1945-1967*, rev. ed. (New York: Oxford University Press, 1968), pp. 309-11.

138. According to Adenauer's memoirs, as cited in Kohl, *French Nuclear Diplomacy*, pp. 279-80.

139. From an English translation in W. W. Kulski, *De Gaulle and the World: The Foreign Policy of the Fifth Republic* (Syracuse, N.Y.: Syracuse University Press, 1966), pp. 276-77.

140. Carmoy, *Foreign Policies of France*, p. 409.

141. Kohl, *French Nuclear Diplomacy*, p. 282.

142. Kissinger, *Troubled Partnership*, p. 205.

143. In 1958, the Gaullist regime had terminated tentative moves by the Fourth Republic to secure some form of West German participation in the French nuclear program. See Kohl, *French Nuclear Diplomacy*, pp. 54-61.

144. Speech of 7 September 1962 in *Discours et messages*, 4: 13.

145. *La France et l'arme atomique* (Paris: René Juillard, 1964), p. 43. For an official presentation of the views of Sanguinetti and the Defense Committee of the National Assembly, see *Avis présenté au nom de la commission de la défense nationale et des forces armées sur la loi de programme (no. 1155) relatif à certains équipements militaires*, Séance du 26 novembre 1964, annexe no. 1192, pp. 227-39. France, Assemblée nationale, *Journal officiel de la république française: Documentaires parlementaires*, sessions ordinaires, 1964-65.

146. *Le Monde*, 4 December 1964.

147. France, Ambassade de France, "Our Military Policy," *French Affairs*, no. 155 (May 1963), p. 12. Originally appeared as "Notre Politique militaire," *Revue de défense nationale* 19 (May 1963): 745-61.

148. *New York Times*, 25 September 1963. At the time, Habib-Deloncle was secretary of state for foreign affairs.

149. But not a unilateral French guarantee, which most West Germans judged to be an insufficient replacement for the American one. See Strauss's prescriptions for Europe in *The Grand Design: A European Solution to German Reunification* (New York: Frederick A. Praeger, 1965).

150. *Franfurter Allgemeine Zeitung*, 17 February 1964 as cited in Kohl, *French Nuclear Diplomacy*, p. 287.

151. Erhard interview in *Neue Zürcher Zeitung*, 8 March 1967, cited in Kohl, *French Nuclear Diplomacy*, p. 288.

152. Kohl, *French Nuclear Diplomacy*, p. 290.

153. See the article by Defense Minister Kai-Uwe von Hassel, "Détente through Firmness," *Foreign Affairs* 42, no. 2 (January 1964): 184-94.

154. "The Basis of Partnership," *Foreign Affairs* 42, no. 1 (October 1963): 84-95.

155. Speech at Grenoble, quoted in Passeron, *De Gaulle parle*, p. 431.

156. Speech to the American Press Association on 20 June 1963, quoted in Dorothy Pickles, *The Uneasy Entente: French Foreign Policy and Franco-British Misunderstandings* (London: Oxford University Press, 1966), p. 46.

157. See von Hassel, "Detente through Firmness."

158. They are succinctly analyzed in Alfred Grosser's "France and Germany: Divergent Outlooks," *Foreign Affairs* 44, no. 1 (October 1965), pp. 26-36. For a discussion of West Germany's unique strategic position on the forward line, see Commandant Champeau, "Les Problèmes de défense de la République fédérale d'Allemagne," *Revue de défense nationale* 22 (November 1960): 1760-73.

159. On 27 January 1964, without the prior consultations mandated by the 1963 treaty, France had announced her intention of establishing diplomatic relations with the People's Republic of China. Washington predictably criticized the move and Bonn did not follow France's lead.

160. France, Ambassade de France, *Major Addresses, 1964-1967*, p. 23.

161. Ibid., p. 24.

162. On the crisis, see John Newhouse's informative *Collision in Brussels: The Common Market Crisis of 30 June 1965* (New York: W. W. Norton & Co., Inc., 1967); and Miriam Camps, *European Unification in the Sixties: From the Veto to the Crisis* (New York: McGraw-Hill Book Co., 1966).

163. For a succinct analysis of the commission's proposal, see Pierre Drouin, "Le Seuil," in *Le Monde*, 11 May 1965.

164. See de Gaulle's remarks to this effect, made during a French cabinet meeting on 15 September and reported in *L'Année politique, économique, sociale et diplomatique en France, 1965* (Paris: Presses universitaires de France, 1966), pp. 297-98.

165. *Le Monde*, 18 June, 1965.

166. Quoted in *Le Monde*, 26 November 1965.

167. See Couve de Murville's speech to the National Assembly, in *Le Monde*, 22 October 1965. On 3 November, Pompidou told the Assembly that a collapse of the EEC would have minimal effects on French industry and agriculture (*L'Année politique, 1965*, p. 315).

168. De Gaulle received only 44.6 percent of the first ballot vote and was forced into a runoff election with François Mitterrand. For an analysis of the effect of the EEC crisis on this election, see Michael M. Harrison, *French Politics and the European Crisis of 1965: Perspectives on the Presidential Election*, Institute on Western Europe (New York: Columbia University, 1970).

169. See C. L. Sulzberger's articles in the *New York Times*, 2 and 6 January 1965.

170. *Discours et messages*, 4, esp. p. 341.

171. As Newhouse, for one, does. See *De Gaulle and the Anglo-Saxons*, pp. 37-38.

172. De Gaulle cited this as the first condition for a general European settlement. See, for example, the press conference of 4 February 1965, in *Discours et messages*, 4: 341.

173. For an interesting discussion of Gaullist and non-Gaullist French perspectives on détente and Soviet inclinations, see Jean Laloy, "Perspectives et limites des rapports Est-Ouest," *Politique étrangère* 31, nos. 5-6 (1966), pp. 451-72.

Chapter 4

1. There is no attempt here to provide a thorough discussion and analysis of French military policy under de Gaulle. Such an analysis, generally objective but written from the distinctive perspective of a German "European," is available in Lothar Rühl's *La Politique militaire de la V*e *république* (Paris: Presses de la Fondation nationale des sciences politiques, 1976). Most of the citations below (specified by date, 1971) are from Rühl's dissertation: "La Politique militaire du gouvernement français, 1958-1970" (Thèse pur le doctorat de recherches, Fondation nationale des sciences politique, Cycle supérieure d'études politiques, 1971). On a more specialized topic, see also Wilfrid L. Kohl's *French Nuclear Diplomacy* (Princeton, N.J.: Princeton University Press, 1971).

2. Text in Charles de Gaulle, *Discours et messages*, (Paris: Plon, 1970), 3: 125-29.

3. Ibid., p. 379.

4. Strasbourg, 23 November 1961, ibid., p. 369.

5. Press conference of 15 May 1962, in France, Ambassade de France, *Major Addresses, Statements, and Press Conferences of General Charles de Gaulle, May 19, 1958-January 31, 1964* (New York: Service de presse et d'information, 1964), pp. 180-81.

6. *De Gaulle and the French Army: A Crisis in Civil-Military Relations* (New York: Twentieth Century Fund, 1964), p. 246.

7. Kohl, *French Nuclear Diplomacy*, p. 130.

8. For an account of Valluy's role in this movement, see Paul-Marie de la Gorce, *The French Army: A Military-Political History* (New York: George Braziller, 1963), pp. 528-31.

9. See the interview by Claude Delmas on 31 January 1961, published as "Entretien avec le Général Challe," *Revue de défense nationale* 17 (April 1961), esp. p. 586.

10. See Furniss, *De Gaulle and French Army*, pp. 54-55; and David Schoenbrun's interview with Salan in January 1961, reported in *The Three Lives of Charles de Gaulle* (New York: Atheneum, 1966), pp. 278-79.

11. De la Gorce, *French Army*, pp. 543-44.

12. *Discours et messages*, 3: 370.

13. See chapter 5, below.

14. *Une Politique étrangère, 1958-1969* (Paris: Librarie Plon, 1971), p. 75.

15. Quoted in Stikker, "France and Its Diminishing Will to Cooperate," *Atlantic Community Quarterly* 3, no. 2 (Summer 1965): 201.

16. General Valluy, *Se Défendre? Contre qui? Pourquoi? Et Comment?* (Paris: Plon, 1960), pp. 107-9. See also Pierre Gerbet, "Les Rapports entre pouvoir civil et pouvoir militaire en France dans l'élaboration de la politique de défense," mimeographed (Paris: Association internationale de science politique, Cinquième congrès mondial, 26-30 September 1961).

17. "Ordonnance no. 59-147 du janvier 1959 portant sur l'organisation générale de la défense," in *Journal officiel de la république française*, no. 1003, *Organisation générale de la défense* (1 February 1970) (with supplements), pp. 1-14. On the prime minister's role, see Alain Claisse, *Le Premier Ministre de la V*e *république* (Paris: Librarie générale de droit et de jurisprudence, 1972), esp. pp. 148-57.

18. "Décret no. 62-808 du 18 juillet, 1962, relatif à l'organisation de la défense nationale," *Journal officiel: Organisation,* pp. 17-18.

19. "Décret no. 62-809 du 18 juillet 1962 fixant les attributions du secrétaire général de la défense nationale," ibid., pp. 21-22. Under Fourquet, this body also assumed responsibility for initiating and coordinating military research. It was abolished (and its functions transferred elsewhere) under the Messmer government in July 1972.

20. Decree of 18 July 1962, cited in Rühl, "Politique militaire," p. 691.

21. "Décret no. 68-370 du 26 Avril 1968 fixant les attributions du Chef d'état-major des armées," *Journal officiel: Organisation,* pp. 25-27.

22. Jean Planchais, "L'Armée après l'Algérie," *Le Monde,* 22 June 1963.

23. "Décret no. 64-46 du 14 janvier 1964 relatif aux forces aériennes stratégiques," *Journal officiel: Organisation,* pp. 33-34.

24. See "Notre politique militaire," *Revue de défense nationale* 13 (July 1957), esp. pp. 1043-44; and J.-L. Lecerf, "Partage des engins ou réforme des armées," *Revue de défense nationale* 15 (March 1959): 474-89.

25. On the early development of the nuclear force, see Wolf Mendl's *Deterrence and Persuasion: French Nuclear Armament in the Context of National Policy, 1945-1969* (New York: Praeger, 1970), pp. 122-54. Kohl's study, *French Nuclear Diplomacy,* is more thorough but is no longer up to date. For an official history, see "Le Développement nucléaire français depuis 1945," *Notes et études documentaires,* no. 3246 (Paris: La Documentation française, 18 December 1965). See also the excellent series of articles by Marc de Lacost Lareymondie, "L'Arme nucléaire française," in *Le Monde,* 5, 6, 7, 9, and 10-11 May 1964.

26. The Evian Accords should have permitted further tests in the Sahara until 1 July 1967, but the new Algerian government prohibited them. On recent policy, see above, pp. 184-85.

27. Messmer, p. 1.

28. *New York Times,* 10 October 1963.

29. See Kohl, *French Nuclear Diplomacy,* pp. 182-83.

30. "Système de transmission et de représentation des informations de défense aérienne." It is described in France, Ministère des armées, Service d'information et d'études du ministère des armées, "La Défense: La Politique militaire française et ses réalisations," *Notes et études documentaires,* no. 3343 (6 December 1966), p. 12.

31. Ibid., p. 11.

32. *Le Monde,* 21 April 1970.

33. The viability of this part of the French deterrent is discussed below, in chapter 5. The construction of a sixth submarine is now definitely scheduled.

34. See Kohl, *French Nuclear Diplomacy,* pp. 192-200, for an analysis of the armed forces budgets between 1960 and 1970.

35. Carl H. Amme, Jr., *NATO without France: A Strategic Appraisal* (Stanford, Calif.: The Hoover Institution on War, Revolution, and Peace, Stanford University, 1967), p. 158. Of the 1971 figure, 322,160 were in the army, 67,969 navy, 102,213 air force, and 65,490 gendarmerie. See France, Ambassade de France, "Reorganization of the National Service in France," document 71/187 (New York: Service de presse et d'information, 1971).

36. "Evolution nécessaire de nos structures militaires," *Revue de défense nationale* 21 (June 1965): p. 949.

37. Each division included two infantry brigades, one armored brigade, nuclear and heavy artillery, reconnaissance aircraft, and helicopters. A brigade had approximately 4,600 men, a division around 14,000. See E. J. Baude, "Chronique militaire," *Revue de défense nationale,* 16 (February 1960): 360-61, and Rühl, "La Politique militaire," pp. 661-62.

38. Pierre Messmer, "Our Military Policy," *French Affairs,* series no. 155 (May 1963), p. 4.

39. The government actually ordered only 810 of the tanks (Rühl, "La Politique militaire," p. 610).

40. Messmer, "Our Military Policy," p. 3.

41. Ailleret, "Evolution nécessaire," p. 950.

42. On this dispute, see Army Chief of Staff General Le Puloch's "Avenir de l'armée de terre," *Revue de défense nationale* 20 (June 1964): 947-60; and Air Force General André Martin, "L'Armée de l'air dans le contexte nucléaire," *Revue de défense nationale* 20 (October 1964): 1499-1517.

43. Messmer, "Our Military Policy," p. 5.

44. Ailleret, "Evolution nécessaire," pp. 953-54.

45. On this issue, see Michel L. Martin, "Cónscription and the Decline of the Mass Army in France, 1960-1975," *Armed Forces and Society* 3, no. 3 (Spring 1977): 355-406.

46. Ministère des armées, "La Défense," p. 10.

47. *The Balance of Terror* (Boston: Houghton Mifflin Co., 1961).

48. Ibid., pp. 144-45.

49. Ibid., and Gallois's article, "L'Alliance atlantique et l'évolution de l'armement," *Politique étrangère* 23, no. 2 (1959): 179-203.

50. France, Ambassade de France, *Major Addresses, Statements and Press Conferences of General Charles de Gaulle, March 17, 1964-May 16, 1967* (New York: Service de presse et d'information, 1967), p. 25.

51. Ministère des armées, "La Défense," p. 8.

52. See Raymond Aron's criticism of Gallois in *The Great Debate: Theories of Nuclear Strategy* (Garden City, N.Y.: Doubleday & Co., 1965), esp. chap. 4.

53. (New York: Frederick A. Praeger, 1965). See also Beaufre's articles, such as "Stratégie de dissuasion et stratégie de guerre," *Revue de défense nationale* 18 (May 1962): 761-68; and "Le Problème du partage des responsabilités nucléaires," *Stratégie,* no. 5 (July-September 1965), pp. 7-20.

54. Beaufre, *Deterrence and Strategy,* p. 84.

55. Ibid., pp. 100-102.

56. *Le Monde,* 4 December 1964.

57. France, Assemblée Nationale, Avis présenté au nom de la commission de la défense nationale et des forces armées sur le projet de loi de programme (no. 1155) relative à certains équipements militaires," *Journal officiel de la république française: Documents parlementaires,* Sessions ordinaires (1964-65). Séance du 26 novembre 1964, annexe no. 1192, p. 228.

58. Radio-TV speech of 10 August 1967, *Discours et messages,* 5: 203.

59. See this important French critique of American strategy, reprinted as "Opinion sur la théorie stratégique de la 'flexible response,'" *Revue de défense nationale* 20 (August 1964): 1323-40.

60. Messmer, "Our Military Policy," p. 2.

61. Ibid., p. 1.

62. Quotations from an unpublished speech cited at length in Rühl, "Politique Militaire," pp. 417-20.

63. "Note sur les relations franco-américaines," dated 21 March 1966, in J.-R. Tournoux, *La Tragédie du général* (Paris: Plon, 1967), p. 653.

64. See Ailleret, "Evolution nécessaire."

65. Ministère des Armées, "La Défense," p. 11.

66. Speech of 15 February 1963, *Discours et messages,* 4: 86-87.

67. See Jean Planchais in *Le Monde,* 19 January 1965.

68. See, for example, "Pour une neutralité militaire," *Le Monde,* 18 December 1964; "La Force de frappe et le neutralisme," *Le Monde,* 20 May 1966; and Léo Hamon's interesting article, "Puissance nucléaire et dissuasion: Alliance et neutralité," *Revue de défense nationale* 22 (February 1966): 234-57.

69. Radio-TV address of 11 December 1965 in *Discours et messages* 4: 411.

70. "Speech by M. Georges Pompidou before the National Assembly, April 20," in France,

Ambassade de France, *French Foreign Policy, 1966* (New York: Service de presse et d'information, 1967), p. 58.

71. Press conference of 21 February 1966, *Discours et messages* 5: 18.

72. This position is suggested by Rühl in "Politique militaire," p. 414.

73. "Letter from General de Gaulle to President Lyndon B. Johnson," Ambassade de France, *French Foreign Policy, 1966*, p. 24 (emphasis added).

74. "La France et l'alliance atlantique," *Note d'information* 17 (August 1966).

75. Speech of 3 November 1959, *Discours et messages* 3: 27.

76. *Revue de défense nationale* 23 (December 1967): 1923-32. Citations are from an English translation, "Defense in All Directions," *Atlantic Community Quarterly* 6, no. 1 (Spring 1968): 17-25.

77. In remarks to the *Centre des hautes études militaires*, quoted in *Le Monde*, 30 January 1968.

78. "L'Atome, cause et moyen d'une politique militaire autonome," *Revue de défense nationale* 24 (March 1968): 395-402. An English version appeared as "The Atom, Cause and Means of an Autonomous Military Policy," *Atlantic Community Quarterly* 6, no. 2 (Summer 1968): 270-77.

79. According to information furnished me during an interview with Gaullist defense expert and deputy Joël le Theule, in the summer of 1972.

80. Interview with M. Debré in the summer of 1972.

81. See the analysis by Edmond Combaux, "Défense tous azimuts? Oui mais . . . ," *Revue de défense nationale* 24 (November 1968): 1600-1618, and his "French Military Policy and European Federalism," *Orbis* 13, no. 1 (Spring 1969): 144-59. See also the analysis by Jacques Isnard in *Le Monde*, 30 January 1968.

82. See, for example, Claude Krief, "Les Azimuts du général Ailleret," *Le Nouvel Observateur*, 6 December 1967. On the treaty issue itself, see chapter 5.

83. See the discussion in chapter 5, below.

84. *Le Monde*, 18 June and 9 July 1959.

85. See *Stars and Stripes*, 20 April 1966, cited in Francis A. Beer, *Integration and Disintegration in NATO: Processes of Alliance Cohesion and Prospects for Atlantic Community* (Columbus, Ohio: Ohio State University Press, 1969), p. 57.

86. Baude, "Chronique militaire," *Revue de défense nationale* 16 (August-September 1960): 1524.

87. See Tournoux, *Tragédie du général*, pp. 336-38.

88. Jean Planchais, "La France dans l'organisation militaire atlantique," *Le Monde*, 27 and 28 February 1959.

89. *Le Monde*, 15 December 1959.

90. *Le Monde*, 21 April 1966.

91. See descriptions of this operation in *Le Monde*, 21 April 1966, and Joannes H. Knoop's article, "The Evolution of Air Defense in Allied Command Europe," in North Atlantic Treaty Organization, *SHAPE and Allied Command Europe: Twenty years in the Service of Peace and Security, 1951-1971* (Belgium: SHAPE, 1971), pp. 99-112.

92. See Ely, "Perspectives stratégiques d'avenir," *Revue de défense nationale* 14 (November 1958): 1631-40.

93. But he was not in charge, because his superiors were Britain's Admiral Bingley at Malta and U.S. Admiral Nomy, the NATO naval commander for the entire Mediterranean region.

94. *New York Times*, 3 February 1959.

95. See Marshall Juin's proposal in a speech delivered to the French Association for the Atlantic Community, in *NATO Letter* 4, no. 8 (1 August 1956), esp. p. 13.

96. The Mediterranean fleet totaled 135,000 tons, including the cruiser *De Grasse*, three aircraft carriers, various destroyers, submarines, etc. (*Le Figaro*, 16 March 1959).

97. An "authorized military source," *Le Figaro*, 20 March 1959.

98. *Discours et messages* 3: 92-93.

99. Press conference of 5 September 1960, ibid., p. 249.

100. See General Norstad's reaction in *Le Monde*, 21 March 1959.

101. André Reussner, "Chronique maritime," *Revue de défense nationale* 15 (July 1959): 1303.

102. *Combat*, 29 December 1959.

103. *Le Monde*, 24 June 1963.

104. Claude Valette, "Chronique de l'O.T.A.N.," *Revue de défense nationale* 19 (August-September 1963): 1417-21.

105. *Le Monde*, 18 July 1963.

106. Ibid., 30 April 1964.

107. Ibid., 29 April 1964.

108. Ibid., 2 May 1964.

109. Ibid., 15 September 1964.

110. Information supplied by NATO officials and allied delegations to NATO, during interviews in 1972.

111. *New York Herald Tribune*, 2 July 1963.

112. *Forces nouvelles*, 30 October 1963.

113. *New York Times*, 13 May 1965 and *New York Herald Tribune*, 14 October 1965.

114. See, for example, C. L. Sulzberger in *New York Times*, 28 December 1964. Sulzberger, who saw de Gaulle regularly, often misinterpreted the General's intentions, or was fed erroneous information by de Gaulle.

115. *Le Monde*, 3 November 1964.

116. For details of the reactions, and the somewhat conflicting versions of how the memorandum's contents were leaked, see: Michael M. Harrison, "France and the Atlantic Alliance: The Process of Political and Military Dealignment" (Ph.D. diss., Columbia University, 1974), pp. 131-36; Rühl, "Politique militaire," p. 80; and John Newhouse, *De Gaulle and the Anglo-Saxons* (New York: Viking Press, 1970), p. 72.

117. The exchange is reported in *Le Monde*, 15 May 1964. See also Spaak's account of the incident in *The Continuing Battle: Memoirs of a European, 1936-1966* (Boston: Little, Brown & Co., 1969), pp 463-66.

118. "Speech by M. Couve de Murville before the National Assembly, April 14," in *French Foreign Policy, 1966*, p. 48.

119. Johnson stopped the bombing during January 1966, but renewed it on 31 January against French advice. For an account of French efforts at mediation, see Couve de Murville, *Politique étrangère*, pp. 131-36.

120. See Hervé Alphand's recollection of his discussion with de Gaulle during this period, in *Le Nouvel Observateur*, 12-18 September 1977, esp. p. 100.

121. De Gaulle offered this as an explanation to the cabinet (see André Fontaine in *Le Monde*, 12 March 1966).

122. Rühl, "Politique militaire," p. 179. Most of the other information discussed in this paragraph comes from my own 1972 interviews of the former Elysée staff.

123. *NATO: The Transatlantic Bargain* (New York: Harper & Row, 1970), p. 101.

124. According to a statement by Pompidou during a television interview (see *Le Monde*, 20 March 1966). It is unclear when Pompidou was actually informed.

125. *New York Herald Tribune*, 21 September 1965. This was thought to be a reaction to charges that in November 1964 the United States had airlifted Belgian paratroopers to Stanleyville from bases in France without obtaining the permission of Paris. Dean Rusk asserted that consent had been obtained (interview in *Paris-March*, 16 April 1966) and an American diplomat formerly at the Paris embassy told me that normal authorization channels had been used, but

they did not include notifying the Elysée. There was another incident in 1965, when an American reconnaissance plane based in France flew over the nuclear installation at Pierrelatte (*New York Times*, 21 July 1965).

126. Ambassade de France, *Major Addresses 1964-1967*, p. 98.

127. From an interview Rühl had with Brosio ("Politique militaire," p. 177).

128. Couve de Murville, "Politique étrangère," p. 78.

129. *Discours et messages* 5: 19.

130. "Memorandum Handed by the French Government to the Fourteen Representatives of the Governments that are Members of NATO," *French Foreign Policy, 1966*, p. 27.

131. Ibid., p. 26.

132. "French Memorandum to the Fourteen Governments of the Member Countries of NATO," *French Foreign Policy, 1966*, pp. 36-38. France also announced her intention to deposit with the United States a denunciation of the NATO Headquarters Agreement that, by virtue of Article 16, would take effect a year later, on 31 March, 1967.

133. "Declaration by 14 NATO Member Countries," in Western European Union, Assembly, Committee on Defense Questions and Armaments, 13th ordinary sess., *France and NATO*, ed. L. Radoux (Paris, June 1967).

134. Cleveland, *NATO*, p. 107.

135. "First Reply from President Johnson," *French Foreign Policy, 1966*, p. 25.

136. "Second Reply from President Johnson to General de Gaulle," ibid., p. 33. Johnson made a similar rejoinder in a speech to the Foreign Service Institute on 23 March. Relevant excerpts are in Western European Union, *France and NATO*, p. 53.

137. Much of the information on American reactions is from interviews with officials at the departments of State and Defense. See also reports in the press: *Guardian*, 14 June 1966, and *Economist*, 9 April 1966.

138. *New York Times*, 21 March 1966. See also Reston's report in the *New York Times*, 17 March 1966. For an example of the kinds of passion de Gaulle's actions raised, see the ill-considered proposals in Horst Mendershausen's *From NATO to Independence: Reflections on de Gaulle's Secession* (Washington, D.C.: Washington Center of Foreign Policy Research, March 1966).

139. *Guardian*, 30 March 1966.

140. See, for example, Ball's address to the American Society of International Law on 29 April: "The Larger Meaning of the NATO Crisis," mimeographed (London: American Embassy, U.S. Information Service, 2 May 1966).

141. See *Times*, 16 March 1966.

142. *Le Figaro*, 18 March 1966.

143. Speech in Illinois on 12 June 1966 (*Financial Times*, 14 June 1966).

144. For German reactions, see reports in *Le Figaro*, 18 March 1966, and *Le Monde*, 17 May 1966.

145. Cleveland, *NATO*, p. 105.

146. For a previous statement on this issue, see Dean Rusk's press conference on 5 November 1965 in *Le Monde*, 8 November 1965.

147. The former were Chateauroux, Evreux, Toul-Rosières, and Laon; the latter, Chaumont, Etain, Thalsbourg, and Chambley (the base at Dreux was then functioning only as an American high school).

148. All figures are from *Le Monde*, 9 March 1966, and France, Ministère des affaires étrangères, *La France et l'OTAN* (Paris: Direction des services d'information et de presse, n.d.), p. 16. According to the *New York Times* (14 March 1973), there were 189 American military installations of all types in France in 1966.

149. "Reply from the United States Government to the Memorandum of the French Government Dated March 29, 1966," *French Foreign Policy, 1966*, pp. 41-42. Only a communications agreement of 8 December 1958 provided for unilateral denunciation and a two-year waiting period for actually terminating the agreement.

150. *New York Herald Tribune*, 6 September 1966.

151. See "Extracts from Mr. McNamara's Statement on Defense before the U.S. Senate," *NATO Letter* 17, no. 3 (March 1968): 25-26.

152. *New York Herald Tribune*, 24 November 1966.

153. The agreement can be denounced by either party, effective one year later. "Agreement between the United States of America and the Republic of France on the Operation, Maintenance and Security of the Donges-Metz Pipeline System," in Western European Union, *France and NATO*, pp. 92-93.

154. By agreement between Couve de Murville and Ambassador Bohlen, in discussions that began on 18 July 1966. See Beer, *Integration and Disintegration in NATO*, p. 184.

155. The claims were reported in the *New York Times* for 14 March 1973. The settlement was reached during the Martinique meeting of Presidents Ford and Giscard d'Estaing (*Le Monde*, 18 December 1974).

156. *Le Monde*, 6 April 1966.

157. *France-Observateur*, 23 May, 1966.

158. *Le Monde*, 31 March 1967. See also a later report in the *International Herald Tribune*, 18 August 1975.

159. Testimony on 21 June 1966, in U.S., Congress, Senate, Committee on Government Operations, Subcommittee on National Security and International Operations, *The Atlantic Alliance: Hearings*, 89th Congr., 2nd sess., 1966, p. 187.

160. See K. Hunt, *NATO without France: The Military Implications*, Adelphi Paper, no. 32 (London: Institute for Strategic Studies, 1966), pp. 12-13.

161. See "Explanatory Memorandum," in *Western European Union, France and NATO*, pp. 9-10; and Hunt, *NATO without France*, p. 12.

162. On this issue, see Gilles Mullens, "Le Retrait de la France de l'OTAN" (Memoir presented to obtain a degree in political and diplomatic sciences, Université libre de Bruxelles, Faculté des sciences sociales, politiques et économiques, July 1971), p. 29.

163. See Hunt, *NATO without France*, p. 15, and Jurgen Bennecke, "The Challenge in the Center," in North Atlantic Treaty Organization, *SHAPE and Allied Command Europe*, esp. p. 84.

164. *Le Monde*, 4 November 1966.

165. *New York Herald Tribune*, 6 May 1966.

166. *Atlantic Alliance: Hearings*, pp. 151-52.

167. Couve de Murville, *Politique étrangère*, p. 83.

168. *French Foreign Policy, 1966*, p. 36.

169. The texts of these agreements can be found in North Atlantic Treaty Organization, *NATO: Facts and Figures* (Brussels: NATO Information Service, 1971), pp. 306-34.

170. "Reply of the Government of the Federal German Republic to the Memorandum of the French Government, Dated March 29," *French Foreign Policy, 1966*, p. 69.

171. See the report in *Le Monde*, 29 April 1966.

172. "Reply of the French Government to the Memorandum of the Government of Germany, Dated May 3rd," *French Foreign Policy, 1966*, p. 73. See also the statement made by Yvon Bourges, secretary of state to the prime minister, after a meeting of the Council of Ministers, in *Le Monde* on 8 May 1966.

173. They had met in Bonn from 1 to 3 May (*Le Monde*, 6 May 1966).

174. See the unpublished speech to the NATO Council by the West German delegate, Greuve, cited in Rühl, "Politique militaire," pp. 202-22.

175. *Le Monde*, 22 May 1966. See also Couve de Murville's memoirs, *Politique étrangère*, p. 85.

176. Earlier, on 13 June, the French had announced that some air and antiaircraft units would be returned to France by October (see the report in *L'Année politique, économique, sociale et diplomatique en France, 1966* [Paris: Presses universitaires de France, 1967], p. 254).

177. "Memorandum of the Federal German Government Relative to the Maintenance of French Forces on West German Soil," *French Foreign Policy, 1966,* p. 90.

178. General Massu, the French Commander in West Germany, informed SHAPE of this on 1 July.

179. France had been notified on 12 April that this action would be taken. In September, after a bit of haggling, the United States also recovered the Nike-Hercules ground-to-air missiles held by the French, on the grounds that the warhead delivery systems were not French property (*New York Herald Tribune,* 29 September 1966).

180. See "Letters Exchanged between the Foreign Affairs Ministers of France and Federal Germany on the Stationing of French Troops in Germany," *French Foreign Policy, 1966,* pp. 218-20.

181. Statement of 21 December 1966, in ibid., p. 227.

182. See reports in *Le Monde* for 23 June and 21 July 1966.

183. Information from interviews of French military officials. See also the report by Waverly Root in the *Washington Post,* 10 November 1966.

184. Information from interviews conducted in the summer of 1972.

185. In an unpublished speech delivered on 26 April 1966 (NATO/D.C.V. 24/534) cited at length in Rühl, "Politique militaire," pp. 427-28.

186. Interview with Rühl, "Politique militaire," p. 256.

187. Speech to the Atlantic Treaty Association General Assembly, reported in the *New York Herald Tribune,* 16 October 1968.

188. In 1966 (and later), NATO still theoretically planned for a ninety-day conventional war in Europe as a guideline for maintaining stockpiles. At the December council meeting, British Defense Minister Healey suggested that fifteen days was a more realistic estimate, but McNamara refused to revise the schedule (*Economist,* 24 December 1966).

189. Some exceptions were made for low-level support personnel (*Le Monde,* 15 May 1966).

190. The mission's status at SHAPE was later defined in a bilateral agreement signed on 1 April 1967. At the time, it had a staff of thirty-three members (*Le Monde,* 3 April 1967). For more information on the NMRs and the French Mission, see Frederick J. Gruber, "Links to the NATO Nations: The National Military Representatives at SHAPE," *NATO Letter* 15, no. 3 (June-July 1970): 15-19.

191. *New York Herald Tribune,* 29 July 1966.

192. Because of the politically sensitive nature of their duties, details of these missions' activities have been kept in obscurity. The Ministry of Defense several times refused to consent to an article on the subject after approaches from the *Revue de défense nationale.*

193. For a description of the IMS, see North Atlantic Treaty Organization, *NATO: Facts and Figures,* p. 197.

194. *New York Herald Tribune,* 18 October 1966.

195. *Le Monde,* 9 June 1966.

196. *New York Herald Tribune,* 8 December 1966.

197. These decisions were announced by Ambassador de Leusse in September 1966., For descriptions of the work of the organizations mentioned here, see North Atlantic Treaty Organization, *NATO: Facts and Figures,* pp. 127-37 and 205-11.

198. Mullens, "Retrait de la France."

199. *Le Monde,* 15 November 1966.

Chapter 5

1. During the press conference of 21 February 1966. See the statement in France, Ambassade de France, *French Foreign Policy, 1966,* p. 20.

2. "Letter from General de Gaulle to President Johnson," ibid., p. 24.

3. Press conference of 28 October 1966, in *Discours et messages* (Paris: Plon, 1970), 5: 104.

4. See, for example, Claude Krief, "Les Azimuts du général Ailleret," *Le Nouvel Observateur,* 6 December 1967; and Maurice Duverger, "Le Bon Plaisir du roi," *Le Nouvel Observateur,* 10 January 1968.

5. Article XIII states that a party may denounce the treaty after it has been in force for twenty years, and that the denunciation takes effect one year after notice is given. In 1966, de Gaulle mistakenly said that 1 April 1969 was the date for a denunciation to become effective, whereas the treaty had come into force on 24 August 1949. It is unclear whether denunciations could have been made after nineteen years, to take effect in the twentieth year, or whether an additional year was necessary. This is, of course, a moot point now.

6. See *Le Nouvel Observateur,* 18 October 1967.

7. In the same poll, 59 percent said that France could not assure her defense alone over the next three years, whereas 17 percent felt she could.

8. Fear of left-wing radicalism was widespread in France after May 1968, so much so that the French Association for the Atlantic Community, a pro-Alliance group, was secretly given one million francs by fifteen top industrialists as a contribution to a campaign against denunciation of the Atlantic Treaty. For the association's position, see "AFCA Delaration on NATO," *NATO Letter* 16, no. 5 (May 1968): p. 26,.

9. Statement before the Council of Ministers on 3 April 1968, in France, Ambassade de France, *French Foreign Policy, 1968,* p. 149.

10. Statement by Georges Gorse, Minister of Information, during the Council of Ministers meeting on 8 May (ibid., p. 154).

11. "General de Gaulle's reply to US Ambassador Shriver," 25 May 1968, in ibid., pp. 103-4.

12. See Nixon's toast to de Gaulle on 28 February, in France, Ambassade de France, *French Foreign Policy, January-June 1969,* p. 70; see also Nixon's support for a Gaullist conception of Europe, expressed in remarks after his return to the United States: "Extracts from President Nixon's Press Conference after His Trip to Europe." *NATO Letter* 17, no. 4 (April 1969): p. 29.

13. Press conference of 9 September 1968, in *Discours et messages,* 5: 334.

14. Communiqué of 16 November 1968, in North Atlantic Treaty Organization, *NATO: Facts and Figures* (Brussels: NATO Information Service, 1971), pp. 369-71.

15. Harlan Cleveland, *NATO: The Transatlantic Bargain* (New York: Harper & Row, 1970), p. 153.

16. Press conference at the National Press Club, 9 April 1969, in Ambassade de France, *French Foreign Policy, January-June, 1969,* p. 98.

17. For a representative expression of Debré's views, see his article, "France's Global Strategy," *Foreign Affairs* 49, no. 3 (April 1971): 395-406; see also his speech at I.H.E.D.N. on 19 October 1971, printed as "La France et sa défense," *Revue de défense nationale* 28, no. 1 (January 1972): 5-21.

18. See *Le Monde,* 27 January 1971.

19. Material from interviews of French and NATO officials. See also *Le Monde,* 9 May 1976.

20. See the report by Jacques Isnard in *Le Monde,* 17 February 1971.

21. Quotations from the speech are from the text issued as a brochure entitled "Current Foreign Policy 1973: The Year of Europe" (Washington, D.C.: Department of State, Bureau of Public Affairs, Office of Media Services).

22. On the background to the Year of Europe policy initiatives, see Wilfrid L. Kohl, "The Nixon-Kissinger Foreign Policy System and U.S.-European Relations: Patterns of Policy-Making," *World Politics* 27, no. 1 (October 1975): 1-43. Although Kissinger's own assessment of the Year of Europe awaits the second volume of his memoirs, some indications can be

found in the first volume, *The White House Years* (Boston: Little, Brown, & Co., 1979), cf. pp. 69, 86, 382.

23. On this background, see Anthony Hartley, *American Foreign Policy in the Nixon Era,* Adelphi Paper, no. 110 (London: International Institute of Strategic Studies, Winter 1974-75).

24. Michel Jobert, *Mémoires d'avenir* (Paris: Grasset, 1974), p. 231.

25. From the European draft of 20 September, published along with suggested American revisions in the *New York Times* of 9 November 1973.

26. *New York Times,* 12 October 1973.

27. *United Nations Energy Statistics, 1973.*

28. In 1972, the United States was importing only 5 percent of its oil, and only 2 percent from the Middle East and North Africa.

29. *Le Monde,* 10 October 1973.

30. "Resolution of Oil Ministers of OAPEC." 17 October 1973, reprinted in *Survival* 16, no. 11 (January/February 1974): 38-39.

31. From the text in the *Washington Post,* 7 November 1973.

32. See *Strategic Survey, 1973* (London: International Institute for Strategic Studies, 1974); and *New York Times* for 11 and 12 October 1973. The American decisions were taken on 11 and 12 October, launching an emergency effort that ended on 14 November.

33. See the statement by Foreign Minister Xanthopoulos in *New York Times,* 4 October 1973.

34. "U.S., Soviets Boost Mideast Airlift," *Aviation Week and Space Technology* (22 October 1973), pp. 18-21.

35. Italy was a major source (*New York Times,* 11 November 1973).

36. See comments made during Secretary Schlessinger's news conference on 26 October, reported in the *New York Times,* 27 October 1973.

37. *Washington Post,* 31 October 1973, and a report on the German-American dispute in the *New York Times,* 11 November 1973.

38. Quotations from Nixon's letter as reported in the *New York Times,* 11 November 1973.

39. See the agreement reached between Schlesinger and West German Defense Minister George Leber, *New York Times,* 10 November 1973.

40. "Agreement between the USSR and the USA on the Prevention of Nuclear War," text in *Survival* 15, no. 5 (September/October 1973): 243-44.

41. See Kissinger's comments in *New York Times,* 23 June 1974.

42. See Robert Kleiman's account in *New York Times,* 11 December 1973. Kissinger insisted that there had been adequate advance discussions; see his remarks in the *New York Times,* 23 June 1974.

43. See reports in the *Washington Post,* 22 November 1973; and Marvin Kalb, and Bernard Kalb, *Kissinger* (Boston: Little, Brown, 1974), pp. 489-90.

44. *Washington Post,* 1 November 1973.

45. Herbert J. Coleman, "U.S. Forces Stay on Alert As NATO Politicians Fume," *Aviation Week and Space Technology* (5 November 1973), pp. 14-16.

46. U.S., Congress, Senate, Committee on Foreign Relations, Subcommittee on U.S. Security Agreements and Commitments Abroad, *U.S. Security Issues in Europe: Burden Sharing and Offset, MBFR and Nuclear Weapons,* 93rd Cong., 1st sess., September 1973.

47. See reports in the *New York Times* on 10 November and 11 December 1973.

48. Quoted in *Survival* 16, no. 1 (January-February 1974).

49. *New York Times,* 13 November 1973. See the complete text of Jobert's remarks in "Chronique: Institutions internationales," *Revue de défense nationale* 30, no. 1 (January 1974): 154.

50. *New York Times,* 22 November 1973.

51. See the text in the *New York Times,* 19 November 1973.
52. "The United States and a Unifying Europe: The Necessity for Partnership," speech in London, 12 December 1973 (*Department of State Bulletin* [31 December 1973], pp. 777-82).
53. Speech on 11 February (*Department of State Bulletin* [4 March 1974], p. 233).
54. Speech to the Executive Club of Chicago on 15 March (*Department of State Bulletin,* [8 April 1974], pp. 363-66).
55. See Giscard's exposition of his views in his book, *French Democracy* (Garden City, N.Y.: Doubleday, 1977).
56. See the conclusions of John Zysman in his book, *Political Strategies for Industrial Order: Market, State, and Industry in France* (Berkeley, Calif.: University of California Press, 1977), and idem, "The French State in the International Economy," *International Organization* 31, no. 4 (Autumn 1977): 839-77.
57. Declaration of general policy to the National Assembly, in *Le Monde,* 7 June 1974. See also a TV interview of the president in *Le Monde* on 22-23 December 1974 and James Goldsborough's interview of Foreign Minister Jean Sauvagnargues in the *International Herald Tribune,* 16 October 1974.
58. Ottawa Declaration of 19 June 1974 (*New York Times,* 20 June 1974).
59. *Le Monde,* 20 May 1976.
60. *Le Monde,* 14 September 1977. French policy under Giscard has continued to stress this theme, despite intermittent conflicts or differences of opinion with the United States. In May 1979, for example, Foreign Minister François-Poncet reminded the National Assembly that both the Atlantic Alliance and the U.S. presence were essential to stability in Europe, adding that "a permanent element of our foreign policy is the equilibrium based, in Europe, on the Atlantic Alliance, with the solidarities that it involves" (*Le Monde,* 5 May 1979).
61. This subject is discussed below, pp. 204-21.
62. *Le Monde,* 8 June 1974.
63. See Guy de Carmoy, *Energy for Europe: Economic and Political Implications* (Washington, D.C.: American Enterprise Institute, 1977).
64. Much of this information comes from Edward A. Kolodziej, "French Disarmament and Arms Control Policy: Challenge to the Gaullist Heritage" (Paper presented at a conference on "The Impact of the Fifth Republic on France: Two Decades of Gaullism," State University College, SUNY, Brockport: N.Y., 9-11 June 1978).
65. Kolodziej, "French Disarmament," p. 17. For an informative discussion of the French position, see the articles by Paul Granet in *Le Monde* on 22 and 23 July 1978.
66. See the resolution of the suppliers' meeting in January 1978 in the *New York Times,* 16 January 1978.
67. See *Le Monde,* 27 January 1978, and the *New York Times,* 26 January 1978.
68. *Le Monde,* 3 July 1978. For the text of Giscard's UN speech, see *Le Monde,* 27 May 1978.
69. See, for example, the statement by Foreign Minister Sauvagnargues to the National Assembly, in *Le Monde,* 8 November 1978. The fate of SALT II and the prospects for future SALT III negotiations (perhaps involving nuclear weapons systems in the European theater) are uncertain at this writing, but the French government has already stated that France definitely would not participate in any such talks—because her nuclear weapons are "central systems" and cannot be equated with the intermediate-range weapons of the superpowers themselves. (See the remarks of Foreign Minister François-Poncet to the National Assembly, *Le Monde,* 5 May 1979.)
70. *Le Monde,* 10 February 1976, and *International Herald Tribune,* 11 February 1976.
71. See the text of Giscard's television interview, when this spontaneous statement was made (*Le Monde,* 19 September 1979). The issue arose somewhat artificially—because of an

interview with Gaullist Alexandre Sanguinetti and General George Buis (*Le Nouvel Observateur*, 29 August 1979), when the two men proposed some form of Franco-German nuclear collaboration (primarily industrial, it seems) as a way of counteracting the growing vulnerability of the FNS to technologically superior superpower weapons.

72. See *Le Nouvel Observateur*, 22 May 1978, and *New York Times*, 15 May 1978.

73. See reports in *Le Monde* during this period, and de Guiringaud's statements in the issue of 16 April 1977.

74. The conference is described in the "Chroniques" section of *Défense nationale* 33 (June 1977): 171-75.

75. See reports in *Le Monde* for this period.

76. *Le Monde*, 20 and 25-26 December 1977.

77. This has been a charge raised by the left in France and elsewhere. See, for example, *Le Nouvel Observateur* for 29 May 1978, pp. 37-40, and the article by Barry Cohen, "L'Enjeu africain," in *Le Monde diplomatique* (July 1978), p. 7. Giscard, on the other hand, has made rather modest and realistic assessments of France's capabilities and intentions in Africa. See hist reports to the fifth Franco-African Conference on 22 May 1978, in *Le Monde*, 24 May 1978. On France's African involvements, see also Pierre Lellouche and Dominique Moise, "French Policy in Africa: A Lonely Battle against Destabilization," *International Security* 3, no. 4 (Spring 1979): 108-33; and James O. Goldsborough, "Dateline Paris: Africa's Policeman," *Foreign Policy*, no. 33 (Winter 1978-79), pp. 174-190.

78. See the English translation published as "Use of Different Force Systems in the Strategy of Deterrence," *NATO Letter* 17, no. 6 (June 1969): 18-22.

79. France, Ambassade de France, *French White Paper on National Defense* (New York: Service de presse et d'information, 1972), 1: 13.

80. Interview granted me in July 1972.

81. Ambassade de France, *French White Paper*, esp. p. 12.

82. Ibid., p. 13.

83. See, for example, his speech of 19 October 1971, printed as "La France et sa défense."

84. The reader should also consult earlier discussions by Colonel Lucien Poirer, who worked with the Ministry of Defense's *Centre de prospective et d'évaluation*, which is responsible for elaborating defense strategy in France. See, for example, Poirer's article "Deterrence and Medium-Sized Powers," published by the Ambassade de France, Service de presse et d'information; it is a translation of an article that appeared in the *Revue de défense nationale* in March 1972. See also, Poirer's recent views in his book, *Des Stratégies nucléaires* (Paris: Hachette, 1977).

85. Guy Méry, "Une Armée pour quoi faire et comment?" *Défense nationale* 32 (June 1976): 11-33. The speech was reprinted in a sometimes misleading translation as "Comments by General Guy Méry, 15 March 1976," in *Survival* 18, no. 5 (September/October 1976): 226-28.

86. Valéry Giscard d'Estaing, speech delivered to I.H.E.D.N. on 1 June 1976, reprinted in *Défense nationale* 32 (July 1976): 5-20.

87. Méry, "Armée."

88. There is some doubt now that a less than strategic nuclear attack on French soil would also bring an automatic strategic nuclear retaliation on the aggressor. Apart from a general shift away from pure nuclear deterrence, some critics' worst fears were confirmed in May 1976, when Giscard d'Estaing stated on television that the strategic nuclear force was a means "of deterring aggression of the same type against France." The Elysée text of his remarks deleted the offending words "of the same type" from the printed version circulated later (see *Le Monde*, 20 May 1976).

The president evidently meant what he said, however, for in June 1980 he confirmed the impression created by earlier remarks when he noted that "any nuclear attack on the soil of France would automatically provoke a strategic nuclear response" (*Le Monde*, 28 June 1980).

89. From the *Survival* text of the Méry speech.

90. See Giscard d'Estaing's speech, in *Défense nationale* 32 (July 1976): 17.

91. See Giscard's television interview reported in *Le Monde*, 11 February 1978,

92. Méry, "Armée," p. 17.

93. Giscard's June 1976 sppech, *Défense nationale* 32 (July 1976): 15. Later statements of Méry, Giscard (*Le Monde*, 11 February 1978), and Defense Minister Bourges (*Le Monde*, 17 June 1978) were designed to correct this impression and downgrade the battlefield role of TNWs.

94. Franco-German discussions on this issue began in 1971 and reached an impasse in the summer of 1972, when the French refused Bonn's request that any French TNWs stationed in West Germany be subject to a double-key arrangement. Thus, French launching platforms, which have dual capability anyway, can cross into West Germany, but not the nuclear warheads.

95. French development of a neutron bomb started in December 1976, by order of Giscard d'Estaing. Production could begin as early as 1982-83, with a more sophisticated model available by 1984-85. According to Giscard's announcement in June 1980, a decision actually to produce the weapon will not be made until 1982 or so. (See the report in *Le Monde* for 28 June 1980, and representative samples of the political debate in *Le Monde* for 20 June 1980.)

96. From "Sur la programmation des dépenses militaires et des équipements des forces armées pour la période 1977-1982," *Le Monde*, 7 May 1976.

97. Méry article in *Survival*, p. 227.

98. See, for example, Pierre M. Gallois, "French Defense Planning: The Future in the Past," *International Security* 1, no. 2 (Fall 1976): 16-31. By mid-1980, debate over defense strategy and force structure was intensifying in step with presidential election politics in France. The defense statement of Giscard's supporters in the U.D.F. centrist coalition (see *Le Monde*, 26 April 1980, and esp. 28 May 1980) was clearly Atlanticist and pro-NATO in its orientation, whereas the Gaullist party tract (*Le Monde*, 4 June 1980) reflected a strict adherence to defense autonomy, absolute deterrence, and nonparticipation in any forward battle.

99. *Le Monde*, 7 May 1976. As a percentage of GNP, the French defense budget has declined from 6.5 percent in 1960 to 5.2 percent in 1965, 4.2 percent in 1970, 3.8 percent in 1975, but moved up slightly to 4 percent in 1979. The 1979 performance was under that of the United States (5.2 percent) and Britain (4.9 percent), but ahead of West Germany (3.3 percent). (Sipri figures, reported in *Le Point*, 23 June 1980.)

100. See 1980 budget analyses in *Le Monde* for 7 September and 5 October 1979.

101. For a detailed analysis of Gaullist armed forces structure and organization, see Lothar Rühl, *La Politique militaire de la Ve république* (Paris: Presses de la Fondation nationale des sciences politiques, 1976).

102. *Le Monde*, 10 June 1976.

103. This amounts to a total of 750 combat units. The armored divisions will have two tank regiments each, with 109 AMX-30 tanks, two mechanized regiments (40 AMX-30 tanks each), and one artillery regiment, plus support facilities. Each infantry division will have three infantry regiments and one armored regiment with AMX-10 tanks. (See the analysis by Jacques Isnard in *Le Monde*, 5 May 1978.)

104. In mid-1980, the *Forces françaises en Allemagne* (F.F.A.) included around 50,000 troops, of which 14,000 were career soldiers and 36,000 were conscripts. The second army corps, along with some air units, made up the bulk of the F.F.A. It comprised an army corps headquarters, three armored divisions (each with 7,500 soldiers and 490 armored vehicles), one logistics brigade, and various other units. The second army corps fell under the authority of the First French Army, headquartered at Strasbourg. Dependents and civilian employees working with the F.F.A. brought the French defense presence in West Germany to over 90,000 persons (*Le Monde*, 10 July 1980).

105. *Le Monde*, 13 May and 20 May 1978.

106. The navy had 69,000 men in 1976, the air force 106,000, for an armed forces total of 505,000 at the start of the program. The projected total in 1980 is 485,000 (*Le Monde,* 17 November 1976). By contrast, the West German Bundeswehr had 496,000 men in 1976, divided into 340,000 for the army, 108,000 for the air force, and 38,000 for the small navy. The West German land army had 2,052 tanks and planned for a total of 2,700 (*Le Monde,* 26 January 1977).

107. On the issue of conscription in France, see Michel L. Martin, "Conscription and the Decline of the Mass Army in France, 1960-1975," *Armed Forces and Society* 3, no. 3 (Spring 1977): 355-406.

Whereas President Giscard d'Estaing confirmed, in June 1980, that France would retain a one-year universal military service, the Gaullists have proposed a reduced initial training period followed by one-week annual sessions until age twenty-five (*Le Monde,* 3 July 1980). Leftist perspectives are discussed below.

108. See plans discussed by General Guy Méry (now head of the General Staff), 3 April 1978, available in a translation by the New York French Embassy Press and Information Division, document #78/68, entitled "France's Defense Policy."

109. Much of this discussion of France's arms industry and exports relies on the research of Edward A. Kolodziej. See "French Disarmament," and "The Success of French Arms (Sales)" (Paper presented at the 1978 APSA meeting, New York). In current francs, a National Assembly report (by RPR deputy Jacques Cressard) contends that French arms exports for 1978 amounted to 17.3 billion francs, divided into 10.6 billion for the aeronautics sector, 3.9 billion for army equipment, 1.2 billion for naval equipment, and 1.5 billion for various electronics equipment. With exports totaling 345 billion francs in 1978, armaments, therefore, amounted to about 5 percent of exports (*Le Monde,* 4 October 1979). Orders (rather than deliveries) for arms exports amounted to 23.2 billion francs in 1978, and rose only slightly to around 25 billion in 1979 (preliminary figures in *Le Monde,* 29 January 1980).

110. *Le Monde,* 16 March 1977.

111. Ibid., 16 May 1977.

112. *L'Express,* 21-27 November 1977. By 1979, the French army was able to insist on its own tank specifications.

113. Early plans for the French mobile missile, baptized "SX" in initial studies at SNIAS (*Société nationale industrielle aérospatial*), favored a two-stage missile, with either single or triple warheads, mounted on wheeled flatbeds suitable for towing (*Le Monde,* 28 June 1980). In mid-1980, it was unclear whether or not this kind of system would be installed alone, or in conjunction with a cruise missile system. The French general staff was reported to favor a mobile land missile over cruise missiles, if required to choose (*Le Monde,* 16-17 March 1980).

114. This modernization program was expected to be finished during 1979 (*Le Monde,* 28-29 May 1978).

115. See the discussion of capability requirements in two essays by Geoffrey Kemp: *Nuclear Forces for Medium Powers:* part 1, *Targets and Weapons Systems,* and parts 2 and 3, *Strategic Requirements and Options,* Adelphi Papers, nos. 106 and 107 (London: International Institute for Strategic Studies, Autumn 1974).

116. See a discussion of the National Assembly debate on this issue in *Le Monde,* 17 June 1978 and the report of Giscard's concession to the Gaullists later in the summer, in *L'Express* for 30 September-7 October 1978.

117. See explanations given for the delay in *Le Monde,* 20-21 November 1977.

118. The discussion of left-wing policies in this section is based on earlier essays of mine on this subject, especially a paper entitled "Consensus, Confusion, and Confrontation in France: The Left in Search of a Defense Policy," in *The Fifth Republic at Twenty,* ed. Stanley Hoffmann and William G. Andrews (Albany, N.Y.: SUNY Press, 1981). For an early analysis of Socialist party foreign policy perspectives, see my "A Socialist Foreign Policy for France?" *Orbis* 21, no. 4 (Winter 1976): 1471-98.

119. See the SF10 statements reported in *Le Monde* on 11 and 15 March 1966. See also Jean Lecanuet's pro-European position, reported in *Le Monde* on 24 March 1966; and socialist

accusations of "pouvoir personnel" (by Gaston Deferre and Guy Mollet) during National Assembly debates on 19 and 20 April, reported in *Le Monde* on 21 and 22 April 1966.

120. The text of the censure motion can be found in *Le Monde*, 15 April 1966.

121. A more detailed discussion of the censure debate can be found in Michael M. Harrison, "France and the Atlantic Alliance: The Process of Political and Military Dealignment" (Ph.D. Diss., Columbia University, 1974).

122. For discussions of Communist policies and perspectives, see Annie Kriegel, "The French Communist Party and the Fifth Republic," in *Communism in Italy and France*, ed. Donald L. M. Blackmer and Sidney Tarrow (Princeton, N.J.: Princeton University Press, 1975), pp. 69-86; and Ronald Tiersky, "Le P.C.F. et la détente," *Esprit*, no. 2 (February 1975), pp. 218-41).

123. A thorough discussion of the Socialist Party's evolution and structure since its swing to the left in 1971 would unduly tax the reader's patience. See Vincent Wright and Howard Machin, "The French Socialist Party: Success and the Problems of Success," *Political Quarterly* 46, no. 1 (January-March 1975): 36-52; and Jean-François Bizot's *Au Parti des socialistes: Plongée libre dans les courants d'un grand parti* (Paris: Bernard Grasset, 1975).

124. This discussion naturally simplifies the diversity of views found in the PS, although the positions described here correspond to the attitudes and rhetoric of many party leaders. See the analysis by Richard Gombin, "Le Parti socialiste et la politique étrangère," *Politique étrangère*, no. 2 (1977), pp. 199-212.

125. See the Marchais reports in Etienne Fajon, *L'Union est un combat* (Paris: Editions sociales, 1975).

126. For a concise communist critique of the PS that reveals the PCF's own attitude, see Daniel Debatisse, "La Crise internationale, réalités et prétextes," *Cahiers du communisme* (December 1977), pp. 32-43.

127. On these elections, see *Le Monde*, Dossiers et Documents, *Les Elections législatives de mars 1978* (March 1978).

128. Jean Marrane, *L'Armée de la France démocratique* (Paris: Editions sociales, 1977). This official defense policy statement of the PCF cites only Western threats to France.

129. It was surprising to see such notions discussed even by moderate Socialist Party military experts such as General Becam. See Becam's wide-ranging and confusing interview in *Repères: Le Cahier du CERES* (April 1977), esp. p. 32. For a more balanced socialist view, see Charles Hernu's *Soldat-Citoyen: Essai sur la défense et la sécurité* (Paris: Flammarion, 1975).

130. From the program of Mitterrand's *Convention des institutions républicaines* (CIR), entitled *Un Socialisme du possible* (Paris: Seuil, 1970), p. 96.

131. Parti socialiste, *Changer la vie: Programme de gouvernement du parti socialiste* (Paris: Flammarion, 1972), p. 198.

132. Quoted in Jean-Pierre Chevènement, "Essai de prospective socialiste," *Preuves* (1972), p. 82.

133. Parti socialiste, Parti communiste, Mouvement des Radicaux de gauche, *Programme commun de gouvernement* (Paris: Flammarion, 1973), p. 85. For a discussion emphasizing this more radical period in Socialist Party foreign policy, see my article "A Socialist Foreign Policy for France?"

134. See *Le Monde*, 11 November 1977, for the text of the motion finally approved in January of 1978.

135. *Le Monde*, 10 January 1978.

136. The phrase is from Robert Pontillon's report, "La Défense nationale française dans son environnement international: Contribution au débat sur la politique de défense," in *Comité directeur* (6 and 7 November 1976), p. 10, mimeographed.

137. Charles Hernu, "Faut-il assurer la sécurité de la France? Crises et menaces: Perspectives du Programme commun," in Parti socialiste, *Comité directeur* (6 and 7 November 1976), p. 14, mimeographed.

138. See the Marchais report in Fajon, *L'Union*, esp. pp. 95-96.

139. See Jean Kanapa's report to the party Central Committee, in *Le Monde*, 24 June 1976.

140. In the foreword to the program of his CIR, Mitterrand noted that "the only possible path for France is to combat the domination of the two blocs. Everything that loosens their double grip is good in itself" (*Un Socialisme du possible,* p. 21). The PS program of 1972 takes up the same goal (*Changer la vie,* p. 197).

141. Fajon, *L'Union,* pp. 96-97.

142. See the communist proposals in: Parti communiste français, *Programme commun de gouvernement actualisé* (Paris: Editions sociales, 1978), p. 143; also, Mitterrand's statement on the matter in *Le Monde,* 24 February 1978.

143. See the Marchais interview in *Le Monde,* 3 March 1978.

144. For the PCF view of these negotiations, see: Pierre Juquin, *Programme commun: L'Actualisation à dossiers ouverts* (Paris: Editions sociales, 1977).

145. See the Pontillon report, "La Défense nationale française."

146. For example, Jean-Pierre Chevènement, "La Gauche, le gouvernement, le pouvoir," *Le Monde,* 17 July 1976. CERES reservations about the European Community are summarized in annex 1 to their motion presented at the party's 1977 Nantes Congress and printed in *Le Poing et la Rose,* no. 62 (June 1977), p. 25.

147. Hernu, *Soldat-Citoyen,* p. 88.

148. From Mitterrand's "Seven Options" of the 1965 presidential campaign, given in Pascal Orly et al., *Les Chemins de l'unité* (Paris: Téma-editions, 1974), p. 100.

149. *Changer la vie,* p. 206.

150. See Mitterrand's statements reported in *Le Monde* on 4 and 16 May 1974.

151. Hernu, *Soldat-Citoyen,* p. 55.

152. See Pontillon, "La Défense national française," and Hernu, "La Sécurité." Jean-Pierre Chevènement's contribution to this meeting reflected the fact that the party's left-wing elites were mostly in agreement; see "La Conception d'une défense indépendante dans la stratégie du Programme commun," November 1976, mimeographed. Also interesting is the forthright discussion of the party's new perspective by Gilles Martinet, "Les Socialistes et la bombe," *Le Nouvel Observateur,* 22 November 1976.

153. The possibility was first raised in public in remarks made by PCF defense expert Louis Baillot, at a meeting of the *Fondation pour les études de défense général* in April 1976. See the initial report in *Le Monde* on 18-19 April 1976 and qualifications in *L'Humanité* for 19 April as well as *Le Monde* on 20 and 23 April. Until the decisions of May 1977, the most forthright communist statements in favor of the FNS came from Jean Elleinstein, the party's leading "Eurocommunist." See *Le Monde,* 10 November 1976.

154. See a summary of the Kanapa report and Jacques Isnard's analysis in *Le Monde,* 13 May 1977.

155. For example, see the debate between Jacques Huntzinger and Dominique Taddei in *Faire: Mensuel pour le socialisme et l'autogestion,* nos. 21/22 (July-August 1977), pp. 7-16. See also Taddei's article in *Le Monde* on 7 January 1978. *Le Nouvel Observateur* (22 October 1977) reported that PS militants were hostile to nuclear power in all its forms by a majority of 48 percent to 42 percent.

156. See, for example, the Marchais interview in *Le Monde* on 3 March 1978, Marchais's statements in *L'Humanité* on 9 August 1977, and Juquin, *Programme commun,* pp. 46-47.

157. The amendment submitted by this group was defeated. It stated that "in the only foreseeable hypothesis of a territorial intervention of the USSR in Europe, Western solidarity is infinitely more of a deterrent than a specifically French threat" (*Le Monde,* 8-9 January 1978).

158. The leadership's resolution was approved by 68.2 percent of the federation mandates voted at the convention.

159. From the defense motion text, in *Le Monde,* 15 December 1977.

160. See the communist suggestions in Marrane, *L'Armée,* and Parti communiste français, *Programme commun actualisé.*

161. Hernu's 1976 report, "La Sécurité," also recommended construction of the sixth submarine. For the PS Defense Committee's brief recommendations, see *L'Armée nouvelle,* September 1978, mimeographed.

162. *Le Monde,* 15 December 1977.

163. *Le Monde,* 10 January 1978.

164. The Kanapa report also favored a sixth submarine (then in doubt) and specified that the Mirage-IVs should not be replaced as they wear out.

165. *Le Monde,* 26 July 1977. Later, in December 1978, Giscard d'Estaing decided to develop a national French early warning sytstem (apparently only for detecting aircraft flying at low altitudes) to ensure the independence and autonomy of the FNS. Thus, France would not take part in the NATO AWACS system, partly because participation might somehow compromise the independence of military decisions in a crisis (*Le Monde,* 9 December 1978.)

166. Hernu, *Soldat-Citoyen,* p. 156.

167. *Le Nouvel Observateur,* 18 August 1977.

168. See comments by Marchais and Mitterrand in *Le Monde,* 9, 10, and 12 August 1977. The PCF also proposed abandoning the anticity targeting strategy for the FNS, but quickly backed down under socialist criticism. Communist proposals for a no-first-use of nuclear weapons commitment met a similar fate.

169. See the Marchais interview, *Le Monde,* 3 March 1978.

170. On the Pluton, see Hernu, "La Sécurité," p. 6; see also his *Chroniques d'attente: Réflexions pour gouverner demain* (Paris: Téma-éditions, 1977).

171. *Le Monde,* 10 January 1978.

172. See *Le Monde,* 20 and 27 June, 1980. The CERES faction was critical of this decision.

173. See the interview of Mitterrand in *Le Monde,* 31 July 1980. The PS secretary-general appeared to be moving closer to the views of his principal rival within the party, Michel Rocard.

Chapter 6

1. The persistence of the basic postwar settlement and two-bloc system in Europe is stressed in the informed and thought-provoking analysis by A. W. DePorte, *Europe between the Superpowers: The Enduring Balance* (New Haven: Yale University Press, 1979).

2. Thus, the sources of French alliance policy are the opposite of those Roger Morgan identified for West Germany, in *The United States and West Germany, 1945-1973: A Study in Alliance Politics* (London: Oxford University Press, 1974).

3. The oligarchical thrust of Gaullist policy was singled out as potentially beneficial by Edward Kolodziej in *French International Policy under de Gaulle and Pompidou* (Ithaca: Cornell University Press, 1974).

4. These trends have been discussed by numerous authors. See, for example, Edward L. Morse, "The Transformation of Foreign Policies: Modernization, Interdependence, and Externalization," *World Politics* 22 (April 1970): 371-92; and Robert O. Keohane and Joseph S. Nye, *Power and Interdependence: World Politics in Transition* (Boston: Little, Brown, & Co., 1977).

5. See the discussion of diverse theories in Ole R. Holsti et al., *Unity and Disintegration in International Alliances: Comparative Studies* (New York: John Wiley & Sons, 1973).

6. For a convenient survey of these developments, see Jacques Menoncourt, "Dangereuse Rivalité gréco-turque en Méditerranée orientale," *Défense nationale* 32 (May 1976): pp. 75-81.

7. *Washington Post,* 29 September 1977.

8. By March 1980, an agreement had been reached in which the United States was granted continued use of important military facilities in Turkey, while Ankara, in return, received substantial commitments of military and economic aid (*New York Times,* 30 March 1980).

9. On French and Italian left security policies and the problems they may raise for the West, see the forthcoming study undertaken for the Ford Foundation by Simon Serfaty and me tentatively entitled *Security Perspectives of the Left in France and Italy.*

10. See the text of Giscard d'Estaing's television interview on 26 February, as given in *Le Monde,* 28 February 1980.

11. See Prime Minister Barre's speech in New York, reported in *Le Monde,* 10-11 February 1980; see also Giscard d'Estaing's comments on the Franco-German declaration on Afganistan, in *Le Monde,* 7 February 1980.

12. The need for vigilance, and a recognition that détente was entering a new and uncertain phase, was stressed by Giscard d'Estaing during televised remarks reported in *Le Monde* on 28 February 1980.

13. See Chirac's statement, reported in *Le Monde* on 14 February 1980.

14. See reports of the February meeting between the two leaders, in *Le Monde* on 5 February 1980.

15. As this book went to press in February 1981, it seemed unwise to speculate at length on the long-term implications of the most recent pattern of developments. It was notable, nevertheless, that France and Germany were continuing to distinguish their positions from those of the United States at a time when events in Poland, as well as the anti-Soviet thrust of the new Reagan adminstration, were exacerbating the crisis in détente. By the time of the Franco-German summit in February 1981, Giscard d'Estaing and Schmidt had exchanged roles to the extent that Paris seemed to be taking a firm line a bit closer to the initial posturing of the new American leadership, whereas Bonn was confirming the extreme West German reluctance to sanction further escalation of East-West tensions. The growing impression that the Federal Republic, not France, had become the strongest proponent of maintaining good relations and ties with the East, perhaps at the expense of Western security interests, was difficult to allay. Developments in French and German policies on such matters were conditioned by impending presidential elections in France and the volatile politics of faction in the SPD, so that clear national interests and positions remained obscure at a time of rapid changes in the international situation. Nevertheless, barring a major tragedy in Poland or some other great crisis with unpredictable consequences, it seems likely that the basic complementarity of long-range Franco-German interests on key issues related to détente will remain intact, while the potential for these interests to conflict with the policies of President Reagan and his advisers is substantial.

Bibliography

Documents

France. *Textes et notes* (series). Paris: La Documentation Française.

France. Ambassade de France. *French Affairs* (series). New York: Service de presse et d'information.

France. Ambassade de France. *French Foreign Policy* (series). New York: Service de presse et d'information.

France. Ambassade de France. *French White Paper on National Defense.* Vol. 1. New York: Service de presse et d'information, 1972.

France, Ambassade de France. *Major Addresses, Statements, and Press Conferences of General Charles de Gaulle, May 19, 1958-January 31, 1964.* New York: Service de presse et d'information, 1964.

France. Ambassade de France. *Major Addresses, Statements, and Press Conferences of General Charles de Gaulle, March 17, 1964-May 16, 1967.* New York: Service de presse et d'information, 1967.

France. Ambassade de France. *Speeches and Press Conferences* (series). New York: Service de presse et d'information.

France. Assemblée Nationale. *Journal officiel de la république française: Débats parlementaires.* Paris: Imprimerie de l'Assemblée Nationale.

France. Assemblée Nationale. *Journal officiel de la république française: documents parlementaires.* Paris: Imprimerie de l'Assemblée Nationale.

France. Assemblée Nationale. *Journal officiel de la république française: Organisation générale de la défense.* Paris: Imprimerie des journaux officiels, 1 February 1970.

France. Ministère des Affaires Etrangères. *La France et l'OTAN.* Paris: Direction des services d'information et de presse, n.d.

France, Ministère des Armées. Service d'information d'études et de cinématographie des armées. "La France et l'Alliance atlantique." *Note d'information,* no. 17 (August 1966).

France, Ministère des Armées. Service d'information et d'études du Ministère des Armées. "La Défense: La Politique militaire et ses réalisations." *Notes et études documentaires,* no. 3343. Paris: La Documentation Française (6 December 1966).

France. Ministère de la Défense Nationale. *Livre blanc sur la défense nationale.* Vol. 1. Paris: 1972.

273

France. Ministère de la Guerre. *L'Organisation militaire atlantique: O.T.A.N.* Bulletin officiel du Ministère de la Guerre, no. 110-1. Paris: Charles—Lavauzelle et Cie., 1956.

France: Secrétariat d'état à l'information. *Le Dossier de l'alliance atlantique.* Paris: 1966.

North Atlantic Treaty Organization. *NATO: Facts and Figures.* Brussels: NATO Information Service, 1971.

North Atlantic Treaty Organization. *SHAPE and Allied Command Europe: Twenty Years in the Service of Peace and Security, 1951-1971.* Brussels: SHAPE, 1971.

U.S. Congress. Senate. Committee on Foreign Relations. *North Atlantic Treaty: Documents Relating to the North Atlantic Treaty.* 81st Cong., 1st sess., 1949.

U.S. Congress. Senate. Committee on Foreign Relations. Subcommittee on U.S. Security Agreements and Commitments Abroad. *U.S. Security Issues in Europe: Burden Sharing and Offset, MBFR and Nuclear Weapons.* 93rd Cong., 1st sess., September 1973.

U.S. Congress. Senate. Committee on Government Operations. Subcommittee on National Security and International Operations. *The Atlantic Alliance: Hearings.* 89th Cong., 2nd sess., 1966.

U.S. Department of State. *Department of State Bulletin* (series). Washington, D.C.: Government Printing Office.

U.S. Department of State. *Foreign Relations of the United States* (series). Washington, D.C.: Government Printing Office.

Western European Union. Assembly. Committee on Defense Questions and Armaments. 9th ordinary Sess. *State of European Security: The NATO Nuclear Force after the Nassau Agreement.* Report submitted by Mr. Duynstee. Paris: 1964.

Western European Union. Assembly. Committee on Defense Questions and Armaments. 13th ordinary Sess. *France and NATO,* edited by L. Radoux. Paris: June 1967.

Books, Manuscripts, and Pamphlets

Acheson, Dean. *Present at the Creation: My Years at the State Department.* New York: W. W. Norton & Co., 1969.

Adenauer, Konrad. *Erinnerungen, 1959-1963: Fragmente.* Stuttgart: Deutsche Verlags-Anstalt, 1968.

Ambler, John Steward. *Soldiers against the State.* Garden City, N.Y.: Doubleday & Co., 1968.

Amme, Carl H., Jr. *NATO without France: A Strategic Appraisal.* Stanford: The Hoover Institution on War, Revolution, and Peace, Stanford University, 1967.

Anonymous. *L'Année politique, économique, sociale et diplomatique en France, 1965.* Paris: Presses universitaires de France, 1966.

————. *L'Année politique, économique, sociale et diplomatique en France, 1966.* Paris: Presses universitaires de France, 1967.

Aron, Raymond. *The Great Debate: Theories of Nuclear Strategy.* Garden City, N.Y.: Doubleday & Co., 1965.

————. *Peace and War: A Theory of International Relations.* Translated by Richard Howard and Annette Baker Fox. Garden City, N.Y.: Doubleday & Co., 1966.

Autin, Jean. *20 Ans de politique financière*. Paris: Editions du Seuil, 1972.

Ball, George. *The Discipline of Power: Essentials of a Modern World Structure*. Boston: Little, Brown, & Co., 1968.

Ball, Margaret M. *NATO and the European Union Movement*. New York: Frederick A. Praeger, 1959.

Beaufre, André. *Deterrence and Strategy*. Translated by Major General R. H. Barry. New York: Frederick A. Praeger, 1965.

_____.*NATO and Europe*. Translated by Joseph Green. New York: Alfred A. Knopf, 1966.

Beer, Francis A. *Integration and Disintegration in NATO: Processes of Alliance Cohesion and Prospects for Atlantic Community*. Columbus, Ohio: Ohio State University Press, 1969.

Béliard, J. "La France et l'OTAN." Mimeographed. Paris: 28 March 1966.

Bell, Coral. *The Debatable Alliance: An Essay in Anglo-American Relations*. London: Oxford University Press, 1964.

Bertram, Christoph. *Mutual Force Reductions in Europe: The Political Aspects*. *Adelphi Paper, no. 84*. London: The International Institute for Strategic Studies, 1972.

Beugel, Ernst H. Van der. *From Marshall Aid to Atlantic Partership: European Integration As a Concern of American Foreign Policy*. Amsterdam: Elsevier Publishing Co., 1966.

Bidault, Georges. *Resistance: The Political Autobiography of Georges Bidault*. New York: Praeger, 1967.

Bizot, Jean-François. *Au Parti des socialistes: Plongée libre dans les courants d'un grand parti*. Paris: Bernard Grasset, 1975.

Bodenheimer, Susanne J. *Political Union: A Microcosm of European Politics, 1960-1966*. Leyden: A. W. Sijthoff, 1967.

Brzezinski, Zbigniew K. *The Soviet Bloc: Unity and Conflict*. Rev. ed. Cambridge, Mass.: Harvard University Press, 1967.

Buchan, Alastair. *Crisis Management: The New Diplomacy*. Paris: Atlantic Institute, April 1966.

_____. *NATO in the 1960's*. Rev. ed. New York: Frederick A. Praeger, 1963.

Calleo, David P. *The Atlantic Fantasy: The U.S., NATO, and Europe*. Baltimore: Johns Hopkins Press, 1970.

_____. *Europe's Future: The Grand Alternatives*. New York: W. W. Norton & Co., 1967.

Camps, Miriam. *European Unification in the Sixties: From the Veto to the Crisis*. New York: McGraw-Hill, 1966.

Carmoy, Guy de. *L'Alliance atlantique disloquée*. Paris: Editions (A.F.C.A.), 1966.

_____. *Energy for America: Economic and Political Implications*. Washington, D.C.: American Enterprise Institute, 1977.

_____. *The Foreign Policies of France: 1944-1968*. Chicago: University of Chicago Press, 1960.

Center for Strategic Studies. *NATO after Czechoslovakia*. Special Report Series, no. 9. Washington, D.C.: Georgetown University, April 1969.

Cerny, Karl H., and Briefs, Henry W. *NATO in Quest of Cohesion*. New York: Frederick A. Praeger, 1965.

Charlot, Jean. *The Gaullist Phenomenon: The Gaullist Movement in the Fifth Re-public*. London: George Allen & Unwin, 1971.

Cleveland, Harlan. *NATO: The Transatlantic Bargain*. New York: Harper & Row, 1970.

Cleveland, Harold van B. *The Atlantic Idea and its European Rivals*. New York: McGraw-Hill, 1966.

Convention des institutions républicains. *Un Socialisme du possible*. Paris: Seuil, 1979.

Cottrell, Alvin J., and Dougherty, James E. *The Politics of the Atlantic Alliance*. New York: Frederick A. Praeger, 1964.

Couve de Murville, Maurice. *Une Politique étrangère, 1958-1969*. Paris: Librarie Plon, 1971.

Crozier, Michel. *The Bureaucratic Phenomenon*. Chicago: University of Chicago Press, 1964.

Debré, Michel. *Au Service de la nation: Essai d'un programme politique*. Paris: Editions Stock, 1963.

de Gaulle, Charles. *The Army of the Future*. Philadelphia: J. B. Lippincott Co., 1941.

_____. *Citations du Président de Gaulle*. Edited by Jean Lacouture. Paris: Editions du Seuil, 1968.

_____. *The Complete War Memoirs of Charles de Gaulle*. Translated by Richard Howard. New York: Simon & Schuster, 1960.

_____. *Discours et Messages*. 5 vols. Paris: Plon, 1970.

_____. *Le Fils de l'épée*. Paris: Editions Berger-Levrault, 1961.

_____. *Memoirs of Hope: Renewal and Endeavor*. Translated by Terence Kilmartin. New York: Simon & Schuster, 1971.

de la Gorce, Paul-Marie. *La France contre les empires*. Paris: Grasset, 1969.

_____. *The French Army: A Military-Political History*. Translated by Kenneth Douglas. New York: George Braziller, 1963.

Delmas, Claude. *L'Alliance atlantique: Essai de phénoménologie politique*. Paris: Payot, 1962.

_____. *L'O.T.A.N.* Paris: Presses universitaires de France, 1960.

DePorte, Anton W. *De Gaulle's Foreign Policy, 1944-1946*. Cambridge, Mass.: Harvard University Press, 1968.

_____. *Europe between the Superpowers: The Enduring Balance*. New Haven: Yale University Press, 1979.

Deutsch, Karl. *France, Germany, and the Western Alliance*. New York: Charles Scribner's Sons, 1967.

_____. *The Nerves of Government: Models of Political Communication and Control*. New York: The Free Press, 1966.

Duchêne, François. *Beyond Alliance*. Paris: Atlantic Institute, 1965.

Duroselle, Jean-Baptist, ed., "The Future of the Atlantic Community." Paper read at the Royaumont Conference. Paris: Atlantic Institute, 7-10 July 1966. Mimeographed.

_____. *La Politique étrangère et ses fondaments*. Paris: Librarie Armand Colin, 1954.

Elgey, Georgette. *Histoire de la IVᵉ république*, vol. 1, *La République des illusions, 1945-1951*. Paris: Fayard, 1965.

_____. *Histoire de la IVᵉ république,* vol. 2, *La République des contradictions, 1951-1954.* Paris: Fayard, 1968.

Ely, Paul. *L'Armée dans la nation.* Paris: Librarie Arthème Fayard, 1961.

_____. *Mémoires: Suez . . . Le 13 Mai.* Paris: Plon, 1969.

Fajon, Richard. *L'Union est un combat.* Paris: Editions sociales, 1975.

Farrell, John C., and Smith, Asa P., eds. *Image and Reality in World Politics.* New York: Columbia University Press, 1967.

Fauvet, Jacques. *La IVᵉ République.* Paris: Fayard, 1959.

Fedder, Edwin H. *NATO: The Dynamics of Alliance in the Postwar World.* New York: Dodd, Mead, & Co., 1973.

Fontaine, André. *L'Alliance atlantique à l'heure du dégât.* Paris: Calmann-Lévy, 1959.

_____. *History of the Cold War: From the Korean War to the Present.* New York: Vintage Books, 1970.

Fox, William T. R., and Fox, Annette B. *NATO and the Range of American Choice.* New York: Columbia University Press, 1967.

Frankel, Joseph. *The Making of Foreign Policy.* London: Oxford University Press, 1963.

Friedman, Julian R., et al., eds. *Alliance in International Politics.* Boston: Allyn & Bacon, 1970.

Furniss, Edgar S., Jr. *De Gaulle and the French Army: A Crisis in Civil-Military Relations.* New York: Twentieth Century Fund, 1964.

_____. *France: Keystone of Western Defense.* Garden City, N.Y.: Doubleday & Co., 1954.

_____. *Weaknesses in French Foreign Policy-Making.* Memorandum no. 5. Princeton, N.J.: Center of International Studies, Princeton University, 5 February 1954.

Girardet, Raoul. "Problèmes généraux de défense nationale," Vols. 1 and 2. Mimeographed. Paris: Fondation nationale des sciences politiques, 15 April 1972.

Grosser, Alfred. *French Foreign Policy under de Gaulle.* Boston: Little, Brown & Co., 1967.

_____. *La IVᵉ République et sa politique extérieure.* Paris: Librarie Armand Colin, 1961.

Haas, Ernst B. *Tangle of Hopes: American Commitments and World Order.* Englewood Cliffs, N.J.: Prentice-Hall, 1969.

Harrison, Michael M. "France and the Atlantic Alliance: The Process of Political and Military Dealignment." Ph.D. dissertation, Columbia University, 1974.

Hartley, Anthony. *American Foreign Policy in the Nixon Era.* Adelphi Paper, no. 110. London: International Institute of Strategic Studies, Winter 1974-75.

Hassner, Pierre. *Change and Security in Europe,* Part 2, *In Search of a System.* Adelphi Paper, no. 49. London: Institute for Strategic Studies, 1968.

Hernu, Charles. *Chroniques d'attente: Reflections pour gouverner demain.* Paris: Téma-éditions, 1977.

_____. *Soldat-Citoyen: Essai sur la défense et la sécurité.* Paris: Flammarion, 1975.

Hess, John L. *The Case for De Gaulle: An American Viewpoint.* New York: William Morrow & Co., 1968.

Hobbes, Thomas. *Leviathan.* Edited by Michael Oakeshott. New York: Collier Books, 1962.

Hoffmann, Stanley. *Decline or Renewal? France since the 1930s.* New York: Viking Press, 1974.

_____, ed. *Conditions of World Order.* Boston: Houghton Mifflin Co., 1968.

_____, et al. *In Search of France.* New York: Harper Torchbooks, 1963.

Holsti, Ole R., et al. *Unity and Disintegration in International Alliances: Comparative Studies.* New York: John Wiley & Sons, 1973.

Hovey, Harold A. *United States Military Assistance: A Study of Policy and Practices.* New York: Frederick A. Praeger, 1965.

Hunt, K. *NATO without France: The Military Implications.* Adelphi Paper, no. 32. London: Institute for Strategic Studies, 1966.

Huntington, Samuel P. *The Common Defense: Strategic Programs in National Politics.* New York: Columbia University Press, 1961.

Iklé, Fred Charles. *How Nations Negotiate.* New York: Frederick A. Praeger, 1964.

Imbert, Armand. *L'Union de L'Europe Occidentale.* Paris: Bibliothèque de droit internationale, 1968.

Inglehart, Ronald. *The Silent Revolution: Changing Values and Political Styles among Western Publics.* Princeton, N.J.: Princeton University Press, 1977.

Institute for Strategic Studies. *The Military Balance* (annual series). London.

Irving, R.E.M. *The First Indochina War: French and American Policy, 1945-54.* London: Croom Helm, 1975.

Ismay, Hastings Lionel, Lord. *NATO: The First Five Years, 1949-1954.* N.p., n.d.

Jacob, Philip E., and Toscano, James V. *The Integration of Political Communities.* Philadelphia: J. B. Lippincott Co., 1964.

Jervis, Robert. *The Logic of Images in International Relations.* Princeton, N.J.: Princeton University Press, 1970.

Jobert, Michel. *Memoirs d'avenir.* Paris: Grasset, 1974.

Juquin, Pierre. *Programme commun: L'Actualisation à dossiers ouverts.* Paris: Editions sociales, 1977.

Kalb, Marvin, and Kalb, Bernard. *Kissinger.* Boston: Little, Brown, & Co., 1974.

Kaufman, William W. *The McNamara Strategy.* New York: Harper & Row, 1964.

Kelleher, Catherine McArdel. *Germany and the Politics of Nuclear Weapons.* New York: Columbia University Press, 1975.

Kemp, Geoffrey. *Nuclear Forces for Medium Powers.* Part 1, *Targets and Weapons Systems.* Parts 2 and 3, *Strategic Requirements and Options,* Adelphi Papers, nos. 106 and 107. London: International Institute for Strategic Studies, Autumn 1974.

Keohane, Robert O., and Nye, Joseph S. *Power and Interdependence: World Politics in Transition.* Boston: Little, Brown & Co., 1977.

Kissinger, Henry A. *Nuclear Weapons and Foreign Policy.* New York: Harper & Brothers, 1957.

_____. *The Troubled Partnership: A Re-appraisal of the Atlantic Alliance.* New York: Anchor Books, 1966.

_____. *The White House Years.* Boston: Little, Brown, & Co., 1979.

Klieman, Robert. *Atlantic Crisis: American Diplomacy Confronts a Resurgent Europe.* New York: W. W. Norton & Co., 1964.

Kohl, Wilfrid L. *French Nuclear Diplomacy.* Princeton, N.J.: Princeton University Press, 1971.

Kolodziej, Edward. *French International Policy under de Gaulle and Pompidou.* Ithaca: Cornell University Press, 1974.

Kraft, Joseph. *The Grand Design: From Common Market to Atlantic Partnership.* New York: Harper & Brothers, 1962.

Kulski, W. W. *De Gaulle and the World: The Foreign Policy of the Fifth Republic.* Syracuse, N.Y.: Syracuse University Press, 1966.

Lazareff, Serge. *Le Statut des forces de l'O.T.A.N. et son application en France.* Paris: Editions A. Pedone, 1964.

Lefranc, Robert. *Aux Premiers Temps de l'OTAN: D'Eisenhower à Ridgway.* Paris: Editions municipales, 1966.

Legaret, Jean, and Martin-Dumesnil, E. *La Communauté européenne de défense: Etude analytique du traité du 27 mai 1952.* Paris: Librarie J. Vrin, 1953.

Lerner, Daniel, and Aron, Raymond, eds. *France Defeats EDC.* New York: Frederick A. Praeger, 1957.

Lindberg, Leon, and Scheingold, Stuart A., eds. *Regional Integration: Theory and Research.* Cambridge, Mass.: Harvard University Press, 1971.

Liska, George. *Nations in Alliance: The Limits of Interdependence.* Baltimore: Johns Hopkins Press, 1962.

Lyon, Peyton V. *NATO as a Diplomatic Instrument.* Toronto: Atlantic Council of Canada, 1970.

Macmillan, Harold. *Pointing the Way, 1959-1961.* New York: Harper & Row, 1969.

Mahncke, Dieter. *Nukleare Mitwirkung: Die Bundesrepublik Deutschland in der Atlantischen Allianz, 1954-1970.* Berlin: Walter de Gruyter, 1972.

Marcus, John T. *Neutralism and Nationalism in France: A Case Study.* New York: Bookman Associates, 1958.

Marrane, Jean. *L'Armée de la France démocratique.* Paris: Editions sociales, 1977.

Mendershausen, Horst. *From NATO to Independence: Reflections on de Gaulle's Secession.* P-3334. Washington, D.C.: Washington Center of Foreign Policy Research, March 1966.

_____. *Unrest and Cohesion in the Atlantic Alliance: NATO and the German Question.* Memorandum RM-4936-PR. Santa Monica, Calif.: Rand Corporation, April 1966.

Mendl, Wolf. *Deterrence and Persuasion: French Nuclear Armament in the Context of National Policy, 1945-1969.* New York: Praeger, 1970.

Meusy, Martine. *La Défense de l'Europe occidentale.* Paris: Presses universitaires de France, 1972.

Moldeski, George. *A Theory of Foreign Policy.* New York: Frederick A. Praeger, 1962.

Le Monde. Dossiers et Documents. *Les Elections législatives de mars 1978.* (March 1978).

Moore, Ben T. *NATO and the Future of Europe.* New York: Harper & Brothers, 1958.

Morgan, Roger. *The United States and West Germany, 1945-1973: A Study in Alliance Politics.* London: Oxford University Press, 1974.

Morse, Edward L. *Foreign Policy and Interdependence in Gaullist France.* Princeton, N.J.: Princeton University Press, 1972.

Mullens, Gilles. "Le Retrait de la France de l'OTAN." Master's thesis. Université Libre de Bruxelles, Faculté des sciences sociales, politiques, et économiques, July 1971.

Neustadt, Richard E. *Alliance Politics.* New York: Columbia University Press, 1970.

Newhouse, John. *Collision in Brussels: The Common Market Crisis of 30 June 1965.* New York: W. W. Norton & Co., 1967.

_____. *De Gaulle and the Anglo-Saxons.* New York: Viking Press, 1970.

New York Times. The Pentagon Papers As Published by the New York Times. New York: Bantam Books, 1971.

Nye, Joseph S., Jr., *International Regionalism: Readings.* Boston: Little, Brown & Co., 1968.

Orly, Pascal, et al. *Les Chemins de l'unité.* Paris: Téma-éditions, 1974.

Osgood, Robert E. *Alliances and American Foreign Policy.* Baltimore: Johns Hopkins Press, 1968.

_____. *NATO: The Entangling Alliance.* Chicago: University of Chicago Press, 1962.

Parti communiste français. *Programme commun de gouvernement actualisé.* Paris: Editions sociales, 1978.

Parti socialiste, Parti communiste, Mouvement des Radicaux de gauche. *Programme commun de gouvernement.* Paris: Flammarion, 1973.

Passeron, André. *De Gaulle parle: Des institutions, de l'Algérie, de l'armée, des affaires étrangères, de la communauté, de l'économie et des questions sociales.* Paris: Plon, 1962.

Pattison de Ménil, Lois. *Who Speaks for Europe? The Vision of Charles de Gaulle.* New York: St. Martin's Press, 1977.

Pickles, Dorothy. *The Uneasy Entente: French Foreign Policy and Franco-British Misunderstandings.* London: Oxford University Press, 1966.

Pierre, Andrew. *Nuclear Politics: The British Experience with an Independent Strategic Force, 1939-1970.* London: Oxford University Press, 1972.

Planchais, Jean. *Une Histoire politique de l'armée: De de Gaulle à de Gaulle, 1940-1967.* Paris: Editions du Seuil, 1967.

Pleven, René. *L'Avenir de l'alliance atlantique.* Association française pour la communauté atlantique, General Assembly, Paris: 7 July 1966.

Poirer, Lucien. *Des Stratégies nucléaires.* Paris: Hachette, 1977.

Reynaud, Paul. *La Politique étrangère du gaullisme.* Paris: Julliard, 1964.

Richardson, James L. *Germany and the Atlantic Alliance: The Interaction of Strategy and Politics.* Cambridge, Mass.: Harvard University Press, 1966.

Riekhoff, Harald von. *NATO: Issues and Prospects.* Contemporary Affairs, no. 38, Toronto, Ont.: Canadian Institute of International Affairs, 1967.

Riker, William H. *The Theory of Political Coalitions.* New Haven: Yale University Press, 1962.

Rosecrance, R. N. *Defense of the Realm.* New York: Columbia University Press, 1968.

Rosenau, James N. *The Scientific Study of Foreign Policy.* New York: Free Press, 1971.

Rothstein, Robert L. *Alliances and Small Powers.* New York: Columbia University Press, 1968.

Rouanet, Pierre. *Mendès-France au pouvoir (18 juin 1954-6 fevrier 1955).* Paris: Robert Laffont, 1965.

Rühl, Lothar. *La Politique militaire de la Ve république.* Paris: Presses de la Fondation nationale des sciences politiques, 1976.
————. "La Politique militaire du gouvernement français, 1958-1970." Ph.D. dissertation, Fondation nationale des sciences politiques, Cycle supérieure d'études politiques, 1971.
Sanguinetti, Alexandre. *La France et l'arme atomique.* Paris: René Julliard, 1964.
————. *Rapport sur la politique militaire.* Troisièmes Assises Nationales U.N.R.-U.D.T., Nice, 22-24 November 1963.
Schoenbrun, David. *The Three Lives of Charles de Gaulle.* New York: Atheneum, 1966.
Schütze, Walter. *European Defense Co-operation and NATO.* Paris: Atlantic Institute, November 1969.
Scott, Andrew M. *The Functioning of the International System.* New York: Macmillan Co., 1967.
Serfaty, Simon. *Fading Partnership: America and Europe After 30 Years.* New York: Praeger, 1979.
————. *France, de Gaulle, and Europe: The Policy of the Fourth and Fifth Republics toward the Continent.* Baltimore: Johns Hopkins Press, 1968.
Smart, Ian. *Future Conditional: The Prospect for Anglo-French Nuclear Cooperation.* Adelphi Paper, no. 78. London: Institute for Strategic Studies, 1971.
Spaak, Paul-Henri. *The Continuing Battle: Memoirs of a European, 1936-1966.* Boston: Little, Brown & Co., 1969.
Stanley, Timothy W. *NATO in Transition.* New York: Frederick A. Praeger, 1965.
Stehlin, Paul. *Retour à zero: L'Europe et sa défense dans le compte à rebours.* Paris: Robert Laffont, 1968.
Steinbrunner, John D. *The Cybernetic Theory of Decision: New Dimensions of Political Analysis.* Princeton, N.J.: Princeton University Press, 1974.
Stikker, Dirk. *Men of Responsibility: A Memoir.* New York: Harper & Row, 1966.
Strauss, Franz-Josef. *The Grand Design: A European Solution to German Reunification.* New York: Frederick A. Praeger, 1965.
Tatu, Michel. *Le Triangle: Washington-Moscou-Pékin et les deux Europe(s).* Paris: Casterman, 1972.
Tiersky, Ronald. *French Communism, 1920-1972.* New York: Columbia University Press, 1974.
Tournoux, J.-R. *Jamais dit.* Paris: Plon, 1971.
————. *La Tragédie du général.* Paris: Plon, 1967.
Valluy, Jean. "La Défense militaire de l'Occident." Mimeographed. Association française pour la communauté atlantique, 1960.
————. *Honneur et patrie: Nation et supranation.* Paris: Nouvelles Editions Latines, 1964.
————. *Se Défendre? Contre qui? Pourquoi? Et Comment?* Paris: Plon, 1960.
Vandevanter, E., Jr., *Some Fundamentals of NATO Organization.* Memorandum RM-3559-PR. Santa Monica, Calif.: Rand Corporation, April 1963.
————. *Studies on NATO: An Analysis of Integration.* Memorandum RM-5006-PR. Santa Monica, Calif.: Rand Corporation, August 1966.
Warne, J. D. *N.A.T.O. and Its Prospects.* New York: Frederick A. Praeger, 1954.
Williams, Philip M., and Harrison, Martin. *The French Parliament: Politics in the Fifth Republic.* New York: Frederick A. Praeger, 1968.

————. *Politics and Society in de Gaulle's Republic.* London: Longman, 1971.
Willis, F. Roy. *France, Germany, and the New Europe, 1945-1967.* Rev. ed. New York: Oxford University Press, 1968.
Wolfers, Arnold, ed. *Changing East-West Relations and the Unity of the West.* Baltimore: Johns Hopkins Press, 1962.
Zysman, John. *Political Strategies for Industrial Order: Market, State, and Industry in France.* Berkeley, Calif.: University of California Press, 1977.

Articles and Papers

Ailleret, Charles. "Defense in All Directions." *Atlantic Community Quarterly* 6, no. 1 (Spring 1968): 17-25.
————. "Evolution nécessaire de nos structures militaires." *Revue de défense nationale* 21 (June 1965): 947-55.
————. "Opinion sur la théorie stratégique de la 'flexible response.'" *Revue de défense nationale* 20 (August 1964): 1323-40.
Allard, Jacques. "L'OTAN et Afrique du Nord." *Revue de défense nationale* 14 (June 1958): 907-11.
————. "Vérités sur l'affaire algérienne." *Revue de défense nationale* 14 (January 1958): 5-41.
Anonymous. "Legal Problems Set by the North Atlantic Treaty Organization." *NATO Letter* 4, no. 2 (1 February 1956): 26-34.
————. "U.S., Soviets Boost Mideast Airlift." *Aviation Week and Space Technology* (22 October 1973), pp. 18-21.
Armstrong, Hamilton Fish. "Postscript to E.D.C." *Foreign Affairs* 33, no. 1 (October 1954): 17-27.
Aron, Raymond. "Défense nationale et unification européenne." *Revue de défense nationale* 26, no. 4 (April 1970): 556-70.
————. "France in the Cold War." *Political Quarterly* 22, no. 1 (January-March 1951): 57-66.
————. "From Independence to Neutrality." *Atlantic Community Quarterly* 6, no. 2 (Summer 1968): 267-69.
Backmann, René. "Les Nouveaux Soldats perdus." *Nouvel Observateur,* 7 April 1969.
Ball, George. "The Larger Meaning of the NATO Crisis." London: American Embassy, United States Information Service, 2 May 1966. Mimeographed.
————. "U.S. Policy toward NATO." In *NATO in Quest of Cohesion,* edited by Karl H. Cerny and Henry W. Briefs, pp. 11-19. New York: Frederick A. Praeger, 1965.
Bourget, P.-A. "Stratégie périphérique." *Politique étrangère* 19, no. 1 (February-March 1954): 59-72.
Burgess, Philip M., and Robinson, James A., "Alliances and the Theory of Collective Action: A Simulation of Coalition Processes." In *International Politics and Foreign Policy: A Reader in Research and Theory,* edited by James N. Rosenau, pp. 640-53. Rev. ed. New York: Free Press, 1969.
Cabanier, G. "L'Evolution de la marine francaise." *Revue de défense nationale,* 21 (July 1965): 1128-46.

Carpentier, Marcel. "Stratégie, tactique et structures classiques." In *L'Avenir de l'alliance atlantique*. Paris: Editions Berger-Levrault, 1961. Pp. 73-109.

Carter, Jack E. "The International Staff Officer." *NATO's Fifteen Nations* 9, no. 6 (December 1964-January 1965): 49-52.

Catroux, Georges. "L'Union française, son concept, son état, ses perspectives." *Politique étrangère* 18, no. 4 (September-October 1953): 233-66.

Challe, Maurice. "Entretien avec le Général Challe" (interview by Claude Delmas). Revue de défense nationale 17 (April 1961): 577-94.

Chambrun, Gilbert de. "Y a-t-il une alternative à la politique étrangère de la France?" *Politique étrangère* 14, no. 4 (July 1949): 355-64.

Champeau, Commandant. "Les Problèmes de défense de la République fédérale d'Allemagne." *Revue de défense nationale* 22 (November 1966): 1760-73.

Chassin, L. M. "Vers un encerclement de l'occident." *Revue de défense nationale* 12 (May 1956): 531-53.

Chevènement, Jean-Pierre. "Essai de prospective socialiste." *Preuves* (1972).

Clermont-Tonnerre, Thierry de. "L'Armée européenne: Une Analyse sans passion." *Politique étrangère* 19, no. 2 (April-May 1954): 169-94.

Cogny, René. "Mirages et réalités de la défense." *Revue politique et parlementaire*, no. 788 (April 1968), pp. 27-34.

Coleman, Herbert J. "U.S. Forces Stay on Alert As NATO Politicians Fume." *Aviation Week and Space Technology* (5 November 1973), pp. 14-16.

Combaux, Edmond. "Au dela de Clausewitz: Une Nouvelle Doctrine de la guerre." *Revue de défense nationale* 13 (April 1957): 518-32.

_____. "La Défense de l'Eurafrique." *Revue de défense nationale* 14 (January 1958): 59-71.

_____. "Défense tous azimuts? Oui mais . . . ." *Revue de défense nationale* 24 (November 1968): 1600-1618.

_____. "French Military Policy and European Federalism." *Orbis* 13, no. 1 (Spring 1969): 144-59.

Coste-Floret, Alfred. "Bilan et perspectives de la politique européenne." *Politique étrangère* 17, no. 5 (November 1952): 321-34.

Dawson, Raymond H., and Nicholson, George E., Jr. "NATO and the SHAPE Technical Center." *International Organization* 21, no. 3 (Summer 1967): 565-91.

Dawson, Raymond, and Rosecrance, Richard. "Theory and Reality in the Anglo-American Alliance." *World Politics* 19, no. 1 (October 1960): 21-52.

Debatisse, Daniel. "La Crise internationale, réalités et prétextes." *Cahiers du communisme* (December 1977), pp. 32-43.

Debau, E. J. "La France vue de Washington à travers l'O.T.A.N." *Revue de défense nationale* 12 (March 1956): 332-36.

Debré, Michel. "Contre l'armée européenne." *Politique étrangère* 18, no. 5 (November 1953): 387-98.

_____. "La France et sa défense." *Revue de défense nationale* 28, no. 1 (January 1972): 5-21.

_____. "France's Global Strategy." *Foreign Affairs* 49, no. 3 (April 1971): 395-406.

_____. "In Memoriam." *Revue de défense nationale* 26, no. 12 (December 1970): 1763-65.

_____. "La Politique nationale de défense." *Revue de défense nationale* 26, no. 12 (December 1970): 1767-84.

_____. "Les Principes de notre politique de défense." *Revue de défense nationale* 26, no. 8 (August-September 1970): 1245-58.

Deener, David R. "Internationalism, Party Politics and the New French Constitution." *Journal of Politics* 15, no. 3 (August 1953): 399-423.

de Guiringaud, Louis. "Trois Aspects de la politique étrangère de la France: Défense, détente, désarmament," *Défense nationale* 34 (March 1978): 11-22.

de Lagarde, Claude. "The Meaning of NATO for France and Europe." *Annals of the American Academy of Political and Social Science.* Vol. 288, *NATO and World Peace,* edited by Ernest Minor Patterson (July 1953): 63-66.

de Larminat, Général. "La Communauté européenne de défense: I. Les données techniques." *Politique étrangère* 13, nos. 2-3 (May-June 1953): 149-60.

Delmas, Claude. "L'Alliance atlantique et la solidarité des alliés." *Politique étrangère* 23, no. 2 (1959): 220-40.

_____. "Bilan de l'O.T.A.N." *Revue de défense nationale* 13 (December 1959): 1920-38.

_____. "La France et sa défense nationale." *Revue de défense nationale* 13 (October 1957): 1434-48.

_____. "L'Occident devant le 'défi global.'" *Revue de défense nationale* 15 (February 1959): 227-42.

_____. "Quel est l'avenir du pacte atlantique?" *Revue de défense nationale* 14 (July 1958): 1103-15.

_____. "Les Retombées diplomatiques de l'explosion de Reggane." *Revue de défense nationale* 16 (April 1960): 604-20.

Deutsch, Karl, and Merritt, Richard L. "Effects of Events on National and International Images." In *International Behavior: A Social-Psychological Analysis.* Edited by Herbert C. Kelman, pp. 132-87. New York: Holt, Rinehart & Winston, 1965.

_____. "External Influences on the Internal Behavior of States." In *Approaches to Comparative and International Politics,* edited by R. Barry Farrell. Evanston: Northwestern University Press, 1966.

_____. "Political Community and the North Atlantic Area." In *International Political Communities: An Anthology.* Garden City, N.Y.: Anchor Books, 1966. Pp. 1-91.

Devillers, Philippe. "La Politique française et la seconde guerre de Vietnam." *Politique étrangère* 32, no. 6 (1967): 569-604.

Devisse, Jean. "Les Forces spirituelles et la politique extérieure de la France." In *La Politique étrangère et ses fondements,* edited by J.-B. Duroselle, pp. 35-61. Paris: Librarie Armand Colin, 1954.

Dours, J., and Duhoc, J. "La Nouvelle Organisation générale de la défense." *Revue de défense nationale* 15 (February 1959): 219-26.

Duroselle, Jean-Baptiste. "Changes in French Foreign Policy since 1945." In *In Search of France.* New York: Harper and Row, 1965. Pp. 305-58.

_____. "German-Franco Relations since 1945." *Review of Politics* 14, no. 4 (October 1952): 513-24.

_____. "The Turning Point in French Politics: 1947." *Review of Politics* 13, no. 3 (July 1951): 302-28.

Duverger, Maurice. "America the Superpower." *Interplay* (October 1967), pp. 12-14.

Eckelen, W. F. van. "Development of NATO's Nuclear Consultation." *NATO Letter* 18, nos. 7-8 (July-August 1970): 2-6.

Ely, Paul. "Notre Politique militaire." *Revue de défense nationale* 13 (July 1957): 1033-51.

————. "Perspectives stratégiques d'avenir." *Revue de défense nationale* 14 (November 1958): 1631-40.

————. "Les Problèmes français et l'équilibre mondial." *Revue de défense nationale* 15 (November 1959): 1709-25.

Enthoven, Alain C. "American Deterrent Policy." In *Problems of National Strategy: A Book of Readings,* edited by Henry A. Kissinger, pp. 129-34. New York: Frederick A. Praeger, 1965.

Erler, Fritz. "The Basis of Partnership." *Foreign Affairs* 42, no. 1 (October 1963): 84-95.

Eyraud, Michel. "L'Alliance atlantique: Court terme et moyen term." *Stratégie* (January-March 1966), pp. 103-20.

————. "La France face à un eventual traité de non-dissemination des armes nucléaire." *Politique ètrangère* 32, nos. 4-5 (1967): 441-52.

Ferro, Maurice. "France Today." *Annals of the American Academy of Political and Social Science: The National Interest—Alone or with Others?* 282 (July 1952): 41-44.

Fontaine, André. "The ABC of MLF." *Reporter,* 31 December 1964.

————. "The Legacy of the Sixties." *Atlantic Community Quarterly* 8, no. 1 (Spring 1970): 31-35.

————. "Options without the Oracle." *Atlantic Community Quarterly* 6, no. 4 (Winter 1969/70): 566-570.

————. "Two Views of France after de Gaulle: Great Arguments in Softer Tones." *Atlantic Community Quarterly* 7, no. 3 (Fall 1969): 378-83.

Fontainebleau, Colonel [pseud.]. "NATO Handicap: The Integrated Staff." *NATO Letter* 11, no. 5 (October-November 1963): 30-35.

Fourquet, Michel. "Use of Different Force Systems in the Strategy of Deterrence." *NATO Letter* 17, no. 6 (June 1969): 18-22.

François-Poncet, André. "La Crise de l'OTAN." Paris: 10 December 1957. Mimeographed.

Furniss, Edgar S. "French Attitudes toward Western European Unity." *International Organization* 7, no. 2 (May 1953): 199-215.

Gallois, Pierre M. "L'Alliance atlantique et l'évolution de l'armement." *Politique ètrangère* 23, no. 2 (1959): 179-203.

————. "L'Alliance entre deux stratégies." *Politique ètrangère* 31, no. 3 (1966): 217-36.

————. "French Defense Planning: The Future in the Past." *International Security* 1, no. 2 (Fall 1976): 16-31.

————. "La Logique de l'ère nucléaire et ses incidences sur l'OTAN." In *L'Avenir de l'Alliance atlantique.* Paris: Berger-Levrault, 1961. Pp. 110-78.

————. "New Teeth for NATO." *Foreign Affairs* 39, no. 1 (October 1960): 67-80.

————. "Les Sophismes de M. McNamara et le départ du Général Norstad." *Revue de défense nationale* 18 (October 1962): 1454-71.

————. "This Is a Policy Move by Washington." *NATO's Fifteen Nations* 8, no. 6

(December 1963-January 1964): 18-21, 91.

Gascuel, Jacques. "Vers une politique européenne." *Politique étrangère* 15, no. 4 (August-September 1950): 437-46.

Gazin, Général. "Réplique ou représailles." *Revue de défense nationale* 14 (October 1958): 1488-95.

Génevey, Pierre. "Sur les aspects militaires du dégagement en Europe." *Politique étrangère* 23, no. 2 (1959): 248-55.

Gérardot, Paul. "La Compétition pour la suprématie thermonucléaire." *Revue de défense nationale* 14 (April 1958): 568-84.

————. "Plaidoyer pour l'attaque." *Revue de défense nationale* 12 (March 1956): 285-305.

Géraud, André. "Rise and Fall of the Anglo-French Entente." *Foreign Affairs* 32, no. 3 (April 1954): 374-87.

Gerbet, Pierre. "L'Influence de l'opinion publique et des parties sur la politique étrangère de la France." In *La Politique étrangère et ses fondements.* Edited by Jean-Baptiste Duroselle, pp. 83-106. Paris: Librarie Armand Colin, 1954.

————. "Les Rapports entre pouvoir civil et pouvoir militaire en France dans l'élaboration de la politique de défense." Paper read at the Cinquième congrès mondial, Association international de science politique. Paris: 26-30 September 1961. Mimeographed.

Giscard d'Estaing, Valéry. "Allocution de M. Valéry Giscard d'Estaing, président de la république, à l'occasion de sa visite à l'Institut des hautes études de défense nationale " (Paris, 1 June 1975). *Défense nationale* 32 (July 1976): 5-20.

Godard, Jean. "L'Aide américaine à la France." *Revue de science financière* 48, no. 3 (July-September 1956): 438-54.

————. "La Contribution alliée aux charges militaires de la France." *Revue de défense nationale* 12 (April 1956): 436-45.

Goldsborough, James O. "Dateline Paris: Africa's Policeman." *Foreign Policy,* no. 33 (Winter 1978-79), pp. 174-90.

Gombin, Richard. "Le Parti socialiste et la politique étrangère." *Politique étrangère,* no. 2 (1977), pp. 199-212.

Goodpaster, Andrew J. "The Development of SHAPE, 1950-1953." *International Organization* 9, no. 2 (May 1955): 257-62.

Grosser, Alfred. "Après le référendum, quelle politique extérieure?" *Etudes* (June 1972), pp. 835-48.

————. "Divergences franco-allemandes." *Revue de défense nationale* 21 (January 1965): 13-20.

————. "General de Gaulle and the Foreign Policy of the Fifth Republic." *International Affairs* (London) 39, no. 2 (April 1963): 198-213.

Gruber, Frederick J. "Links to the NATO Nations: The National Military Representatives at SHAPE." *NATO Letter* 15, no. 3 (June-July 1970): 15-19.

Haagerup, Niels J. "Réactions scandinaves à la politique atlantique du président de Gaulle." *Politique étrangère* 31, no. 3 (1966): 237-52.

Hamon, Léo. "Puissance nucléaire et dissuasion: Alliance et neutralité." *Revue de défense nationale* 22 (February 1966): 234-57.

————. "Relations between Europe and America: A French Viewpoint." *NATO Letter* 15, no. 11 (November 1967): 20-22.

Hanrieder, Wolfram F. "Compatibility and Consensus: A Proposal for the Conceptual Linkage of External and Internal Dimensions of Foreign Policy." *American Political Science Review* 61, no. 4 (December 1967): 971-88.

Harrison, Michael M. "Consensus, Confusion, and Confrontation in France: The Left in Search of a Defense Policy." In *The Fifth Republic at Twenty,* edited by William G. Andrews and Stanley Hoffmann, pp. 430-49. Albany, N.Y.: SUNY Press, 1981.

_____. "The PCI and Eurocommunism: Implications for Atlantic Relations." In *The Italian Communist Party,* edited by Lawrence Gray and Simon Serfaty, pp. 157-89. Westport, Conn.: Greenwood Press, 1980.

_____. "A Socialist Foreign Policy for France?" *Orbis* 21, no. 4 (Winter 1976): 1471-98.

_____. "The Socialist Party, the Union of the Left, and French National Security." In *The Foreign Policies of the French Left,* edited by Simon Serfaty, pp. 22-47. Boulder, Colo.: Westview Press, 1979.

Hassel, Kai-Uwe von. "Détente through Firmness." *Foreign Affairs* 42, no. 2 (January 1964): 184-94.

_____. "Organizing Western Defense." *Foreign Affairs* 43, no. 2 (January 1965): 209-16.

Hinterhoff, Eugene. "Reflexions sur la force multilatérale." *Politique étrangère* 30, no. 1 (1965): 45-74.

Hoag, Malcolm W. "Nuclear Policy and French Intransigence." *Foreign Affairs* 41, no. 2 (January 1963): 286-98.

_____. "Nuclear Strategic Options and European Force Participation." In *Problems of National Strategy: A Book of Readings,* edited by Henry A. Kissinger, pp. 213-36. New York: Frederick A. Praeger, 1965.

Hoffmann, Stanley. "Heroic Leadership: The Case of Modern France." In *Political Leadership in Industrialized Societies: Studies in Comparative Analysis,* edited by Lewis J. Edinger, pp. 108-54. New York: John Wiley & Sons, 1967.

_____. "Obstinant or Obsolete? The Fate of the Nation-State and the Case of Western Europe." In *International Regionalism: Readings,* edited by Joseph S. Nye, Jr., pp. 177-230. Boston: Little, Brown & Co., 1968.

_____. "Perceptions, Reality, and the Franco-American Conflict." *Journal of International Affairs* 21, no. 1 (1967): 57-71.

Hoffmann, Stanley, and Hoffmann, Inge. "The Will to Grandeur: De Gaulle As Political Artist." In *Philosophers and Kings: Studies in Leadership,* edited by Dankwart Rustow, pp. 248-316. New York: George Braziller, 1970.

Holmes, John W. "The Advantages of Diversity in NATO." In *NATO in Quest of Cohesion,* edited by Karl H. Cerny and Henry W. Briefs, pp. 289-302. New York: Frederick A. Praeger, 1965.

_____. "Fearful Symmetry: The Dilemmas of Consultation and Coordination in the North Atlantic Treaty Organization." *International Organization* 22, no. 4 (Autumn 1968): 821-40.

Holsti, K. J. "National Role Conceptions in the Study of Foreign Policy." *International Studies Quarterly* 14, no. 3 (September 1970): 233-309.

Isnard, Jacques. "Re-vamping French Military Strategy." *Atlantic Community Quarterly* 7, no. 2 (Summer 1969): 241-44.

Jacob, Philip E. "The Influence of Values in Political Integration." In *The Integration of Political Communities,* edited by Philip E. Jacob and James V. Toscano, pp. 208-46. Philadelphia: J. B. Lippincott Co., 1964.

Joxe, Alain. "Fin de la prépondérance stratégique américaine I." *Politique étrangère* 34, no. 4 (1969): 451-70.

————. "Fin de la prépondérance stratégique américaine II." *Politique étrangère* 34, nos. 5-6 (1969): 581-614.

Kaminsky, Elijah Ben-Zion. "The French Chief Executive and Foreign Policy." In *Sage International Yearbook of Foreign Policy Studies,* edited by Patrick McGowan. Beverly Hills: Sage, 1973. Vol. 1.

Kaplan, Lawrence A. "The United States and the Origins of NATO, 1946-1949." *The Review of Politics* 31, no. 2 (April 1969): 210-22.

Kelly, George A. "The French Army Re-enters Politics, 1940-1955." *Political Science Quarterly* 76, no. 3 (September 1961): 367-92.

Kissinger, Henry A. "Coalition Diplomacy in a Nuclear Age." In *International Regionalism,* edited by Joseph S. Nye, Jr., pp. 126-45. Boston: Little, Brown & Co., 1968.

————. "Current Foreign Policy, 1973: The Year of Europe." Washington, D.C.: Department of State, Bureau of Public Affairs, Office of Media Services, 1973.

————. "Domestic Structure and Foreign Policy." In *Conditions of World Order,* edited by Stanley Hoffmann, pp. 164-90. Boston: Houghton Mifflin Co., 1968.

————. "Missiles and the Western Alliance." *Foreign Affairs* 36, no. 3 (April 1958): 383-400.

————. "Strains on the Alliance." *Foreign Affairs* 41, no. 2 (January 1963): 261-285.

————. "The Unsolved Problems of European Defense." *Foreign Affairs* 40, no. 4 (July 1962): 515-41.

Knorr, Klaus. "Perspective on Nuclear Policy." In *NATO in Quest of Cohesion,* edited by Kerl H. Cerny and Henry W. Briefs, pp. 149-60. New York: Frederick A. Praeger, 1963.

Knowlton, William A. "Early Stages in the Organization of SHAPE." *International Organization* 13, no. 1 (Winter 1959): 1-18.

Kohl, Wilfrid L. "The French Nuclear Deterrent." *The "Atlantic Community" Reappraised: Proceedings of the Academy of Political Science* 29, no. 2 (November 1968): 80-94.

————. "The Nixon-Kissinger Foreign Policy System and U.S.-European Relations: Patterns of Policy-Making." *World Politics* 27, no. 1 (October 1975): 1-43.

————. "Nuclear Sharing in NATO and the Multilateral Force." *Political Science Quarterly* 80, no. 1 (March 1965): 88-109.

Kohn, Hans. "Nationalism and Integration: NATO in the Perspectives of 1949 and 1969." *Orbis* 13, no. 1 (Spring 1969): 30-47.

Kolodziej, Edward A. "France and the Arms Trade: Where Foreign and Domestic Policy Meet." Paper presented at the 1979 American Political Science Convention, Washington, D.C.

————. "France and the Atlantic Alliance: Alliance with a De-aligning Power." *Polity* 2, no. 3 (Spring 1970): 241-66.

————. "French Disarmament and Arms Control Policy: Challenge to the Gaullist Heritage." Paper presented at a conference on "The Impact of the Fifth Republic on France: Two Decades of Gaullism," 9-11 June 1978, State University College, SUNY, Brockport, N.Y.

_____. "Revolt and Revisionism in the Gaullist Global Vision: An Analysis of French Strategic Policy." *Journal of Politics* 33, no. 2 (May 1971): 448-77.

_____. "The Success of French Arms (Sales)." Paper presented at the 1978 American Political Science Convention, New York.

Kriegel, Annie. "The French Communist Party and the Fifth Republic." In *Communism in Italy and France,* edited by Donald L. M. Blackmer and Sidney Tarrow, pp. 69-86. Princeton, N.J.: Princeton University Press, 1975.

Laborde, Maxime. "Universalité de la défense nationale." *Revue de défense nationale* 16 (April 1960): 590-603.

Labrousse, de Fregate. "La Marine et la défense de la Communauté." *Revue de défense nationale* 16 (October 1960): 1651-66.

Lacarrière, Philippe. "Problèmes financiers de la défense." *Défense nationale* 33 (January 1977): 11-30.

Laloy, Jean. "Perspectives et limites des rapports Est-Ouest." *Politique ètrangére* 31 nos. 5-6 (1966): 451-72.

Lecanuet, Jean. "Relations between Europe and America: Another French Viewpoint." *NATO Letter* 15, no. 12 (December 1967): 10-13.

Lecerf, J.-L. "Partage des engins ou réforme des armées." *Revue de défense nationale* 15 (March 1959): 474-89.

Legatte, Paul. "Économie d'armement et économie française." *Politique étrangère* 17, no. 2 (April-May 1952): 71-91.

Leites, Nathan, and de la Malène, Christian. "Paris from EDC to WEU." *World Politics* 9, no. 2 (January 1957): 193-219.

Lellouche, Pierre, and Moisi, Dominique. "French Policy in Africa: A Lonely Battle against Destabilization." *International Security* 3, no. 4 (Spring 1979): 108-33.

Lemnitzer, Lyman L. "Collective Defence: The Basis of Military Security." *NATO Letter* 16, no. 1 (January 1968): 2-7.

Lepotier, Contre-Amiral. "Pourquoi la 'force de frappe'." *Revue de défense nationale* 16 (March 1960): 411-29.

Le Puloch, General. "Avenir de l'Armée de terre." *Revue de défense nationale* 20 (June 1964): 947-60.

Lucien, René. "L'Aspect économique de la défense de l'Europe." *Revue de défense nationale* 21 (February 1965): 223-28.

McLachlan, Donald H. "Rearmament and European Integration." *Foreign Affairs* 29, no. 2 (January 1951): 276-86.

McNamara, Robert. "Extracts from Mr. McNamara's Statement on Defense before the U.S. Senate." *NATO Letter* 17, no. 3 (March 1968): 25-26.

Manet, Olivier. "La Communauté européenne de défense: II. Les Données politiques." *Politique étrangère* 18, nos. 2-3 (May-July 1953): 160-68.

Manue, Georges R. "La Leçon de Suez." *Revue de défense nationale* 12 (October 1956): 1155-64.

Marchat, Henry. "A Propos d'un plan de communauté méditerranéenne." *Revue de défense nationale* 14 (August-September 1958): 1339-53.

Marcus, John T. "Neutralism in France." *Review of Politics* 17, no. 3 (July 1955): 295-328.

Marshall, Charles Burton. "Détente: Effects on the Alliance." In *Changing East-West*

Relations and the Unity of the West, edited by Arnold Wolfers, pp. 17-54. Baltimore: Johns Hopkins Press, 1964.

Martin, André. "L'Armée de l'air dans le contexte nucléaire." *Revue de défense nationale* 20 (October 1964): 1, 1499-1517.

Martin, Michel L. "Conscription and the Decline of the Mass Army in France, 1960-1975." *Armed Forces and Society* 3, no. 3 (Spring 1977): 355-406.

Martinet, Gilles. "Le Paravent renversé." *France-Observateur,* 20 April 1968.

Mayer, René. "Organisation atlantique et communauté européenne." *Politique étrangère* 18, no. 6 (December 1953-January 1954): 457-62.

————. "Organisation européenne et coexistence pacifique." *Politique étrangère* 19, no. 3 (June-July 1954): 249-56.

Megret, Maurice. "Les intérêts intellectuels de l'O.T.A.N." *Politique étrangère* 23, no. 2 (1959): 256-67.

Menoncourt, Jacques. "Dangereuse Rivalité gréco-turque en Méditerranée orientale." *Défense nationale* 32 (May 1976): 75-81.

Méry, Guy. "Une Armée pour quoi faire et comment?" *Défense nationale* 32 (June 1976): 11-33.

————. "French Defense Policy." Mimeographed document #78/68. New York: French Embassy Press and Information Division.

Messmer, Pierre. "The Atom, Cause and Means of an Autonomous Military Policy." *Atlantic Community Quarterly* 4, no. 2 (Summer 1968): 270-77.

————. "Our Military Policy," Ambassade de France, Service de presse et d'information, *French Affairs,* series no. 155 (May 1963).

Michel, Pierre. "La Nouvelle Orientation de la défense operationnelle du territoire." *Défense nationale* 34 (January 1978): 35-50.

Middleton, Drew. "NATO Changes Direction." *Foreign Affairs* 32, no. 3 (April 1953): 427-40.

Miksche, F. O. "Western Europe: Security through Integration." *Orbis* 13, no. 1 (Spring 1969): 67-89.

Mitterrand, Jacques. "La Place de l'action militaire extérieure dans la stratégie française." *Revue de défense nationale* 26, no. 6 (June 1970): 887-901.

Mollet, Guy. "France and the Defense of Europe: A Socialist View." *Foreign Affairs* 32, no. 3 (April 1954): 365-73.

Monaque, Paul. "Aperçus sur la politique navale française." *Revue de défense nationale* 14 (March 1958): 385-99.

Monsabert, Général de. "North Africa in Atlantic Strategy." *Foreign Affairs* 31, no. 3 (April 1953): 418-26.

Morse, Edward L. "The Transformation of Foreign Policies: Modernization, Interdependence, and Externalization." *World Politics* 22 (April 1970): 371-93.

Nixon, Richard M. "Extracts from President Nixon's Press Conference after His Trip to Europe." *NATO Letter* 17, no. 4 (April 1969): 26-29.

Norstad, Lauris. "Entretien avec le Général Norstad, Commandant suprême des forces alliées en Europe" (interview by Claude Delmas). *Revue de défense nationale* 13 (December 1957): 1803-13.

Nouël, Elise. "NADGE: The Last Word in Computerized Air-Defense." *NATO Review* 19, nos. 7-8 (July/August 1971): 8-12.

Parisot, Colonel. "Valeur stratégique de l'Afrique pour l'O.T.A.N." *Revue de défense nationale* 14 (March 1958): 430-35.

Pezet, Ernest. "Une Force allemande autonome, serait-elle une nouvelle Wehrmacht?" *Politique étrangère* 19, no. 4 (August-October 1954): 467-87.

Pierre, Andrew J. "Implications of the Western Response to the Soviet Intervention in Czechoslovakia." *Atlantic Community Quarterly* 9, no. 1 (Spring 1969): 59-75.

Pigasse, Jean-Paul. "Armée: La Révolution de la dissuasion continue." *Entreprise,* 18 March 1968.

————. "La Coopération économique entre la France et l'U.R.S.S.: Champ d'application et limites." *Politique étrangère* 32, no. 2 (1967): 155-72.

Pleven, René. "France in the Atlantic Community." *Foreign Affairs* 38, no. 1 (October 1959): 19-30.

Poirer, Lucien. "Deterrence and Medium-Sized Powers." New York: Ambassade de France, Service de presse et d'information, 1972.

Portmann, Georges. "Un bilan." *Revue politique et parlementaire,* no. 789 (May 1968), pp. 17-18.

Pruitt, Dean G. "Definition of the Situation as a Determinant of International Behavior." In *International Behavior: A Social-Psychological Analysis,* edited by Herbert C. Kelman, pp. 393-432. New York: Holt, Rinehart & Winston, 1965.

Radoux, Lucien. "The New Strategy of the Atlantic Alliance." *NATO Letter* 17, no. 1 (February 1968): 2-7.

Ravail, Jean. "Bilan d'application de l'Ordonnance du 7 janvier 1959," *Revue de défense nationale* 26 (February 1970): 189-98.

Rose, François de. "Atlantic Relationships and Nuclear Problems." *Foreign Affairs* 41, no. 3 (April 1963): 479-90.

————. "The Future of SALT and Western Security in Europe." *Foreign Affairs* 57, no. 5 (Summer 1979): 1065-74.

Russett, Bruce M. "Components of an Operational Theory of International Alliance Formation." *Journal of Conflict Resolution* 12, no. 3 (September 1968): 285-301.

Scheinman, Lawrence. "Politics and Nationalism in Contemporary France." *International Organization* 23, no. 4 (Autumn 1969): 834-58.

Schelling, Thomas C. "Nuclears, NATO, and the 'New Strategy.'" In *Problems of National Strategy: A Book of Readings,* edited by Henry A. Kissinger, pp. 169-85. New York: Frederick A. Praeger, 1965.

Schuman, Robert. "France and Europe." *Foreign Affairs* 31, no. 3 (April 1953): 349-66.

Schumann, Maurice. "De la continuité du gaullisme." *Revue de défense nationale* 16 (January 1960): 201-16.

————. "Europe's Role in a New World: A French Viewpoint." *NATO Letter* 15, no. 11 (November 1966): 2-7.

————. "How de Gaulle Hopes to Save the Atlantic Alliance, and Why." *Western World* (September 1959), pp. 10-15.

Schütze, Walter. "La France et l'OTAN." *Politique étrangère* 31, no. 2 (May 1966): 109-18.

Slessor, John. "Western Strategy after Nassau." *NATO Letter* 8, no. 5 (October-November 1963): 33-41.

Smouts, Marie Claude. "French Foreign Policy: The Domestic Debate." *International Affairs* (London) 53, no. 1 (January 1977): 36-50.

Sommer, Theo. "Détente and Security: The Options." *Atlantic Community Quarterly* 9, no. 1 (Spring 1971): 35-49.

Soustelle, Jacques. "France and Europe: A Gaullist View." *Foreign Affairs* 30, no. 4 (July 1952): 545-53.

————. "Indo-China and Korea: One Front." *Foreign Affairs* 29, no. 1 (October, 1950): 56-66.

Spaak, Paul-Henri. "Hold Fast." *Foreign Affairs* 41, no. 4 (July 1963): 611-20.

————. "Nous devons passer de l'alliance à la communauté atlantique." *Revue de défense nationale* 13 (November 1957): 1617-25.

Spofford, Charles M. "NATO's Growing Pains." *Foreign Affairs* 31, no. 1 (October 1952): 95-105.

Stehlin, Paul. "The Evolution of Western Defense." *Foreign Affairs* 42, no. 1 (October 1963): 70-83.

————. "French Thoughts on the Alliance." *NATO's Fifteen Nations* 1, no. 4 (August-September 1964): pp. 20-26.

Stikker, Dirk U. "Effect of Political Factors on the Future Strength of NATO." *Atlantic Community Quarterly* 6, no. 3 (Fall 1968): 331-42.

————. "France and Its Diminishing Will to Cooperate." *Atlantic Community Quarterly* 3, no. 2 (Summer 1965): 197-206.

Sulzberger, C. L. "De Gaulle and the U.S." *Atlantic Community Quarterly* 6, no. 1 (Spring 1968): 26-28.

Sunder, Richard. "AFCENT Leaves France for the Netherlands: Goodbye to Fontainebleau." *NATO Letter* 15, no. 3 (March 1967): 12-13.

Taylor, Edmond. "The Long NATO Crisis." *Reporter,* 21 April 1966, pp. 16-21.

Tiersky, Ronald. "Le P.C.F. et la détente." *Esprit,* no. 2 (February 1975), pp. 218-41.

Tournoux, Raymond. "De Gaulle: La Crise est devant nous, je le sais." *Paris Match,* no. 888 (16 April 1966), pp. 62-63.

Treverton, Gregory F. "Nuclear Weapons and the 'Gray Area.'" *Foreign Affairs* 57, no. 5 (Summer 1979): 1075-89.

Valluy, Jean. "L'OTAN à l'ère atomique." *Revue de défense nationale* 15 (July 1959): 1137-47.

Vandevanter, Elliott, Jr. "The Politics of Integration." *NATO's Fifteen Nations* 12, no. 2 (April-May 1967): 21-23.

Verba, Sidney. "Assumptions of Rationality and Non-Rationality in Models of the Integral System." In *International Politics and Foreign Policy: A Reader in Research and Theory,* pp. 217-31. New York: Free Press, 1969.

Vernant, Jacques. "L'Alliance en mouvement." *Revue de défense nationale* 26, no. 7 (July 1970): 1168-73.

————. "Après le conseil de l'O.T.A.N.: Nouveaux Aspects du dialogue Europe-Etats-Unis." *Revue de défense nationale* 14 (February 1958): 336-41.

————. "Armement nucléaire français ou force de frappe européenne." *Politique étrangère* 24, no. 6 (1959): 591-604.

————. "La Crise cubaine." *Revue de défense nationale* 18 (December 1962): 1919-25.

_____. "Défense et indépendance nationale: L'Example britannique." *Revue de défense nationale* 15 (December 1959): 2033-40.

_____. "Les Entretiens de Paris et la politique étrangère américaine." *Revue de défense nationale* 16 (February 1960): 327-33.

_____. "France-Tunisie-Maroc." *Revue de défense nationale* 14 (August-September 1958): 1398-1405.

_____. "Le général de Gaulle et la politique extérieure." *Politique étrangère* 35, no. 6 (1970): 619-29.

_____. "L'OTAN: Les Raisons des décisions françaises." *Revue de défense nationale* 22 (May 1966): 898-903.

_____. "Perspectives franco-allemandes." *Politique étrangère* 32, no. 1 (1967): 22-34.

_____. "Politique et diplomatie de la Ve république." *Revue de défense nationale* 15 (May 1959): 895-901.

_____. "Politique et diplomatie: Les Etats-Unis et les pays arabes." *Revue de défense nationale* 12 (October 1956): 1252-56.

_____. "Stratégie et politique à l'âge atomique." *Revue de défense nationale* 14 (May 1958): 855-62.

Villiers de l'Isle-Adam, Colonel de. "Cette Guerre de notre siècle." *Revue de défense nationale* 12 (July 1956): 874-93.

Walton, Clarence C. "Background for the European Defense Community." *Political Science Quarterly* 68, no. 1 (1953): 42-69.

Wohlstetter, Albert. "Nuclear Sharing: NATO and the N+1 Country." In *Problems of National Strategy: A Book of Readings,* edited by Henry A. Kissinger, pp. 186-211. New York: Frederick A. Praeger, 1965.

Wright, Vincent, and Machin, Howard. "The French Socialist Party: Success and the Problems of Success." *Political Quarterly* 46, no. 1 (January-March 1975): 36-52.

Zysman, John. "The French State in the International Economy." *International Organization* 31, no. 4 (Autumn 1977): 839-77.

X. "A propos des bases étrangères en France." *Revue de défense nationale* 22 (May 1966): 894-97.

XXX. "Chronique militaire: L'Armée de terre en 1956." *Revue de défense nationale* 13 (January 1957): 140-50.

XXX. "Faut-il réformer l'alliance atlantique?" *Politique étrangère* 30, no. 3 (1965): 230-44.

** "Faut-il réformer l'alliance atlantique? Examen critique." *Politique étrangère* 30, nos. 4-5 (1965): 324-29.

XXX. "Union française et institutions européennes." *Politique étrangère* 18, no. 4 (September-October 1953): 267-76.

List of Abbreviations

ABC	Atomic, biological, chemical (weapons)
ACE	Allied Command Europe
AFCENT	Allied Forces Central Europe
AFSOUTH	Allied Forces Southern Europe
AIRCENT	(Allied) Air Forces Central Europe
BTO	Brussels Treaty Organization
CATAC	Commandement aérien tactique (Tactical Air Command, France)
CDU	Christlich-Demokratische Union (Christian Democratic Union, West Germany)
CERES	Centre d'études, de recherches, et d'education socialiste (Center for Socialist Studies, Research, and Education; faction in the French Socialist Party)
CINCENT	Commander-in-Chief Allied Forces Central Europe
CIR	Convention des institutions républicaines (Convention of Republican Institutions; leftist political group in France, fused with the Socialist Party in 1971)
CODA	Centre d'opération de la défense aérienne (Air Defense Operations Center, France)
CSU	Christlich Soziale Union (Christian Social Union, Bavaria)
DOT	Défense opérationelle du territoire (Territorial Defense Operations, part of the French armed forces structure)
DPC	Defense Planning Committee (NATO)
EDC	European Defense Community
EEC	European Economic Community (Common Market)
EMGDN	Etat-major général de la défense nationale (Joint Chiefs of Staff, France)
ERP	European Recovery Program
FFA	Forces françaises en Allemagne (French Forces in Germany)
FNS	Force nucléaire stratégique (Strategic Nuclear Force, France)
ICBM	Intercontinental Ballistic Missile
IHEDN	Institut des hautes études de défense nationale (Institute of Advanced Studies of National Defense; the French national war college)

IMS	International Military Staff (NATO)
IRBM	Intermediate Range Ballistic Missile
JCAE	Joint Committee on Atomic Energy
JCS	Joint Chiefs of Staff
LANDCENT	(Allied) Land Forces Central Europe
MBFR	Mutual and Balanced Force Reductions
MLF	Multilateral Force
MRP	Mouvement républicain populaire (Popular Republican Movement; French Christian democratic party)
MSBS	Mer-sol ballistique stratégique (SLBM)
NADGE	NATO Air Defense Ground Environment System
NATO	North Atlantic Treaty Organization
NDAC	Nuclear Defense Affairs Committee (NATO)
NMR	National Military Representative (to SHAPE)
NPG	Nuclear Planning Group (NATO)
NSC	National Security Council
OAPEC	Organization of Arab Petroleum Exporting Countries
OTAN	Organisation du traité de l'Atlantique nord (North Atlantic Treaty Organization)
PCF	Parti communiste français (French Communist Party)
PS	Parti socialiste (Socialist Party, France)
PSU	Parti socialiste unifié (Unified Socialist Party, France)
SACEUR	Supreme Allied Commander Europe
SACLANT	Supreme Allied Commander Atlantic
SEATO	Southeast Asia Treaty Organization
SFIO	Section française de l'internationale ouvrière (French Section of the Workers' International; name of the French socialist party until the 1970s)
SHAPE	Supreme Headquarters Allied Powers Europe
SLBM	Sea-launched ballistic missile
SPD	Sozialdemokratische Partei Deutschlands (Social Democratic Party of Germany)
SSBS	Sol-Sol ballistique stratégique (Land-launched ballistic missile, or IRBM)
TNW	Tactical Nuclear Weapon
USAF	United States Air Force
WEU	Western European Union

Index